D0844429

Alan Jay Lerner

Alan Jay Lerner

A Lyricist's Letters

EDITED WITH COMMENTARY BY DOMINIC McHUGH

OXFORD
UNIVERSITY PRESS

Oxford University Press is a department of the University of Oxford.
It furthers the University's objective of excellence in research, scholarship,
and education by publishing worldwide.

Oxford New York
Auckland Cape Town Dar es Salaam Hong Kong Karachi
Kuala Lumpur Madrid Melbourne Mexico City Nairobi
New Delhi Shanghai Taipei Toronto

With offices in
Argentina Austria Brazil Chile Czech Republic France Greece
Guatemala Hungary Italy Japan Poland Portugal Singapore
South Korea Switzerland Thailand Turkey Ukraine Vietnam

Published in the United States of America by
Oxford University Press
198 Madison Avenue, New York, NY 10016

*Research for this book was generously supported by the
Tim Rice Charitable Trust and The Mackintosh Foundation*

Library of Congress Cataloging-in-Publication Data

Alan Jay Lerner: a lyricists letters / edited with commentary by Dominic McHugh.
p. cm.
Includes bibliographical references and index.
ISBN 978-0-19-994927-4 (hardcover : alk. paper) 1. Lerner, Alan Jay, 1918-1986—Correspondence.
2. Lerner, Alan Jay, 1918-1986—Friends and associates. 3. Lyricists—United States—Biography.
I. McHugh, Dominic, editor.
ML423.L3A4 2014
782.14092—dc23
[B]
2014001790

9 8 7 6 5 4 3 2
Printed in the United States of America
on acid-free paper

For my partner,
LAWRENCE BROOMFIELD

CONTENTS

INTRODUCTION AND ACKNOWLEDGMENTS

In one of the letters reproduced in Chapter 6 of this book, Jule Styne—the great composer of *Gypsy, Funny Girl,* and numerous other hit musicals—suggests to Alan Jay Lerner that "one day someone may do a musical based on our letters to one another." Although to write a Broadway musical is well beyond my capabilities, I believe the impulse behind Styne's frivolous suggestion is exactly the same as that behind this book. When researching my monograph, *Loverly: The Life and Times of "My Fair Lady"* (Oxford University Press, 2012), one of my most riveting discoveries was a letter of November 1955 from Lerner to Rex Harrison, who would start rehearsing the show a few weeks later. In it, Lerner discusses various aspects of Higgins's character, of writing lyrics generally, and of the show's overall progress. Having by that time plowed through hundreds of letters to and from other members of the production team and cast of *My Fair Lady,* all of which were interesting as documents but hardly remarkable as pieces of writing, I felt this single letter stood out for its charm, insights, and penmanship.

Of course, it ought to have come as no surprise that the person who wrote *My Fair Lady* also wrote beautiful letters. Yet Lerner has somehow never been given full credit for his prose facility, in spite of writing several Academy Award–winning movies. Too often he has been blindly portrayed as an able but old-fashioned lyricist who added a few songs to Shaw's *Pygmalion* to great effect, repeated the "Cinderella" formula in *Gigi,* and went off the rails after the end of his collaboration with Frederick Loewe on *Camelot.* As an artist, he has rarely been discussed as having the vision and ambition to write musicals based on Nabokov's controversial novel *Lolita* (*Lolita, My Love*), the history of the White House (*1600 Pennsylvania Avenue*), or extra-sensory perception (*On a Clear Day You Can See Forever*), however problematic these may have turned out, nor as the writer of as critically admired a film as *An American in Paris.*

His collaborators, too, make an extraordinary list. In addition to the eminent composers with whom he completed work—Frederick Loewe, Leonard

Bernstein, Burton Lane, Michel Legrand, Kurt Weill, Charles Strouse, and John Barry—we can also add two titans of the Broadway canon, Richard Rodgers and Andrew Lloyd Webber, with whom he was on the verge of collaborating on musicals. Nor should we overlook Arthur Schwartz, Jule Styne, Harold Arlen, and Hoagy Carmichael, with whom Lerner discussed or (in Schwartz's case) started projects. He wrote material for many of the greatest performers of his day, including Fred Astaire, Gene Kelly, Julie Andrews, Richard Burton, Rex Harrison, Maurice Chevalier, Katharine Hepburn, and Barbra Streisand, and worked with the best producers (Arthur Freed, Cheryl Crawford), directors (Vincente Minnelli, Moss Hart) and designers (Cecil Beaton, Oliver Smith).

None of this is a guarantee of quality, of course, and Lerner himself would never have denied that *My Fair Lady*'s unprecedented success was offset by the dismal failure of shows like *Lolita, My Love* (which closed out of town), *1600 Pennsylvania Avenue* (7 performances), *Carmelina* (17 performances), or *Dance a Little Closer* (1 performance). The downward trajectory of his career after 1970 led to derision in his own lifetime and beyond, to the extent that one might almost think he had never been responsible for such an important body of work. His biography, too, has been an intrusive agent in the interpretation of his output: gossip about his marriages, financial insecurity, and association with Dr. Max Jacobson has overwhelmed the reason he was famous: his musicals.

It is for this reason that the main focus of this book is on his work and not on his private life. By now, more than enough has been written on Lerner's divorces, and the writer himself was very open in his attitude toward the subject in his book, *The Street Where I Live*. Almost none of the letters I found in the research for this project shed any light on his family life, so in the absence of any new information I decided not simply to turn the wheel on that subject but instead to focus on his work and working relationships, on which there is a great deal more to be said. Previous books on Lerner's life and works—which are pretty much limited to three volumes: Gene Lees's *Inventing Champagne*, Stephen Citron's *The Wordsmiths*, and Edward Jablonski's *Alan Jay Lerner: A Biography*—tend to repeat most of the same stories about his career and focus much more on the main Lerner and Loewe years than on the rest. This is a striking bias, given that after *Camelot* Lerner worked for another twenty-six years. Since the relationship with Burton Lane was never particularly close, little has ever been written about the four musicals Lerner wrote with him (*Royal Wedding, On a Clear Day, Carmelina*, and the unproduced *Huckleberry Finn*), and because most of his other musicals were unsuccessful, they have been the focus only of the most intense Broadway fanatics and connoisseurs.

Yet many of the letters included in this book present windows into the writer's workshop that confirm that the level of Lerner's imagination, technical ability, and dedication was much higher than we are usually told, even taking into account his unquestionable flaws and failures. The correspondence is often quite personal, too, though not in the family sense. The few letters from Lerner to Loewe prove just how close they were in the mid-1950s and how formal their relationship had become by the 1980s; those to Burton Lane suggest they rarely agreed on anything. Lerner's exchanges with Bernstein seem affectionate and deeply respectful, and he also seems to have got on very well with Arthur Freed, producer of his musicals at MGM. The correspondence with other leading figures of the day also reminds us of Lerner's stature: he wrote with warmth to Irving Berlin, Ira Gershwin, Cole Porter, and Richard Rodgers, four of the heroes of his youth, and in other correspondence we can also see how fondly he felt toward Julie Andrews, Rex Harrison, Richard Burton, Katharine Hepburn, and Robert Goulet, all of whom starred in his musicals. The next generation was also important to him, and a few letters at the end of the book reveal details of his collaboration with Cameron Mackintosh on the London revival of *My Fair Lady* and his brief involvement with Andrew Lloyd Webber's *The Phantom of the Opera* in the final months of his life.

Rather than simply reproduce a stack of letters with a few explanatory footnotes, I felt it would be more useful to place them in the context of Lerner's career. That is why the commentary in the book is quite extensive, though it is not in any way meant to provide a full biography. To compile a collection of Lerner's correspondence was a particular challenge, because he kept very few of his own letters. He seems even to have destroyed or given away most of his manuscripts. Consequently, there is no significant archive of his work, other than a small one at the Library of Congress, which may further explain why so little research has gone into Lerner's oeuvres. The present collection was pieced together from dozens of resources, including the private collections of many of the recipients of the letters (including Lloyd Webber and Mackintosh) and special collections at major archives and universities in the United States and the United Kingdom (including the Library of Congress, the New York Public Library, Yale University, and the University of Southern California).

The collection on *Coco* is especially rich because both its producer (Frederick Brisson) and star (Katharine Hepburn) donated their papers to public institutions; the 1980s are also well covered thanks to the wonderful collection of Liz Robertson, Lerner's widow. There are also some disappointing and frustrating gaps: I could find nothing of significance before 1951, for instance, and some of the Hollywood projects from the 1960s are lacking coverage. Such is the nature of archival research, though, and it seems to me that the omissions are less important than the quality of the letters I did discover, most of which are important to our understanding of this major writer and his times. Few edits have been made to the letters; in most cases, I have silently corrected obvious typographical errors, but a couple of major changes (made in agreement with the Lerner estate) have been indicated with ellipses.

* * *

Many people have helped to make this book possible, but it would never have happened without the incredible passion and support of Liz Robertson, Lerner's widow. From the start, Liz has helped me to gather letters, not only from her own attic but from those of many of Lerner's friends, colleagues, and collaborators across the globe. She has been patient and encouraging over the past three fascinating years. To her, and to the entire Lerner family, I owe many thanks. Equally, I am grateful for the continued assistance and support of David Grossberg, Lerner's attorney and the executor of his estate, who kindly supplied me with the permission to reproduce much of the material in this volume.

Extremely generous financial assistance from the Tim Rice Charitable Foundation and the Mackintosh Foundation also helped to get the project off the ground, with funding for a research trip to the United States in the summer of 2011. Tim in particular met with me on several occasions and immediately understood the value of this collection of letters. For giving me permission to reproduce copyrighted material, I am also indebted to Lynn Lane (Burton Lane), Gabrielle Kraft (Herman Levin), Paul Schwartz (Arthur Schwartz), Chris Hart (Moss Hart), Margaret Styne (Jule Styne), and Robin Walton (Irving Berlin). Ned Comstock at USC was especially helpful in the early stages of the book in helping me to trace letters from Lerner's MGM years, and to the various archives I visited or corresponded with across the globe, I'm enormously indebted.

At Oxford, Norm Hirschy has been a dream of an editor. It seems that no query is too small or large for him to deal with, and it never fails to impress me how quickly and cheerfully he responds to all my problems. I'm honored to count him a good friend, too, and look forward to many more collaborations in the future. My thanks are due to the rest of the team at Oxford as well, including the project manager (Mary Jo Rhodes) and copyeditor (Patterson Lamb), who have both done a sterling job. To Geoffrey Block and Mark Eden Horowitz I also extend my deepest thanks for their endless support and help, which have been essential in making this book possible. As always, thanks to my friend and mentor Cliff Eisen for his ongoing support, and for taking the trouble to acquire Lerner's letters to James Barton for me. I'm also particularly grateful to Richard C. Norton for locating several letters and articles for use in the book.

Not long after starting this book, I was honored to join the staff of the Department of Music at the University of Sheffield, where I have enjoyed perhaps the happiest three years of my life. To my colleagues and students, I am very grateful. In particular, I have to thank Danielle Birkett, Debra Finch, and Hannah Robbins, for their help with this book: Danielle very kindly copied quite a number of letters for me on one of her research trips and brought them back, while Debra and Hannah closely scrutinized and skilfully criticized a draft of the book, vastly improving it in the process.

As ever, my friends have been enduringly patient and loving toward me, so my thanks go to Vanessa Ashbee, Stephen Banfield, Ross Bellaby, Nick Bland, Larry Blank, Dorothy and Michael Bradley, Matthew Brett, Tracy and Darren Bryant, Rexton S. Bunnett, Jo Burrows, Elliot J. Cohen, the late Jere Couture, Nikki Dibben, Jeff Dunne, Bill Everett, Michael Feinstein, Ian Marshall Fisher, Marilyn Flitterman, Andrea Gray, Paul Guinery, Patrick Hayward, Loie Horowitz, Simon Keefe, Barry Kirk, Jeffrey Magee, Candice Majewski, Nelly Miricioiu, Adrian Moore, Larry Moore, George Nicholson, Stephen Pettitt, Stephanie Pitts, Sophie Redfern, Helen Reynolds, Marina Romani, Gary Schocker, Nigel Simeone, Anna Stevens, Richard Tay, Arlene and Roy Tomlinson, Mark and Katy Warman, Joseph Weiss, and Walter Zvonchenko. Space doesn't allow me to describe what they (and many others) all did and do for me, but they know and I know.

To my family, I am likewise grateful, and my particular thanks go to Terry and Sue Broomfield, Linda and John Riley, Alistair, Natallia, and Ophelia. Especial thanks go to my Mum and Dad, Gilly and Larry McHugh, who constantly prove that their love for me knows no bounds. This book is dedicated to Lawrence Broomfield, my dearly beloved partner, who is a constant source of love, patience, and support.

Dominic McHugh
Sheffield, December 2013

Alan Jay Lerner

CHAPTER 1

"From This Day On"

THE RISE OF THE PLAYWRIGHT-LYRICIST, 1918–1951

Compared to the rather sketchy biography of the formative years of his collaborator Frederick Loewe,[1] details of the early life of Alan Jay Lerner are fairly well known. His birth into a privileged family, his excellent and varied education, and his youthful experiments in writing for the theater all paved the way for his rise to prominence in the 1940s and the peak of his fame in the late 1950s, following the success of *My Fair Lady* and *Gigi*. However, little has survived in the way of significant correspondence from his childhood or the first decade of his career. Presumably, letters from the pre-*Brigadoon*, pre-celebrity Lerner must have seemed of little significance to their recipients at the time, even if the contents were witty or interesting. Therefore, this chapter briefly outlines how he came to be one of the leading writers of his generation through the use of alternative sources, such as interviews, newspaper articles, and other contemporary documentation, as well as Lerner's own incredible account of some of his career, *The Street Where I Live*.

Alan Jay Lerner was born in New York City on August 31, 1918, into a home where business was a family concern: his father, Joseph, had established the Lorraine Stores Corporation in 1917 with his brothers Michael and Samuel, and under a new name it grew into the popular nationwide Lerner chain, specializing in budget-priced ladies' fashion. This guaranteed the financial security of Lerner's upbringing, and he was educated at Columbia Grammar School, Bedales (in England), and Choate. But on his own admission, the relationship between his parents was frequently strained: "My Pappy was rich and my Ma was good lookin', but by the time I was born my father no longer thought so," he

[1] Frederick Loewe (1901–88) was the composer of most of Lerner's greatest successes, including *Brigadoon* (1947), *Paint Your Wagon* (1951), *My Fair Lady* (1956), *Gigi* (1958), and *Camelot* (1960).

later recalled. "As far back as I can remember, their life together was a familiar symphony in three movements: arguing, separating, reuniting."[2]

He was his father's favorite, and this led to a fundamental influence in his life: they would regularly attend the theater together, which meant that Lerner saw most musicals that appeared on Broadway starting from roughly his fifth birthday. Consequently, he grew up with a vast knowledge of the output of George and Ira Gershwin,[3] Richard Rodgers[4] and Lorenz Hart,[5] Irving Berlin,[6] Vincent Youmans,[7] and all the other major writers of Broadway shows from the mid-1920s onward. His later comment, "By the age of twelve I had only one ambition and that was to be involved, someday, somehow, in the musical theatre,"[8] therefore comes as no surprise—and when he eventually came to write his own history of the musical theater, published posthumously in 1986, he was particularly qualified for the task.[9] Two works stood out from his early theatergoing days: Jerome Kern[10] and Oscar Hammerstein II's[11] *Show Boat* ("The entire score was studded with both brilliance and depth, almost as if each man had suddenly opened a door in his creative soul behind which a greater artist had been waiting to see the sunlight") and DuBose Heyward[12] and the Gershwins' *Porgy and Bess* ("It was the first of its kind and remains to this day the greatest triumph of the modern musical theatre").[13] Already, Lerner's taste was starting

[2] Alan Jay Lerner, *The Street Where I Live* (London: Hodder and Stoughton, 1978),16.

[3] Brothers George Gershwin (1898–1937) and Ira Gershwin (1896–1983) formed one of the most successful composer-lyricist teams of the 1920s and 1930s. Their songs were used extensively in Lerner's screenplay for *An American in Paris*. As one of the leading lyricists of the previous generation, Ira Gershwin was revered by Lerner, while the Gershwins' *Porgy and Bess* was one of Lerner's favorite works.

[4] Richard Rodgers (1902–79) was one of the most prolific and successful Broadway composers of the twentieth century, particularly noted for his rich collaborations with Lorenz Hart and Oscar Hammerstein II. He also briefly collaborated with Lerner on an aborted project in the 1960s.

[5] Lorenz Hart (1895–1943) was the first of Richard Rodgers's two major lyricists. Their hit musicals include *On Your Toes* (1936), *Babes in Arms* (1937), and *Pal Joey* (1940).

[6] Irving Berlin (1888–1989) was the composer and lyricist of numerous musicals, including *Annie Get Your Gun* (1946) and *Call Me Madam* (1950). Among his dozens of successful songs are "Cheek to Cheek," "Let's Face the Music and Dance," "White Christmas" and "God Bless America."

[7] Vincent Youmans (1898–1946) wrote a number of successful musicals in the 1920s and 1930s, most notably *No, No, Nanette* (1925).

[8] Lerner, *Street*, 17.

[9] Alan Jay Lerner, *The Musical Theatre: A Celebration* (Glasgow: Collins, 1986).

[10] Jerome Kern (1885–1945) was a prolific composer of musicals including *Show Boat* (1927) and *Roberta* (1933).

[11] Oscar Hammerstein II (1895–1960) was one of Broadway's most beloved librettists and lyricists and was best known as the second major collaborator (along with Lorenz Hart) of composer Richard Rodgers.

[12] DuBose Heyward (1885–1940) wrote the play *Porgy* (1927) and collaborated with Ira Gershwin on the libretto and lyrics for its operatic adaptation, *Porgy and Bess* (1935).

[13] Lerner, *The Musical Theatre*, 69 and 133. *Show Boat* opened on December 27, 1927, and ran for 572 performances. *Porgy and Bess* opened on October 10, 1935, and ran for 124 performances.

to emerge. Both of these shows are based on strong literary material that had already enjoyed an independent identity, both engage fiercely with social issues, and both feature finely drawn music, book, and lyrics.

Though Lerner's career was entirely focused on words, his initial inclination was more in the direction of music. From the age of five he learned how to play the piano, and he started to compose songs (including Choate's football song) in his early teens.[14] While his father's love of the theater ultimately had more of an impact on him, his mother's musical talents also contributed to his development: she was a competent singer in her youth and (according to Lerner) had been accompanied at one time by Richard Rodgers's mother. Furthermore, she took Lerner on "educational sightseeing tours ranging from concert hall to museum, from ancient ruin to European cathedral."[15] Relatively untouched by the economic unrest of the late 1920s and early 1930s, Lerner enjoyed a privileged upbringing of culture and sport, and like his classmate, the future president John F. Kennedy,[16] he went straight from Choate to Harvard. Originally, Lerner's father had intended him to study at the Sorbonne in Paris and to become a diplomat, but Lerner was apparently expelled from Choate shortly before graduation for being caught smoking on the school's golf course (though, in fact, his name is included in the *New York Times*'s list of graduates from Choate that year, so perhaps he exaggerated the event in his autobiography).[17] The sentence for his disobedience was to be sent to Harvard instead of the Sorbonne, but Lerner was delighted to be "twenty-eight hundred miles closer to Times Square" than he would have been in the French university and said "it was a little like punishing a prisoner by kicking him out of jail."[18]

He arrived at Harvard in September 1936, and his period there was to be perhaps the most formative of his life. Ostensibly, he specialized in the Romance languages and also spent time boxing and taking flying lessons, though a boxing accident left him with impaired vision and unable to fly in the air corps during the war as he had intended. Yet his heart lay in the Hasty Pudding Club, several of whose shows (or "Theatricals") he contributed to as writer or performer. In *The Street Where I Live* Lerner refers to the Theatricals as "the annual undergraduate musical romp," but in spite of their lack of sophistication, the experience was invaluable. He contributed to the script and score of both *So Proudly We Hail!* (1938) and *Fair Enough* (1939). Though the Hasty Pudding Theatricals

[14] Reproduced in Stephen Citron, *The Wordsmiths* (New York: Oxford University Press, 1996), 107.

[15] Lerner, *Street*, 19.

[16] John F. Kennedy (1917–63) was the 35th president of the United States from January 1961 until he was assassinated in November 1963.

[17] "Awards Bestowed at Choate School," *New York Times*, May 24, 1936, N10.

[18] Lerner, *Street*, 24.

were not "book musicals" (where the script is usually substantial and the songs relate closely to it) as such, the opportunity to write songs for a dramatic context of sorts was a first for Lerner. Given that his later career was devoted purely to writing lyrics and librettos, it perhaps comes as a surprise that for all these songs he wrote both words and music. But he had studied the piano for many years, and leading songwriters such as Irving Berlin and Cole Porter[19] wrote both words and music for their scores, so theirs was clearly the model Lerner aimed to emulate at this point.

In October 1937, he registered for copyright numbers called "You're Not My Type," "You're My Song," "Then I'll Forget You," "My First Night with You," "Man about Town," and "Living the Life," and the following March a further song of his, "Chance to Dream," was published by Chappell.[20] Presumably many of these were intended for *So Proudly We Hail!*, on which Lerner's collaborators were Benjamin Welles (book and songs),[21] Nathaniel Benchley (book),[22] John MacDougal Graham (book), David Lannon (additional lyrics), and Stanley Miller (songs).[23] Welles went on to be a lifelong friend of Lerner's, corresponding with him regularly right up to the 1980s. The show was described in the *Harvard Crimson* as "a satire on Cafe Society with international implications involving Mussolini, Hitler, and Roosevelt and their respective countries, and the small nation of Cafeteria, bounded by Central Park East and 42nd street. Cafeteria is a pawn in the power politics of the three dictators, and these complications form the plot."[24] The paper's reporter noted furthermore that "The directors are finding some difficulty in casting the part of Princess Elizabeth"—an ironic reference to the fact that the Hasty Pudding Theatricals had all-male casts. On March 23, 1938, highlights from the show were broadcast on the radio, including Lerner's "Living the Life," but the script was banned due to its subversive nature, and special skits had to be prepared for the occasion.[25] The official first night was March 29, then it moved to the Copley Theatre in Boston for two performances before the traditional annual show at the Waldorf-Astoria in New York, where it played on April 8. The *Crimson*'s anonymous reporter noted of the first night

[19] Cole Porter (1891–1964) was the composer and lyricist of musicals including *Anything Goes* (1934) and *Kiss Me, Kate* (1948).

[20] Copies of the songs were consulted in the Library of Congress's copyright deposit.

[21] Benjamin Welles (1916–2002) was a famous biographer and journalist.

[22] Nathaniel Benchley (1915–81) was a major novelist and children's author.

[23] Stanley Miller (1916–77) went on to work as a Voice of America aide in Washington, D.C.

[24] "Hasty Pudding Show Socks Café Society," *Harvard Crimson*, February 29, 1938. (Accessed at http://www.thecrimson.harvard.edu/article/1938/2/19/hasty-pudding-show-socks-cafe-society/?print=1 on January 9, 2013.)

[25] "Hasty Pudding Goes on National Hookup in Preview Tonight," *Harvard Crimson*, March 23, 1938. (Accessed at http://www.thecrimson.com/article/1938/3/23/hasty-pudding-goes-on-national-hookup/ on January 9, 2013.)

that "Cheers and hoots greeted the appearance of the hefty chorus 'girls' in scanty corsets for one scene," and anticipated "raised eyebrows" at the Boston and New York venues.[26] Furthermore, the *New York Times* reported that 1,800 alumni and friends attended the gala in the grand ballroom at the Waldorf, and observed that the show "pokes fun at nearly every one."[27]

A year later, Lerner contributed to the 93rd annual Hasty Pudding Show, *Fair Enough*. This time, the book was written in collaboration with Morgan O. Preston and David Lannon, and Lerner shared the score with Elliot Forbes,[28] Francis C. Lawrance,[29] and Sherwood Rollins;[30] no less a figure than Leroy Anderson, future composer of *Sleigh Ride, The Typewriter,* and the Broadway musical *Goldilocks,* was the conductor.[31] The review in the *Crimson* indicated that this show was more successful than *So Proudly We Hail!* had been. "The Hasty Pudding has gone Broadway and vanished are the touches of Minsky that labelled past shows as 'college,'" it was remarked, and the first night was given "a tumultuous reception."

Whereas *Proudly* had represented a departure from previous Hasty Pudding shows in its tone of political satire, *Fair Enough* returned to lighter themes and dealt with "the troubles of Homer Leland in raising enough cash to stage the World's Fair."[32] The production gave birth to Lerner's second and third published songs, "From Me to You" and "Home Made Heaven," both of which are slightly generic but very charming. Typical of his gently witty writing is the opening line of the verse of the latter song: "Didn't you ever dream you owned a palace/Or were an Alice/In Wonderland?" Lerner was the only member of the team to contribute to the music, lyrics, and script, hinting at the emergence of his all-encompassing theatrical vision. The show toured extensively and to great acclaim, stopping off in Boston, Providence, Hot Springs, Washington, Baltimore, and Philadelphia, before reaching the Waldorf on April 8. Lerner's

[26] "Hasty Pudding's Graduates See Show," *Harvard Crimson,* March 29, 1938. (Accessed at http://www.thecrimson.com/article/1938/3/29/hasty-puddings-graduates-see-show-eat/ on January 9, 2013.)

[27] "Harvard Players Give a Satire Here," *New York Times,* April 9, 1938.

[28] Elliot Forbes (1917–2006) was an eminent musicologist, perhaps best known for revising *Thayer's Life of Beethoven.*

[29] Francis C. Lawrance (?–2004) was president of J. S. Frelinghuysen Insurance Co. of New York.

[30] Sherwood Rollins (1919–82) formed his own executive search firm, Sherwood Rollins Company, in New York, and went on to write musical shows for charity benefits as a longtime member of the Tavern Club in Boston.

[31] Leroy Anderson (1908–75) was a major composer and conductor who specialized in "light" music.

[32] C. L. B., "Hasty Pudding Theatricals," *Harvard Crimson,* March 28, 1939. (Accessed at http://www.thecrimson.com/article/1939/3/28/the-playgoer-pin-its-93rd-production/ on January 9, 2013.)

Figure 1.1 A portrait of Alan Jay Lerner. Credit: Photofest

ballad "Home Made Heaven" was singled out in the *New York Times* as a highlight of the evening.[33]

As if to confirm that Lerner had set his sights firmly on the theater as a career, in October 1939 it was revealed that he had co-written the score with Stanley Miller (of *So Proudly We Hail!*) for "an intimate revue" called *The Little Dog Laughed*. Edward Clarke Lilley[34] was slated to produce, and the sketches had "mostly" been written by Arthur Pierson,[35] who would go on to be involved in Lerner and Loewe's first Broadway musical.[36] Nothing much seems to have happened with the show, but its announcement meant Lerner's entrance into the theatrical gossip column of the *New York Times*, in which his name would be a regular fixture for the next four decades. The next we hear of him is in March

[33] "Revue Given Here by Harvard Group," *New York Times*, April 9, 1939, G6.

[34] Edward C. Lilley (1896–1974) was active on Broadway as a director of musicals and operettas, especially in the 1930s.

[35] Actor and director Arthur Pierson (1901–75) was born in Norway but raised in Seattle and worked as both an actor and director on Broadway and in Hollywood. His appearances included playing Lorenzo in Hal Roach's film *The Devil's Brother* (1933) and Demetrius in Max Reinhardt's famous production of *A Midsummer Night's Dream* (1937) on Broadway.

[36] "News of the Stage," *New York Times*, October 6, 1939, 35.

1940, when he announced his forthcoming marriage to Ruth O'Day Boyd, a fellow New Yorker, following his graduation from Harvard. They were married on June 26, and while continuing to pursue his theatrical ambitions Lerner worked as a scriptwriter for radio, later crediting himself with creating over 500 programs between 1940 and 1945.[37] Two further unpublished songs in the Library of Congress's copyright deposits relate to these events: he wrote the lyrics and music for "Evening at the Stork," evidently inspired by his visits to the Stork Club with Boyd, and "Cities Service Signature" is a radio theme tune for which he wrote the music. Again, neither piece is of huge artistic consequence but these early examples of Lerner's work help to reveal the length of his apprenticeship, a period that is often mistakenly thought to date only from his first professional musical.

That show, *Life of the Party*, marked the start of Lerner's greatest collaboration, namely, with the German composer Frederick Loewe. He was fond of telling how they came to meet in the summer of 1942 at the Lambs Club, where he had also met and been encouraged by his mentor, Lorenz Hart:

> I was having lunch in the grill when a short, well-built, tightly strung man with a large head and hands and immensely dark circles under his eyes strode to a few feet from my table and stopped short. His destination was the men's room and he had gone the wrong way. He turned to get back on the right road and suddenly saw me. He stared for a moment. I knew who he was. His name was Frederick Loewe, Fritz to the membership, a Viennese-born, ex-concert pianist and a talented, struggling composer. He came to my table and sat down. 'You're Lerner, aren't you?' he asked. I could not deny it. 'You write lyrics don't you?' he continued. 'I try,' I replied. 'Well,' he said 'would you like to write with me?' I immediately said, 'Yes.' And we went to work."[38]

Alternative versions of the meeting have been told, changing the date or hinting at Lerner's initial reluctance, but they are all credibly based on their meeting at some point at the Lambs Club, of which they were both members.[39] In any case, their first assignment did not require them to "go to work" quite in the way Lerner suggests. *Life of the Party* was a revision of a show called *Patricia* for a Detroit theater company, which had been produced the previous November in San Francisco by Henry Duffy. *Patricia* itself was an adaptation of Barry Conners's

[37] Lerner's self-entry in the Harvard Class report of 1946 is quoted in Edward Jablonski, *Alan Jay Lerner: A Biography* (New York: Henry Holt, 1996), 13.

[38] Lerner, *Street*, 27–28.

[39] Gene Lees usefully indicates some of the other versions in *Inventing Champagne: The Worlds of Lerner and Loewe* (New York: St. Martin's Press, 1990), 41–42.

largely forgotten comedy *The Patsy* (1925).[40] The idea was to take a few songs from an earlier piece by Loewe and his regular lyricist Earle Crooker, called *Salute to Spring* (1937), and redraft them for *Life of the Party*, along with some new material. Lerner's input was only on the book, since Crooker was responsible for the lyrics, which is why this is by no means the first "Lerner and Loewe" musical; after all, Lerner's lyrics would become integral to the formula of their later shows. *Life of the Party* opened at Detroit's Wilson Theatre on October 8 with a cast including Dorothy Stone, Charles Collins, and Charles Ruggles, and it ran until December 5.

It is clear from a notification in the *New York Times* that there was no plan for the show to have an afterlife.[41] But it hardly mattered, for Lerner and Loewe were now destined to act as a team for the foreseeable future. Back in New York, they set to work on a new musical, *What's Up?*, to be produced by the bandleader Mark Warnow.[42] As with *Life of the Party*, there was a third, familiar collaborator: Arthur Pierson, with whom Lerner had written the unproduced *The Little Dog Laughed* several years previously. Pierson's obvious inclination toward farce is betrayed in the book for *What's Up?*, which he co-wrote with Lerner: the plot describes how an aircraft carrying an Eastern potentate makes a crash landing in the grounds of Miss Langley's School for Girls, where the passengers are forced to be quarantined due to an outbreak of measles. Recounting the plot in the *New York Times*, Sam Zolotow added with a hint of sarcasm that "For good measure, the President's voice is introduced on the telephone and he, being a good sport, even obliges by bringing the lovers together at the final curtain. What more can anyone ask?"[43]

In spite of the presence of ballet legend George Balanchine[44] on the production team (choreography and staging), much of the show carried the atmosphere of a slapstick revue, starring a mostly young cast alongside popular comedian Jimmy Savo,[45] who was responsible for much of the broad comedy. Rehearsals began in September 1943 and the show opened at Broadway's National Theatre on November 11 after tryouts in Wilmington and Philadelphia.[46] Unfortunately,

[40] Barry Conners (1882–1933) was an actor and writer of a number of successful plays, including *Hell's Bells* (1925), which featured the Broadway debuts of Humphrey Bogart and Shirley Booth.

[41] "Revival Tonight for Capek's R.U.R.," *New York Times*, December 3, 1942, 34.

[42] "News and Gossip Picked Up on the Rialto," *New York Times*, August 8, 1943, X2. Mark Warnow (1900–49) was a conductor and violinist. *What's Up?* is his only Broadway credit, though he worked with success for CBS/Columbia, including as a conductor and arranger for Frank Sinatra.

[43] Sam Zolotow, "Warnow Musical Opening Tonight," *New York Times*, November 11, 1943, 30.

[44] George Balanchine (1904–83) choreographed more than 400 ballets, including work with Rodgers and Hart on *On Your Toes* and *Babes in Arms*.

[45] Comedian Jimmy Savo (1895–1960) enjoyed success on Broadway in the original production of Rodgers and Hart's *The Boys from Syracuse* (1938).

[46] "'Land of Fame' Will Open Sept. 21," *New York Times*, August 9, 1943, 19. Sam Zolotow, "The Franken Play Coming to Royale," *New York Times*, October 5, 1943, 30.

the reviews were by no means kind: Lewis Nichols found it "curiously lacking" and added that while "No one expects a musical comedy book to rank as high literature... something a little this side of embarrassing does no harm."[47] The show ran only 63 performances and barely lasted to the New Year.[48]

But undeterred by a second disappointment, Lerner and Loewe set about writing their next piece, *The Day before Spring*. This time, Lerner was to write the book and lyrics on his own, and regardless of the failure of *What's Up?* the progress of the new show was regularly charted in the press. In mid-November 1944, the two were ready to announce their new project: "Stanley Gilkey, general manager for Guthrie McClintic, says he will have first call on a musical comedy which Alan Jay Lerner and Frederick Loewe are working on entitled 'The Day before Spring.' Mr Gilkey would like John Murray Anderson to do the staging."[49]

However, five months later it was revealed that John C. Wilson,[50] who had enjoyed recent success as the producer of *Bloomer Girl*, would direct and produce the show, which was due to appear in September.[51] In June 1945, backing was provided for *Spring* by MGM, which put up $75,000 (half the production costs) and signed a deal for the movie rights, too. Eventually, this would reap $250,000 for Lerner and Loewe (though they did not each receive that figure, as Loewe later claimed).[52] The article announcing the deal is revelatory: Irene Dunne[53] was mentioned as a potential star for the eventual film adaptation, while for the stage version Wilson had hired Bill Johnson (for the lead male), Robert Davison (scenery), and Miles White (costumes). Even more tantalizingly, the first mention is made of the next Lerner-Loewe musical, tentatively called *Rigadoon*. Wilson had an option on the show, whose plot was vaguely revealed to deal with "a couple of Americans in the Scottish Highlands."

That the concept for *Brigadoon* had been determined before *Spring* was completed is important in light of Lerner's later account of his career progression. He says that in *Spring* he "set out to try to combine the dramatic lyrics of Hammerstein with the wit and tenderness of Larry [Hart]," resulting in "The sort of play George Kaufman used to call a 'succes d'estime,' i.e., a success that runs out of steam." He continues that "then I got off the track" and both "*Brigadoon*

[47] Lewis Nichols, "A Group of Young People Sing and Dance the Measures of 'What's Up' at the National," *New York Times*, November 12, 1943, 24.

[48] Sam Zolotow, "Draper and Adler at the City Center," *New York Times*, December 31, 1943, 18.

[49] "Ethel Barrymore May Return Dec. 4," *New York Times*, November 18, 1944, 17.

[50] John C. Wilson (1899–1961) had a prolific career on Broadway as producer or director of *Kiss Me, Kate* (1948), *Gentlemen Prefer Blondes* (1949), and *Make a Wish* (1951), among many plays and musicals.

[51] Sam Zolotow, "New Musical Play Due in September," *New York Times*, April 27, 1945, 23.

[52] Sam Zolotow, "Rights to 'Spring' Sought by Metro," *New York Times*, June 13, 1945, 28.

[53] Irene Dunne (1898–1990) was a film star whose hits included *Show Boat* (1936), *The Awful Truth* (1937), and *I Remember Mama* (1948).

and *Paint Your Wagon* were much more along the *Oklahoma[!]* road than the one I had set out on."[54] Lerner tries to imply that with *Spring* he started to explore the kind of theater that he would later return to and perfect in *My Fair Lady*. Yet it is clear that *Brigadoon* was conceived more in conjunction with its predecessor than with the show that followed it, which perhaps helps us to understand it as being more a part of his experimental phase than might be assumed.

Casting for *Spring* took a long time, and the female leads (Irene Manning[55] and Patricia Marshall)[56] were only hired in August, pushing back the production schedule.[57] Rehearsals started on September 24,[58] with tryouts in New Haven (October 25) and Boston (October 30).[59] A scheduled three-week extended additional tryout in Philadelphia was canceled when Wilson's Broadway theater of preference (the National) suddenly became vacant, allowing the production to open on November 22, 1945.[60] The attenuated preview period might have been partly to blame for some of the show's weaknesses, which had been noted even in its previews: an anonymous reviewer from the *Harvard Crimson* reported in early November that although it was "superior entertainment" it was "burdened by a book that gets it off to a slow start." The acting of the two leads was also severely criticized, suggesting that casting strong singers rather than actors might have been the fault rather than the writing.[61] This perspective is likewise apparent in some of the Broadway reviews: Lewis Nichols, for instance, notes that Manning, Johnson, and Marshall "know how to sing" Loewe's "very pleasant tunes" but "Albert [*sic*] Jay Lerner . . . has chosen to be austere rather than light."[62] Weak acting is again mentioned in a later interview with Maurice Abravanel,[63] the show's conductor, who thought it was "very interesting" but "badly cast."[64]

[54] Lerner, *Street*, 33 and 34.

[55] Irene Manning (1912–2004) appeared in the films *Yankee Doodle Dandy* (1942) and *The Desert Song* (1943), as well as stage productions and her own TV show.

[56] Patricia Marshall (1928–) appeared in the Broadway productions of *What's Up?*, *The Pajama Game* (replacement cast), and *Mr. Wonderful*.

[57] " 'Carib Song' Listed for Sept. 25 Debut," *New York Times*, August 11, 1945, 14.

[58] "Jed Harris Plans 2 Shows This Fall," *New York Times*, August 24, 1945, 15.

[59] "Claiborne Foster in New Lang Play," *New York Times*, October 13, 1945, 21.

[60] Sam Zolotow, "National to House J. C. Wilson Show," *New York Times*, November 1, 1945, 20.

[61] Anon, "Playgoer at the Shubert," *Harvard Crimson*, November 6, 1945. (Accessed on 10 January 2013 at http://www.thecrimson.com/article/1945/11/6/playgoer-pmusicals-like-lady-in-the/.)

[62] Lewis Nichols, "The Play," *New York Times*, November 23, 1945, 27.

[63] Maurice Abravanel (1903–93) was an American conductor who performed with many of the world's great orchestras and opera companies, as well as a number of Kurt Weill's Broadway musicals (including *Lady in the Dark*, *One Touch of Venus* and *Street Scene*).

[64] Lees, *Inventing Champagne*, 45.

The heavy tone may also have been partly due to the direction, which was shared between Edward Padula[65] (book direction) and Wilson (staging).

In spite of the mixed reception, the show certainly put Lerner and Loewe on the map. In February 1946, MGM took up their option on the screen rights, and the movie version went into pre-production for an early summer filming. Tom Helmore[66] was to repeat his stage role, and Arthur Hornblow Jr. was set to produce.[67] But this extra publicity failed to improve the show's fortunes, and in mid-March Wilson had to declare the production would close on April 14 after only 165 performances, though it went on to have a brief run in Chicago.[68] The financial impact of the early closure hit Wilson hard, and in June he declared he would produce no more musicals for the time being, thereby relinquishing his right to *Rigadoon*.[69] Inevitably, this delayed the show's premiere, though other producers were interested. In September, Billy Rose[70] and Oscar Hammerstein II discussed a co-production of *Brigadoon*, as it was now called,[71] but Lerner felt that Rose's demanding contract (which included the right to call in other authors to add material) "negated Abraham Lincoln's Emancipation Proclamation that freed the slaves."[72] Instead, Lerner took the project to Cheryl Crawford,[73] one of the powerful managing directors of the American Repertory Theatre, and she immediately signed up to produce the show. She announced the project on October 2 and had already managed to engage Agnes de Mille (of *Oklahoma!* and *Carousel* fame)[74] for the choreography—quite a coup, considering De Mille's stature at the time, but perhaps also one of the reasons Lerner felt *Brigadoon* led him more in the direction of *Oklahoma!* than he had wanted.

[65] Edward Padula (1916–2001) had a long career on Broadway that included *Seventh Heaven* (1955, assistant director), *Rumple* (1957, stage manager), *Bye Bye Birdie* (1960, producer), and *All American* (1962, producer).

[66] British actor Tom Helmore (1912–95) appeared in numerous plays on Broadway; his turn as Gerald in *The Day before Spring* was his only major credit in a musical.

[67] "Helmore to Play in Metro Musical," *New York Times*, February 25, 1946, 31.

[68] Sam Zolotow, "'Flamingo Road' Arriving Tonight," *New York Times*, March 19, 1946, 33.

[69] Sam Zolotow, "Karson May Offer a Musical in Fall," *New York Times*, June 4, 1946, 33.

[70] Billy Rose (1899–1966) was a major impresario (with credits including *Jumbo* and *Carmen Jones*) and occasional lyricist.

[71] Sam Zolotow, "'Playboy' to Open at Booth Oct. 2," *New York Times*, September 6, 1946, 17.

[72] Lerner, *The Musical Theatre*, 166.

[73] Cheryl Crawford (1902–86) co-founded The Group Theatre and the American Repertory Theatre. She produced the original Broadway productions of *One Touch of Venus* (1943), *Paint Your Wagon* (1951), and *Jennie* (1963).

[74] Agnes de Mille (1905–1993) was one of the leading choreographers of Broadway's Golden Age, with additional credits including *Paint Your Wagon* (1951), *Gentlemen Prefer Blondes* (1949), and *Goldilocks* (1958).

Crawford's name brought a strong budget of about $160,000 (though she later disclosed that this was difficult to raise),[75] as well as a director (Robert Lewis),[76] designer (Lemuel Ayers),[77] and cast (including Marion Bell, whom Lerner went on to marry, David Brooks, and George Keane), all of whom were excellent.[78] After many months of trying unsuccessfully to secure an appropriate theater, at the last minute, in January 1947, Crawford managed to book the Ziegfeld (which, ironically, was owned by Billy Rose).[79] Rehearsals began in the second week of January, with previews at New Haven (February 6–8), Boston, and Philadelphia (two weeks each) followed by the Broadway opening on March 13. Finally, Lerner and Loewe had made it: the reviews not only praised their work lavishly but equally showed an appreciation for their artistry and imagination. Brooks Atkinson, for instance, observed that "For once the modest label 'musical play' has a precise meaning. For it is impossible to say where the music and dancing leave off and the story begins in this beautifully orchestrated Scotch idyll.... [A]ll the arts of the theatre have been woven into a singing pattern of enchantment."[80] Ward Morehouse of the *New York Sun* raved in a similar fashion about the "stunning show," declaring it to be "by far the best musical play this season has produced, and it is certainly one of the best within my entire play-going experience." Even better, Richard Watts Jr. in the *New York Post* commented that there were few musicals "for which I have a deeper admiration.... [T]here is no denying that the authors have matured as craftsmen."[81]

Brigadoon became the signature work for the "Lerner and Loewe" brand, and the five years they had been working to make it on Broadway finally paid off. The production ran for 581 performances and went on an extensive American tour; the London production (1949) lasted 685 performances. The show also enjoyed a number of revivals, the 1954 MGM film adaptation with Gene Kelly,[82] and a 1966 telecast with Sally Ann Howes[83] and Robert Goulet[84] that won five Emmy Awards.

[75] Sam Zolotow, "News of the Stage," *New York Times*, March 17, 1947, 26. This article gives some fascinating statistics on the show's weekly gross ($43,000) and running costs ($22,00), as well as a list of the 38 backers.

[76] Robert Lewis (1909–97) was a prolific actor and director, who co-founded the Actors Studio in New York in 1947.

[77] Lemuel Ayers (1915–55) was responsible for the designs of the original Broadway productions of *Kiss Me, Kate* (1948), *Kismet* (1953), and *The Pajama Game* (1954).

[78] Sam Zolotow, "'Set 'Em Up, Tony' Halts This Week: Signed for New Show," *New York Times*, December 6, 1946, 29.

[79] Louis Calta, "New Opera Troupe Is Reviving 'Topaz,'" *New York Times*, January 4, 1947, 11.

[80] Brooks Atkinson, "The New Play," *New York Times*, March 14, 1947, 28.

[81] Reviews quoted in Suskin, *Opening Night*, 103–107.

[82] Gene Kelly (1912–1996) was the star of *An American in Paris* (1951) and *Singin' in the Rain* (1952), among dozens of stage and screen projects; he was also a prolific director.

[83] Sally Ann Howes (1930–) is a stage and screen actress, perhaps best known for appearing in the film *Chitty Chitty Bang Bang* (1968). Her numerous credits include Eliza in *My Fair Lady* on Broadway.

[84] Robert Goulet (1933–2007) appeared in dozens of musical productions, including the original production of *Camelot* on Broadway.

But two things were to overshadow the immediate aftermath of *Brigadoon*'s opening for Lerner: the dissolution of his working relationship with Loewe, and the accusation that he had plagiarized the story of *Brigadoon* from a German source. The latter was flatly denied in a letter to the *New York Times* on March 30. Lerner wrote:

> The existence of the German story *Germelshausen* comes as no surprise to me at this time. It was not long after I had completed the first draft of *Brigadoon* that a friend informed me of it. At that time I obtained a copy and read it; and I was, of course, amazed at the resemblance. Then, upon delving into the matter a little further, I discovered that there existed another German legend much older than *Germelshausen* upon which the latter was either based or to which it bore an equally striking resemblance. On doing still more research, I was again astounded to learn that legends of disappearing towns can be found in the folklore of many, many countries. For instance, there is the old Irish tale that was recorded by James Stephens which is very similar.
>
> Literary history being filled with unconscious coincidence, I could do nothing more than deduce that this was another and let it go at that. I was, of course, aware that many theatregoers might notice similarities between *Brigadoon* and any one of the ancient legends and question me about it. So Miss Harber's letter is not something I did not anticipate. However, I'm sure the thought has occurred to anyone who questioned the originality of *Brigadoon* that, after all, if the story were based on or suggested by another, why didn't I mention it? Artistically it would certainly not have been personally detrimental, nor would it have prevented the play's achieving success. Shakespeare borrowed plots indiscriminately and it didn't seem to disturb his reputation. And financially, all the legends on this theme are in the public domain, so there was no royalty problem involved.[85]

In spite of defending himself so extensively, the accusation festered with Lerner all his life; he even raises the point in *The Street Where I Live*, even though *Brigadoon* is scarcely mentioned otherwise.[86]

On the same day he wrote this letter, Lerner flatly denied "reports he has split with Frederick Loewe, his tune writer. They simply haven't yet thought of a new vehicle on which they could work together."[87] But there was no smoke without fire, and when Lerner's name was mentioned in connection with a new show

[85] Alan Jay Lerner, "Explanation," *New York Times*, March 30, 1947, X3.

[86] Lerner, *Street*, 26–27.

[87] Lewis Funke, "News and Gossip Gathered on the Rialto," *New York Times*, March 30, 1947, X1.

Figure 1.2 Alan Jay Lerner and Frederick Loewe working on the screen version of *Brigadoon*. Credit: Photofest

for star actress Mary Martin[88] in late July, it was clear that the composer would not be Loewe but rather Kurt Weill,[89] who had written the music for Martin's hit *One Touch of Venus* (1943). As with *Brigadoon,* the producer was to be Cheryl Crawford, but little other information was disclosed at that time.[90] In itself, this seems significant: the announcement effectively divulges nothing but Lerner's split from Loewe, bearing in mind that the new project with Weill was clearly in its very early stages. Of course, the new relationship made artistic sense: an article by Howard Taubman in the *New York Times* in October, headlined "Musicians Return to the Theatre," discussed how Broadway in the mid-1940s had seen the rise of composers of art music, such as Leonard Bernstein (*On the Town*),[91] Morton Gould (*Billion Dollar*

[88] Mary Martin (1913–1990) was one of the preeminent musical theater actresses of her generation. Her Broadway appearances included *One Touch of Venus* (1943), *South Pacific* (1949), *Peter Pan* (1954), *The Sound of Music* (1959), and *I Do, I Do* (1966), as well as a number of film and television roles.

[89] Kurt Weill (1900–50) was one of the most important composers of his generation, both in art music and on Broadway (for which his credits include *Lady in the Dark*, 1941).

[90] Sam Zolotow, "New Team May Do Song, Dance Show," *New York Times*, July 30, 1947, 27.

[91] Leonard Bernstein (1918–90) was well known as a composer, conductor, and teacher. His Broadway musicals include *On the Town* (1944), *Wonderful Town* (1953), *Candide* (1956), and *West Side Story* (1957).

Baby),[92] Weill (*Lady in the Dark*), and Loewe, who was the main subject of the article.[93] (Intriguingly, the article also mentions that Lerner and Loewe had tried to obtain the musical rights to J. M. Barrie's *The Little Minister* (1891) before settling on *Brigadoon*. This refutes the idea that *My Fair Lady* was Lerner and Loewe's first attempt at a musical adaptation.) Taubman wrote, "The success of Frederick Loewe with *Brigadoon* is another proof that a Broadway musical can be written by a musician who can compose a concerto for symphony orchestra and, if need be, appear as his own soloist."[94] Thus the combination of Lerner and Weill had as much potential as that of Lerner and Loewe, and for the next two years it seemed the new team was permanent.

In September 1947, Lerner started to pursue talent for the show. Gertrude Lawrence[95] was now mentioned as the potential star,[96] and the musical at this point was designed to tell "the history of a woman"; Robert Lewis was slated to direct, following his success with *Brigadoon*.[97] By November, Lerner and Weill had already written several songs, and the provisional title was *A Dish for the Gods*, but they declared that "as for a star to play the lead, there'll be no more dickering with anyone until the final script is delivered."[98] As time went on, it was clear that the musical would be deferred until the following season,[99] though in early February Lerner and Weill revealed that their work would be completed "within two or three weeks" and screen star Ginger Rogers[100] was now in the running for the lead.[101] Then on February 16 they announced that the piece was complete, but Crawford had decided to delay the production until the following year in order to have a few major actresses to choose from.[102] Martin and Lawrence were apparently still in the running, but Lerner and Weill went to visit Rogers in Hollywood with the script and score, which she liked; her film schedule ultimately prevented her from taking part.[103] In the interim, the new writing

[92] Morton Gould (1913–96) was a well-known composer and conductor of art music, though his career included several musicals.

[93] Howard Taubman, "Musicians Return to the Theatre," *New York Times*, October 26, 1947, X1.

[94] Little research has been published on Loewe's early career, so it is difficult to verify details of his output of art music.

[95] Gertrude Lawrence (1898–1952) was a popular stage actress, famous in particular for her collaborations with Noel Coward.

[96] Louis Calta, "News of the Stage," *New York Times*, September 13, 1947, 8.

[97] Sam Zolotow, "Another Musical Draws Top Notice," *New York Times*, September 17, 1947, 30.

[98] Lewis Funke, "News and Gossip of the Realto," *New York Times*, November 2, 1947, X1.

[99] Sam Zolotow, "Premire Tonight for 'Bedfellows,'" *New York Times*, January 14, 1948, 30.

[100] Ginger Rogers (1911–95) was one of the most popular screen actresses of the mid-twentieth century, best known for her ten films with Fred Astaire.

[101] Sam Zolotow, "'Cradle' to Close Saturday Night," *New York Times*, February 4, 1948, 27.

[102] Lester Bernstein, "Ibsen Drama Due to Arrive Tonight," *New York Times*, February 16, 1948, 16.

[103] Sam Zolotow, "'Inside U.S.A.' Cast Rehearses Today," *New York Times*, February 27, 1948, 26.

team set to work on planning a musical for Lerner's wife Marion Bell, who was still appearing in *Brigadoon*. Lerner described it to a reporter as "a musical play, halfway between *Street Scene* and *Brigadoon*," and said "the locale is the eastern end of the Mediterranean."[104]

Meanwhile, Lerner maintained contact with Loewe while discussions were under way for the screen version of *Brigadoon*. For many months, J. Arthur Rank pursued the rights to make the film in England, with Bing Crosby[105] as the lead.[106] The writers were seeking $500,000, though they later accepted less than half that sum from MGM, which eventually made the movie under the direction of Vincente Minnelli.[107] Despite these negotiations, it was clear that Lerner was still fully committed to Weill, and work continued on their show, regardless of their claims to have finished in February. On May 2, further details were disclosed: the title was to be changed, and the script had been amended to increase the importance of the male lead character in the hopes of attracting Alfred Drake[108] or Eddie Albert[109] for the role.[110] Ultimately, Nanette Fabray[111] was named as the female star, following rave reviews for her performance in Jule Styne's *High Button Shoes*, with Ray Middleton (the original Broadway Frank Butler in *Annie Get Your Gun*)[112] as the male lead, and Robert Lewis was replaced by Elia Kazan[113] as director.

Renamed *Love Life*, the show started rehearsals on August 9 ahead of a New Haven tryout in September.[114] Lerner's innovative libretto recounted "the story of 130 years of American home life involving a couple and their two children," and even as *Brigadoon* closed on July 31, Lerner looked forward to his next musical on Broadway.[115] Four days before the October 7 opening, an imaginary

[104] Sam Zolotow, "Lawrence's Cold Cancels Showing," *New York Times*, March 12, 1948, 28.

[105] Bing Crosby (1903–77) was one of the most successful screen and recording artists of his generation, perhaps best remembered for his rendition of Irving Berlin's "White Christmas."

[106] A. H. Weiler, "By Way of Report: Life of Gandhi in the Offing?" *New York Times*, March 28, 1948.

[107] Vincente Minnelli (1903–86) was the director of such beloved musicals as *Meet Me in St Louis* (1944) and *The Band Wagon* (1953).

[108] Alfred Drake (1914–92) was popular at the time because of his appearance in the original production of *Oklahoma!* Later, he would appear in the original Broadway production of Lerner's *Gigi* (1973).

[109] Eddie Albert (1906–2005) had appeared alongside Drake in *Oklahoma!* in the role of Ali Hakim.

[110] Lewis Funke, "News and Gossip of the Rialto," *New York Times*, May 2, 1948, 81.

[111] Nanette Fabray (1920–) starred in several important musicals of the 1940s and '50s, and appeared in the movie *The Band Wagon* (1953).

[112] Ray Middleton (1907–84) appeared in numerous musicals and films, including the original Broadway *Man of La Mancha*.

[113] Elia Kazan (1909–2003) was one of the most influential directors of his generation, with credits including the landmark films *On the Waterfront, A Streetcar Named Desire,* and *East of Eden*.

[114] Louis Calta, "Lead in 'Love-Life' to Nanette Fabray," *New York Times*, May 29, 1948, 9.

[115] Louis Calta, "Hartman Opposes Equity Proposals," *New York Times*, July 6, 1948, 20.

conversation between Weill, Lerner, and a man on the street was printed in the *New York Times*, in which they tried to explain the concept of their new show. As can be seen from the following excerpt, they were clearly aware that they were pushing the envelope in terms of what audiences might be expecting:

MAN: Pardon me. Do either of you know anything about this show?
LERNER: Yes, we saw it in New Haven.
MAN: What is it? I am a little confused. It says here on the sign it's a vaudeville.
WEILL: That's right, it is.
MAN: You mean it has vaudeville acts?
WEILL: Lots of them.
MAN: That's fine. Then I don't have to worry about following a plot. That's a relief.
LERNER: No. There's a plot.
MAN: I thought you said it was a vaudeville.
LERNER: It's a vaudeville with a plot.
MAN: How does that work?
WEILL: Well, the sketches and the vaudeville acts have a continuity and supplement each other.
MAN: (Scratching his head) Did you understand?
WEILL: I did.
LERNER: So did I.[116]

Unfortunately, the tone of this conversation was an indication of things to come. Even on the day of the opening, Lerner was still desperately explaining that it was "an experiment with form," and a "serious subject treated, most of the way, lightly."[117] He elaborated that this "serious subject" was "the decline of American home life in the past century or so and the resultant unhappiness and confusion of the average family." Hours later, it was branded by the critics as a "disappointment... cute, complex and joyless,"[118] and it only lasted one season (252 performances).[119] A musicians' union strike resulted in no cast album being recorded, and in spite of its huge ambition it remains an obscure, rarely heard show that Lerner was always reluctant to allow to be revived (perhaps in part because he reused some of the material from one of the numbers, "I Remember It Well," in the movie *Gigi*).

[116] Kurt Weill and Alan Jay Lerner, "Two on the Street," *New York Times*, October 3, 1948, X3.

[117] Louis Calta, "'Love Life' in Bow to Rialto Tonight," *New York Times*, October 7, 1948, 33.

[118] Brooks Atkinson, "At the Theatre," *New York Times*, October 8, 1948, 31.

[119] Sam Zolotow, "Abbott Play Quits Tomorrow Night," *New York Times*, May 6, 1949, 30. Crawford reported that the show had made back $40,000 toward the production costs of $180,000.

Lerner spent the early weeks of 1949 in Hollywood writing a film musical for Fred Astaire[120] and Ginger Rogers, an intended follow-up to their reunion movie *The Barkleys of Broadway*, though in the end only Astaire appeared in the movie, which became *Royal Wedding*.[121] As it became clear that *Love Life* was faltering, the collaboration with Weill was severed and their second project abandoned. Looking around for a replacement writing partner, Lerner discussed a project with Leonard Bernstein, a fellow Harvard graduate whose work he admired. But within four weeks after the closure of *Love Life*, Lerner and Loewe buried the hatchet and decided to collaborate on another show.[122] Indeed, they seem literally to have set to work immediately on the show that became *Paint Your Wagon*, because on July 20 it was revealed that Cheryl Crawford had agreed to oversee the production, which would be "set in the United States in the nineteenth century."[123] This ability to move on from a disappointing situation very quickly would set the model for Lerner's entire career, motivated by his imagination and unflagging optimism.

First, though, he had to complete work on two Hollywood projects that were demanding urgent attention: *Royal Wedding*, which was now to star the young Jane Powell[124] opposite Astaire,[125] and *An American in Paris*, which would provide a vehicle for Gene Kelly, using the song catalogue of George and Ira Gershwin. His contract with producer Arthur Freed[126] at MGM would become increasingly pressing over the course of the 1950s, because he was obliged to write several movie musicals for an industry in swift decline, and at the same time he was pursuing various Broadway projects on the opposite coast. Though *Paris* was always to have a Lerner screenplay and *Royal Wedding* was also in the works, the third film was to prove elusive. For instance, he was offered *Mr. Imperium*, a vehicle for Ezio Pinza[127] (the star of Rodgers and Hammerstein's *South Pacific*), which would have brought him a new collaborator in composer Harold Arlen[128]

[120] Fred Astaire (1899–1987) was one of the most celebrated dancers and screen actors of all time. He appeared in more than two dozen movie musicals, including *Top Hat* (1935), *Swing Time* (1936), and *The Band Wagon* (1953).

[121] Louis Calta, "Stage Role Likely for E.G. Robinson," *New York Times*, January 1, 1949, 10.

[122] Sam Zolotow, "'Along Fifth Ave.' Closes Saturday," *New York Times*, June 13, 1949, 16.

[123] J. P. Shanley, "Lerner and Loewe Work on a Musical," *New York Times*, July 20, 1949, 31.

[124] Jane Powell (1929–) is the star of films such as *Seven Brides for Seven Brothers* (1954).

[125] Powell was cast after Rogers, June Allyson, Vera-Ellen, Judy Garland, and Moira Shearer turned it down, were unavailable, or were rejected.

[126] Arthur Freed (1894–1973) started out as a successful lyricist but became the most important and influential producer of film musicals of all time, thanks to his work at MGM in the 1940s and '50s.

[127] Ezio Pinza (1892–1957) was a leading bass with the Metropolitan Opera before his appearance in the original production of Rodgers and Hammerstein's *South Pacific* (1949).

[128] Harold Arlen (1905–86) was a prolific composer, best remembered for his music for *The Wizard of Oz* (1939).

(*The Wizard of Oz*), but Lerner rejected the idea.[129] Additionally, Lerner was briefly named as screenwriter of the remake of *The Belle of New York*, perhaps as a result of his successful ongoing relationship with Astaire (the intended star) on *Royal Wedding*, but he quickly passed on the option.[130] Eventually, Lerner did complete the songs and screenplay for a film version of *Huckleberry Finn* with Burton Lane,[131] composer of the score for *Royal Wedding*, though it went unproduced. At a time when Freed was among the most powerful figures in Hollywood and only engaged the best, it is telling that Lerner was hired for or associated with all these films, in spite of barely having passed his thirtieth birthday.

May 1950 brought Lerner back into the newspapers with the return of *Brigadoon* to New York's City Center after its successful national tour. The reviews again gave him credit for his "constantly fascinating" book, and the show was referred to as "one of the milestones in the latter-day history of the musical stage."[132] No wonder Lerner was determined to resume the partnership with Loewe. Returning from Hollywood to see *Brigadoon* in mid-May, he had now completed most of his work on *An American in Paris* and *Royal Wedding* and could spend the rest of the year concentrating on his next Broadway show. By the end of the month, Lerner and Loewe were happy to divulge the fact that the new production would recall "the rip-roaring days of the wild and woolly West" and announced it was to be called *Paint Your Wagon*. In the show's announcement in the New York Times, columnist Sam Zolotow explained, "If you're mystified by the connection between the title and the hectic Western Era, hearken to the following explanation: During the gold rush the wagons used by the pioneers carried the inscription of 'Pike's Peak or Bust' lest the absent-minded lost sight of the objective. The story covers the birth, life and death of a gold mining town."[133]

Work on the new show went slowly, presumably not helped by the fact that *Royal Wedding* was being shot until October 1950.[134] *Wagon*'s book and several songs were drafted, but by January 1951 the production had been deferred to the next season, ostensibly because of the lack of availability of the intended star, veteran James Barton.[135] If the delay was also partly Lerner's fault (as seems

[129] Thomas F. Brady, "Play by Saroyan Is Made into Film," *New York Times*, April 19, 1950, 35.

[130] Thomas Bady, "Metro Acquires Two New Stories," *New York Times*, May 11, 1950, 35. *The Belle of New York* was eventually written for the screen by Chester Erskine and released in 1952.

[131] Burton Lane (1912–97) was a respected composer whose works include *Finian's Rainbow* (1947) and *On a Clear Day You Can See Forever* (1965). The *Huckleberry Finn* project had been offered to numerous writers, including E.Y. Harburg.

[132] Brooks Atkinson, "At the Theatre," *New York Times*, May 3, 1950, 36.

[133] Sam Zolotow, "Cheryl Crawford to Sponsor Show," *New York Times*, May 26, 1950, 31.

[134] Thomas F. Brady, "Leslie Caron Gets Metro Film Role," *New York Times*, June 3, 1950, 9.

[135] James Barton (1890–1962) was a popular figure from revue and vaudeville, but his theatrical credits also included Eugene O'Neill's *The Iceman Cometh* (1946). Sam Zolotow, "Broadway to See Sarah Churchill," *New York Times*, January 5, 1951, 16.

likely from his busy schedule and *Paint Your Wagon*'s well-known book problems), Loewe cannot have been annoyed for long because in February the lyricist's relationship with MGM helped him close a deal for Freed to produce the long-mooted movie version of *Brigadoon.*[136] In March, *Royal Wedding* opened to mixed reviews: in his appraisal for the *New York Times,* Bosley Crowther didn't even mention Lerner's name as lyricist or screenwriter. Crowther's reference to the "spider-web story-line" was less than flattering,[137] and Lerner himself mentioned the film only with embarrassment later in his career: "Although Burton Lane wrote some spiffy songs and Fred [Astaire] danced in a way that made all superlatives inadequate, my contribution left me in such a state of cringe that I could barely straighten up."[138] Nevertheless, the film made almost $4 million at the box office, against costs of around $1.5 million.

It had also provided him with the opportunity to write for one of his idols, Fred Astaire, adding to the extraordinary list of stars for whom Lerner created musicals, and he must have been proud of the double feat of writing for both the major male Hollywood dancers of the Golden Age—Astaire and Kelly. *Royal Wedding* was an underwhelming screen debut for a young writer who had always loved the movies, but with the much more ambitious *An American in Paris* due to be released later in the year, plus the new contract to write the screen version of *Brigadoon,* all was not lost.[139] Freed's confidence in him was high: $225,000 was paid for the rights to *Brigadoon,* and star names were associated with it from the start (Gene Kelly and Kathryn Grayson,[140] who was soon replaced by Cyd Charisse).[141] In turn, Lerner's spirits were on the rise, and by June 1951 *Paint Your Wagon* neared completion, with previews set to start in September.[142]

After *Brigadoon,* Lerner and Loewe were starting to be regarded as serious competition for Rodgers and Hammerstein, and the new show boasted a stellar list of investors including Mary Martin and Josh Logan (star and director, respectively, of *South Pacific*), Theresa Helburn and Lawrence Langner (directors of the Theatre Guild, who had produced *Oklahoma!* and *Carousel*), and producer Billy Rose.[143] The curtain went up on the first Philadelphia preview of the

[136] Thomas F. Brady, "Ferrer Is Leaving Play for Film Role," *New York Times,* February 27, 1951, 39.

[137] Bosley Crowther, "The Screen in Review," *New York Times,* March 9, 1951, 30.

[138] Lerner, *Street,* 140.

[139] Thomas F. Brady, "*Brigadoon* Listed by Metro for Fall," *New York Times,* March 12, 1951, 20.

[140] Kathryn Grayson (1922–2010) was one of MGM's top stars, with screen appearances including *Show Boat* (1951) and *Kiss Me Kate* (1953).

[141] Thomas F. Brady, "Paramount Names Stallings to Post," *New York Times,* March 14, 1951, 52. Cyd Charisse (1922–2008) was a leading actress and dancer for MGM in the 1950s, with credits including *The Band Wagon* and *Silk Stockings.*

[142] Louis Calta, "*Paint Your Wagon* Will Arrive Oct. 15," *New York Times,* June 19, 1951, 33.

[143] Lewis Funke, "News and Gossip Gathered on the Rialto," *New York Times,* September 2, 1951, 53.

musical on September 17, but it opened to very mixed reviews. Problems with the script, on which Lerner had been working for several years, led to the addition of a three-week Boston preview through most of October, with an extra week after that for final polishing before the Broadway debut on November 12. As part of this process, several songs were added to the score.[144]

In the middle of the stress, Lerner could at least enjoy a momentary respite with the successful opening of *An American in Paris* in October. The film, which starred Gene Kelly, Oscar Levant,[145] and Leslie Caron[146] under the direction of Vincente Minnelli, received glowing reviews and became instantly admired for its artistic vision and ingenious sets, going on to win six Oscars, including one for Lerner's screenplay.[147] But his mind was entirely on his current production, which had been in his head for years and brought him back into contact with Loewe. In an article titled "Painting the Wagon," published the night before the opening, Lerner admitted that it had not been an easy project:

> The show itself was a brute to write. There was too much material. It was hard to coordinate it all and distill it to its purest meaning. Many of the incidents in the show are based upon actual fact. Comstock, of the Comstock Silver Lode, bought his wife from a man who didn't want her and a bill of sale was actually drawn up to consummate the purchase. In *Paint Your Wagon* Ben Rumson (played by James Barton) becomes involved in a variation of that incident. There is a scene where a woman and a child arrive in a camp that has not seen a woman or a child for over a year and a half. The incident is verbatim from an old record. There is a courtroom scene held in a saloon on a Sunday morning after services in which the judge is sentencing a man. His speech is based upon an actual one. These are only a few incidents that come readily to mind, but there are others.
>
> Musically, Fritz went through the same trial and error that I did on the book. Over thirty songs were actually written. Half that number are in the show now. The reason so many songs were discarded was mostly a matter of style. The Western flavor is a hard thing to pin down. James Barrie once said that he could not define charm but he knew when somebody didn't have it. That's very much like Western flavor. In the writing of the songs we weren't sure what we had but we certainly knew when it wasn't there.[148]

[144] Sam Zolotow, "*Paint Your Wagon* to Open on November 5," *New York Times*, September 26, 1951, 37.

[145] Oscar Levant (1906–72) was a pianist, screen actor, personality, and writer.

[146] Leslie Caron (1931–) is an award-winning actress who later appeared in Lerner's *Gigi* (1958).

[147] Thomas M. Pryor, "Decca Would Buy Universal Stock," *New York Times*, October 4, 1951, 38.

[148] Alan Jay Lerner, "Painting the Wagon," *New York Times*, November 11, 1951, X1.

After seven weeks on the road and two delays to the New York opening, the show's critical reception was not as immaculate as might have been hoped, but neither was it a disaster. Brooks Atkinson, for instance, called it "bountiful and exultant," and although he said it was not up to the "artistic standard" of *Brigadoon* because it was "not quite so meticulously edited and organized," for the most part "good humor and romantic beauty" made *Paint Your Wagon* "a very happy evening in the theatre."[149] In an additional article, written five days later, Atkinson commented specifically on Lerner's work: "For *Paint Your Wagon* Alan Jay Lerner, author of *Brigadoon*, has written a more literate book. He is trying to recapture some of the comic naiveté of life in an old mining town. In the second act he runs into some mass resistance that impedes the movement of the production but the first act is freely sketched, spontaneous and convivial. As a whole *Paint Your Wagon* is so heartily enjoyable that a job of loosening and shortening the second act might still be worth attempting."[150] Others were less kind: Robert Garland (*Journal-American*) called it "monotonous" and "quite repetitious," William Hawkins (*World-Telegram and Sun*) said it had "gigantic faults," Walter Kerr (*Herald Tribune*) commented that "Mr. Lerner seems more interested in the authenticity of his background than in the joy of his audience," and Richard Watts Jr. (*New York Post*) simply said "there is something just a little flat about it."[151] Nonetheless, the score included a series of Lerner and Loewe's finest songs, such as "I Talk to the Trees" and "They Call the Wind Maria."

Early the following May, James Barton announced his intention to leave the show, citing the need to take a rest as his reason for his departure after only about half a year. This left the production in trouble, because Barton's name was a huge commercial draw and artistic linchpin, as Lerner explained to him in the following letter:

To James Barton

May 4, 1952

Dear Jim,

I was heartbroken to hear this week that you are leaving the show. It goes without saying that, to me, the show will never be the same without you.

[149] Brooks Atkinson, "At the Theatre," *New York Times*, November 13, 1951, 32.
[150] Brooks Atkinson, "Swell Folks," *New York Times*, November 18, 1951, X1.
[151] Suskin, *Opening Night*, 531–532.

As you know, neither Cheryl [Crawford], Fritz [Loewe] nor I expected you to leave so soon, and although I certainly do not blame you for feeling the need of a rest, it does put us in a kind of difficult position. We are trying very, very hard to find a replacement, but so far we have been unsuccessful. Both Joe E. Brown[152] and Jack Oakie[153] are unavailable. We have two or three other ideas, as of yesterday, that we will get into immediately. If you have any notions on it, please tell Dick LaMarr.[154]

In the meantime, June 1st is just a few weeks away and we may not be able to find a replacement, rehearse him and put him in, in that short a period. At the same time, it would not be possible to play the show without a star of your caliber, in other words, with the understudy, and expect either business or the show to hold up. Therefore, Jim, if there is a one- or two-week delay, would you help us out? You can rest assured we will do our damnedest to find somebody so that you can leave June 1st, but if it isn't possible in that short a period, we would all appreciate it more than we can say if you would stay a little longer, certainly not more than two weeks, and undoubtedly not more than a week.

California is the same - and you know what that means. I can't wait to get finished and get back to my natural habitat. I'll be looking forward to seeing you and Katherine then.

Best love to you both,
Alan

It is interesting to see how keenly and personally Lerner engaged in the running of his musicals, even when he was not the producer. Barton obliged, and in mid-June actor Eddie Dowling[155] took over the role of Rumson.

Dowling's characteristics as an actor were clearly very different to Barton's, and when helping to rehearse Dowling with the existing Broadway company, Lerner evidently made a comment about the differences between the two personalities. He felt his remarks had been misrepresented to Barton, who had heard about it, and Lerner wrote to confirm his respect for the actor:

[152] Joe E. Brown (1891–1973) was an American actor and comedian, perhaps best remembered today for his appearances in movies such as *Show Boat* (1951) and *Some Like It Hot* (1959).

[153] Jack Oakie (1903–1978) was an American actor, whose Hollywood career lasted from the 1920s through to the Doris Day–Rock Hudson film *Lover Come Back* (1961).

[154] Richard LaMarr was a regular casting agent for Lerner and Loewe's Broadway productions, including the original productions of *The Day Before Spring* and *Brigadoon*.

[155] Eddie Dowling (1889–1976) had a wide-ranging career as an actor, producer, director and writer. He appeared in, produced, and directed the original Broadway production of *The Glass Menagerie*.

To James Barton

[Undated; early June 1952]

Dear Jimmy:

I just heard from the theater that my remarks introducing Eddie Dowling to the company were repeated to you in the usual out of shape condition of most second hand things. Actually, all I said was that because Eddie was a different artist than you and had a different interpretation of the part, the play would at first seem different to the company. How this innocent and accurate statement could be twisted is something beyond me. But it seems to have been. I beg you to rest assured that nothing detrimental to you was intended or implied. As you well know, this show was written for <u>you</u> from the very beginning and, as I wrote you not long ago, would always be your show as much as mine.

Anything you've heard to the contrary please ignore. There's obviously a malicious little gremlin loose in the theater.

See you tomorrow.

As always,
Alan

In spite of Lerner's efforts to ensure a smooth transition into the new cast, *Paint Your Wagon* only ran until July 19. Then the writers took the opportunity to revise the piece for the national tour. Looking back over the creative process in December 1952, Lerner explained in *Theatre Arts* that his vision had taken a long time to come into focus:

I started *Paint Your Wagon* in 1947. I began thinking about it the month after *Brigadoon* opened. *Brigadoon* was my first real success. I discovered after it opened that I was guilty of the success illusion just like anyone else. You somehow expect your emotional tensions of the past to disappear overnight. Well, it just doesn't work that way. Realizing this, I decided to write about it, and that's how *Paint Your Wagon* started. My original thought was of the first scene. I visualized two wagons: one going *hopefully* to the gold country, and the other coming back in *despair*. I guess this more or less symbolically represented the reaching for and achieving of personal success. I wanted to tell the story of these two wagons and what lay between their coming and going. Actually, as

> things developed, I finally decided to write the life and death of a ghost town, and to do it in a serious tone.
>
> I did enormous research. It may be that I did too much for the play's good. I think that I became so impassioned with realistic values that I forgot that musical theater is not really interested in that kind of truth. I realize now that I was trying to write what the British call a *gutsy* musical: a lusty, bawdy reproduction of an era. I even tried to write realistic, non-theatrical lyrics.
>
> The reason for so many changes [to the score] was that as we rehearsed each scene in Philadelphia, the show was fine. But when we put all the scenes together, the show fell apart. From the third week of rehearsals to the third week out of town, we were still making changes. Most of the work was done in Boston—two weeks before coming to New York.
>
> One of the problems was a confusion of style. The scenery and the dancing matched; they were both done impressionistically. The music and the book also matched, but they were done realistically. This conflict hurt the unity of the show.
>
> Looking back, I realize that the play got watered down by compromise after compromise.... I talked to a lot of people about the show, and I listened to their criticisms. Finally, I sat down and rewrote it. The really important thing is that my original intentions for the show are still valid and worthwhile. I believe in an honest reproduction of life on the musical stage. I believe in the *gutsy* musical I tried to do. What's more, I believe that musical theatre has to welcome that kind of treatment of earthy people.[156]

But even the revised touring version folded quickly, and *Wagon* never quite repeated the success of *Brigadoon*. Curiously, the London production (1953: 477 performances) ran longer than its Broadway incarnation (289 performances), suggesting that perhaps the exoticism of the Wild West was more appealing to a British audience. Then again, it hardly mattered any more. *Brigadoon* hinted at what was to come from the Lerner and Loewe team, and *Love Life* was among the most ambitious musicals Broadway had yet seen. With the appearance of *An American in Paris, Royal Wedding,* and *Paint Your Wagon* in quick succession, Lerner was now a force to be reckoned with.

[156] Armand Aulicino, "A Musical that Kept on Growing," *Theatre Arts*, December, 1952, 33–35.

CHAPTER 2

"Open Your Eyes"

LERNER WITHOUT LOEWE AND THE MGM YEARS, 1952–1955

In March 1952, Lerner and Loewe entered into discussions with The Theatre Guild about the possibility of writing a musical version of George Bernard Shaw's hit play *Pygmalion* (1912). The rights to the play were owned by Gabriel Pascal, the Hungarian producer who had been responsible for its 1938 film adaptation. Shaw had forbidden all attempts to write a musical version of any of his plays after the popularity of Oscar Straus's operetta *The Chocolate Soldier* (1908) had completely eclipsed that of his play *Arms and the Man* (1894), on which it was based. But following Shaw's death in 1950, Pascal joined forces with The Theatre Guild—the guiding force behind the early Rodgers and Hammerstein musicals *Oklahoma!* and *Carousel*—to try to bring about a musical *Pygmalion*. Rodgers and Hammerstein pondered the idea but could not find a way of developing the adaptation, then Irving Berlin, Frank Loesser, and Cole Porter all considered but turned down the project, mostly because they were too busy with other musicals.

However, Lerner and Loewe sensed the play might suit them and spent several months working on it in 1952. In the following letter, Lerner writes to Pascal about his initial ideas for the adaptation. He also expresses his eagerness for Mary Martin—the star of Rodgers and Hammerstein's *South Pacific* (1949),in which she was appearing in London's West End at the time—to take the role of Eliza Doolittle:

> *To Gabriel Pascal*
>
> 10 May 1952
>
> Dear Gabriel,
>
> I can't find a typewriter on the premises so you'll have to put up with my penmanship. If you have any trouble reading it, call the cryptology division of the F.B.I. and they'll help you.

I had a lovely flight down and for the past two days I've been eating, sleeping, swimming, and sunbathing, and in general catering to all the sensual pleasures. In my books, Hawaii is one of the garden spots of the world. I love it dearly.

Naturally, I've been giving a lot of thought to *Pygmalion* (or shall we start calling it *Lady Liza*?).[1] The more I brood upon it the more excited I become. It really can be a great musical. It's so unusual to find high comedy on such a touching, warm level. The more I think about it, the more convinced I am that the locale should remain England and that it should be designed and styled completely modern, with no references, however, to anything contemporary. At heart, it's a timeless fable and bigger than any period. By treating it in a stylized modern fashion it can not only be a great treat to the eye but can give Liza the opportunity to wear magnificent clothes, all of which is very important dramatically as well as visually. In other words it can be sumptuous but, of course, in infinite taste.

As far as the actual conversion into musical form is concerned, there are two basic problems that I see at this moment—both of which [are] easily overcome. The first is to get it out of the drawing room and into the open; and the second is to tighten the story. By that I mean to give characters such as Mr. Doolittle a more important role in the plot and not just be a highly amusing interlude as he is now. Too, Freddie should be developed into more attractive a fellow so that he can become more of a real threat. In the first instance of getting it out of the drawing room, Fritz and I have several ideas which we didn't have time to discuss with you. The scene in Mrs. Higgins's home for example—the "gin to her was mother's milk" scene—could be played at the opening of Ascot.[2] It could be extremely colorful and lend itself to great humor both musically and otherwise. The calmness of the British aristocracy at the races I always thought very funny. Now, of course, following the motion picture,[3] there are the ball scenes and the wonderfully touching sequence when she returns to Covent Garden and nobody recognizes her. A scene like that could be developed so that the second scene at Mrs. Higgins's when the Professor finds her after his long search could

[1] *Lady Liza* or *My Lady Liza* was the working title of the show until late 1955. For a more detailed genesis of the show, see Dominic McHugh, *Loverly: The Life and Times of "My Fair Lady"* (New York: Oxford University Press, 2012).

[2] The addition of a scene at the Ascot races was one of Lerner's main inventions in the adaptation of *Pygmalion*.

[3] Lerner used Shaw's screenplay for the 1938 film of *Pygmalion*, which contained numerous additions and changes from the original play text, as the basis for the musical.

be obviated. The end of the first act, of course, can be one of the great moments of any musical I can remember. It should be Liza's preparation for the ball, her excitement, her desire to please the Prof., her dressing, her rehearsing, her manners, etc. Musically it should be one of her big, big numbers—ending with her going off with the Prof. for the great and final test.[4] It could be really wonderful, don't you think?

Of course, no matter how excited I get about the play, I always stop when I come to the question: can we get Mary Martin? Although there are undoubtedly others who could play it, I do feel anybody after Mary is second choice. Liza is one of the great parts for a woman ever written. In music it will be even greater. And Mary is obviously the greatest star the musical theater has produced—there's no doubt about that. Somehow it seems like a perfect marriage. It doesn't bother me at all that she is American because if the King's English as taught to her by the Prof. doesn't seem completely compatible with her, neither was it with Liza in the play. And the cockney she can do easily. From a show business point of view it would be a great tour-de-force for her. Then, too, Mary is the only one I know who has naturally that odd combination of the little girl and the great lady. I can't think of another part when both these qualities could be better employed—or on the other side, when Mary could run more of a gamut of all her talents. This is one play that should be written *for* her and *with* her. If you could persuade her and Dick[5] to be as enthusiastic as we are, Fritz and I would gladly fly over and discuss it with her when we have the actual layout completed.

If you fail, Gabriel old boy, then fly right home and persuade me to write it anyhow. I know it's a superb property but at the moment I'm stuck with Mary Martin in my head and in my heart.

On a secondary level of importance, I would love to get Michael Kidd[6] for the choreography. He could do wonderfully humorous things with the cockneys as well as "the swells" and he'd be first rate for Mary. (There I go again with Mary.) He's about the only choreographer who thinks of the show first and thinks that by some chance the star may be more important than his itty-bitty dances. I've already mentioned the project to Mike and he's highly enthusiastic.

[4] Lerner and Loewe wrote a long sequence depicting Eliza's final preparations for the ball, including the songs "Come to the Ball" and "Say a Prayer for Me Tonight," and a ballet. They were cut after the first preview of *My Fair Lady* in New Haven.

[5] Richard Halliday (1905–73), a theater producer, was Mary Martin's husband.

[6] Michael Kidd (1915–2007), choreographer of numerous shows such as *Finian's Rainbow* (1947), *Love Life* (with book and lyrics by Lerner, 1948), and *Guys and Dolls* (1950). Later, he went on to direct and choreograph many projects.

Well, I guess that's about all at the moment. The surf is beginning to call me so I think I'll drop my tired body into the brine. Just wanted you to know that *Pygmalion* haunts me and that I'm hoping and praying God will be with you on your trip to London. Give Mary and Dick my love and tell them I'm ready to do anything short of homicide to see Mary as Liza. I'll be leaving here Sunday, May 18th and I'll be in N. Y. Tuesday, the 20th. Fritz and I have to fly home for a week on matters of *Paint My Wagon* [*sic*]. I'll be at the Algonquin that week and then back on the coast the following Monday.

Bon voyage—and keep us posted.

Faithfully,
Alan

Lerner's relish for the show is palpable. With the benefit of hindsight, it is curious to see how a couple of his initial ideas for the adaptation were very different from the finished product. In particular, the notion of designing the show in a "completely modern" setting seems at odds with the ultimate decision to set it in period (which is central to the depiction of Eliza's social mobility in the show). Equally striking is Lerner's emphasis on his original ideas for the first-act finale, which were woven into a ballet sequence and included in the show's out-of-town tryout in New Haven in February 1956 but cut after one performance. The idea of "obviating" the great Eliza-Higgins encounter at Mrs. Higgins's house is also surprising in light of the brilliance of the "Without You" scene in the finished show. Perhaps most interesting and amusing are the enthusiastic references to actress Mary Martin and choreographer Michael Kidd. According to Lerner's memoir, both of them reacted critically to the show's score when he and Loewe later performed it for them, and both turned it down. It's clear he held this against them, because the accounts of their reactions in his memoir are comically exaggerated, but this letter shows that Lerner desperately wanted both of them at the beginning.[7] Further work on the show was announced in the press in June, but Lerner and Loewe temporarily abandoned it later in the year and only returned to it in 1954.[8]

Pygmalion was by no means the pair's only musical prospect at the time. Barely a month after writing to Pascal, Lerner set his sights on another high-profile property: a musical adaptation of the beloved 1942 Humphrey Bogart-Ingrid Bergman movie, *Casablanca*. It was announced on April 9 that "In the event

[7] Alan Jay Lerner, *The Street Where I Live* (London: Hodder and Stoughton, 1978), 49–51 (on Martin) and 83–84 (on Kidd).

[8] Lewis Funke, "Miss Hepburn and Theatre Guild Await London Reaction to 'Millionairess,'" *New York Times*, June 22, 1952, X1.

Alan Jay Lerner and Frederick Loewe, who co-wrote *Paint Your Wagon,* convert the film, *Casablanca,* into a musical they would like to join hands with Monte Proser and Jack Small in the sponsorship."[9] Though Lerner and Loewe went on to sign provisional contracts to gain the rights to *Casablanca,* the project never seems to have gone beyond the discussion stage, unlike *Pygmalion.*[10] Throughout their working relationship, various projects were mulled over but abandoned, and this period was no exception. They were also beginning to talk about the possible film adaptation of *Paint Your Wagon,* which continued to run on Broadway. As early as January 1952, the newspapers were talking about the competition between the major studios to bid for the screen rights to the show—Paramount wanted it as a Bing Crosby vehicle, while Warner Bros. saw it as perfect material for their leading lady, Doris Day—and in February it was announced that Louis B. Mayer had outbid his rivals.[11] Loewe then departed for Hollywood on March 24 to work with Lerner on the film, which was presumed to be going ahead; their work was broken in May and June when they returned to New York to hire and coach veteran Eddie Dowling to replace James Barton in the stage version of *Wagon* (as noted in the previous chapter).[12] But in the end, the show would take over a decade further to reach the screen, and without Loewe's participation.

February and March also saw Lerner enjoy success in the awards season for his screenplay for *An American in Paris.* On February 18, the Screen Writers Guild of America commended him in the category for the best screenplay for a musical, and the following month saw the ultimate accolade: the Oscar.[13] For all that Lerner is often thought of as a more talented lyricist than scriptwriter, his achievement in this landmark film (which won a total of seven Oscars), and in *Gigi* later in the decade, proves his ability for writing prose when dealing with the right (usually lyric-romantic) material. Buoyed up by the success of *Paris,* Lerner spent the summer of 1952 investing time in a series of ongoing film projects, including the long-awaited adaptation of *Huckleberry Finn* for Gene Kelly and Danny Kaye, as well as improving the book for the tour of *Paint Your Wagon.* Burl Ives, whom the *Times* described as "the troubadour of the ancient and romantic ballad," was set to star in the tour, which was due to start in October, and it was

[9] Sam Zolotow, "Delay in Staging *The Baker's Wife,*" *New York Times,* April 9, 1952, 26.

[10] Thanks to Richard C. Norton for sharing the contracts for *Casablanca* with me.

[11] A. H. Weiler, "Paint Your Wagon Eyed by Coast," *New York Times,* January 20, 1952, X5. Sam Zolotow, "Williams to Open Solo Bill Tonight," *New York Times,* February 4, 1952, 14.

[12] Louis Calta, "Lesser Seeks Cast for *Moulin Rouge,*" *New York Times,* March 25, 1952, 24. Sam Zolotow, "New Unit to Send Six Plays on Tour," *New York Times,* May 21, 1952, 22.

[13] Thomas M. Pryor, "Film Writers Cite Buckner for Movie," *New York Times,* February 19, 1952, 24. "Humphrey Bogart Wins Movie 'Oscar,'" *New York Times,* March 21, 1952, 25.

announced that his part was to be drastically expanded.[14] Indicating Lerner's insatiable appetite for movie work, yet another title was discussed in September, when Arthur Freed announced that plans were under way for a screen adaptation of David Belasco's play *The Girl of the Golden West*, to be filmed on location and adapted by Lerner.[15] It would have been the fourth adaptation of the play for the screen. He didn't always say yes, however. For instance, he turned down the opportunity to make a musical out of Ludwig Bemelmans's[16] novel *Hotel Splendide* (1941), as the following letter to Sam Byrd, a producer acquaintance from the Lamb's Club, reveals:

To Sam Byrd

July 1, 1952

Dear Sam:

Please forgive the long period of silence. I was called suddenly back to California and upon my return found my father seriously ill. All is quiet and well now and I can start thinking again about writing.

I have given *Hotel Splendide* a lot of thought. I think as you do that there is definitely a show there, but where it is, at the moment, I don't know. As I told you, I am a very slow worker and I have to live with things a long time. I wouldn't have the slightest idea when I would find the solution for this project. It might be next week and it might be two years from now. Consequently, rather than subject you to my intellectual vagaries, I feel I must regretfully withdraw from the venture. I will drop the book by at the club the beginning of the week.

I do hope I haven't held you up too long and I wish you all good luck and success.

Thanks for thinking of me in the first place.

Fondly,
Alan

[14] Thomas M. Pryor, "Billy Wilder Lists 'Oedipus Rex' Film," *New York Times*, September 5, 1952. Louis Calta, "Dassin Will Stage Bette Davis Revue," *New York Times*, September 2, 1952, 19. Several of the musical numbers were changed, too, including the addition of the song "Take the Wheels Off the Wagon."

[15] Thomas M. Pryor, "Metro to Remake *Girl of the West*," *New York Times*, September 26, 1952, 18.

[16] Ludwig Bemelmans (1898–1962) was a writer and illustrator, best known for his children's books.

Of note here is Lerner's candid self-assessment about his slow progress as a writer and adapter, which frequently caused him to delay or abandon his plans.

This period spelled the temporary end of the Lerner-Loewe collaboration, following a disagreement. Although Lerner, always eager to be politically involved, took time out in October to participate in a major Democratic rally at Madison Square Garden in order to boost Adlai Stevenson's bid for the presidency of the United States, the remainder of the year was spent in developing movie projects without his old partner. A new collaborator was needed, and Lerner found one in the person of Arthur Schwartz, composer of 1930s hits such as *The Band Wagon* as well as producer of movies including *Cover Girl*. Schwartz's witty, elegant style was the perfect foil for Lerner's lightness of touch as a lyricist, and a slew of projects was announced. First up was the movie adaptation of *Paint Your Wagon*. Only a few of the original Lerner-Loewe songs were now to be retained, and Lerner and Schwartz wrote nine new numbers; although they were never used, copies of the songs are held in the Library of Congress's Arthur Schwartz Collection. This was the surest sign yet that the rift between Lerner and Loewe was serious. On February 11, 1953, it was suggested in the press that the movie would be "the first feature-length entertainment film to be made in the Cinerama process." It was due to go into production in June and be released in October, with Louis B. Mayer still onboard as producer[17].

A month later, a further Lerner-Schwartz venture was announced: "Arthur Schwartz and Alan Jay Lerner have reached an agreement with Al Capp to make a musical of his popular cartoon, *Li'l Abner*," reported Louis Calta.[18] The article also claimed that Lerner was writing a play for Schwartz to produce on Broadway with him, though there is no evidence that he ever began work on it. By June, yet another production was on the cards for the new team: Lerner was to create the script and lyrics for an MGM movie of *Kismet*, to music by Schwartz. Cyd Charisse was lined up to star in this revamp of the old 1944 film of the same name, but the studio went on to make the film as a straightforward adaptation of Wright and Forrest's Broadway hit version of the story, which opened out of town in the summer of 1953 and reached Broadway in December of the same year.[19] With so many plans for the future, Lerner was evidently happy with his new creative partner, though the article also mentions

[17] Thomas M. Pryor, "Cinerama Slates Full-Length Film," *New York Times*, February 11, 1953, 35.

[18] Louis Calta, " 'Li'l Abner' Baged by Two Showmen," *New York Times*, March 17, 1953, 26.

[19] Thomas M. Pryor, "Disney Is Testing Fox' Cinemascope," *New York Times*, June 27, 1953, 7. The adaptation of the Wright-Forrest version was released in 1955.

Figure 2.1 Frederick Loewe and Alan Jay Lerner in the early 1960s. Credit: Photofest

two forthcoming MGM-Lerner projects that did not involve Schwartz, namely, *Brigadoon* (whose Frederick Loewe score was to be left largely intact), due for production in September, and *Huckleberry Finn* (still with its Burton Lane music), tentatively scheduled for February 1954.

But the cracks started to show only a few weeks later. On July 15, *Li'l Abner* was suddenly postponed to the 1954–55 season—more than a year ahead.[20] This was the first indication that insufficient work was being produced. Lerner and Schwartz were supposedly "busy" with unspecified "Hollywood matters." In reality, personal worries had begun to stunt Lerner's progress. The first was health related, as he told his good friend Irene Mayer Selznick[21] in mid-July:

[20] Sam Zolotow, "'Mr. Byculla' Is Set for Broadway Run," *New York Times*, July 15, 1953, 21.

[21] Irene Mayer Selznick (1907–90) was an American theater producer of several important plays, including *A Streetcar Named Desire* (1947).

To Irene Mayer Selznick

July 20, 1953

Dear, dear Irene:

Just so you won't think I am in California and haven't called you, I wanted you to know there's been a change in my plans. Chances are I won't leave for the Coast for at least two weeks. There is also the possibility that I may not come at all.

The reason for the change is that I just spent three enchanting weeks in the hospital with an old fashioned case of spinal meningitis. Considering the fact that this is the first time I have been sick since I was eleven years old, you can imagine how irksome the whole business has been. I've always taken it as a personal affront when anybody I know is indisposed, and I have absolutely no sympathy for myself when it happens to me. However, aside from feeling as weak as a whore when the Navy is in town, I am my old alarming self again, and, outside of a few missing reflexes in one leg, which should return shortly, all parts of me function as usual.

I do hope I'll be able to get to the Coast. I would love to see you and the boys again. The day you all came up was one of the nicest I can remember. Be sure and give them my warmest regards, and as for you, darling,

All my love,
Alan

Lerner's other ongoing problem was the infirmity of his beloved father, who was his hero and role model. The following letter to Goddard Lieberson,[22] the head of Columbia Records, hints at Lerner's efforts to make his father's final months as enjoyable as possible, as well as at his own continuing health troubles:

To Goddard Lieberson

July 23, 1953

My boy:

Forgive me for bothering you with a seeming triviality, except, it is not quite a triviality to me.

[22] Goddard Lieberson (1911–77) was the president of Columbia Records (from 1956 to 1971 and 1973 to 1975) and the producer of a string of original cast albums, including that of *My Fair Lady*.

As you probably know, my father is an invalid, and anything I can do to brighten his days, I rush to do. His favorite record is an old one by Buddy Clark of "In My Dreams I Kiss Your Hand, Madame." He has now worn it out and cannot get another pressing. If it isn't too much trouble, do you think you could pass this along to somebody in the appropriate department and ask him to send me C.O.D. two copies of that record? I would appreciate it ever so much.

I am just out of the hospital myself, after a long siege. As soon as I feel a little more like my old Democratic self, I'll call you, and let's get together. It's been a long time. Too long.

I hope the above request won't be too much trouble.

Fondly,
Alan

Lieberson, one of Lerner's close friends, soon acceded to his request, commenting that "These records are to serve for a long time and I hope that your father will get many hours of enjoyment out of them." Lieberson added: "I must see you soon because there is a dance we've got to practice. It's called the Eisenhower Glide. If you want to work on it without me, here are the directions: One step forward, two steps back; turn to the left, hesitate; turn to the right, hesitate; turn to the left, hesitate; turn to the right, hesitate; side-step. Do you think you can do it?" This reference to General Eisenhower,[23] who had become president of the United States in January 1953, indicates that Lieberson was, like Lerner, a diehard Democrat. Lerner quickly replied to thank him for his support:

To Goddard Lieberson

August 10, 1953

Dear Goddard:

Thanks ever so much for helping me out with the records. I appreciate it more than you know.

I'm still recuperating in the country from a bout with spinal meningitis, and I doubt if I'll be coming to New York for another two weeks. When I do, I'll certainly call you, and perhaps we'll be able to break gluten toast at "21." If you absolutely insist, I will bring Fritz Loewe along.

[23] Dwight D. Eisenhower (1890–1969) was president from January 20, 1953, to January 20, 1961.

Hope your brood is all well. Give Brigita . . . I mean, Brigitta . . . I mean, Briggitta . . . well anyhow, please give your wife my love.

Fondly,
Alan

The bitter allusion to Loewe shows the extent to which the writers of *Brigadoon* had burned their bridges.

A few days later, Lerner and Schwartz signed up to yet another project that would never see the light of day—a children's television musical for the Ford Foundation[24]—and Lerner clearly felt *Abner* could be a major show, as the following telegram to Schwartz proves:

To Arthur Schwartz

July 21, 1953

JUST HAD AND [*SIC*] EXHILARATING MEETING WITH AL CAPP. CONTRACTS WERE SIGNED. I HAVE COLLECTED YOUR $20. I AM MORE ENTHUSIASTIC THAN EVER AND CAN'T WAIT TO GO TO WORK. HOPE YOU WILL BRUSH ASIDE ALL NEGATIVE FEELINGS AND THROW YOURSELF INTO WHAT I AM CONVINCED CAN BE ONE OF THE MOST EXCITING EXPERIENCES OF BOTH OUR LIVES.

ALAN

But although movie star Van Johnson was rumored to have been cast in the musical in September, Schwartz's impatience with Lerner reached an impasse in November. He decided to collaborate with Dorothy Fields[25] on her new show, *By the Beautiful Sea*, instead. Burton Lane was to have written the music for Fields, but he withdrew after major changes were made to *Beautiful Sea*'s story line, providing Schwartz with the perfect last-minute opportunity to find an alternative to working with Lerner.[26] A clue to the reason for Schwartz's frustration was revealed on October 29, when Lerner announced he had started writing the screenplay for the non-musical movie version of the W. H.

[24] Val Adams, "News and Notes Gathered from the Studios," *New York Times*, August 16, 1953, X9.

[25] Dorothy Fields (1905–74) was perhaps the most successful female librettist and lyricist of her era. She was responsible for writing the book for *Annie Get Your Gun* (1946) and the lyrics for *Sweet Charity* (1966), among many others.

[26] Louis Calta, "News of the Stage," *New York Times*, November 12, 1953, 37.

Hudson novel *Green Mansions* for Arthur Freed, thereby delaying all plans for his musical projects.[27] Left with nothing to do, Schwartz was glad to jump ship, even if it meant the end of the relationship with Lerner and, sadly, thereby wasting the nine well-honed songs they had written for the *Wagon* film. These seem to have been the only products of the collaboration, and none of the other announced projects were ever written.

In an unusual twist of fate, Lane took Schwartz's place as the composer of *Abner*, and it seemed like the *Royal Wedding* team was to reunite for at least a couple of new musicals (including *Huckleberry Finn*). In a letter from this period, Freed wrote to Lerner about the end of his association with Schwartz, as well as mentioning his screenplay adaptation of *Brigadoon*, which had been submitted in early October.[28] "Naturally, I've been giving a lot of thought to *Brigadoon* because at long last the starting date is getting closer and closer. In going over the music I realize more than ever what a great score it is," he commented. "Confidentially, I've been a little put out about Arthur Schwartz's conduct," he added, "and while I would be the last person in the world not to fight for the proper credit of any creator, I certainly resented the ultimatums and, it seems to me, the pettiness of the whole affair. Frankly, I've lost my desire and enthusiasm for working with him. It seems to me the desire to work with you and, incidentally, myself should have made anything else secondary. I'm a funny guy; I just don't like one-sided love affairs."

Aside from his main projects, friends and colleagues constantly wrote to Lerner to ask him for favors or help. For instance, a letter arrived in September from Lotte Lenya, the widow of Kurt Weill, asking him to reminisce with her about his time with Weill on writing the groundbreaking *Love Life*. "A publisher has asked me to write a biography of Kurt," she reported. "Of course, the whole story of your collaboration on *Love Life* must be told, and I want to get all the facts down with complete accuracy." Although brief, Lerner's reply reveals the affection with which he regarded the composer:

To Lotte Lenya

October 5, 1953

[27] Thomas M. Pryor, "Metro Will Film *Green Mansions*," *New York Times*, October 29, 1953, 42.

[28] This letter is reproduced in Hugh Fordin, *MGM's Greatest Musicals* (New York: Da Capo, 1996), 423–424.

Lenya dear,

I'm off to California for about ten days. As soon as I return I'll put down all I can remember about *Love Life*. I hate to do it. It's going to make me very sad.

See you soon.

Love to you and George.[29]

Fondly,
Alan

Many of the letters that were found during the research for this book but omitted from it are notes such as this, arranging meetings or offering assistance to a range of friends and acquaintances.

Lerner's work during the second half of 1953 revolved around Arthur Freed, and specifically *Green Mansions* and *Huckleberry Finn*. The latter was to be a musical adaptation of Mark Twain's novel and was probably first mooted as an immediate follow-up to *Royal Wedding* for Lerner and Lane (though a few manuscripts in the Burton Lane Collection at the Library of Congress suggest that E. Y. Harburg was briefly intended as the lyricist). Danny Kaye was cast as the Dauphin, with Gene Kelly as the Duke. As with *An American in Paris* and *Brigadoon,* Vincente Minnelli was to direct. In this letter, Lerner discusses details of the plot structure, which was still in development:

To Arthur Freed

December 29, 1953

Dear Arthur:

Under separate cover I am sending you *Huck Finn*. I have included all the lyrics, some of which were not in the studio script, and all in all, including the lyrics I have added, I think I will have cut around twenty-five to thirty pages.

As you know from our discussions, there was no major problem in cutting and editing up to the arrival at the Grangerford's. The Grangerford sequence, as I worked on it, seemed to me to present two major problems, and I am not sure even now that they are licked. That's

[29] The influential fiction editor George Davis (1906–57) was Lenya's second husband.

something that may well require not only further work, but possibly even a whole new idea—although I doubt the latter.

The two problems were: 1) It seemed to get farcical and therefore over-plotty, and 2) The section is on the skimpy side musically. It seemed to get out of lyric theatre and to fall more into a picture with songs.

As you will see from reading the script, I tried to handle the first problem by simply cutting the fat and therefore placing the story line that much more in relief. In dealing with the second problem, I put in a montage to "The World's Full of Suckers," which montage leads directly into "When You Grow Up You'll Know." The incidents of the montage are a little sketchy even now, but if you and Vincente like the dramatic theme of the montage, when the time comes to prepare the final script for shooting I am sure they can be improved upon. There is no doubt that the montage gives us a great musical pickup and telescopes an awful lot of story line and lapses of time.

It was great fun working on the script again, even though I felt like I was buying a marriage license for a wedding next year. It's really a wonderful project, and I can't wait for "the big push," when you, Vincente and I really tear into it, with production imminent. If everything goes off according to schedule, I imagine that moment will be some time next winter. Needless to say, when that time does come I will be at your disposal wherever and for how long you want me to be.

From my experience with you and Vincente on *An American in Paris* and *Brigadoon,* it's only when the three of us are working together for immediate production that a really final script can be prepared. However, I think the cut version I just finished is a pretty good scaffolding for that last period of concentrated work.

In the meantime, have a wonderful New Year.

Devotedly,
Alan

The letter refers to the cutting of an earlier studio script, a copy of which is currently housed in the New York Public Library, and unlocks some of Lerner's techniques for improving his work. The references to "cutting the fat" and adding a "montage" attest to his high level of self-awareness as a writer. Whether his judgments on improving this specific script were well placed is impossible to confirm because the film was never made, but as a window into the atmosphere of his "workshop" this letter is invaluable.

Lerner worked hard during this period on his MGM assignments, and both he and Minnelli were particularly enthusiastic about the *Green Mansions* project. In the absence of Loewe, Minnelli almost seemed to become Lerner's replacement collaborator, and in view of their mutual inclination toward fantasy on the screen—something that comes explicitly into *An American in Paris, Brigadoon,* and *On a Clear Day You Can See Forever*—their attitudes to the movie musical were evidently sympathetic with one another. But the adaptation of Hudson's fantasy about a traveler to a Venezuelan jungle who encounters a forest dweller, Rima the Bird Girl, was a complicated process. MGM had owned the rights for eight years by the time Lerner was given the go-ahead to make his adaptation in September 1953.[30] By early 1954, he in turn was starting to have his doubts, which he underlines in the following letter to Freed:

To Arthur Freed

January 12, 1954

Dear Arthur:

Enclosed is a kind of general outline for *Green Mansions*. I use the words "general outline" loosely, because what you will find is certainly more of an expression of my general approach to the book and an indication of some of the scenes I intend to omit and some of the relatively minor changes I intend making.

I think what is very important to keep in mind is that *Green Mansions,* even as a novel, is not a perfect work of art, as is, for example, *Huckleberry Finn,* and that it is generally conceded even by the most ardent Hudson admirers in the literary world that his character delineation and plot development were far less perfect than his exquisite prose facility. I'll be more specific in the "outline."

I'll call you next weekend. I'm glad all is well with *Brigadoon*.

Love,
Alan

The agony lingers in the next two letters, as Lerner continued to ponder the *Green Mansions* material. More than one ending to the film was considered, and increasingly it became apparent that the strength of the source material was its linguistic surface (as Lerner indicates above), rather than its narrative structure. He also hints at the ongoing development of *Huckleberry Finn* in

[30] Thomas M. Pryor, "Metro Will Film *Green Mansions*," *New York Times*, October 29, 1953, 42.

these letters, particularly in the second. Ironically, Lerner's problem with *Finn* was the opposite of the one with *Mansions*: Twain's book is episodic in nature, with lots of action but perhaps lacking the simple teleological structure of most musicals' plots. As Lerner said, the problem with adapting a serialized story is that "there are so many ways of doing it"—words that bring to mind Stephen Sondheim's discussion of his own struggles when trying to make a musical out of the episodic *Mary Poppins* stories when he was a teenager (he ultimately abandoned his attempt).[31] *Green Mansions* and *Finn* were developed in tandem while *Brigadoon* was being made (production started the second week of December)[32]—a sign of Lerner's central importance to the Freed Unit at this period of high activity for MGM:

To Arthur Freed

January 15, 1954

Dear Arthur:

Since I spoke to you on the phone, I've been going through a one-man debate about the ending—my feeling about it swinging back and forth for the last few days. Hence the delay in sending the outline.

The ending that you read is, of course, the one I am certain now is right. When I see you I'll tell you what the alternative in my mind was.

Huck will go out over the weekend.

Love,
Alan

To Arthur Freed

January 16, 1954

Dear Arthur:

Here are the changes for *Huck*.

There was no problem cutting the Grangerford section. As for the beginning, I went over it with a fine toothcomb and gave it a great deal of thought, and actually in the present structure there isn't too much that can be done about revealing Huck himself before the song, unless

[31] Stephen Banfield, *Sondheim's Broadway Musicals* (Ann Arbor: University of Michigan Press, 1994), 18-20.

[32] Hugh Fordin, *MGM's Greatest Musicals*, 427.

we include some new situations. One of the dangers of that, of course, is that it would be such a long time before a song. As you remember, in the first draft I had a huge court trial about whether Huck should go to Widow Brown or Pap. When Huck finds out he is to go to Pap, he runs away. Before that scene, however, there was a small scene between Huck and Jim, leading into the song, "Huckleberry Finn." In that way we had a song practically in the first three minutes. Unfortunately, the trial scene was just too long for the balance of the picture. That was when we got the idea of the present opening of having everyone think Huck is dead.

This situation is so tight, I would hesitate to cloud it with extraneous matter. Therefore, what I have tried to do is establish Huck a little more before the song and a little more after. If this still seems inadequate and it still seems that Huck is not established properly, then I think we have to re-examine the whole opening idea.

My own personal opinion is that the present opening idea is absolutely right, and that we may have to include another sequence with Huck and Jim before introducing the Duke and Dauphin, in order to put everything in the right proportion.

One of the peculiarities of *Huck* as a project is that there are so many ways of doing it, any one of which can be made right. In the final analysis, it will be a matter of choice what we do, rather than the usual procedure of suddenly recognizing the one and only way and doing it that way.

This aside, I am now into *Green Mansions*, and you will be receiving the opening sequence within the next ten days. I see Tyrone Power[33] more and more as I work on it. He has the well-born look and air of a gentleman that Brando[34] lacks, plus the lyricism that Robert Taylor[35] lacks. Of course (and I am assuming the man I am about to suggest is still young enough), I suppose the most really ideal casting of all would be Laurence Olivier.[36] I have had him in my mind, too, for a long time,

[33] Stage and film actor Tyrone Power (1914–58) was the star of Hollywood blockbusters such as *The Mark of Zorro* (1940). In this section of the letter, we can see Lerner discussing the attributes of various possible stars for the film, as was characteristic of his work: he preferred to write with specific actors in mind.

[34] Marlon Brando (1924–2004) was the Academy Award–winning star of films such as *A Streetcar Named Desire* (1951), *Julius Caesar* (1953), *On the Waterfront* (1954), and *The Godfather* (1972), among many others.

[35] Robert Taylor (1911–69) appeared in a wide range of films including the musical *Broadway Melody of 1936* and the drama *Waterloo Bridge* (1940).

[36] One of the most versatile and powerful actors of the twentieth century, Laurence Olivier (1907–89) was discussed in connection with several Lerner projects, though he never appeared in any of them.

and the only reason I haven't mentioned him is that I thought he was impossible to get. But he, obviously, is in the great tradition of classic actors. Whereas, José Ferrer,[37] also in that tradition, has great equipment, but the soul of a pistachio nut. Olivier, at least as an actor, has a soul as big as his talent. The nearest thing to him in the quality we need for *Green Mansions*—for me, anyhow—is Power.

I'm also terribly excited about that "future project" I mentioned on the phone. I think it's a better and fresher venture even than *Marco Polo*,[38] and absolutely marvelous for Gene [Kelly]. Also, an absolutely ideal part for Cyd [Charisse], or Leslie [Caron], for that matter. (One of these days, we've got to do another picture for Gene and Leslie.) So prepare yourself, when I come out I'm going to try and sell the pants off you.

If you want any more changes in *Huck*, let me know.

Love,
Alan

P.S. Forgive the paper—I left my stationery in the office.

As well as the explanation of his changes to the screenplay, this letter is useful for explaining some of Lerner's ideas about casting, with frank comments about a handful of the leading actors of the time.

In the next two letters, which are undated but are relevant to this period, Lerner writes to Minnelli and Freed about *Huckleberry Finn*, on which he was working in earnest:

To Vincente Minnelli

[Undated]

Dear Vince –

I think this is right, but if it isn't, at least you have something to correct.

I've had a bitch of a time with the river lyric.[39] I thought I was finished yesterday but then this morning it looked rotten to me, so I'm working on it again.

[37] José Ferrer (1912–92) was another star of stage and screen whom Lerner considered for several shows, and he directed Lerner's *Carmelina* (1979) on Broadway.

[38] No further evidence survives to explain Lerner's reference to *Marco Polo*, but presumably it was a subject he briefly considered turning into a film for Freed.

[39] A song called "I'll Wait for You by the River."

However, be of good cheer. Rehearsals start tomorrow morning[40] and if all goes well at the first reading, and I have every reason to think it will, I'm going up to the country for a few days and finally finish up all the lyric work on the picture. I'll call you over the weekend to talk about Gene's number.

I hope I haven't been too much of a problem. I'll try to make up for the delay with quality.

I miss you. We must do a picture together sometime.

Love,
Huck

To Arthur Freed

[Undated]

Dear Chief,

Yes, I'm really enclosing a lyric. And there isn't one line missing![41] I hope the shock won't be too great.

"I'm from Missouri" is in the works and I'll have it in a few days at the latest. "I'll Wait for You by the River" has two lines missing. Gene's number I'll get to next week-end.

I now weigh twenty-two pounds and have the color of the pages of a first edition of Dante's Inferno. Other than that I'm fine.

Glad everything is going well. Keep me posted.

Love, love, love,
Alan
Alan Jay Lerner
Fourth Assistant
To The Second Secretary
Of the First Ass-Kisser
Of The Head of Music Department

Though it is perhaps difficult to appreciate every detail contained in these letters, it is nevertheless fascinating to see how Freed continued to push his team to produce new material, even in the face of the imminent collapse of the movie musical as a commercial genre. Freed's active involvement in the

[40] Presumably a reference to Paint Your Wagon.

[41] Lerner famously agonized over his lyric writing, by his own admission; see Lerner, *Street*, 68–69.

content of the development of the material is also striking: perhaps this is one of the key reasons that so many of his movies have endured, compared to those of some of his contemporaries. This correspondence is all we have left of what could have been two major films of the decade, given the personnel involved.

As much as Hollywood provided plenty to distract him, Lerner's heart was always drawn toward the stage. Excited though he clearly was about *Finn* and *Green Mansions*, he showed renewed interest in a Broadway project that had been brewing for almost a year, *Li'l Abner*. By early February 1954, the personnel for the show started to take shape. Herman Levin was to produce, with Michael Kidd as choreographer, and Lane had firmly taken Schwartz's place as composer.[42] But the lynchpin of the project was to be the director, Robert Lewis (1909–97), who had directed the original Broadway production of *Brigadoon* and went on to direct Lerner's later work *On a Clear Day You Can See Forever*. This letter offers him the job as director of *Abner* and outlines the timescale of the project:

To Robert Lewis

February 3, 1954

Dear, dear Bobbie:

Sorry I missed seeing you before you left, but life ganged up on me that week, and by the time I disentangled myself, you were already sipping 11:00 o'clock bouillon in your deck chair. Anyhow, I hope you "voyaged bon."

Not too much has happened since you left. I haven't even had another daughter. The only slightly good news I can relate is that there is a great possibility that Billy Rose is about to have a crashing flop. His production of *The Immoralist*[43] opened in New York Monday night, and he publically asked the critics not to come for a week, while they doctored things up a bit. From all I can glean, the critics will come next Monday night and publically ask the audience not to come from then on. Oh, happy day![44]

Everything has finally been straightened out on *Li'l Abner*. Burton Lane is doing the music, and Herman Levin will produce. (On the

[42] Louis Calta, "New Play Bought by Theatre Guild," *New York Times*, February 2, 1954, 19.

[43] The Immoralist was a play by Augustus and Ruth Goetz, based on André Gide's novel (1902) of the same name.

[44] As noted in Chapter 1, producer and songwriter Billy Rose was to have produced the original *Brigadoon* on Broadway, but Lerner and Loewe parted ways with him after he wanted to rewrite some of their material; Lerner never forgave him for his disrespectful attitude toward Loewe's work.

production end, I will be kind of a silent partner.) Herman is a very close friend of Al Capp's and came into the picture at a crucial moment. He turned out to be indispensable in helping us hurdle several problems with Capp and making the entire project possible. Not only that, he is an old friend of Burton's. He is in complete sympathy with the project, and I feel he is ideal on all counts.

I mention all this because I know you and he had difficulties in the past, and I am hoping that those difficulties won't stand in the way of our working together again—at long last. From Herman's point of view, all I can tell you is that he is as enthusiastic about the possibility of your doing the play as I am, and you know how much my heart is set on it.

We now have a definite schedule. We are planning rehearsals for somewhere between the 15th of September and October 1st. Under ordinary circumstances we would wait on a choreographer until the director were signed, so that he would be a part of that choice. However, you and I have spoken about the choreographic problem together, and I know that we are in agreement about the rightness of Michael Kidd. Consequently, Herman and I are going to the Coast sometime this month, at which time Herman can talk to him about it.

I have been working terribly hard on the book, and I am more excited about the project than ever. I have an outline, but I would prefer not sending it to you, but waiting until you return, when we will have a few songs and a few scenes either written or laid out in detail. The basic reason we feel confident in scheduling rehearsals now is because of the general enthusiasm about the outline and because we all feel that the road is clear for the writing.

If you are still as interested in doing the show as you were before you left (and I hope to God you are), the time has now come to make everything official. And so, old boy, please write me and tell me: a) That you can't wait to do *Li'l Abner* and that if you don't do it you will die, and b) Whom we should talk to about drawing up a contract.

I finally saw *Teahouse*[45] and was completely enchanted. I am sure it will be as big a hit in London as it is here. I hope all is going well.

I'll be looking forward to hearing from you. If you have no time to write, a cable will do.

Devotedly,
Alan

[45] *Teahouse of the August Moon* was a play by John Patrick that had opened to huge acclaim on Broadway in October 1953.

By June, *Abner* was one of three musicals that Lewis was "wondering about" for his next project, according to the *New York Times*,[46] and a November rehearsal date was now mentioned, but in the end Lerner did not see the project to completion.

This was hardly surprising, considering how much work he had on at the time. With *Brigadoon* being filmed and *Finn* still on the backburner, he resumed work on *Green Mansions* and started to develop the outline into a script. In the following letter, Lerner nervously submits the first 25 pages to Freed and Minnelli for their opinion. His passion for the movie is palpable, but it is also clear that he is still unsure as to how to overcome the unevenness of the source material.

To Arthur Freed

February 9, 1954

Dear Arthur:

Here are the first twenty-five pages of *Green Mansions*. I am also sending a copy to Lillie,[47] with instructions to read it and then pass it along to Vincente, so that there will be two copies in the studio.

It goes without saying that at this point in the writing, the script is my lover. I don't know whether she's bad or good—I only know I love it. Consequently, after you and Vincente have read it and we speak on the phone, I hope you will discuss it in violent terms. I hope it's either wonderful or it stinks. If it's mediocre, I'll be lost. If it stinks, it'll be obvious why.

I am hoping you will be able to tell even from these few pages that I am trying to make the narrative as pure and simple as possible, and make every scene pertinent to the story and, here in the beginning, to the humanizing of Abel. I am resisting desperately the temptation to write "charm" and "local color." I feel very keenly that it must never look like a fantasy, but at the same time the story must be tight from beginning to end. I am also trying to write it economically, not only to preserve the mood and narrative flow, but also so that there will be adequate room for the visual.

[46] Sam Zolotow, "Lewis Wondering about 3 Musicals," *New York Times*, June 21, 1954, 20.

[47] Lily Messenger (dates unknown) was Freed's assistant, responsible for carrying out many responsible duties for him, including negotiations with writers and stars (as is clear from the many mentions in Fordin, *MGM's Greatest Musicals*).

I was delighted to talk to you three Highlanders[48] Monday. If I seemed a little vague, it's because while you are punting on the Doon, I am cruising up the Orinoco. I'll call you Sunday. Can't wait for your reaction.

Love,
Alan

The spring of 1954 saw Lerner continuing to work on his Hollywood projects, as well as collaborating with Lane on *Abner*. Then on July 18, his father Joseph J. Lerner died of cancer in New York's Memorial Hospital at the age of 67, after more than 50 grueling operations.[49] Naturally, this came as a huge blow to Lerner: he idolized his father, who had introduced him to musical theater as a boy and to whom he owed his all-round cultural education. Years later, he wrote with affection of his father's final weeks: "One day when I was pushing his bed into the elevator to take him into the operating room, he wrote to me: 'I suppose you're wondering why I want to live.' It was precisely what I was thinking and I nodded. He wrote another note and just before the nurses took him away, he tore it from the pad and stuffed it into my hand.... It read: 'Because I want to see what happens to you.' "[50] This story is one of the most affectionate in Lerner's autobiography, and underlines the pain he clearly still felt many years later.

Lerner tried to battle on with his portfolio of work, now turning back to *Green Mansions*. As Vincente Minnelli geared up to create a screen test for Pier Angeli[51] to play Rima the Bird Girl, Lerner wrote hurriedly to Freed to inform him that he intended to be on hand to observe Angeli's suitability for the role (he hoped she would speak in a bird-like voice):

To Arthur Freed

August 9, 1954

Dear Arthur:

No word from Clift[52] as yet. I am also awaiting the call from Metro about the appointment with the professor at Cornell.[53] I think it's very important that I see both of them before I come out.

[48] A reference to *Brigadoon*, which was currently in production.

[49] Unknown, "Joseph J. Lerner of Chain Stores," *New York Times*, July 19, 1954, 19.

[50] Lerner, *Street*, 23.

[51] Italian screen actress Pier Angeli (1932–71) was under contract for a series of films for MGM in 1950s.

[52] Montgomery Clift (1920–66) was one of the top movie stars of the 1950s thanks to a string of popular appearances including *From Here to Eternity* (1953). Evidently Lerner was interested in discussing *Green Mansions* with him.

[53] Although it is unclear to whom Lerner is referring, this sentence suggests he was again being tempted to over-research his projects, in spite of his comments cited earlier about the problems of doing this with *Paint Your Wagon*.

I spoke to Vincente a couple of days ago, and we both thought it would be a good idea if I were on the Coast while he's making the test of Pier Angeli. I had planned to come around the 18th, but because of some meetings that have just come up concerning my father's estate, for which my brother is flying here next Monday, I think it will now be next weekend, or around the 21st. I hope this is satisfactory. If it isn't, please let me know.

I'll call you as soon as I know something about Clift.

Love,
Alan

A week later, the *New York Times* reported that the film was still on schedule to begin filming in October on location in Venezuela. The article included a couple of quotations from Lerner (flatteringly referred to as "a man of tomorrow"),[54] who said, "The idea is to photograph that lush jungle terrain at its peak; as the rains end, the dry season begins." Of the adaptation, he commented, "The novel is an allegory, not always the easiest thing to handle, but I've tried to be as faithful as was humanly possible to the story, translating it into terms of pure action and understanding." [55] Though he was confident enough to announce the project (and even draw attention to his approach), the vagueness of his words reveals his persistent struggle with this material.

The article also mentioned that Lerner was "busy collaborating with Burton Lane on the forthcoming stage musicalization of the 'Li'l Abner' comic strip." Yet fate was quickly to bring this project to a final standstill. In July, Gabriel Pascal had died, and his obituary called Lerner's attention back to the *Pygmalion* project for Broadway. It was a bittersweet decision to take on this material only a few weeks after his father's death, since Lerner owed his love of language to his elder parent, to whom as a student he never sent a letter "that he did not return to me with notes in the margin suggesting more interesting ways of saying the same sentence";[56] perhaps Higgins came to represent a putative father-figure for Lerner. Around a month later, probably in early September, he was reconciled with his old collaborator Fritz Loewe. It is surely no accident that the move to patch things up coincided with Lerner's reminder of human mortality in his father's death. They joined forces with Herman Levin, who was due to produce *Abner* but agreed to take on *Pygmalion* as well. The show was announced on October 11 and immediately incurred the wrath of The Theatre Guild, which had

[54] I.e., Superman.

[55] Howard Thompson, "The Local Screen Scene," *New York Times*, August 15, 1954, X5.

[56] Lerner, *Street*, 17.

brought the *Pygmalion* project to Lerner and Loewe in 1952. Theresa Helburn and Lawrence Langner wrote to Lerner on behalf of the Guild in disgust and demanded justice, but, as Lerner reminds them in this letter, they had long relinquished their rights to the play and no "dirty trick" was involved:

To Theresa Helburn and Lawrence Langner

October 19, 1954

Dear Terry and Lawrence:

I returned from California a few days ago and found your disturbing, but flattering, letter. Because I was the one who withdrew from the project originally, I am answering your letter myself rather than in conjunction with Fritz, even though Fritz and I have discussed the matter thoroughly and I am, in a sense, speaking for both of us.

My reaction is puzzlement[57] and bewilderment. Pascal, not The Theatre Guild, was the owner of the rights, and it was he who approached us about the project in California, much before any arrangement with The Theatre Guild. Our obvious obligation, if not legal, but definitely ethical, is to Pascal. When I came to New York two or three months later, Fritz and I were told by Gaby that he was entering into a producing partnership with the Guild. I can only believe that, in your great love for the property itself, and your highly complimentary enthusiasm for Fritz's and my participation in it, which we both remember well, you have forgotten some of the facts. After all, Gaby was negotiating with Thompson and Allen[58] before he died. Suppose that negotiation had been concluded and they had approached Fritz and me and we had accepted? Would you have written us as you did? Of course not. The property belonged to Pascal as it now belongs to his estate, and it is with his estate we negotiated.

That disposed of, perhaps you are wondering why Fritz and I didn't come to you now, when we suddenly found a solution for some of the artistic problems. The answer is very simple. I am sure you remember the difficulty you and I had over the royalty agreement. Nothing discouraged me as much at the time as the fact that everybody held firm on their royalty and only the author was asked to accept less than minimum.

[57] Perhaps a reference to the King of Siam's song in Rodgers and Hammerstein's *The King and I.*

[58] Thompson and Allen were perhaps rival producers or agents.

My ego was not troubled, but my sense of fairness was definitely jarred. Suffice to say I have improved my lot with Herman Levin.

In spite of the above, I found my brief association with you most pleasant and cannot but hold you both in the highest esteem and greatest respect. Fritz and I sincerely hope we will receive another letter from you soon, wishing us both good luck on a very difficult venture.

Sincerely,
Alan Jay Lerner

They replied the following day, reminding him, "You withdrew from the project because you said you were unable to lick the book. It was a blow to us because everything had been agreed upon and we were under the illusion that everything was going forward." But in spite of Helburn and Langner's indignation, Lerner was immovable, not least because he was indebted to Levin, to whom he had promised *Abner.*

While Levin started to negotiate with various actors (including Noël Coward and Michael Redgrave) to star in the musical, Lerner hastened to complete the work for which he was under contract at MGM. September had seen the premiere of the screen adaptation of *Brigadoon*—neatly bringing a new "Lerner and Loewe" product into the public eye at just the moment the team reunited—but the combination of Gene Kelly and Cyd Charisse, under Vincente Minnelli's direction, did not meet with universal acclaim from the critics.[59] Nevertheless, Minnelli and Lerner pushed on with their next movie together. The director completed the screen test for *Green Mansions* with Angeli and Edmund Purdom,[60] and in this letter Lerner gives Freed his detailed reaction to the two of them, as well as updating him on *Pygmalion* and asking when shooting would begin on *Huckleberry Finn*:

To Arthur Freed

November 15, 1954

Dear Arthur:

I have thought about the test a very great deal.

Let me begin by saying that obviously Vincente did a wonderful job, despite the limited time and the handicap of shooting indoors.

[59] The *Times* described it as "pretty weak synthetic Scotch" and bemoaned the fact that some of the stronger songs had been omitted from the original score. Bosley Crowther, "The Screen in Review," *New York Times*, September 17, 1954, 18.

[60] Edmund Purdom (1926–2009) was a British actor best known for his roles in *The Student Prince* (1954) and *The Egyptian* (1954).

As for judging Angeli and Purdom, it is, of course, exceedingly difficult. I suppose the reason it is difficult reveals all the basic fallacies in judging anybody or anything by a test. A play is not one scene. A performance is in a sense a parabola, with a beginning, a middle, and an end, and one section of the arc cannot indicate the whole arc. So, in the final analysis I suppose one has to fall back on that awful word called "quality." And when it comes to quality, I sincerely believe that Angeli does not have it. I don't believe it is humanly possible to make somebody something they're not. I don't think you can act "purity," at least the kind of purity and innocence that Rima possesses. Leslie Caron[61] has it, and she may be a far worse actress than Angeli. I also have grave misgivings about the way Angeli moves. It would seem to me that a real balletic background is an essential. When Rima moves through the woods it should be poetry. Audrey Hepburn[62] moves that way, and again, so does Caron.

As for Purdom, I just simply couldn't tell. Seeing only one scene, it is hard to know what light and shade, ferocity and aggressiveness, deep feeling and joy he is capable of. If you and Vincente think he has all that potential, I suppose that would clinch it. My basic negative feeling about him, however, was I didn't feel any "burn" inside him. I didn't feel his sex putting her on the spot. I didn't feel any real animal in him. But that, perhaps, could be directed.

One thing I did find out very positively from the test is about the script. I could see more than ever how cut to the bone it must be. Within the next ten days I will send you a copy of the script with my suggested cuts. Incidentally, I would appreciate it if you would ask Mildred to send me an additional copy right away so that I have one here.

Pygmalion is progressing smoothly, and much faster than I expected. About forty percent of the score is completed, and the book is completely broken down into a clear-cut story line, with all the new characters included. However, even though the writing will be completed in the next couple of months, we decided not to go into rehearsal until August. We've been doing a lot of preliminary work on casting, and I don't think it's going to be as difficult as we anticipated.

[61] Lerner was keen to write another project for Caron after the success of her appearance in his *An American in Paris*. His ambition came to pass with *Gigi* (1958).

[62] Lerner was interested in beloved film actress Audrey Hepburn (1929–93) for various roles in this period (the height of her career), including the Broadway production of *My Fair Lady*. Eventually, she played Eliza in the 1964 movie version.

All in all it's wonderful fun, in fact the most fun I've had writing in a long time.

Is there a shooting schedule yet on *Huck Finn*? I am hoping and praying that whatever additional work is needed I will be able to do before the middle of May. I'm trying assiduously to avoid any more of doing two things at once. Please let me know as soon as you have decided.

Give my love to Renee,[63] Oscar[64] and Ira.[65] I miss you.

Devotedly,
Alan

Aside from the comments on the screen test, several things in this letter are arresting. In particular, there is a wonderful sense of Lerner's joy at working with Loewe ("the most fun I've had writing in a long time"), so much so that previous struggles with adapting Shaw's play into a musical no longer seemed to be getting in the way; it is surprising that "about forty percent of the score" had been written in only a couple of months of the old team getting back together. The other interesting aspect of the letter is the mention of a habit that had impeded Lerner's recent progress (and which would also cause problems at other points in his career): "doing two things at once." By sweeping aside his Hollywood work, Lerner was able to craft what would become unquestionably his most important work, *My Fair Lady*. It wasn't entirely his decision, however. *Huckleberry Finn* was written and in rehearsal when Gene Kelly decided to withdraw and move to Europe to commence work on a dance film for MGM, *Invitation to the Dance*, which was a pet project of his.[66] As a result of losing the star, and the growing problems with financing movie musicals in the 1950s, Freed eventually cancelled *Finn*.[67] Much of the musical material is today housed in the Burton Lane Collection at the Library of Congress, and there is a complete screenplay in the New York Public Library. These suggest that had the movie come to fruition, it could have been a colorful addition to the Lerner-Minnelli-Freed canon.

With *Finn* and then *Green Mansions* canceled, Lerner's mind was firmly set back toward Broadway. Happy in his setup as a silent co-producer with Herman

[63] Renee Klein was Freed's wife.

[64] Oscar Levant.

[65] Ira Gershwin.

[66] Kelly's departure was also part of a plan to avoid paying high taxes; see Fordin, *MGM's Greatest Musicals*, 369.

[67] See Fordin, *MGM's Greatest Musicals*, 369. Fordin claims the production was closed down in 1951, though it is clear from Lerner's letter that it was still on the cards as late as 1954.

Figure 2.2 Frederick Loewe and Alan Jay Lerner in 1962. Credit: Photofest

Levin, Lerner decided to add a second production to his portfolio: a musical by Hugh Martin and Ralph Blane (of *Meet Me in St. Louis* fame) called *Three Tigers*.[68] The relationship with Loewe was obviously harmonious, and *Pygmalion* proceeded well. In addition, a new subject was planned: a musical adaptation of Edna Ferber's best-selling novel *Saratoga Trunk*. For both his new shows with Loewe, Lerner hoped to hire Robert Lewis, following from the aborted Lerner-Lane *Li'l Abner* (which was ultimately brought to Broadway with a completely different production and creative team, bar choreographer Michael Kidd). But Lewis was unavailable for *Pygmalion*, and Lerner wrote to tell him how sorry he was to have lost his director of preference:

[68] Sam Zolotow, "Inge's 'Bus Stop' Due in February," *New York Times*, December 3, 1954, 30. *Three Tigers* never actually came to the stage, in fact, and *My Fair Lady* became Lerner and Levin's only co-production.

To Robert Lewis

May 20, 1955

Dear, dear Bobby:

I'm absolutely heartsick that we can't work together on *Pygmalion*. I think you must know that, were it left to me alone, I would wait till March or even later for you without a moment's hesitation. Unfortunately, [just] as you have ethical obligations to *Mr. Johnson*, we have actual legal obligations to Rex Harrison,[69] Stanley Holloway,[70] Julie Andrews[71] *and* the Pascal Estate. In all four of the above agreements we are obligated to go into production no later than January 1st. If there is a delay, we would either lose the people or pay a whopping penalty. As a matter of fact, it was only in the last two days that we successfully managed to persuade the Chase Bank, who represents the Pascal interests, to give us the outside date of January 1st. Up until then we had been legally bound to *open* by January 1st. So you can see how tied our hands are. I know that I shall miss you every moment of rehearsal, not only professionally, but personally as well.

For God's sake let's have nothing go wrong with *Saratoga Trunk*. It's being planned so far ahead that we should be able to work out a time schedule satisfactory to us all. At the moment the plan is to go into production sometime before the end of '56. It might well come after *Teahouse* on your schedule. (That's just a guess.) Please, Bobby, let's try and work that one out. I think it could be a wonderful show, and I hope you're still interested in doing it.

They're trying to set up some sort of corporation for which not only the play, but the motion picture would be financed by a motion picture company, and all of us would not only do the play, but the picture as well—participating in the profits of each accordingly. I think Fryer[72] will be getting in touch with Bill[73] about it in the next few days—if he hasn't already.

[69] Tony- and Oscar-winning actor Rex Harrison (1908–90) was the star of two stage productions and the film of *My Fair Lady*, as well as various acclaimed movies, including *Anna and the King of Siam* (1946) and *Cleopatra* (1963).

[70] Stanley Holloway (1890–1982) was a renowned English film and stage actor, as well as a comedian and singer. He played Alfred P. Doolittle in *My Fair Lady*.

[71] Julie Andrews (b. 1935) was the most popular actress in movie musicals of the 1960s, and also appeared in the original stage productions of Lerner's *My Fair Lady* and *Camelot*.

[72] Robert Fryer was a prolific Broadway producer, usually in collaboration with Lawrence Carr.

[73] The attorney, H. William Fitelson, represented many leading names in show business, including Lerner and Loewe.

How sad about *Pygmalion*!

Oh, well...!

How's the picture coming? Will you be coming East soon? Call me when you do.

All my love,
Alan

By June, Lerner's work for MGM had completely stalled, though he was still under contract to write another film for them. The costly movie musical genre was nearly at the end of its slow decline, with fewer projects emanating from all the studios, and both Lerner as writer and Freed as producer were coming to the end of their Hollywood years. Still, they kept in close touch, and in this letter to Freed, Lerner describes at length his approach to his current project, *Pygmalion*, as well as the casting and financing of the show:

To Arthur Freed

June 21, 1955

Dear Arthur,

It seems so long since I have seen you or spoken to you that I thought I'd just drop you a line and let you know I'm still alive.

Naturally, I've been working around the clock on the show, and I think it's coming along well, albeit slowly. The book is completely broken down, a lot of the writing has been done, and the layout looks first rate. The reason for the slowness in writing is that the song requirements are so specific that there is very little room to move around. We sort of have to hit each one precisely on the nose. The reason for this, as you undoubtedly would imagine, is the very precise style that Shaw created, and by which we must abide.

We played the new things for Oliver[74] the other night, and I'm pleased to report he was terribly excited. Also, Moss Hart[75] has agreed

[74] Oliver Smith (1918–94) was one of the most prolific and important designers in Broadway history. Among his credits were *On the Town* (1944), *Gentlemen Prefer Blondes* (1949), *Candide* (1956), *West Side Story* (1957), *The Sound of Music* (1959), and *Hello, Dolly!* (1964), as well as several Lerner projects: *Paint Your Wagon* (1951), *My Fair Lady* (1956), *Camelot* (1960), *On a Clear Day You Can See Forever* (1965), *Gigi* (1973), and *Carmelina* (1979).

[75] Moss Hart (1904–61) was a leading writer and director on Broadway for roughly 30 years. Equally acclaimed for his collaborations with George S. Kaufman on plays such as *You Can't Take It with You* (1936) and *The Man Who Came to Dinner* (1939) and his direction of musicals such as *My Fair Lady*, he was a close friend of and key inspiration to Lerner.

to direct it, and we're all delighted. He made great good sense about the whole thing and, even though we've only had two meetings together, he already has given us a couple of wonderfully creative ideas.

We haven't done much more on the casting than when I saw you. So far, just Rex, Julie Andrews, Stanley Holloway and an English boy we signed in London for the young lover.[76] Of course, Oliver and Cecil Beaton[77] will be designing and costuming.

On the financing side of it, we made an excellent deal with CBS, who are financing the entire venture for 40%. The main advantage to that, other than the financial, is, of course, the national exploitation and advertising which they are committed to give us for nothing.

Rehearsals are scheduled for the 15th of November, and Fritz and I have to go to England for a week in August to teach Rex his songs. I come in to town only about once a week now—the rest of the time I'm up in the country[78] writing. In my usual fashion, half the songs still have one line missing in each.

I saw Howard Dietz[79] the other day, and he told me that "Fair Weather"[80] is one of the best pictures you've ever made. I was thrilled to hear it and I can't wait to see it.

Do you plan on coming East at all? I could let you know when the hot spell starts, so that you could be sure and make it. Seriously, I would love to see you and, seeing that there's no chance of my coming out, I am hoping that you'll come East.

How are Vincente [Minnelli], Oscar [Levant] and the Gershwins? Please give them all my love and tell them I miss them.

I miss you, too.

Faithfully,
Alan

[76] In the end, American actor John Michael King (1926–2008) played Freddy Eynsford-Hill on Broadway.

[77] Cecil Beaton (1904–80) was an English designer of theatrical sets and costumes, as well as a popular photographer. His costume designs for *My Fair Lady* solidified his reputation and led to many other engagements, such as Arthur Freed and Lerner's film *Gigi* (1958).

[78] A reference to Rockland County, where Lerner spent much time writing.

[79] Howard Dietz (1896–1983) was an American lyricist and librettist, most famous for his collaborations with the composer Arthur Schwartz (on shows such as *The Band Wagon*). Dietz was also a leading Hollywood publicist.

[80] *It's Always Fair Weather* was Gene Kelly's latest film; like *Invitation to the Dance,* it was a commercial flop.

As well as adding to our knowledge of the dates when progress was being made on the show, this letter is also fascinating for the way in which Lerner discusses the specific challenge of writing the songs for the show: he says that their requirements are "so specific that there is very little room to move around" and they had to "hit each one precisely on the nose" due to "the very precise style that Shaw created." The particularity of this approach is arguably one of the reasons for the musical's success.

The summer of 1955 saw the completion of much of the work on *Pygmalion*, and in September Hanya Holm signed on as choreographer. Aside from the problems associated with maintaining Shaw's tone of writing in the songs, Lerner and Loewe's main challenge in this piece was to create the right kind of material for actor Rex Harrison. Many years after the show had closed, Lerner reminisced on how he came to hear of Harrison's musical ability:

> About two years before the show was readied, Rex was in New York for *Anne of a Thousand Days*. I was living up in Rockland County, and Maxwell Anderson and Kurt Weill lived up there. I had the house next door. Rex and Lilli Palmer used to come up over the weekends to Max's Saturday nights and we had poker games on Sunday night.
>
> One day, Kurt said we ought to do a revival of *The Threepenny Opera*, and he wanted me to consider writing the new version of it. And I said, "Well, who would play it, in the name of God?" And he said, "Rex." And I said, "Does he sing?" And he said, "Yes." That was the first time I ever knew that Rex was musical. I never heard him sing, so when we started working on *My Fair Lady*, the first person I suggested was Rex.[81] And everybody asked: "Does he sing?" And I said, "Well, Kurt says he does. I don't know how he knew it, but if Kurt Weill said he was musical, he must be."[82]

Lerner consulted Harrison at every stage of the composition, keeping him up to date with progress and sending him demo recordings of the new songs as they were written. In this letter from late November, Lerner employs his legendary charm to appease Harrison, who was unhappy with their first attempt at "Why Can't the English?" and tells him all about the new song they had just written for him, "I've Grown Accustomed to Her Face." He also discusses his approach to writing song lyrics, and in the postscript mentions current thoughts on the title for the show. Just over three months later, *My Fair Lady* would open

[81] In fact, Harrison was at least third choice for the role of Higgins. See McHugh, *Loverly*, 20–21.

[82] From an interview with Lehman Engel, transcript held in the Lehman Engel Papers, Gilmore Music Library, Yale University, box 32, folder 623, 3–4.

on Broadway to the most glowing reviews of Lerner's career and become the longest-running musical in history.

To Rex Harrison

November 29, 1955

Rex, old boy:

Absolutely delighted with your report on your voice, plus "the recommendation" from Roy Lowe.[83] Fritz and I always have believed it was merely a matter of developing the tonal quality you naturally had, and we were both confident of the result. Suffice to say we are very happy that confidence is now shared by you.

I was very interested in your comments about "Why Can't The English," and want you to know that I feel your reservations, as far as you are concerned, are completely justifiable. As I said in my cable, don't let it tinge one hair with gray—we are rewriting it completely in a way that will be not only simpatico with you, but with the character of Higgins. I can do no other but agree with you when you are right, but I would fight you like a wounded tiger if I thought you were wrong.

I might add, before closing the matter, that there are certain lyric liberties one can take when they are framed by certain kinds of melodies. There are "song songs" and "character songs." A "character song," which is basically free and is accompanied by an emotion or emotions, as is the case in "I'm An Ordinary Man," must pretty much stay within the bounds of reason. In a "song song," certain extravagances are not only permissible, but desirable. "Why Can't The English," written as it was, was definitely a "song song" and therefore contained a certain amount of satiric extravagance. The minute the same idea is written in a freer way, so that it almost seems like normal conversation set to music, those extravagances would seem definitely out of place. When one reads the lyric of a "song song" over and compares it to the character who is singing it, very often there will seem to be a discrepancy. For example, what business does a young Navy lieutenant have singing a poetic song like "Younger Than Springtime"?[84]

[83] Roy Lowe, Harrison's vocal coach.

[84] A reference to Lieutenant Cable's song "Younger than Springtime" from Rodgers and Hammerstein's *South Pacific*.

But all this is part of the tricks of our trade, which you are gradually discovering now that you're in the "music racket." The reason we will be changing the song is to give you a broader scope and longer line musically, and this will automatically entail a different kind of lyric. In other words, the original song as one entity of words and music was entirely appropriate. Torn apart, it wouldn't be possible. As a matter of fact, I'm quite surprised you went ahead and tried it out on the stage. It seems to me you just added to your worries and frustrations. If something doesn't sound right in a room, the chances are it won't sound right on the stage.

I hope by this time you have received the music to "Come To The Ball."[85] Of course, the tempo that I read the dialogue in, in the middle of the song, is not the tempo that you will read it in. Actually, Fritz hasn't even bothered to write the final background music to that sequence yet. He will do it with you. We have millions of ideas of how "Come To The Ball" should be done, so should you have any questions, I beg you not to get an ulcer about it, but wait until we're all together. We all feel it will work like a dream. Moss has some enchanting ideas about the way you'll do the last chorus of the song itself (the new one). In the meantime, use Roy Lowe to get it under your belt, so that you'll have the freedom you want with it when we start setting the business.

The big news of the letter is that we are practically finished with your second act number and our collective enthusiasm is boundless. I think it's going to be one of the most important things you'll do in the show—funny, touching in an odd way, and "Higgins" to a tee. We wrote a new song, which frames an entire interlude of a soliloquy that contains bits of "I Can See Her Now" and "I'm An Ordinary Man," all with new lyrics, of course. We want to let it marinate for a few days after it's finished, which is our custom. Because the melody itself is very simple (only twenty bars), and the music of the interlude is all music with which you are well familiar, you will have no trouble with it. We much prefer, therefore, not sending it over now but waiting until you arrive. I might want to do additional lyrics in a certain place, but I can't tell that until I let it settle a bit and then look at it again. I also, by the

[85] Lerner writes of this cut song in *Street*: "There was to be a scene following Eliza's catastrophic blunder at Ascot in which she refused to go on. The idea of the song was, having tried every form of persuasion from cajoling to steamrolling, Higgins finally resorts to charm. It was written as a waltz and I was on it for three weeks." He continues, "We all felt that undoubtedly this would be Rex's *pièce de résistance* in the first act," but reports that on opening night it was "a disaster in three-quarter time" and was cut after one performance. Lerner, *Street*, 78, 79 and 105.

very fact that rehearsals are growing near, do not have the concentrated time. There are auditions every day for the Ensemble, the final meetings on the script, etc. Besides all that, I'm most anxious to do this whole number for you myself, so that you can see what's intended and not trust to cold acetate being listened to three thousand miles away. I know you're going to be delighted.

We have started on the new version of "English." It's very funny that you mentioned the expression "The King's English," because long, long, long ago when we first started on that number, that was the original title. I'll keep you posted on our progress. I can well understand your desire to have it when you come back from your vacation, and I would certainly love to get it to you by then if I can do it without doing injury to my plodding thought processes.

In the meantime, I beg you not to worry—anyhow, certainly not when you're on vacation. We are as determined as you are that everything Higgins does shall be absolutely right. Can't wait to see you. I received a confirmation from The Pierre yesterday on your reservation. They can't wait to see you either. Give my regards to Laurie[86] and Binky.[87]

Devotedly,
AJL

P.S. *Fanfaroon*[88] has not been abandoned, although there is stiff opposition. But *My Lady Liza* will definitely not be it. I know this will break your heart, because you seem so terribly fond of it.

[86] Laurence Evans, Harrison's agent in London.

[87] Hugh "Binky" Beaumont, the London producer of *Bell, Book and Candle*, the play from which Harrison had to be released in order to appear in *My Fair Lady* on Broadway. Beaumont went on to produce *Fair Lady* in London as part of his deal to release Harrison.

[88] Loewe's own preference for the title—perhaps because of its resemblance to that of *Brigadoon*, as Lerner suggests in *The Street Where I Live*.

CHAPTER 3

"You Did It"

MY FAIR LADY, GIGI, AND BEYOND, 1955–1958

Rehearsals for *My Fair Lady* were due to begin on January 3, 1956. Out of caution for the weather, which often delayed flights in the winter, Lerner and Levin wanted the British stars of the show to arrive in New York before the New Year, and both Rex Harrison and Stanley Holloway readily acquiesced. But Julie Andrews—who had just finished a run of *The Boy Friend* on Broadway and was signed up to appear in *My Fair Lady* for two years—desperately wanted to spend the holiday with her family (including her young brothers) in London. Lerner wrote to try to persuade her to come sooner:

To Julie Andrews

December 5, 1955

Dear Julie,

Nancy[1] tells me you are absolutely first-rate in *High Tor*—which comes as no surprise. And I also received a letter from Arthur Schwartz with a more gushing version of the same report. Suffice to say I couldn't be happier if you were one of my own family, which in a manner of speaking for the next few years I trust you will be.

I don't know whether or not you have been aware of the explosive conversations that have been going on lately between Herman Levin and Lou Wilson.[2] I might add that Herman has been doing the

[1] Nancy Olson (b.1928), Lerner's wife, who appeared with Andrews and Bing Crosby in the then-recent television musical *High Tor* by Arthur Schwartz and Maxwell Anderson.

[2] Lou Wilson, Andrews's representative in London.

conversing and Lou the exploding. What it's all been about is the matter of your being here on December 27th. I, of course, realize how much you would want to be with your family over New Year's, but there are a few things involved that I beg you to consider. I am sure you know in advance that our desire to have you here on that date is no capricious whim on our part.

Both Rex and Stanley Holloway are arriving at that time. It is not at all uncommon for the stars of a play to make it their business to be in town a week before rehearsals for the express purpose of using that time for the good of themselves and the play. You are a star now, Julie, and I do think that as a well-meaning observer, as well as an active participant in these proceedings, it would be most impolitic to have them, who are two great and established artists, follow the usual pattern and you not do so. Even though we will not, of course, be working around the clock during that time, much can be accomplished in those few days. We can go over your new songs with you and get the keys set. If you feel it is necessary, you could freshen up your Cockney with Dixon.[3] We could go over a couple of the scenes, which we would all like to hear, mainly for length, before the first reading on stage January 3rd. Besides that, there is that old devil Publicity, which, annoying as it is, is more annoying when it isn't. It will also give you a chance to make yourself comfortable in your flat, and you will be rested and ready for the official first day of rehearsals January 3rd.

Another thing that worries us about your not leaving London until New Year's Day is the problem of flying conditions at that time of year. Should you run into bad weather and be delayed, or should New York be fogged in, which is not at all unusual at that time of the year, you might find yourself arriving the night of January 2nd, or even the morning of rehearsals. I do feel it would be calling it a bit close.

Lou Wilson—I think a little foolishly—has been defending your "rights" vigorously. His position has been that if we want you here on the 27th, move rehearsals up and you will be here. It's far from my intention to go behind your representative's back, but I think that what is involved here is not a legal matter, but merely one of common sense for all concerned. Hence my writing you directly.

[3] Alfred Dixon (dates unknown) was a high-profile dialect coach, who worked on *My Fair Lady* with both Julie Andrews and Audrey Hepburn (in the movie version). Although Andrews was brought up in and near London, she had to be careful to control her cockney accent as Eliza Doolittle in order to make sure the Broadway audience could understand everything she said.

If I have, I hope successfully, upset your holiday plans, with all my heart I wish you a wonderful Christmas. I'll try to fix up one room in the apartment to look like an English pub, and if you will join us New Year's Eve, at 12:00 o'clock we will all sit around and sing "Sweet Blooming Lavender." As for the new year that comes after, I have a very good feeling it's going to be all yours. I certainly hope so—not only for you, but if it is, the chances are it will be for me too.

Will I see you December 27th? Please. Please.

Fondly,
Alan

The letter shows Lerner at his persuasive best and is an indication of how his input into the show often involved acting as a tacit co-producer, but Andrews understandably decided to put her family duty first.[4] And though her arrival at the start of the next year was famously followed by a challenging rehearsal period for her—in which the director, Moss Hart, had to close down rehearsals for the weekend and spend time with her on her own to polish her interpretation—the decision proved to be wise for Andrews in retrospect: after a long stint in *Fair Lady* on Broadway, she had little break before the start of rehearsals for the London transfer of the show.

On January 1, 1956, the musical began its media campaign with a large photograph in the *New York Times* of the female dancers from the show in rehearsal with Hanya Holm,[5] the choreographer. Ironically, the photograph probably depicts the show's ballet which was ultimately cut, but "Some of the Fair Ladies in *My Fair Lady*," as the photo's caption reads, was the start of Levin's intense effort to guarantee the show's success with extensive press coverage in the weeks leading up to the opening in mid-March. Meanwhile, the onstage success of the show was by this point largely in the hands of one man: Moss Hart. In his memoir, Lerner wrote of Hart, who directed *Camelot* as well as *Fair Lady*: "Moss Hart, as I was to find out, had no understudies. He is and will forever be irreplaceable to more people in more ways than any man I have ever known." As a theater writer and director, Hart was perhaps Lerner's biggest hero: his interest in every aspect of theater was something Lerner admired and often emulated. In the following undated letter, probably written just after the opening of the New Haven tryout of *My Fair Lady*, Lerner pays tribute to everything Hart brought to the show:

[4] For Andrews's explanation of her late arrival and her account of the subsequent rehearsals, see Julie Andrews, *Home* (New York: Doubleday, 2008), 382.

[5] Hanya Holm (1893–1992) was one of the most influential choreographers of American ballet in the twentieth century. Her Labanotation (choreographic notation) for *Kiss, Me Kate* (1948) was the first choreography to be copyrighted in America.

To Moss Hart

[Undated; c. mid-February 1956]

Dear Moss:

I have to type this because I don't have a pen.

Because I'm "rich and Jewish" I've received a lot of nice presents in my time, but in all my graying thirty-seven years none has ever meant as much to me as yours. I've never been sentimental about possessions, but I shall keep these with me always.

Dear Moss—I don't make friends easily and those I love often have to wait years to discover how I really feel. I'm not too good at saying things. That's why I'm writing you. But through the years you will find out that in a very short time I've grown to love you very deeply—and even though you are one of those rare gents who has crowds who adore you there is no one, literally no one, who will ever be in your corner more than I.

As for the show, I shudder to think what would have become of it without you. God knows it's yours as much as mine. And if God doesn't know it, I do.

Oh for a walk on the boardwalk!

Alan

Though the chances of *Fair Lady*'s success seemed high, Lerner also revived a backup plan: on February 22 it was announced that he and Burton Lane were negotiating with MGM to bring their unused *Huckleberry Finn* movie material to the stage.[6] It was to be Lane's first Broadway score since *Finian's Rainbow* in 1947, and he was to co-produce the show with Lerner, helped by financial backing from MGM. But it quickly became apparent that *Fair Lady* was to exceed all expectations, and Lerner was soon busy with the biggest success of his career. The *New York Times* ran a large photo spread on March 4, and two days later Levin announced that ticket prices for the new show would be raised from September—a sure sign that the producer expected sufficient demand to take this risk.[7]

In jovial mood, Lerner wrote to his friend, the legendary theatrical producer Irene Mayer Selznick, to invite her to the Broadway opening. Reference is made in the letter to "gratitude" and to Rex Harrison. During the previous year,

[6] Sam Zolotow, "Many in 'Debut' to Bow Tonight," *New York Times*, February 22, 1956, 23.

[7] Sam Zolotow, "Guiness to Star in London Farce," *New York Times*, March 6, 1956, 27.

Harrison had starred in the play *Bell, Book and Candle* in London, and because of the production's success he was unable to leave to start *Fair Lady* when Lerner and Levin wished. Selznick's intervention (as the play's Broadway producer) played an important role in releasing the actor early; hence, the particular care and enthusiasm with which she was invited to the musical's opening:

To Irene Mayer Selznick

March 7, 1956

Irene darling,

Great fights between Rex and me about who gets to invite you to the opening. So we compromise by saying that we both do—with much love and gratitude.

I'll have the seats delivered to your hotel when I come back to town next week.

Can't wait to see you and have a good "jaw." Will you be in town the week after we open? I'll call you next week.

Devotedly,
Alan

On March 11, Levin announced that he was in discussions with Lerner and Loewe to produce the movie adaptation of the show independently, and the following day a reporter observed that "*My Fair Lady*, whose out-of-town tryout ended in Philadelphia Saturday night, already has taken on legendary stature, although it does not open on Broadway until Thursday.... [N]early everyone is convinced that something pretty hot is cooking."[8] The piece explained that the stars were being bombarded with demands from friends for tickets for opening night: "As it developed quickly that there were at least ten bids for each available ticket, Mr. Harrison, Miss Andrews et al had no choice but to cut off their telephones or leave instructions that no long-distance calls be put through to them."

To this amusing anecdote (which was probably a concoction of the show's press agent, Richard Maney) Lerner himself added to speculation on *Fair Lady* with an article in the *New York Times* on March 11 titled "Shavian Musical Notes,"[9] excerpted below:

[8] Arthur Gelb, "N.B.C. May Finance Musical, Offer It Later as a Spectacular," *New York Times*, March 12, 1956, 23.

[9] Alan Jay Lerner, "Shavian Musical Notes," *New York Times*, March 11, 1956, 129. The omitted passages merely detail the genesis of Shaw's *Pygmalion* in a cursory way, and do not really add to the discussion of Lerner's work.

"Pygmalion" first crossed the path of Frederick Loewe and myself in the winter of 1952. It was suggested to us by Gabriel Pascal, an improbable mid-European impresario, who had, many years before, somehow cajoled, persuaded or amused G.B.S. into handing over to him the motion-picture rights to his plays.... When we met Pascal, he recently had acquired the musical rights [to *Pygmalion*]. Loewe and I were instantly intrigued with the project and spent several months talking it about. For reasons much too diverse and complicated to record here, we then abandoned it. One day in August of 1954, shortly after Pascal had died, we began discussing it again. Our enthusiasm was rekindled immediately.

Since that sultry summer day we have been at it like two men possessed. The more we worked, the more we loved it; the more we loved it, the more we worked. In the process of writing it we got half through twice and started over. There are fifteen musical items in the show that will open Thursday night. We actually wrote more than thirty. Two were dispensed with on the road in the normal process of tightening and perfecting. The rest are in the files under "G" for "Groping." For, in spite of its timeless story, "Pygmalion" is far from a simple play. It would be un-Shavian if it were. Eliza's development is straight-forward enough, but Professor Higgins is as complex as Shaw himself, and is, in fact, very much Shaw.

In a far less tangible way, Higgins goes through as much of a transformation as Eliza, the only difference being that Shaw would never allow the transformation to run its natural course. As a result, for a "potboiler," it has one of the most perverse fifth acts Shaw ever wrote. Thematically it reaches a subtle climax with Eliza acquiring, if you will, a soul, therefore completing her transformation. Therefore, the play is finished. But on the more human level of Higgins and Eliza, nothing is solved. Much is implied, but nothing stated clearly. Shaw compounded his felonious perversity by writing an epilogue which, delicious though it may be, is maddeningly frustrating.

In the epilogue he tells what happens to Eliza and Higgins after the play is over. And it is precisely everything you don't want to hear and don't wish to believe at all. It makes good sense, but it's highly unsatisfactory, as is usually the case when relentless logic is applied to the emotions. I can only assume it's but one more example of Shaw's mischievous refusal to join in the chorus of those who look at Man and Woman and murmur the age-old "Vive la différence." There is a story told that, at the rehearsals of "Pygmalion," Shaw, the most celebrated vegetarian of our time, complained about the way a certain scene was being performed. Somehow the word "love" crept into the discussion. This was too much for Mrs. Campbell, who turned on him and said: "What do you know of love? If you ever ate a lamb chop, there wouldn't be a woman safe in London." I don't know if this story is true, but I hope so.

Naturally, Loewe and I often speculate as to what the old Boy would say if he saw "My Fair Lady." Naturally, we hope he would be pleased. Eventually I, as do all we poor mortals, will pass on to meet my Maker. For all of us earthly sinners, it can be rather terrifying. I should hate to think that I might also have to contend with an irate Shaw standing at the gate waiting for me, too.

This statement represents an important dimension of the generation of *My Fair Lady*'s reception history. From the genesis point of view, this was perhaps the first major public statement in which Lerner swept his disagreements with Loewe in 1952 under the carpet; the phrase "For reasons much too diverse and complicated to record here" rings as a firm ceasefire on previous battles. More important, the article plays a key role in the reception of the Higgins-Eliza relationship. Before the critics had even had their say on the success of his adaptation of the beloved play, Lerner was already defending his approach to the story—which allows the audience to decide whether Eliza and Higgins are romantically united at the end, rather than Shaw's insistence that she marries her young romantic suitor, Freddy—by portraying Shaw as "perverse" and suggesting that he would not let the play "run its natural course." Only a few days later, Brooks Atkinson's review of the show in the *New York Times* would pick up on this theme by remarking that "the hero and heroine never kiss in this original comedy," though he also conceded that the show had "a romantic glow."[10]

The night before the show's Broadway opening, Lerner and Loewe wrote a brief message of thanks to their beloved director, Hart:

To Moss Hart

March 14, 1956

Dear, dear Mossie,

We would like to think that every time you open this in the future and find a play inside that has words and music, they will be by us.

How can we thank you enough for everything?

All our love,
Alan & Fritz

[10] Brooks Atkinson, "My Fair Lady," *New York Times*, March 25, 1956, X1.

From the style of writing, it's clear that Lerner is the author of this note, and the particular tenderness of the message is a sign of the special connection between the two men, though Loewe was also extremely fond of him. Their appreciation was well placed: the musical opened on March 15 to an ecstatic response, the likes of which had rarely been seen before on Broadway. According to Alistair Cooke's report of the event in *The Manchester Guardian*, "This is the show that stunned a knowing first-night audience like nothing since 'Oklahoma' [*sic*] twelve years ago; that had sophisticates crowding to the orchestra pit...for thirteen show curtains; that started a continuous queue shuffling for eight hours through Friday's flailing snowstorm."[11] The *New York Times* added that it "won glowing notices from all New York's drama reviewers" and noted that the day after the opening, an estimated $18,000 was taken at the box office for future ticket sales.[12] Screen icon Fred Astaire (who had worked with Lerner on *Royal Wedding*) wrote to tell Lerner it was "simply the best show that has ever been produced—as you well know" and fellow lyricist Sammy Cahn sent him a message to say "I just had to take the time to let you know that last night (again) I saw *My Fair Lady* and with a capacity audience was again reminded of your monumental achievement." These are just two of numerous letters Lerner received from his peers in the weeks following the opening,[13] all of them expressing a special admiration for the musical.

Now that *Fair Lady* had opened and was a success, it quickly became apparent that something was going to have to be done to safeguard its future when the first cast needed to be replaced. For a while, theater producers and writers had been frustrated by the stringent rules of both the American and British actors' unions, which raised objections whenever successful productions were mooted to cross the Atlantic in either direction. There was a general lack of cooperation between the two sides, as happened in the case of Harrison's delayed departure from *Bell, Book and Candle*, which caused the deferral of the opening of *Fair Lady*. In the case of *My Fair Lady*, of course, the need to retain the original cast for the London transfer was especially sensitive, since it was a Broadway show with all-British leads. The issue also affected producers who wanted to take their Broadway productions to Britain with American casts. Therefore, Lerner called a meeting with others in the same predicament—Rodgers and Hammerstein, and the playwright Augustus Goetz[14]—in order to try to set up a better channel

[11] Alistair Cooke, "Shavian Source of a Delicious Daydream," *Manchester Guardian*, March 20, 1956, 5.

[12] Louis Calta, "Critics Doff Hats to 'My Fair Lady,' " *New York Times*, March 17, 1956, 11.

[13] The letters come from a small scrapbook kindly loaned to me by Liz Robertson, Lerner's widow.

[14] Augustus Goetz (1897–57) was the co-author (with his wife, Ruth) of the play *The Heiress* (1947).

Figure 3.1 Alan Jay Lerner, Leslie Caron, and Frederick Loewe working on *Gigi*.
Credit: MGM/Photofest

of communication between the British and American theater communities on this subject. Lerner wrote to Irene Selznick—who produced the internationally successful plays *A Streetcar Named Desire* and *The Chalk Garden*, and therefore had a special interest in the matter—to report on the plan of action:

To Irene Mayer Selznick

March 30, 1956

Irene, darling,

We had a very successful lunch Tuesday: Dick, Oscar, Gus Goetz and myself. The plan of action goes something like this:

The Dramatists Guild is going to ask Actors Equity if we can appoint a small committee to sit in at the next meeting between the Theatre League and Equity. At that meeting we are going to ask if we, the dramatists, could undertake mediating between Actors Equity and British Equity, either in London or New York, and see if some long-range program can be devised to relax the barriers of each. The idea will come up at the meeting as if it's something spontaneous, just thought of.

We shall also ask them, if they consent to this, to leave their present laws as is and not change them until this meeting has had a chance to take place. One thing that certainly became clear to all at lunch is that those mainly affected by any decision of Equity are the authors, and therefore it's up to the authors to take the lead in their own defense.

I hope you had a nice trip over. Do give Binky [Beaumont] my best regards. Miss you. Will write longer letter in a week or two, when I dig my way out of the telegrams and letters.

Love, darling,
Alan

It is important to note Lerner's keen involvement in these sorts of industry issues, as well as his collegiality toward Rodgers and Hammerstein. Evidently, they were not the bitter rivals that some might imagine, and the Broadway community often came together when issues such as this arose.

With not just a hit but the biggest hit in years on their hands, Lerner, Loewe, and the team reacted strongly to their success. After the opening, Moss Hart immediately left for Barbados with his wife.[15] Sadly, the weather was not quite what the Harts had hoped for, as is clear from the following amusing letter, which Lerner quoted in his autobiography and frequently read out in his public talks:[16]

From Moss Hart

[Undated; c. March/April 1956]

Dear chaps

I am a true friend—the vrai!

I could tell you that it has been marvelous—but it would not be the vrai. Wretched is the word for Mossie! We arrived in a downpour and it has been torrential since. Did you send Richard Ahearne[17] ahead?

Only one thing has dissipated the gloom for me—in yesterday's local newspaper there occurred a glorious—a collectors' item—typo error. They were reporting a wedding and went into great detail on the

[15] Gene Lees, *The Musical World of Lerner and Loewe* (Lincoln: University of Nebraska Press, 1990), 137.

[16] The letter is quoted in Lerner, *Street*, 74. Thanks to Rex Bunnett and The Overtures Trust for allowing me to hear a recording of Lerner's talk at BASCA in 1985, in which he reads out the letter.

[17] Hart perhaps means actor Richard Hearne (1908–79), famous for his portrayal of the bumbling character Mr. Pastry on television (including *The Ed Sullivan Show*) and film.

bride's costume. Then—the last paragraph read—"And the groom, not to be outdone, wore a large red carnation in his bottomhole."

If the rain keeps on I may stick one in mine!

Your dolorous friend,
Moss

My Fair Lady's cast album was recorded on March 25, then, like Hart, Loewe quickly left Manhattan for "a rest in Europe on the advice of his physician."[18] This immediately brought to an end their next planned show, an adaptation of the 1941 novel *Saratoga Trunk* by Edna Ferber (1885–1968). Ferber was one of the most distinguished American writers of the twentieth century, with credits including the novels *Show Boat* (1926) and *Giant* (1952) and the plays *Stage Door* (1926) and *The Royal Family* (1926; both were co-authored by George S. Kaufman). Rodgers and Hammerstein had first considered *Saratoga Trunk* as suitable material for a musical but they decided to pass on it, and with the success of *My Fair Lady* behind them, Lerner and Loewe decided to do the same.

In this letter, Lerner refers to some of the reasons for their decision, including Loewe's health, which had certainly been strained. But by May, they were already discussing the possibility of writing *Gigi* as a film for MGM. This shows that they had simply lost enthusiasm for *Saratoga Trunk* (which was eventually written as a musical by Harold Arlen, composer of *The Wizard of Oz*, and Johnny Mercer, lyricist of *Seven Brides for Seven Brothers* and *Li'l Abner*):

To Edna Ferber

April 9, 1956

Dear Edna,

First off, a million thanks for your opening night wire and charming little notes that you sent me while I was in rehearsal. I've been in the process of writing my "thank yous," and I saved yours for last because obviously I don't consider it among those. It was a wonderful opening night, and I'm so glad you were there.

In the last few days I've been in touch with Fryer and Carr,[19] and thousands of attorneys. I also received your letter of concern. I must

[18] Sam Zolotow, "'Fair Lady' Team Is Out of Action," *New York Times*, April 11, 1956, 30.

[19] Robert Fryer (1921–2000) was the producer of the original productions of *Wonderful Town* (1953), *Mame* (1966), *Chicago* (1975), and *Sweeney Todd* (1979). Lawrence Carr (1917–69), known as Jimmy, was his co-producer on several projects, including *Redhead* (1959) and *Sweet Charity* (1966).

say in fairness to Fryer and Carr, they have not been remiss in any way. The reason no financing deal was made is because Fritz and I have been holding it up on purpose. There would never be any problem of raising money—especially for a property by you, and I suppose after *My Fair Lady*, by Fritz and me, either. The reason we were loathe to make any commitments is quite simple. We did not know from whom we wanted something. In other words, suppose we wanted Howard Keel[20] and he was tied to Metro? Then it naturally would behoove us to try to work out a deal with Metro, freeing Howard Keel. With *My Fair Lady*, we were at one point thinking about Audrey Hepburn (until a strange report that she was pregnant reached our ears—which it seems she wasn't),[21] and so we spent a good deal of time thrashing it all about with Paramount, who own her contract. In short, I think Bobby and Jim have done everything they could, and have acquitted themselves more than fittingly and energetically in their joint role of producer.

As it turns out now, it was a very wise thing that no deal was made. I don't know whether you know it or not, but Fritz had an emergency appendectomy just before we went into rehearsal. He went right from a hospital bed back to work. He is now exhausted and had intended taking a month's vacation. I had breakfast with Bobby this morning and told him that Fritz would be back in June and that we had intended starting work at that time. Since then I have seen Fritz, who incidentally is leaving for Europe tonight, and he tells me that he cannot possible start on anything until at least the fall. He saw his doctor this morning, and acting, not upon his orders, but upon his suggestion, he feels that he really needs a good six-months' rest, and maybe even longer. Therefore, he now intends staying abroad for the next few months. Of course, this bit of news comes as a sad blow to me, but I can certainly understand the position he is in, as I'm sure you do, and would not want to force him into doing anything that would be bad for his health.

[20] Howard Keel (1919–2004) was a leading actor and singer on the West End (*Oklahoma!*) and Broadway (*Saratoga, No Strings*) stages. His fame rests mainly from the series of movie musicals he made in the 1950s, including *Annie Get Your Gun* (1950), *Show Boat* (1951), *Calamity Jane* (1953), and *Kiss Me Kate* (1953). He also appeared as Henry Higgins in a production of *My Fair Lady* at the St. Louis Muny in 1996. When *Saratoga* reached the stage in 1959, Keel was its star, as Lerner and Loewe had intended.

[21] Audrey Hepburn went on to star in the 1964 film version of *My Fair Lady*. Curiously, it is often assumed that Lerner and Loewe did not want her for the role—though they would have tailored the music differently had they written the stage version for her—but here we learn that she was in the running even for the Broadway production.

> Bobby told me this morning how anxious you are to get started. I certainly don't blame you. You have been more than patient with our endless delays in getting *My Fair Lady* launched. I cannot possibly ask you to wait any longer, and don't intend to. Even if you should say that you would wait an additional year or two, which is what would now be involved because of our road company commitments to *My Fair Lady* and the English production of same, I would know very well what anxiety it would cause you, and I simply could not be a party to it. Too, if we were well into the writing, sufficiently to have some estimation of how long it would take to complete the play, we could quite conceivably make production plans, in spite of the delay. However, that is not the case. Although we have done much talking about it and have many notions and many scratch ideas for melodies and lyrics, we are still in fact at the beginning.
>
> Considering all that, this leaves us with no other choice but to withdraw. I say this with great regret and great sadness, but with the time that we can work so vague, I do feel it's the only thing we can do.
>
> I'll send a copy of this letter to Bobby and Jim. I do hope you all won't curse us to high heaven, or places lower, or in any way construe this as a rejection of the property, or think that *My Fair Lady* has changed our attitude about it in any way. It is purely a physical matter over which we have no control.
>
> Fondly,
> Alan

Lerner's letter is masterful, since it explains from several points of view why he and Loewe were now no longer interested in pursuing the project, without making reference to Ferber's work or anything other than practical considerations. Ultimately, had they been passionate about the project, they would probably have stuck with it, in spite of what Lerner writes here.

Ferber was not impressed: in her reply, she described the affair as "sad and dispiriting," and expressed her sorrow and disgust. The huge impact of *My Fair Lady* clearly made her situation even worse because the potential commercial success of *Saratoga Trunk* had suddenly become much greater, had Lerner and Loewe gone ahead with it. She reminded Lerner that a contract had been signed between them, and, with a mixture of irritation and flattery, tried to persuade him to go ahead after all. In response, Lerner rose to Ferber's challenging letter politely but firmly. It seems that one of the most irritating aspects of the "affair" for her was the fact that she had received Lerner's letter withdrawing from the project after having read about it in the *New York Times*. Sam Zolotow's gossip column had announced on April 11 that Lerner and Loewe were "unable to proceed with their next project" due to Loewe's health. "Mr. Lerner feels tuckered out, too," Zolotow further reported, and went on to announce, that Lerner had therefore decided to withdraw from the stage version of the long-planned *Huckleberry Finn,* which Burton Lane would now produce on his own. This article was the first Ferber knew of Lerner and Loewe's withdrawal from *Saratoga,* and she was evidently shocked. She also saw through several of Lerner's other excuses, such as being too busy with further productions of *Fair Lady* to write a new musical (something that *Gigi* was soon to prove untrue). Yet most of her arguments were of little relevance now that Lerner and Loewe had decided it was not for them, as Lerner tried to tell her gently in the following letter:

To Edna Ferber

April 24, 1956

Dear Edna:

I didn't call you the next day because after I read your letter, I wanted to first write you an answer to it before speaking to you again, and this is the first chance I've had to do it. I put my house in the country up for sale and for the last month I have been out practically every day looking for another house to rent for the summer. Yesterday we finally found one—so here I am this morning with your letter before me.

I hate to do what I'm going to do—which is to answer the various points you've raised one at a time. I hate it because it makes me feel like I've been hiding something in the closet that now must be revealed, when actually the closet is as empty as the second night of "Grandma's Diary." However, here goes:

Quite true, I wrote you a letter on the afternoon of April 9th. It was that afternoon that Fritz left for Europe. The next day Zolotow of the *Times* called me about Fritz's departure and about our future places. I saw no reason not to tell the truth. Hence the alacrity with which the story appeared in the press.

I don't know whether you meant it or not, but in your letter you implied some Machiavellian scheme on our part to postpone the financing of the play. Actually, we did it for the best interests of the show. It was no scheme which in any way indicated tentativeness on our part or any hesitancy whatsoever about our intention to do your lovely book. As I explained, we felt it was foolish to make a deal before we knew what motion picture company could best serve us artistically.

You ask quite logically why we did not request an extension. The answer is very simple. I wouldn't have the slightest idea how long to ask an extension for. I have no idea when Fritz and I will be settling down to work together. As a matter of fact, because I am already growing restless, I may even do something in another medium without him over the summer and into the early fall,[22] just to fill up the time until he feels up to going to work again.

I was terribly amused by your reference to your not being a "Tennessee mountain girl." Dear Edna, I swear to you, I have never pictured you bringing the water down from the mountain. I also sigh with relief you were not brought up in the shotgun country or this lovely April breeze might be wafting through my head. However, please don't ever think that the preparations for a second company are any less detailed and time-consuming than those of a first company. It might be easier on a straight play but on a musical the work is prodigious. The only difference is you are sending out an exclamation point and not a question mark.

As for Fritz and I damaging *Saratoga Trunk* in any way, I think you are being too modest. Rodgers and Hammerstein simply turned down *Pygmalion* and said it couldn't be done. Yet when the property became available, the bidding was ferocious. It's absolutely absurd to even think that the likes of Fritz and me could ever in any way injure Edna Ferber's *Saratoga Trunk*, much less "degrade" it by having to withdraw for reasons of health.

And finally, you seem to have misconstrued my saying that I had been "in touch with thousands of attornies." I was merely being facetious about Pilpel, Cohen, Fitelson, Aslan, etc. etc.[23] I must tell you I never consulted our attorney at all before I wrote you the letter. After all, it had nothing to do with him. I don't think it is even a question of a breach of contract. I have always understood that any contract in which an outside date for completion of a play is involved with the penalty of loss of rights automatically contemplates the possibility the play may not be done. Not only that, but from the more important point of view, namely the ethical, Fritz and I feel that we acted on the best of faith by not holding you up any longer.

[22] This may be a reference to the movie *Gigi*, whose script Lerner was considering writing without necessarily creating the songs (see following pages).

[23] Leading New York lawyers: Harriet Pilpel, Irving Cohen, H. William Fitelson, and Benjamin Aslan.

I beg you not to feel the "business is sordid." Sad it undoubtedly us, but sordid, never.

Now I shall phone you.

Fondly,
Alan Jay Lerner

Three days later, the *New York Times* confirmed that "The musical stage rights to Edna Ferber's novel 'Saratoga Trunk' have reverted to the author.... Messrs. Lerner and Loewe were too worn out from their efforts in making 'My Fair Lady' the big hit it is to process 'Saratoga Trunk' immediately."[24]

With these negotiations with Ferber out of the way, Lerner wrote to Selznick to update her on the Equity situation, as well as the arrival of the partners of Rex Harrison and Julie Andrews to Manhattan:

To Irene Mayer Selznick

April 27, 1956

Darling:

Life continues to be hectic—although if you ask me what I am doing that makes it so, I couldn't quite tell you—hence the delay in writing you.

First off, I am thrilled about the success of *The Chalk Garden*,[25] and I know that my pleasure can only be a small portion of what yours is and that makes me doubly happy. Congratulations, and I wish I'd been there on opening night with you.

Oscar, Dick and Howard Lindsay had an informal meeting with some of the Equity officials the other day. According to them, the 60/40 arrangement has <u>not</u> been changed and there is, in fact, no basic alteration of the previous policy. The impression that Oscar, Dick and Howard got was that the executives of Equity feel rather on the spot themselves and wish that even the present laws were not as stringent as they are. It is interesting to note that the rigid laws of British Equity didn't even come up. A permanent committee from the Dramatists Guild is now being appointed and they will continue more detailed discussions with Equity. I'll keep you informed.

[24] Sam Zolotow, "'Lovers' Puts Off Arrival by a Day," *New York Times*, April 27, 1956, 24.

[25] Enid Bagnold's play *The Chalk Garden* had just premiered in London, in a production directed by John Gielgud and starring Edith Evans and Peggy Ashcroft.

How long are you staying over? There still is a slight possibility I might come around mid-May. I'll know definitely within a few days and will cable you accordingly. I am writing Binkie [Beaumont] today to find out precisely when he is coming so that we don't wave to each other from the airplane enroute.

After a devilish search that took me practically every other day for the last three weeks, we finally got a house for the summer in Glen Cove. It has a real human beach for people instead of those usual North Shore jobs that are only for clams and crabs. Quite wonderful really.

Katy[26] arrived a week ago and Rex is now the Governor of the Stage of Euphoria. He got himself a house in Westbury for the summer and he and Katy will probably move out in June. So for the time being, all is quiet, cozy and iniquitous.

Julie's love[27] arrived the same day as did Katy and I must say he came as rather a shock. He couldn't possibly be more than twelve although he claims to be twenty. He's terribly nice but so young you could kick him. He is now ensconced in Julie's hotel and I live in mortal fear that they might get drunk on buttermilk one night, commit the original sin (in a highly unoriginal way), and leave us with the problem of having to let out her costumes. Ah, the arts!

Write soon. Miss you.

All my love,
Alan

Lerner's gently humorous comments on Andrews prefigured the "buttermilk" image that was to overshadow much of her career.[28]

A week later, with *My Fair Lady* set in for a long run, Lerner wrote an extensive letter to Loewe, who was still on retreat in Europe. In this missive, Lerner hints at his unhappiness at the way Herman Levin was running certain aspects of the production, and suggests to Loewe a way forward now that their own importance had suddenly increased. The affection, familiarity, and detail of Lerner's

[26] Actress Kay Kendall (1927–59) was to become Rex Harrison's wife the following year. They were happily married until her tragically early death from leukemia. She is perhaps best remembered for her appearances in the films *Genevieve* (1953) and *Les Girls* (1958).

[27] Theater and movie set and costume designer Tony Walton (b. 1934) was the first husband of Julie Andrews from 1959 to 1967. He was costume designer and visual consultant for Andrews's first movie, *Mary Poppins* (1964), and won the Oscar for *All That Jazz* (1980).

[28] For a critical perspective on Andrews's screen image, see Peter Kemp, "How Do You Solve a 'Problem' Like Maria von Poppins?" in *Musicals and Beyond*, ed. Bill Marshall and Robynn Stilwell (Exeter: Intellect, 2000), 55–61.

letter to Loewe, compared to his communications with most of his other friends and colleagues, is quite arresting:

To Frederick Loewe

May 8, 1956

Dear Meistercocker,[29]

Not having heard from you for the last fortnight, I can only assume the wheel has beaten you and you have shot yourself on the terrace of the Monte Carlo Casino in fine heroic tradition. However, on the supposition that your silence has been due to your usual shit-heel negligence, I am writing you to bring you up to date on our affairs.

Things have been a bit rickety at the theatre. There has been a full scale investigation of the ticket situation of *My Fair Lady* by the city authorities with much blazing of headline every day. Not being able to get anything out of Levin and Adler,[30] I only know what I read in the papers, which is that the main culprits seem to be the theatre party agents. It got so bad there was even an editorial in the Journal American about it the other day, about the disgrace of seats for *My Fair Lady* going for $150 a pair. Thus far, I have been unable to force our "producer" to make any statement to the papers assuring the public that there are seats and that requests are being honored. Irving Cohen's[31] been in California and will be back tomorrow and there will be a full scale meeting then. I have been rather waiting for him to return. Herman assures me that Phil has been keeping the ice down to $1500 a week. Whether Herman is participating is anybody's guess. He sold 20% of his stock three days ago for $425,000 capital gains, so why the hell he would want to, I don't know.

Herman is a very good producer, but he approaches the theatre I think the way all producers seem to. They are basically cigar store operators. He's very good on the little things but he doesn't seem to think in the larger concepts that running a five million dollar business entails—and after all, that's what this is. I mean, for example, the whole coordination of the road company, the English company, and the motion picture deal; the proper time to make a motion picture deal

[29] Probably a comical development of "alter cocker," an affectionate Yiddish phrase meaning "old fart" that Lerner uses fairly regularly.

[30] Philip Adler was general manager of the show; his son Jerry was the stage manager.

[31] Irving Cohen, one of Lerner's attorneys.

(which I believe is within the next few months—prices can't get any higher and they might get lower);[32] the matter of signing Rex by doing it on some tax basis where Rex will profit more but it won't cost the company any more; the proper public relations on the change of price; the proper use of CBS TV in areas where the mail orders are not as great as they are in other geographical areas, etc. etc. Even a little thing like the touring company was about to be done in an offhand way. I was told by both him and Phil that we would have to cut the show down. I know neither of us wants to do that. So I had lunch with Jerry Whyte[33] who toured *Winged Victory*.[34] He told me they toured with turntables by the simple device of having additional turntables which were always sent ahead in advance. It burned me up that they couldn't have found that out and that I had to take the time to explore. All of this is fine but I don't enjoy it very much and when we sit down to write another show, there's no reason why we should have to be bothered by matters such as these when Herman is receiving a handsome sum to be doing it himself. Therefore, I have a very positive suggestion which I am sure you will agree to. I've already spoken to Ben [Aslan] and Irving [Cohen] about it and they both agree. My idea is for Lowal[35] to hire somebody like Eddie Knill[36] who would be a sort of business coordinator for Lowal's activities. Until we go into production with something, we could probably get him for about $150. per week, but it wouldn't take all his time and he could continue business managing whatever show he is doing until we need him full-time. He could then keep on top of all of these things and make a weekly report to us. Being an experienced man around the box office, his very presence would cause the boys to be a little cautious. He could also see that we get the proper business statements every week on such things as what our advance is—believe it or not, it took until yesterday to find out what our actual advance was. It's a little over $600,000, incidentally, which is not nearly as high as it should be. The reason it isn't higher could only be one of two things: either they are not filling the mail orders and are handing seats back for ice, or people are discouraged by all the publicity and aren't buying with

[32] Lerner proved to be wrong about this, as the film rights were much later bought by Jack Warner for a record $5 million.

[33] Jerome Whyte (?–1974), a production supervisor on numerous Richard Rodgers shows.

[34] A play with music, by Moss Hart, that debuted in 1943.

[35] Lowal, Lerner and Loewe's company.

[36] Edwin Knill (?–1997) was an experienced General Manager with Broadway credits including *The Day before Spring* (1945) and *Kiss Me, Kate* (1948).

the abandon they should. Of course, this does not imply that the show is in the slightest bit of trouble. It's such an overwhelming hit that no mistakes can make any difference at this time.

However, as Moss [Hart] says, a continuation of this will shorten the run at some future time. Besides all of this, it's very good for Lowal tax-wise to have someone on the payroll. There is enough money coming in to Lowal all the time from the music business to take care of a salary until we start getting profits from the show.

There has been a lot of interest motion picture wise in the last couple of weeks and Irving has worked out a formula which he will, of course, go over with Ben, whereby whatever sum is paid for the picture rights will <u>exclude</u> GBS.[37] He will get his on the gross later on. In other words, if the property sells for a million dollars, which is certainly the minimum, we will be able to divide it on the usual basis.

The songs are doing absolutely wonderfully. Vic Damone's[38] record in the last seven days has begun to crash through and you hear it all the time. Not only that, but "On The Street Where You Live" is getting wonderful plugging on radio and TV; in fact, all three of the songs are. Rosemary Clooney[39] is making another record of "I Could Have Danced All Night" this week and the old record is being withdrawn. I have been keeping after Goddard [Lieberson] and Mitch[40] and I'm going to try and get them to make another record of "Accustomed" with a male singer.

Did I tell you last time about the Actors Benefit? I don't think so. Anyhow it was the goddamnedest night of all time. It made the opening night look like a Hadassah benefit. The laughter was enormous on every point; practically every song stopped the show and the ovation at the end was something I'll never forget as long as I live. When Rex and Julie stepped out of the line for their final bow, the entire audience stood up like one person and shouted. There were over seven minutes of curtain calls. Comments at the end were something I've never heard before. It was an absolutely incredible experience and I can't tell you how much

[37] A reference to the estate of George Bernard Shaw. Lerner was keen to avoid losing too much of the money from *My Fair Lady* to the Shaw estate because of their rights to *Pygmalion*.

[38] Vic Damone (b. 1928), a popular singer whose recording of "On the Street Where You Live" reached #4 on the US charts and #1 on the UK charts.

[39] American singer and actress Rosemary Clooney (1928–2002), who released singles of "I Could Have Danced All Night" (#49 in the United States) and "I've Grown Accustomed to Your Face" (#70).

[40] Mitch Miller (1911–2010) was the head of Artists and Repertoire at Columbia Records.

I wish you'd been there. Rex told me later it was the most extraordinary night in his entire theatrical career. Incidentally, Rex gave the greatest performance I've ever seen him give and it was fascinating to see how the actors knew that his was the really great performance of the show. His ovation was tumultuous.

I'll send you *The Male Animal*[41] but after reading it over carefully, I'm not as hot on it as I was. It's awfully hard to get steamed up about things for any length of time when we are not together. The French play I told you about looks fascinating and Moss and I have also been kicking other things around from time to time. I am sure when you come home that it won't take too long for us to decide on something. I want you to know, incidentally, that for the first time in my life, I am not bursting to go to work. The only reason I am doing what I am doing is just to keep my mind occupied in a vague way. However, I am sure this lethargy won't last forever and the minute we're together again, the old sparks will begin to fly.

Binkie arrives over the weekend to discuss London. After he leaves, at long last, I'll be able to get away. Can't wait. I'll let you know where I'm going.

Put 500 fr. on number 17 for me some night and let me know what's going on with you and the Poo.[42]

Love,
Alan

P.S. The Loesser show[43] got over, but there was only one out and out rave; Chapman in the *News*—Atkinson was a fine notice with one or two reservations. Kerr had lots of reservations.[44] I'll let you know when I see it.

So little is known about the working relationship between Lerner and Loewe that this letter significantly increases our understanding of their collaboration. At this crucial moment in their joint development, with huge success just under way and a significant business now to manage, it is instructive to see the level of detail in which they discuss the financial and managerial issues at hand. Though *Brigadoon* and *Paint Your Wagon* had brought them to prominence, *Fair Lady*

[41] *The Male Animal* (1940) was a Broadway play by James Thurber and Elliott Nugent that Lerner had evidently considered for a musical treatment.

[42] Presumably Loewe's girlfriend.

[43] Frank Loesser's *The Most Happy Fella*, which had just opened on Broadway.

[44] The leading New York critics: John Chapman, Brooks Atkinson, and Walter Kerr.

catapulted them into the major league, and with it came responsibility. We also learn from the letter that it was thanks to Lerner that the touring production of the show included the complete Broadway sets (with double turntables) by Oliver Smith. Evidently, Levin intended to simplify the show when it went around the country, but Lerner realized that the production was part of the *Fair Lady* brand and, as such, crucial to its continuing success. Equally interesting is Lerner's confession that he was feeling lethargic and was "not bursting to go back to work"; he is known as a workaholic, but on this occasion even he seemed to feel it had been better to journey than to arrive. None of this information has been included in previous biographies of the writer, and the letter paints Lerner in a much more nuanced, serious light than is often the case.

Yet his ennui didn't last for long. Just over a week later, Lerner wrote again to Loewe, this time more briefly, to entreat him to write the score of *Gigi* for MGM. The idea for a film based on Colette's novella *Gigi* (1944) seems to have started at MGM in 1951 as a vehicle for Leslie Caron, but nothing came of it at the time.[45] Anita Loos's stage adaptation (as a play without songs) played Broadway in 1953, and MGM producer Arthur Freed showed renewed interest in the material in late 1955. He visited Lerner during the Philadelphia tryouts of *My Fair Lady* and offered him the project as the third and final movie (after *Brigadoon* and *Huckleberry Finn*) to fulfill his contract with the studio. Lerner agreed, though he anticipated struggling to persuade Loewe to write the music for the film. In the following letter, he writes to Loewe to ask him to take part in the film (probably after having previously mentioned it to him in Philadelphia), as well as passing on an idea for a new stage musical:

To Frederick Loewe

May 17, 1956

Dear Boy:

This is not the long letter I promised you in my cable. I'll write again over the weekend.

Two things have just come up:

David Selznick[46] called last night to offer us *Gone With the Wind* for a stage musical. Are you interested? He's leaving for Europe tomorrow and would like to see you some place on the continent. I told him I'd

[45] For information on the early genesis of the musical *Gigi*, see Fordin, *MGM's Greatest Musicals*, 453–457.

[46] David Selznick (1902–65) was the producer of the Oscar-winning films *Gone With the Wind* (1939) and *Rebecca* (1940).

cable if it's possible. Would you like to meet him or would you rather wait and have me do it the end of June when he gets back? Either way, let me know right away your thoughts.

The second thing is that Metro has started calling again in the last couple of days about *Gigi*. As you know, I am anxious to get rid of my last commitment to them. But I hate like hell to even think about it without you. It wouldn't be much of a job and we could do it July or August here in the East. It could be a Lerner-Loewe picture à la Rodgers and Hammerstein's *State Fair*.[47] And they're going to do it with an all-French cast, Leslie Caron, [Maurice] Chevalier,[48] etc.

Now you know you're going to be sick of toasting your Viennese ass by the first of July, so why don't you be a good fellow and help me out. Please think about it and cable me. You know damn well it would be right up our alley.

Edwin Lester[49] is here from California and Beaumont from London. I've been working on a second company and English company all week. Will write about it over the weekend.

The songs are doing great. I'll send you the last *Variety* music pages to Vienna.

Love to the Poo and a kick in the balls to you.
Alan

Famously, Loewe's reaction to the idea of writing a musical based on *Gone With the Wind* came through a telegram which inadvertently reproduced his German accent: "VIND NOT FUNNY. LOVE FRITZ."[50] He also seems to have turned down *Gigi* at this point (though he is reported to have agreed to read Lerner's screenplay after its completion), partly due to his general antipathy toward Hollywood.[51]

[47] *State Fair* (1945) was the only project Rodgers and Hammerstein wrote directly for the big screen. At 100 minutes in length it was a comparatively short musical, and required only six songs. Lerner makes the comparison to emphasize that the project might not involve as much work as a stage show.

[48] Maurice Chevalier (1888–1972) was a beloved singer and actor who appeared in numerous musical films and was a great favorite of Lerner's. He went on to play Honoré Lachailles in the film *Gigi*.

[49] Edwin Lester (1895–1990) was a hugely successful producer, director, and impresario. He founded the Los Angeles Civic Light Opera in 1938 and later played host to the stage premiere of the musical *Gigi* there in 1973. His other successes included *Kismet* (1953) and *Peter Pan* (1954).

[50] Lerner, *Street*, 143.

[51] Lerner writes: "I desperately wanted to do it with Fritz, but Fritz had always refused to involve himself with a motion picture. Nothing but the theatre was of any interest to him." Lerner, *Street*, 143. See Fordin, *MGM's Greatest Musicals*, 455–457, for information on Loewe's promise to read the script.

In consequence, Lerner proceeded without a composer, and the *New York Times* reported that "Alan Jay Lerner, author of book and lyrics of 'My Fair Lady,' will be here next week to work with Arthur Freed on the script of the musical version of 'Gigi,' "[52] without mentioning who was to write the songs.

One of the pleasures of having such success with *My Fair Lady* was the way in which it allowed Lerner to become good friends with various of his musical idols. These included composer-lyricist Cole Porter (1891–1964), of *Anything Goes* and *Kiss Me, Kate* fame, who loved the show so much that by the end of the year, through Lerner's gift, he was seeing the show almost every Wednesday night. The following letter was written by Lerner to Porter after the two had spent an evening together. Porter had raved about Lerner's work and been promised the weekly tickets:

To Cole Porter

July 2, 1956

Dear Cole:

I enjoyed seeing you so very much the other night. Your enthusiasm for the show means more to me than I can possibly say. I am naturally always pleased when people like it, but especially so when some do, and I can't think of anybody to whom that applies more than you.

I'll have your seats for you in the fall and I do hope we'll be able to have an evening together while you're here.

Have a wonderful summer.

Best regards,
Alan

P.S. Crest Toothpaste is dazzling. I bought a tube the next morning. Best thing since French pastry.

Porter was delighted about the tickets, as he told Lerner in a short note: "My 'subscription' seats for *My Fair Lady* arrived, and I can't tell you how deeply I appreciate it." He added: "From now on, any time you happen to be in your theatre and want a companion between the acts, I shall be there on Wednesday nights."

[52] Oscar Godbout, " 'The Ninth Wave' bought for Film," *New York Times*, July 12, 1956, 15.

During the summer of 1956, Lerner started to grapple with the *Gigi* screenplay, and finished the first draft during the fall. He also managed to persuade Maurice Chevalier to star in the film, though his first choice for the title role, Audrey Hepburn, was unwilling to repeat her performance as Gigi from Anita Loos' stage adaptation of Colette's novella on which the musical was based.[53] At the same time, Lerner and Loewe started to search for material for a new stage project. The novel *Greenwillow* by magazine fiction writer B. J. Chute was proposed in October, though it was declined and eventually taken up by Frank Loesser.[54] An interesting column in the *New York Times* in December indicated the next work by "the *Fair Lady* Team" would involve a co-production by Lerner, Loewe and Moss Hart: "They aim to pool their talents in writing a musical. . . . Their work would be divided on the following basis: book, Mr. Lerner and Mr. Hart; lyrics, Mr. Lerner; music, Mr. Loewe; staging, Mr. Hart."[55] Although the three men did indeed collaborate on their next stage musical, *Camelot* (1960), it is intriguing to note that Hart's name was not in the end associated with writing the book, given his influence on the script of *Fair Lady* and this article announcing his involvement with the script of the new show.

Meanwhile, *Fair Lady* required some attention if the show was to sustain its success. Rex Harrison had only signed up for a year's run, and the team was desperate to have him extend his contract. Therefore, Lerner persuaded John Gielgud (1904–2000), the veteran British stage actor, to agree to play Higgins on Broadway for five months and then take the show to London, if Harrison would not stay in it for a longer run:

Telegram to Herman Levin

November 15, 1956

GIELGUD WILLING TO PLAY BROADWAY NOVEMBER THROUGH MARCH AND THEN LONDON. WE CAN NOW PUT PRESSURE ON HARRISON TO SIGN AT LEAST TILL JUNE OR LOSE LONDON. CABLE PROGRESS OF NEGOTIATIONS. IF NEGATIVE, FRITZ AND I WILL FLY TO LONDON TO SEE GIELGUD ABOUT MUSIC.

ALAN

[53] Hepburn had played *Gigi* in the 1951 Broadway production of the play. Fordin, *MGM's Greatest Musicals*, 457.

[54] Louis Calta, "Lowe [*sic*] and Lerner Asked to Write Musical Score for 'Greenwillow,' " *New York Times*, October 6, 1956. Loesser's *Greenwillow* opened on Broadway on March 8, 1960, and ran for 97 performances.

[55] Sam Zolotow, " 'Mister Roberts' Returns Tonight," *New York Times*, December 5, 1956, 49.

Lerner knew that Harrison was eager to appear in the show's London debut, returning home from his triumph in a Broadway musical, and that this would be the leverage required to make him extend his New York contract. Though he was good friends with Harrison, Lerner knew that he had to step in for Levin and manipulate the situation for the good of the show, and indeed Harrison ultimately agreed to their terms.

On a different front, the script of *My Fair Lady* was published for the first time, but upon opening it Lerner discovered that the name of the choreographer, Hanya Holm, had been omitted. He wrote to apologize:

To Hanya Holm

19 December 1956

Hanya Darling:

I was absolutely devastated when it was brought to my attention that your name had been omitted by the publishers in the published version of the show. Of course, I know, that you know, that it was a typographical oversight and I am moving heaven and earth to try to have it rectified even before the next printing. Aside from your wonderful contribution to the success of the show I was all the more upset because I am so terribly fond of you. Please accept my deepest, deepest apologies.

Devotedly,
Alan

The show made the headlines in January 1957 when American Equity announced that Edward Mulhare,[56] the Irish actor Lerner had lined up to replace Harrison during the latter's vacations during his extension, would not be allowed to undertake the role because he was a non-US actor.[57] Similarly, the three British actors lined up to star in the National Tour were being obstructed from immigrating, and the New York Department of Labor was forced to intercede.[58] The mayor then became involved, and terms between Equity and Levin were only agreed upon a fortnight before Mulhare was due to start.[59] The

[56] Edward Mulhare (1923–97) was an Irish actor with many stage and screen credits, though Higgins was his signature role.

[57] Sam Zolotow, "'Fair Lady' Role Barred to Alien," *New York Times*, January 11, 1957, 17.

[58] Sam Zolotow, "City to Mediate 'Fair Lady' Issue," *New York Times*, January 15, 1957, 24.

[59] Arthur Gelb, "Kheel Will Rule on Stage Dispute," *New York Times*, January 16, 1957, 35.

producer hastily signed him up for three years, first to cover for Harrison during his vacations, then to take over permanently upon Harrison's departure in December.[60]

By early 1957, Lerner was moving ahead with *Gigi*. He showed his screenplay to Loewe, who unexpectedly caved in and agreed to write the score in early February.[61] He was charmed by what he read, and with no Broadway project firmly slated for the future, the prospect of writing a handful of songs for *Gigi* was obviously a viable alternative. But although Leslie Caron (Gigi) and Maurice Chevalier (Honoré) were lined up to head the cast, a male co-star was still needed. Lerner had long wanted to write a project for his friend Dirk Bogarde,[62] and he wrote to him to try to persuade him to play Gaston:

To Dirk Bogarde

February 7th, 1957

Dear Dirk,

Formal studio letter.

Here's the script. As you'll see, a couple of song ideas have been indicated but they are by no means definite. Also, as I told you on the phone, there are bound to be changes (not large ones) when Fritz and I start musicalizing it.[63] Gaston will have at least one solo and one number with Uncle Honoré (Chevalier).

K and R[64] will be in Hollywood the same time as you if you do the picture. I mention it for the sole purpose of influencing you.

I hope you like the script but if you don't I forgive you.

More later in my own inimitable profane style.

Love to Tony.[65]

Aye,
Alan

[60] Sam Zolotow, "'Tunnel of Love' Arrives Tonight," *New York Times*, February 13, 1957, 40.

[61] Thomas M. Pryor, "'Fair Lady' Team to Join in Movie," *New York Times*, February 13, 1957, 39.

[62] Actor Dirk Bogarde (1921–99) was well known for his appearances for the Rank film company, though he later appeared in productions for other studios, such as Visconti's *Death in Venice* (1971).

[63] They had not yet started, showing that Loewe had only just agreed to participate.

[64] Probably a reference to Rex Harrison and his wife Kay Kendall, with whom he was good friends.

[65] Anthony Forwood (1915–88) was an actor, as well as Bogarde's manager and partner.

Sadly, he proved to be unavailable for contractual reasons, and it took time to persuade the eventual choice, Louis Jourdan,[66] to accept the role, given his lack of previous experience in musicals.[67]

As for the designs, after the success of *My Fair Lady* it was natural that Lerner and Loewe should turn to Cecil Beaton for *Gigi*. Lerner wrote to Arthur Freed, the film's producer, to ask whether he could approach Beaton about the project. Evidently, Lerner's enthusiasm for the film largely depended on Beaton's involvement:

Telegram to Arthur Freed

FEBRUARY 11, 1957

DEAR ARTHUR

CECIL BEATON WILL BE ARRIVING IN NEW YORK FROM JAPAN AND CAN BE REACHED AT THE AMBASSADOR HOTEL. PLEASE LET US KNOW IF YOU WANT FRITZ AND ME TO TALK TO HIM ABOUT THE PICTURE BEFORE YOU DO OR AFTER.

LOVE,
ALAN

A day later Freed wrote back to say he was more than happy to let Lerner handle the matter, and all were relieved when the designer said yes.[68]

March was a busy month for Lerner. *Brigadoon* was to have a short run at City Center from March 27, which meant that Lerner and Loewe would have two shows playing in New York concurrently.[69] Then, when Moss Hart fell ill, Lerner had to take over the directorial responsibilities for the National Tour of *My Fair Lady*. Consequently, he had to turn down the offer of a vacation at the house of his friend Marietta Peabody Tree:[70]

[66] Louis Jourdan (1921–) is a French movie actor who had been known for his appearances in films such as *The Paradine Case* (1947) and *Three Coins in the Fountain* (1954) before *Gigi*, his first musical picture.

[67] Fordin, *MGM's Greatest Musicals*, 463.

[68] Telegram from Freed to Lerner, February 12, 1957, Arthur Freed Collection, USC.

[69] Lewis Funke, "News and Gossip of the Rialto," *New York Times*, March 10, 1957, X1.

[70] Marietta Peabody Tree (1917–91) went on to represent the United States on the United Nations Commission on Human Rights (appointed by Lerner's school friend, President John F. Kennedy) from 1961 to 1964. Her husband, Ronald Tree (1897– 1976) was a British journalist and Conservative M.P.

To Marietta Tree

February 20, 1957

Dear Marietta:

Forgive the delay in answering your enticing letter, but I just returned from California a few days ago. I use the word "enticing" with full awareness, because nothing could be more so than to be able to visit you and Ronnie in your tropical Shangri-la, and therefore nothing grieves me more than not to be able to do it.

Unfortunately, March is my frenetic month this year. The National Company[71] goes into rehearsal next week, and I have to see it through until the opening on March 18th. Immediately following, I have to go to Paris on business. When you consider that I don't like Paris and adore the sunny climes, and that I am irritated by the French and always smile at the prospect of seeing you, you can further understand the depth of my grief. However, thank you for thinking of me, and perhaps someday some year you will again have an empty room for me to fill and I will be able to take advantage of it.

Do have a wonderful winter, and give Ronnie my warmest. Will we see you in the spring? I hope so.

Fondly and soulfully,
Alan

Lerner's comments about Paris and the French are patently "niceties" intended to soften the blow of his rejection of Tree's offer: obviously, the author of *An American in Paris* and *Gigi* loved the city.

On March 15, another Lerner premiere took place: the first performance of two new songs, with music by Leonard Bernstein and lyrics by Lerner, written for their alma mater, Harvard University. The songs—called "Dedication" and "Lonely Men of Harvard"—were performed at Carnegie Hall by the Harvard University Glee Club and the Harvard University Band in a concert in aid of Harvard College.[72] The same night, *My Fair Lady* celebrated its first anniversary,[73] and two weeks later the nominees for the Tony Awards were announced; *My Fair Lady* led with ten citations.[74] These, with other events, are among the topics Lerner discusses in the following two conversational letters from the period.

[71] The National Tour of *My Fair Lady*.

[72] H.C.S., "Harvard Unveils 2 New Songs Here," *New York Times*, March 16, 1957, 14.

[73] Milton Z. Esterow, "First Birthday for 'Lady,'" *New York Times*, March 10, 1957, X3.

[74] "Nominees Listed for Stage 'Tonys,'" *New York Times*, March 26, 1957, 36.

A long-term friend of Lerner's, Morys Bruce, Fourth Baron Aberdare (1919–2005), was a Conservative politician and, at the time Lerner wrote this letter, also worked for the BBC. Herman Wouk (b. 1915) is the Pulitzer Prize–winning author of the novel *The Caine Mutiny* (1951), who probably knew Lerner through his early work on writing radio scripts. These letters outline Lerner's general activities during March and April:

To Morys Bruce

March 1, 1957

Dear Morys:

Do forgive me for not answering your first letter, but I was in California and only got back in time for Nancy's opening.[75] They had a miserable opening night audience, who stared at the stage as if they were all under the influence of a heavy narcotic. Considering the play is a comedy, it hardly made for an uproarious evening. The play itself received fair to good notices. Nancy, however, came off wonderfully well, praise Allah. Since the opening night, the regular civilians who go to the theatre have been behaving much more humanly, and I am sure they are in for a long run.

While I was in California your second letter arrived about seats for Mrs. Murray. My secretary for some reason thought you were Ben and answered him to your address. It's all very confusing, but the result of it all is that we have two seats reserved for Mrs. Murray for the night of March 25th and will leave them at the box office in her name. She can pick them up the evening of the performance.

As for me, I had a rather dreary time on the Coast and am decidedly pleased to be back in my old haunts. The second company is in rehearsal now, so I'll be tied up with that until the end of the month.

Immediately following, Fritz and I shall be off to London and Paris. We've decided to write the score for the film version of *Gigi*. [Maurice] Chevalier is going to be in it, and he's in Paris. Profiting by the happy experience we had with Rex [Harrison] of trying every song out with him long before production, we're going to do the same with dear old Maurice. In London, we'll try to find a replacement for Julie Andrews when she leaves next December.[76]

[75] Nancy Olson had just opened on Broadway in the Theatre Guild production *The Tunnel of Love*.
[76] A reference to Andrews's departure from the role of Eliza in *My Fair Lady*.

I do hope you and Sarah[77] will be in town. I'll let you know in the next couple of weeks precisely when we'll be arriving.... Give my love to Sarah. I can't wait to see you both.

Aye,
Alan

To Herman Wouk

April 4, 1957

Dear Herman:

To begin with, old cock, my name is A-L-A-N, not "Allen." I should have thought that after all we have been through together, my name would have been engraved on the wall of one of those dark, dank corridors of your subconscious that you visit when you have nightmares.

My second beef about your letter is that it's quite obvious from its tone that this Western D. H. Lawrence life you're leading, this existence of sandy detachment and wind-swept isolation, with no one to talk to but leather-skinned Neanderthals, has increased your rather irritating self-satisfaction and political perversity. Not only are you going to return tanned and healthy, which is annoying enough, but I fully expect you to be completely converted to Richard Nixon, with the possible exception that here and there he may be a bit too liberal for you. Oh, Sarah,[78] speak up! Don't let this happen to our Herman!

As for the Authors' League, not only have I been shirking my civic duties, but my general attitude these days about the human race in general is one of buoyant disinterest. I am off for Paris next week, where I fully intend to grow a beard, become an Existentialist, and spend the rest of my days sitting in the corner of a shabby bistro thinking up new and exhilarating ways of committing suicide. I did, however, attend one meeting, and all seems to be well. They have more speakers than a ladies' club, and Freedom-To-Write Day will obviously be the most important national event since John Hancock John Hancocked. The invitations have gone out, but I've no idea about the reaction. I have a strange recurring feeling the only authors who will

[77] Bruce's wife.

[78] Betty Sarah Wouk (1920–2011) was Herman's wife and literary agent.

be there will be Rex Stout,[79] Buck Crouse,[80] you and I—and I'm not sure about the last one.

Of myself, my winter has gone something like this:

1. Wrote two dreary songs for Harvard with Leonard Bernstein, which took me weeks and weeks and were presented at Carnegie Hall to a packed house of aged, deaf alumni, who couldn't hear a word and loved them.

2. Spent three appalling weeks in California with my children, whom as a result of which I have since given to Hungarian Relief.

3. Attended the opening of wife Nancy's play, which the authors successfully mangled to pieces on the road, but which nevertheless will enjoy a run.

4. Directed the road company of *My Fair Lady*—Moss Hart having been conveniently taken ill—and saw same through the opening in Rochester—great success.

5. Vaguely assisted in the highly successful and totally undeserved revival of *Brigadoon* at the City Center.[81]

6. Began score for film version of *Gigi*.

7. As mentioned above, leaving for Paris Wednesday for casting, atmosphere and la vie de bohème.

Do hope the book is coming well. Before you make any more fool motion picture deals, you'd better let me read it, in case there's a musical in it. I miss you, old boy, and I'll be glad when you're back in town. Give Sarah a buss for me, and come home soon.

Aye,
Alan

These letters show just how productive Lerner was; the post–*Fair Lady* inertia had not lasted long. Then on April 21 came the great news: *My Fair Lady* had won six Tony Awards, including Best Musical, Actor, Musical Director, Costume Designer, Scenic Designer, and Director.

Out of this busy and elating period came earnest preparations for *Gigi*, which progressed quickly now that Loewe had come on board. Moving to Paris in mid-April, Lerner worked fast to complete changes to the script in time for production. In doing so, he managed to quell the fears of Maurice Chevalier, who had concerns about his role of Uncle Honoré. Because this character is not

[79] Rex Stout (1886–1975) was an American crime novelist.

[80] Russel Crouse (1893–1966) was co-librettist (with Howard Lindsay) of *Anything Goes* (1934), *Call Me Madam* (1950), and *The Sound of Music* (1959).

[81] The revival of *Brigadoon* ran from April 9 to May 5.

fully developed in Colette's novella, he is largely the invention of Lerner and, as such, took time to bring into focus. Lerner was a lifelong fan of Chevalier—"He had been an idol of mine ever since every little breeze started whispering Louise," he commented—and sensed the French star should be the cornerstone of the movie, as he explains in his book: "I felt that a musical personality, such as Chevalier, was essential to the film: there had to be someone whose singing would be expected. The other characters could sing, but they were not singing roles."[82] Therefore, the character that Chevalier initially read on the page did not fully correspond to Lerner's intentions for him, so Lerner met with the actor to calm him down. In response, Chevalier wrote him a short note of thanks, saying "I was very happy to feel yesterday that with Fred[83] you were decided to fortify as much as it is possible with the story my part of Uncle Honoré. I can assure you that I am out in our picture to give the very best acting singing performance I can get out of my blood. I admire and trust our group immensely and you can all be sure of my devotion and sincerity."[84] The movie was in production over the summer, and in spite of various problems with filming on location in Paris, it was completed on October 30, 1957.[85]

For now, Lerner and Loewe had a major movie musical in the can, but, as the *New York Times* asked, "Where Do They Go from 'My Fair Lady?' "[86] They both felt that the show had led them in their "natural" direction as writers, as Lerner commented during November 1957:

> You learn from your failures; they teach you what you've done wrong. But you learn more from a success. When you can get far enough away from it to think it over and analyse it, a success shows you what you've done right.
>
> I see now there were some things I had to get out of my system; hang-overs from youth, fantasy, dream stuff. The "Day Before Spring," "Brigadoon" phase is over.
>
> I know now that what I want to be is a good lyric writer. Larry Hart told me once, "To be a writer, you must be brutal." He didn't mean you must hurt people. He meant you must be ruthless with yourself, you must concentrate on your writing to the exclusion of everything and everyone else, you must devote yourself to learning it, improving it,

[82] Lerner, *Street*, 142.

[83] A reference to Frederick Loewe, whose usual nickname was Fritz.

[84] Note from Chevalier to Lerner, May 31, 1957. Copy in a private collection.

[85] Fordin, *MGM's Greatest Musicals*, 489.

[86] Cecelia Ager, "Where Do They Go from 'My Fair Lady?' " *New York Times*, November 17, 1957, SM22.

> working at it constantly without ever giving yourself an out, without ever settling for less.
>
> For years, Fritz and I floundered around, trying to find our natural way of writing. "My Fair Lady" revealed it to us. The property dictates it. The characters in the story. We are the means by which they express themselves, not vice versa. So it's better they be in somebody else's story. Your own are too accommodating. They stay flat, the easier for you to pin songs on. Without their resistance to give you an original springboard into your lyrics, your score doesn't come off.
>
> Doing "My Fair Lady," for the first time Fritz and I had to come to grips with somebody else's characters, Shaw's. They were too strong, too alive to let us push them around. They compelled us to see things their way so that when we moved them into scenes outside the story framework that had hitherto contained them, they were able to meet their new situations with their emotions, motivations, quirks intact.
>
> When we felt we really knew them, then we began to work on the score. If we were right, their songs came out of what they are, out of the only way they could express themselves.
>
> Writing lyrics from this viewpoint, you don't say "Hey! How about this for a title?," fill in the rest, decide who should sing it, and look for a likely place to spot it. We try to catch some thought of a character that motivates him and, in turn, the story; that's our title. When we've agreed on that thought and its mood, Fritz sets it to music, then writes out the music for me. (I read music.) I go away with it and sketch in the lyric. Next meeting I try out what I've done on Fritz.
>
> His taste is incredibly fine and sensitive. He may find I've got off the track or gone too fancy, or I may feel his music needs development here or calming there, or there may even be a time when we're both delighted—but in the early stages that's rare.
>
> The "Gigi" score gave us the first chance to use what we'd learned from "My Fair Lady"; we wrote it, for us, in a flash.[87]

Here, Lerner acknowledges that his work on *My Fair Lady* had taken him to a new level of craft as a lyricist, and that this had helped *Gigi* to be a much easier project to write.

Apparently at the happiest point of their relationship to date, Lerner and Loewe mulled over some ideas that came their way. First they heard from Jo

[87] Ager, "Where Do They Go from 'My Fair Lady?' "

Mielziner,[88] the veteran scenic and lighting designer. One of his most acclaimed designs was for the Elmer Rice[89] play *Dream Girl* (1945), for which he won the Donaldson Award, and he wrote to Lerner and Loewe to suggest it to them as their next musical. However, they decided to turn it down:

To Jo Mielziner

August 16, 1957

Dear Mr. Mielziner:

I am dictating this long distance, so do forgive me if this letter is a little brief.

Fritz and I have thought about *Dream Girl* most carefully and feel that, for various reasons, it is not for us. I'll be back in town within the month, and if you would like I'll call you and explain in a little more detail why we feel the way we do. Thanks so much for thinking of us.

Give my best regards to Elmer, and all good luck to you both on the project.

Sincerely,
Alan

It wasn't until 1965 that a musical was adapted from the play, under the title *Skyscraper* with a score by Cahn and Van Heusen, and Mielziner's name was not attached.

As for Lerner, this period of theatrical deliberation coincided with separation from his wife, Nancy Olson, in September.[90] Then, he and Loewe finally settled on their future plans: following rumors about the show in August,[91] on October 13 they announced that they were at work with Moss Hart on a musical version of *Father of the Bride*, based on the 1949 novel by Edward Streeter and the 1950 film starring Elizabeth Taylor.[92] Hart would stage the show, and the three of them would produce it. In addition, Lerner and Loewe also intended to produce their first play: Jean Anouilh's *Ornifle*, adapted by Lucienne Hill and starring Rex Harrison. In this way, they proposed to emulate their great forebears,

[88] Jo Mielziner (1901–76) was the scenic and lighting designer of the original Broadway productions of *South Pacific, Carousel, A Streetcar Named Desire,* and *Death of a Salesman,* among others.

[89] Elmer Rice (1892–1967) was an American playwright, known for his plays *The Adding Machine* (1923) and *Street Scene* (1929).

[90] "The Alan Lerners Separate," *New York Times,* October 16, 1957, 40.

[91] Sam Zolotow, "John Kerr to Act in Phoenix Drama," *New York Times,* August 30, 1957, 11.

[92] Lewis Funke, "News and Gossip of the Realto," *New York Times,* October 13, 1957, 121.

Rodgers and Hammerstein, in producing others' work as well as their own, and in both musical and dramatic theater. Another project that briefly came back on the cards was the movie adaptation of *Paint Your Wagon*. After having written the version in 1953 with Arthur Schwartz, Lerner now agreed to write some new songs with Loewe, to a screenplay by John Lee Mahin and William Ludwig.[93] But as before, nothing came of any of the movie. A possible musical based on Sherlock Holmes, suggested by Billy Wilder,[94] also never came to pass.[95]

In the end, after several months' work on *Father of the Bride* they elected to abandon that project too, and they decided to give Herman Levin the rights as a Christmas present:

To Herman Levin

December 23, 1957

Dear Herm:

Fritz and I didn't know what to give you for Christmas, so we finally decided to give you *Father of the Bride*. We're not doing it, and we thought you might like to have it.

Will call you tomorrow, and we must get together before the end of the year about all our casting problems.

Hope you and Dawn[96] have a wonderful holiday.

Aye,
Alan

At around the same time, Lerner remarried, this time to the French lawyer Micheline Musselli Pozzo di Borgo.

By the start of 1958, Lerner and Loewe were back to square one, with no future projects in preparation. But both *Fair Lady* and *Gigi* still required work: the former's original cast was dispersing to prepare for the London transfer in April, and the latter's May premiere required effort from them in advance publicity, as well as some reshooting in February after a slightly disappointing first preview in

[93] Thomas M. Pryor, "Mayer Will Film Broadway Show," *New York Times*, June 7, 1957, 19.

[94] Billy Wilder (1906–2002) was one of the most prolific and respected movie directors of the twentieth century, with credits including *Sunset Boulevard* (1950) and *Some Like It Hot* (1959). Wilder would later make a film inspired by the Holmes stories, *The Private Life of Sherlock Holmes* (1970).

[95] Sam Zolotow, "June Havoc Gets 'One Foot in Door,'" *New York Times*, September 5, 1957, 32. In 1965, Marian Grudeff and Raymond Jessel presented their own musical version of Sherlock Holmes, called *Baker Street*.

[96] Dawn Levin, Herman's wife.

January.[97] After the success of Vic Damone's recording of "On the Street Where You Live" as a marketing tool for *Fair Lady*, Lerner and Loewe were keen to have him record the title song from their next project, and Lerner wrote to the singer to express his approbation when he agreed:

Telegram to Vic Damone

January 22, 1958

I'M SO DELIGHTED YOU WILL BE RECORDING "GIGI." LOEWE AND I HAVE NEVER BEEN HAPPIER WITH A RECORDING THAN YOUR VERSION OF "ON THE STREET WHERE YOU LIVE." WE'RE VERY ANXIOUS FOR YOURS TO BE THE DEFINITIVE RECORD AND HAVE YOU INTRODUCE IT ON THE ED SULLIVAN SHOW.[98] HOPE TO SEE YOU NEXT WEEK IN NEW YORK.

BEST REGARDS,
ALAN JAY LERNER

Again taking up the silent co-producer's role on *Fair Lady*, Lerner also tried to intervene when the *New York Times* did not review the new Eliza Doolittle, Sally Ann Howes, who took over from Andrews. He wrote to Brooks Atkinson,[99] the paper's chief critic, and attempted to persuade him to attend the show again and review it, now that all three of the original stars had left. Harrison and Holloway's contracts ended in December 1957, but Andrews had to stay on until February of the following year due to Howes's schedule. We saw earlier how keen Lerner was to bolster Levin's production strategy, and the following exchange of letters is a useful example of how he got involved in opportunities for publicity:

To Brooks Atkinson

17 February 1958

Dear Mr. Atkinson:

If you get a chance, I would be so happy if you would go in and see Sally Ann Howes playing Eliza Doolittle. We're all very excited about her, and even though the show is undoubtedly old hat to you now, I don't think you would find it a wasted evening.

[97] For details on the reshooting, see Fordin, *MGM's Greatest Musicals*, 490–491, and Lerner, *Street*, 174–179.

[98] The Ed Sullivan Show was an American variety television program that ran from 1948 to 1971.

[99] Brooks Atkinson (1894–1984) was the chief drama critic of the *New York Times* and one of the most respected theater journalists of Broadway's golden age.

Not only that, but if you do go, I promise either to write another article for Harvard, or not write one—whichever you think would help the school more.

Incidentally, the book[100] was absolutely wonderful: touching, interesting, nostalgic and informative. I enjoyed it enormously, even though there isn't a musical in it.

Kindest regards,
Alan Jay Lerner

The much-respected Atkinson was not to be rushed into a review, but assured Lerner that he hoped to run a profile on Howes later in the season.[101] "But not now," he said. "I am always desperately looking for subjects for Sunday articles towards the end of the season. Sally Ann Howes is one of the topics I have tucked away in the back of my head to get me out of the slump towards the end of the season. I hope this schedule will be reasonably satisfactory to you." Atkinson also said he was "glad" that Lerner liked his book. He continued: "I received one irascible letter from a graduate, who had a bad time at Harvard and wishes the whole place would just go away. I console myself by suspecting in something he said in the letter that he had not read the book but only a review that praised it." As on several other occasions in this book, these letters show the level of respect that existed between different members of the Broadway community in this era—even between writers and critics.

With the retakes and new touches done on *Gigi*—including re-filming and re-recording parts of Gaston's "Soliloquy" (incorporating the famous title song)—the movie was now ready for another preview. This time, the audience reaction was much more positive, as Freed wrote to inform Lerner: "We had an absolutely sensational film preview last night at Encino," he commented, adding: "We were able to use the new recording of Jourdan for the Soliloquy, and it was perfect, especially your favorite line, 'The way it clung on one so young.'" The reception of *Gigi* was equally as warm as that for *My Fair Lady*, and Lerner and Loewe had much to celebrate.

Lerner was now in London for the opening of *Fair Lady*. Although the same four leads (Andrews, Harrison, Holloway, and Coote) were to take the main roles, the rest of the cast was new (including Zena Dare[102] as Mrs. Higgins and Leonard

[100] Lerner probably means Atkinson's collection of essays about their alma mater, Harvard University: *College in a Yard: Minutes by Thirty-One Harvard Men* (Cambridge, MA: Harvard University Press, 1957).

[101] Letter from Atkinson to Lerner, February 18, 1958.

[102] Zena Dare (1887–1975) was a beloved English actress who ended her career in the role of Mrs. Higgins.

Weir[103] as Freddy), as was the musical director, Cyril Ornadel.[104] The production also had to be modified in places, since the Theatre Royal, Drury Lane, where the show was to be housed in London, was larger than *Lady*'s Broadway home at the Mark Hellinger. On top of that, there were understandable nerves about how the musical would be received on Shaw's "home territory." Therefore, the rehearsal period was crucial. But the consternation was unnecessary: Drew Middleton, special correspondent to the *New York Times*, was able to report on April 30 that the "spiritual home of the musical" had discovered "it is as good as the Yanks said it was."[105] Two weeks later, Lerner enjoyed a further triumph: the formal premiere of *Gigi* on May 15 at the Royale Theatre in New York. Bosley Crowther's review referred to Lerner and Loewe as "two wizards" and raved about the film, whose success meant that they were enjoying stage and screen hits concurrently, and both could be seen in Broadway theaters. The following week, *Gigi* also drew acclaim when it was the closing gala movie at the Cannes Film Festival.[106]

Lerner received a good luck telegram for the opening of *Gigi* from veteran producer Leland Hayward,[107] who also mentioned a project he was talking about producing for Lerner and Loewe. In place of *Father of the Bride* they were now considering a musical version of Howard Lindsay and Russel Crouse's play *Life with Father* (1939), the longest-running non-musical play on Broadway, and Lerner promised to discuss it with Loewe, who was due to visit him in Paris (where Lerner stayed after the Cannes premiere of the movie):

To Leland Hayward

May 14, 1958

Dear Leland:

It was so kind of you to cable. Thank you, thank you.

Fritz will be joining me in June and after a month of talk I'll write you about "Father." I know that you, Howard and Buck understand the delay in getting to it.

[103] Australian tenor Leonard Weir (dates unknown) played the role of Freddy for five years in the London production.

[104] Cyril Ornadel (1924–2011) was a British conductor and composer, known for conducting a number of major American musicals in their West End transfers in this period, as well as for writing the musical *Pickwick* (1963).

[105] Drew Middleton, "Londoners Greet Their 'Fair Lady,'" *New York Times*, May 1, 1958, 34.

[106] Fordin, *MGM's Greatest Musicals*, 493.

[107] Leland Hayward (1901–71) was an agent and producer whose biggest successes were Rodgers and Hammerstein's *South Pacific* and *The Sound of Music*.

Micheline joins in love to you and Nancy.

Aye,
Alan

While Lerner was basking in his latest Hollywood success, his "other" theatrical collaborator, Hart, was in New York looking after *Fair Lady*. He was then due to go to Chicago to sort out the latest cast in the touring production of the show, and clearly did not relish the task. He wrote to Lerner in teasing fury, communicating his jealousy about their respective plans for the coming weeks:

From Moss Hart

[Undated; c. May 1958]

Poor boy, Poor boy,

Downhearted and depressed

And in a spin:—

Well, thank heaven I understand the reason behind those little jokes so helpless and appealing—the arid jests anent the tall buildings in America—the petty jibes about my book! Ah, dear chap, when the front numeral changes from 3 to 4 the blood chills a bit, the mind grows dimmer and the jokes get a little thinner... ! Don't fight it so, poor boy, don't try so hard. Let you-know-who be your Patron Saint, and lie quietly in a good French lawyer's arms. There's nothing better!

Are the chestnut trees still in blossom? Are the little bistros still in flower? Well, enjoy them all you dirty sonofabitch! I go to see the full show tonight (don't ask what show, you bastard), give notices afterwards, then rehearse Monday, Tuesday, Thursday and Friday with orchestra putting all the new arrangements of the numbers we did in London into the show here, then I go to Chicago (oh, God!), put Michael Evans[108] [the new Henry Higgins] into the show and do all the new numbers with him and Anne Rogers[109] [who played Eliza Doolittle] and after that I'm coming home and breaking every record we have of the show

[108] Michael Evans (1920–2007) was a popular successor to Rex Harrison as Henry Higgins.

[109] Anne Rogers (1933–) is a British actress, who originated the lead role in the original production of *The Boy Friend* (1954), various productions of *My Fair Lady*, and the original London production of *She Loves Me* (1963).

over each child's dear little head, and if your children are still here I'll try to get hold of them and break some over their heads.

Don't ask me how I feel, you shit, you, sitting in Paris! All I can tell you is that I thought *Say Darling*[110] was absolutely glorious! Just to hear some other music! Just to hear some other words! O, my God, it was great!

But there's no reason for me to feel differently towards that darling woman who lives with you, so give her my love. And let me know the exact date of your birthday—I want to think of something appropriate to send you—and I want to have a good long time to think about it.

Your amusing and battered friend,

Moss

Though jovial, Hart's letter communicates his growing eagerness to move on to a new musical with Lerner, though they had still not picked a suitable subject.

On June 30, Herman Levin wrote to Lerner with the idea of a co-production of *Fair Lady* in Europe and South America, in English, with the Ukraine-born American impresario Sol Hurok.[111] Though international productions of musicals had become relatively common, the kind of globalization Levin proposed was innovative. He also brought him up to date with casting problems in the New York and touring companies of the show. By this point, Lerner and Loewe's relationship with Levin had started to sour, not least because he had been shut out of the new Lerner-Loewe-Hart producing partnership, and the tone of Levin's letter is comparatively formal:

From Herman Levin

June 30, 1958

Dear Alan:

Sol Hurok and I have been discussing a joint presentation of *My Fair Lady* on the continent of Europe and in South America, in English.

You will remember that we had a minute or two to discuss this is London, and that you evidenced interest in such a proposition. Before we proceed to go further, will you let me know whether you and Fritz, as authors, are willing seriously to consider an offer to be made by Hurok

[110] *Say, Darling* was a Broadway play by Abe Burrows and Marian and Richard Bissell that opened on April 3. It contained eight songs by Jule Styne, Betty Comden, and Adolph Green, though it was a play about staging a musical and all the songs were diegetic rather than book numbers.

[111] Sol Hurok (1888–1974) managed numerous Russian artists in their appearances in the West, and was responsible for bringing the Bolshoi ballet to America in 1959.

and myself for the rights to present the show throughout the world (except in the United States, Canada, Great Britain and Australia)?

I point out to you that, assuming that we do the show in English, the foreign language versions could still be done a year or two after the English speaking run. I have heard that you have disposed of the Spanish speaking rights. Will you give me the facts on this?

Everything is going along smoothly here except that I have been having my annual fight with Equity, this time about [Michael] Allinson. I think that it will all be settled by an arrangement for Allinson to be the standby understudy on the road and to follow [Edward] Mulhare in New York, we to hire an American Equity member to play Karpathy. If it isn't settled this way today, you will read about it in the papers because my instructions are that Allinson is to go in tonight as Karpathy unless Equity agrees to a settlement as I have just described. My feeling is that if it isn't settled and I put Allinson in the show, Equity will bring some kind of injunctive proceeding in the courts. However, both Irving Cohen and I are reasonably certain that the matter will be settled.

Moss is going to Chicago next week to work with Evans and give the company a general brush-up. The business in Chicago jumped to $71,000 last week because of conventions. Our business this summer in Chicago will vary up and down depending upon whether or not Chicago is harboring a convention, but generally speaking I think we should stay above $60,000 regardless.

With all the best to you, to Micheline and to Fritz —

Very sincerely,
Herman

But in spite of Levin's hopes, Lerner and Loewe preferred to have the show performed in the local language when it traveled abroad because of the risk that the subtle humor of the text might be lost in translation. Additionally, the team was probably reluctant to empower Levin with responsibility for the show's worldwide distribution. Lerner wrote to inform Levin of his misgivings:

To Herman Levin

July 4th, 1958

Dear Herm:

Thought of you the other day. I picked up the London Times and there was a headline: CYDE WEEK OPENS.[112]

[112] Lerner is probably referring to "Clyde Week," an annual regatta held in the Firth of Clyde.

The Hurok idea is an interesting one but both Fritz and I question the wisdom of it. The thing that frightens both of us is that although the critics know the plot, they don't know the lyrics and I think we run the risk of bad notices. The Figaro, for example, saw the opening in London and gave it a rather shabby notice. I found out later in Paris that the critic did not speak English. To him it was just another operetta. Now although a bad press may not hurt business when the show is only going to play a limited engagement, it'll hurt Fritz and me. It seems to us that if it is to be done on the continent at all, it must be with first class translations or not at all. And whether such a thing is possible I don't know. At the moment I'm working on some French lyrics with a French lyricist and I'll have a better idea after we've finished. Anyhow, let me know your thoughts in view of the above opinion and we can talk (or write) some more about it.

How is business holding up? Do you think we'll have any empty seats this summer? Do write and tell me. I'm peculiarly interested.

Hope everything works out with Equity. Please let me know the outcome.

All goes well here. The children are having a ball, and I'm getting so healthy I'm dangerous. Please give our love to Dawn. Hope you're having a good summer.

Pip pip, old cock,

Aye,
Alan

Of particular note is the reference to translations of the Lerner-Loewe material: at the time of *Gigi*'s premiere at Cannes, Lerner had acted to get it properly dubbed into the local language (with only Chevalier of the onscreen cast doing his own dubbing) and also had it translated into German and Italian, which helped to pick up the movie's fortunes around Europe. Apparently, he was eager to control the translations of *Fair Lady*, too, since he considered it essential to understand exactly what was going on.

Levin replied amicably, indicating that he understood Lerner's point of view regarding the translation and promising to leave the matter up to Lerner and Loewe. He also reported that on the Fourth of July holiday, *Fair Lady* was the only Broadway show to completely sell out; that he, his assistants, and Moss Hart were on their way to Chicago to work on the touring production of the show; and that he had gained permission for Michael Allinson to remain in the show:

Figure 3.2 André Previn, Louis Jourdan, Frederick Loewe, and Alan Jay Lerner working on *Gigi*. Credit: MGM/Photofest

From Herman Levin

July 7, 1958

Dear Alan

The last thing I want to do is talk you and Fritz into my idea for the English language version tour. I see your point and of course I cannot deny that the risk exists. I did not know about the Figaro notice, but that illustrates your point very well. I assure you that I am as much concerned that the show receive an enthusiastic reception artistically as I am about making the money.

However, Hurok feels that the reaction to the show critically throughout Europe and South America, in English, would be enthusiastic. Of course, there is only one precedent—*Porgy and Bess*. Hurok told me that Moiseyev thought the show was fabulous and said that it should be done in Russia just as it is done here. Incidentally, it was our idea to provide librettos in the local language in every case. As to the lyrics, however, it is not a question of simple translation. The problem, as you point out, would be to provide their actual quality.

I am not going to urge that you do it. As a matter of fact, I have not gone into the financial side of it at all and have no real opinion as to whether or not it is feasible from that viewpoint. You are certainly in a better position to get some opinions from your French friends. I am going to leave the matter up to you and Fritz. When you have a definite opinion, please let me know.

Business in New York remains at absolute capacity. I don't think we will have an empty seat this summer. We get plenty of returns from the brokers each night—even though we cut them way down—but we sell out just the same. Incidentally, last Wednesday night, according to my information, we were the only completely sold out show in New York. This includes *Sunrise at Campobello, The Music Man,* etc. Chicago varies from a low of 64 to a high, week before last, of almost 72. Last week we did over 65. Our Chicago business during the summer will depend upon the conventions. This week we will probably do 64 or 65; next week, with a convention of Lions International, probably over 70.

Moss, Biff [Liff, the Production Stage Manager], Phil [Adler, Stage Manager] and I are going to Chicago Wednesday, Moss and Biff to work with the company (especially Evans), Phil and I to look over the situation generally as well as to try to make some decision as to when we are likely to close so that we can begin setting up the tour to follow. I would guess that we will close in Chicago sometime in March, play our way to California, replay Los Angeles and San Francisco, then go North West (Seattle, Spokane, Portland, Vancouver, etc) and then work our way back to the Middle West.

The Allinson matter is settled on the following terms. He will be a standby understudy and we will get a new Karpathy. This is the worst that can happen. It may be that in the final analysis he will play Karpathy as well. Moss and I are going to look at the understudy who is playing Karpathy now and if he is good enough we will retain him in the part. Otherwise we will have to get someone else.

As I told your office, I am negotiating for Elizabeth Larner[113] to follow Anne Rogers in November in the National Company. Rogers has definitely refused to continue. Not having heard from your office,

[113] Elizabeth Larner (1931–) is a British actress and singer who appeared in numerous important original British productions of Broadway musicals, including *Kiss Me, Kate, Camelot,* and *Kismet*. She also appeared in the TV shows *The Two Ronnies* and *Up Pompeii!*

I assume this is okay with you, but if for any reason it is not, please let me know at once.

Little remains to be told. New York is, as the paper says, a "Summer Festival." We have stayed in town so far but will begin weekending it soon and may go up to Nantucket during some part of August.

With all the best to you, Fritz, and Micheline—

Sincerely,
Herman

In his response, Lerner mentions a subsequent conversation about the possibility of a European tour of *Fair Lady* and also reveals the derivation of the word "Aye," with which he often closed his letters:

To Herman Levin

July 17th, 1958

Dear Herm:

Thanks for the letter.

Will be home July 26th and we can talk further about the European idea. Binkie wrote me that he is very much opposed to it because he wants everybody who speaks English in Europe to come to London. I see his point.

You probably heard that Rex was out of the show for a couple of days. They hailed Max Oldaker[114] like he was Michael Evans. Ha! How lovely it's not our problem.

Give my love to Dawn. Hope you both haven't melted. Will call you when I get in.

Aye (Scottish for "always"),
Alan

More than anything, this sequence of letters shows how a hit Broadway musical can bring as much trouble as joy to its creators. Tensions were rising, and truthfully neither side could be sure of the most successful strategy, though each was stubborn in his opinion.

Over the summer, *Gigi* gradually opened across America. Arthur Freed kept Lerner informed of its progress in a series of telegrams that expressed his elation

[114] Australian singer and actor Max Oldaker (1907–72) was understudy to Harrison in the London *Fair Lady*.

at the film's success in the face of the collapse of the movie musical genre. The first said that the film had "opened to the most aesthetic reviews I have ever seen in a motion picture," adding, "They all acclaim Lerner and Loewe." The second also mentions the possibility of Louis Jourdan coming in to re-record the soundtrack of the movie in French and then record the songs for a special French soundtrack album, though ultimately he did not participate in either. The costs were to be extensive, including $1,300 round trip airfare plus $350 per week in expenses, as well as Jourdan's fee of $1,000 per day.It is ironic that such detailed negotiation should be gone into regarding an album involving Jourdan, whose singing ability was severely limited, while Leslie Caron's singing voice was dubbed (by Betty Wand)[115] in the original film.

The rest of 1958 was spent quietly and comparatively unproductively for Lerner. Fritz Loewe had suffered a heart attack on the eve of the London opening of *Fair Lady*, and passed the summer recuperating, which meant their next project had to be put on hold.[116] The final existing piece of Lerner's correspondence from this year is the following amusing letter from Arthur Schwartz, his sometime collaborator of 1953, with whom he had remained on friendly terms:

From Arthur Schwartz

December 29, 1958

Dear Alan,

I had a brief note from Ben Welles this morning which contains the following quote: "If you see Alan, tell him he always reminds me of Yul Brynner in a turtle-neck sweater; and he'll know what reminds me of Yul Brynner in a turtle-neck sweater even more!"

This is undoubtedly a reference of pornographic important between you, and long live pornography.

Also, long live the Lerners.

Ever,
Arthur

P.S. I have been attaching my turtle-neck sweater to photographs of Yul Brynner during the last hour, and have gotten nowhere.

[115] Betty Wand is a singer whose credits include dubbing various movie musicals in the 1950s and 1960s, including *Gigi* and *West Side Story*.

[116] Lerner, *Street*, 126–127.

CHAPTER 4

"One Brief Shining Moment"

CHANGING PARTNERS, 1959–1964

After many months of stagnation, and having rejected *Father of the Bride*, *Life with Father*, and *Sherlock Holmes*, Lerner and Loewe finally hit upon their next project. Announcing the show on February 5, 1959, the *New York Times* explained, "The plot will concern King Arthur and his valorous knights of the Round Table, the Pentagon of its day. But everything hinges on the outcome of negotiations, initiated by Mr. Lerner, Mr. Loewe and Moss Hart, director of 'My Fair Lady,' for the rights to 'The Once and Future King.' The reason why they would like to acquire T. H. White's witty and scholarly book was prompted by the author's retelling of the legend and his fluoroscopic examination of the medieval characters. Mr. Lerner, Mr. Loewe and Mr. Hart aim to produce the attraction themselves with the last named gripping the directorial reins again. Barring obstacles, rehearsals should begin in January or February, 1960."[1] This was a promising start for the musical, and since they had taken years to make a choice, it was reasonable to expect another hit was in the making.

But the show that became *Camelot* turned out to be the most troubled of the Lerner-Loewe relationship and effectively brought it to an end. It had been exceedingly difficult to choose material to follow *My Fair Lady* and *Gigi*: with these musicals, Lerner and Loewe had conquered Broadway and Hollywood once and for all, winning an unusually equal level of critical praise and commercial success. The reaction of composer and lyricist to this situation was almost completely opposed: for Lerner, it meant they must go on to bigger and better things; for Loewe, it meant the satisfying climax of a career that had almost run its course. Lerner reports in his autobiography that after Loewe's health scare in 1958, the composer was reticent about working again, and when the prospect of writing *Camelot* arose he said: "My boy, I'll try it one more time. But if it's too tough or if I start to worry so much I can't work the way I want to, the

[1] Sam Zolotow, "'Fair Lady' Team Seeks New Show," *New York Times*, February 5, 1959, 25.

next will be my last." It also did not bode well that although Lerner and Hart were passionate about the story of King Arthur, Guenevere, and Lancelot, the composer was unmoved and "could not even finish" reading White's book. But, Lerner claims, he was "swept along by our enthusiasm and after much persuasion agreed to do it."[2]

About a month after announcing the new musical, the press started to spread rumors about who was to star in the show. On March 8, the *New York Times* suggested that "Laurence Harvey,[3] seen not so long ago at the Broadway Theatre as Old Vic's Henry V, may be with us again. With authentic British reticence he concedes that he has been approached to play the role of Launcelot [*sic*] in the musical that Alan Jay Lerner, Frederick Loewe and Moss Hart hope to make out of T. H. White's 'The Once and Future King.'" The article added that Harvey "confessed that as soon as he returns to London he will seek out Elisabeth Schwarzkopf,[4] eminent artist and vocal instructor, for training."[5] However, according to Lerner's subsequent account, Harvey contacted *him* and announced that he "wanted to play Lancelot." But, the lyricist continued, although they were intrigued, "he was a basso profundo, not at all like his speaking voice," and would require lots of training to enable him to project in the theater. They were looking for a baritone, and eventually found him in the form of a young unknown singer, Robert Goulet,[6] who was signed to play Lancelot on the spot after an outstanding audition; it would be the defining performance of his career.[7] Harvey, meanwhile, went on to appear as Arthur, not Lancelot, in the original London production of the show, in 1964. The next rumor involved the designer Adrian:[8] on March 12, it was announced that he would create the costumes for the musical.[9] Two weeks later, Lerner and Loewe declared that the show would be called *Jenny Kiss'd Me*. They planned to leave for France in May to work on the project and expected to be ready for rehearsal in January 1960.[10] With the source material finally chosen, composition could begin.

[2] Alan Jay Lerner, *The Street Where I Live* (London: Hodder and Stoughton, 1978), 190.

[3] Laurence Harvey (1928–73) appeared in numerous films, including *Romeo and Juliet* (1954), *I Am a Camera* (1955), *Expresso Bongo* (1960), and *The Manchurian Candidate* (1962).

[4] Elisabeth Schwarzkopf (1915–2006) was one of the greatest sopranos of the twentieth century, specializing in Mozart and Strauss.

[5] Lewis Funke, "Rialto Gossip," *New York Times*, March 8, 1959, X1.

[6] Robert Goulet (1933–2007) was a singer and actor who launched his career with *Camelot*. Later in his career, he played the role of King Arthur in the show.

[7] Lerner, *Street*, 197–198.

[8] Gilbert Adrian (1901–59) was one of the most prolific designers of the early days of Hollywood, with credits including *The Wizard of Oz* (1939), *Ziegfeld Girl* (1941), and *Lovely to Look At* (1952).

[9] Sam Zolotow, "Williams' Drama Attracts Throng," *New York Times*, March 12, 1959, 26.

[10] Louis Calta, "Stage Investors to Produce Play," *New York Times*, April 1, 1959, 42.

Just as *Camelot* was part of a strategy to enlarge the "Lerner and Loewe" brand, so too was it necessary to take care of *My Fair Lady* both in New York and on its gradual journey round the world's capitals as the pair started to globalize their product. In January 1959, *Fair Lady* had its Australian premiere at Melbourne and was accorded "one of the most enthusiastic receptions ever given to an Australian performance." The *Melbourne Herald* said it was "the most beautiful piece of spectacular theatre Australia has ever seen," while the *Melbourne Sun* declared it "fabulous."[11] Stockholm saw its own production in mid-February, and a Mexican version called *Mi bella dama* opened in Monterrey a week later.[12] Most important of all, the Broadway production celebrated its third birthday on March 15. A special six-page report in the *New York Times* commemorated the event and noted that the worldwide box office to date was $21,359,000, an extraordinary sum by any standards. The article was illustrated with photographs of some of the productions from around the world, as well as with a caricature of a woman holding the theater's ticket agent at gunpoint, indicating how difficult it had been to obtain a ticket for this most beloved of musicals.[13]

It wasn't all plain sailing, however: when the show reached Mexico City on April 2, the audience was initially so unresponsive that "the artists began putting increasing energy into their contribution. The dancing at one point became so frenzied that one of the male dancers slid halfway into the orchestra pit."[14] Meanwhile, the other representative of the Lerner and Loewe brand, *Gigi,* also enjoyed huge success into 1959. On April 7, it was awarded nine Oscars including best picture, the first musical to do so since *An American in Paris* in 1951; both films, of course, were written by Lerner, directed by Vincente Minnelli, and starred Leslie Caron. In celebration of this achievement, the studio's telephone operators started to identify their place of work as "M-Gigi-M" when people called them up, according to newspaper reports.[15]

Fair Lady was not just a Lerner and Loewe show, though: it was also in the hands of the producer Herman Levin, who had his own ideas about how it should be promoted. For the greater part of 1959, Levin worked to bring it to even greater international prominence than before by organizing the launch of a European-wide tour, in Russia. The show's initial connection with this country was controversial. On May 1, it emerged that "a young Muscovite" by the name of Victor Louis had translated it into Russian and planned to stage it in

[11] "Melbourne Goes for 'Fair Lady,'" *New York Times,* January 27, 1959, 26.

[12] Sam Zolotow, "'Lute Song' of '46 May Be Revived," *New York Times,* February 6, 1959, 22.

[13] Lewis Nichols, "Birthday of the Fairest Lady," *New York Times,* March 15, 1959, SM16.

[14] Paul P. Kennedy, "'Mi Bella Dama' Is No Fair Lady to First-Nighters in Mexico City," *New York Times,* April 4, 1959, 12.

[15] "Hollywood Likes Its Oscar Show," *New York Times,* April 8, 1959, 42.

Sverdlovsk and Kiev in the 1959–60 season. Lerner and Loewe "publicly protested," not least because the production was unauthorized and they would receive no royalties due to the lack of an international copyright agreement between the United States and the USSR at this time. Nevertheless, Louis had apparently asked Lerner and Loewe for a copy of the full score because although he had a script and piano-vocal score, he did not have the orchestrations.[16] This was front-page news for the *New York Times*, and the article started an extensive discussion about the possibility of taking *Fair Lady* to Russia. Four days later, Louis responded to Lerner's protests in the newspaper by saying "I cannot understand why the authors of 'My Fair Lady' would not be pleased to have the Russian people hear this fine example of American culture." He remained adamant that the show would go ahead, though it was noted by the *New York Times*'s anonymous Moscow reporter that "there are few here who believe it would be possible without the sanction of the authorities."[17]

For the time being, the matter rested there, at least in public. In July, Lerner admitted that *Jenny Kiss'd Me* would have to be delayed until November 1960 due to the lack of a suitable theater. At the same time, he also unveiled the musical's "dream team": "Players already lined up are Richard Burton,[18] Julie Andrews, Robert Goulet and Robert Coote. The director will be Mr. [Moss] Hart; choreographer, Hanya Holm; scenic designer, Oliver Smith, and the costumer, Gilbert Adrian."[19] It is impressive that within five months of deciding on their new project, Lerner and Loewe had already recruited such a formidable collection of talent, including major figures from *Fair Lady* (Andrews, Coote, Holm, and Smith), well-established names (Burton and Adrian), and an exciting newcomer (Goulet). The show seemed to be on track, and in announcing that Hart was flying to London on August 1 to rehearse a new Eliza Doolittle for the London *Fair Lady*, the *New York Times* also mentioned that he would "go to Cannes, France, where he will confer with Alan Jay Lerner and Frederick Loewe regarding their next show, 'Jenny Kiss'd Me.' "[20] Lerner confirms that he spent July to September writing with Loewe in Cannes, before returning to New York in the fall.[21]

Back in the United States, the subject of the Russian *Fair Lady* once more arose, but this time in a more official manner. The Soviet Deputy Minister of

[16] Philip Benjamin, " 'Fair Lady' Faces Russian Pirating: Translator Says It Would Be Loverly to Get Score Free," *New York Times*, May 1, 1959, 1.

[17] Unknown, "Russian Adamant on 'Fair Lady,' " *New York Times*, May 5, 1959, 35.

[18] Richard Burton (1925–84) was one of the biggest movie stars of the 1960s and was nominated for seven Academy Awards.

[19] Sam Zolotow, "Stage Bid Made to Miss Truman," *New York Times*, July 9, 1959, 23.

[20] Unknown, "Moss Hart to Fly to London," *New York Times*, July 31, 1959, 11.

[21] Lerner, *Street*, 199.

Culture, Nikolai N. Danilov, issued an invitation for the show to visit Russia as part of an ongoing series of Soviet-American cultural exchanges designed to foster better relations between the two nations during a difficult period of the Cold War. Herman Levin loved the idea and planned for the production to tour Russia before visiting various European capitals (thereby bringing to fruition an ambition for globalization that he had first raised with Lerner in 1958). Initially, Lerner and Loewe gave permission, and the tour was announced in the press in November 1959.[22] But in truth, the writers were fundamentally unhappy with the idea and wanted to call it off, as Lerner indicates in this letter to Levin:

To Herman Levin

January 28, 1960

Dear Herm:

I think the content of this letter will come as a disappointment to you, and even though it may seem infantile to mention it, it in no way influenced our decision. I think you know Fritz and me well enough to know what when it comes to *My Fair Lady* we always try to be dispassionate and objective and to do what we feel is professionally right for it.

It is for that reason that we would like to cast a strong negative vote about going to Russia, and explain to you in full detail our reasons for so deciding. And I am taking the time to write it all out so that you will understand fully why we feel as we do.

1. We have just learned that Rex is unable to go, and when faced with a concrete fact that we would be sending a show that is not at its best, we find ourselves deeply reluctant to let it be seen that way. Even though we have had many discussions about [Edmund] Mulhare versus [Michael] Evans,[23] somehow it always seemed in the vague future, and for myself I was always clinging to the hope that Rex would go. But now that the time is here we find ourselves instinctively withdrawing. We would not like the show to be judged in an international capital without Rex or Julie.

2. Although the morale of a company is not necessarily of major importance, nevertheless we feel the New York company will seriously suffer on that level, if the road company goes. Fritz and I—and I'm sure you too—have been bombarded with letters from the company, and

[22] Sam Zolotow, "Lerner Discusses 'Fair Lady' Tour," *New York Times*, November 24, 1959, 44.

[23] Mulhare and Evans were the two actors currently playing the part of Higgins on Broadway and on tour.

recently we received a long telegram asking us to meet them after a performance to hear their case. So persistent have they been, that we feel their disappointment about not going may be greater than we had at first imagined.

3. There are many risky features about the entire venture. To sum them up quickly, there is the physical risk, and there is the artistic risk if they do not like it.

4. All the above reasons could be balanced if we really believed that there was a great publicity value in our going. After much investigation and inquiry, we are both of the opinion that the publicity value is questionable. At best there may be a brief story on the front page of the *Times* and *Tribune*, and the chances are more likely it is not front page material. *On the Beach* had a formal opening in Moscow recently, the first American motion picture to so do. Gregory Peck was on hand for the premiere, and there wasn't one line about it in any newspaper. Ed Sullivan was there for a month, and neither his presence nor his subsequent television show created a ripple. Bob Hope was there, and his adventures were totally ignored by the press. Max Youngstein of United Artists, a pretty sound public relations fellow who has been back and forth many times to Russia, is even more positive in his opinion that we have nothing to gain. I mention these few instances, but I know many more.

I also know how much work you have put into it, and your own optimism about its value to the show. There have been amazingly few things in connection with *My Fair Lady* about which you, Fritz and I have differed. We are both sorry it has to be on something as large as this, that has involved so much of your time and labor, but we feel that we would be something less than honest with ourselves, and capricious with our professionalism, if we didn't speak up, even at this last moment.

If we can be of any assistance in explaining this to the State Department, we will cooperate in any way you see fit.

Again, forgive us for this last minute decision.

Yours,
Alan

In short, Lerner and Loewe felt there was much more going against the idea than in its favor. The possibility of sending the show out in anything less than its ideal form was not something they were willing to countenance, because, like Levin, they saw the importance of its international reputation but disagreed with him on how to promote it. They were also increasingly keen to take charge of the destiny of their own work, as is shown by their decision to produce *Camelot* themselves (thereby creating tension between Levin and the writers). But, as Levin points out in his irate reply, Lerner and Loewe had already announced plans for the tour the previous November, and it was now too late to pull out:

From Herman Levin

January 29, 1960

Dear Alan:

When I received your letter last night, I telephoned Washington and read it to Mr. Thayer and Mr. Magdanz of The State Department. They were shocked. I am too. You and Fritz agreed to the Russian tour months ago. You confirmed your agreement by announcing it to the press on November 24th, 1959.

Relying on your word, I gave mine to The State Department and they in turn entered into an agreement with the Soviet Government. I do not know what State intends, but if they are unwilling at this late date to release us, I think we are bound.

The work I put into this is unimportant and had your change of mind come before our Government relied on your assent, I would not quarrel with the reasons you advance to justify your new attitude. However, I believe them to be without substance.

1. You were told ten days ago that Rex would not go and besides you never made it a condition that he go. The question has always been[:] Mulhare or Evans?

2. As to the morale of the New York Company, I too received a telegram. I answered it by a memorandum posted on the theatre bulletin board, and I am informed they are resigned to the logic of it and to the fact that our decision to take the road company is the only one we could make. Furthermore, I question the fact that this creates any morale problem at all. I go further—if it does, I'm sorry but we can't help it.

3. As to the risk. It exists but it existed when you and Fritz agreed that we all take it.

4. As to publicity. Leonard Bernstein and the New York Philharmonic is a more analogous situation. Their publicity was tremendous and I think ours will be much greater.

On the Beach is not even a good picture. Youngstein is a nice fellow but certainly knows no more about my business than I know about his. Neither Sullivan nor Hope is the greatest musical of the century. I'll borrow your phrase—you are comparing chalk and cheese. I'd rather listen to my own estimates and to Maney's. He is certain of the publicity value.

Now let me, without waving the flag (or even if I do wave it a little), tell you that your entire letter ignores the most important aspect of the entire project. I think it a privilege to have some part in improving the relations between the United States and the U.S.S.R. May I respectfully suggest that this is a damned sight more important than considerations of personal convenience or whether or not the New York Company is annoyed for a day or two. In fact—if we do not get one line of publicity, it will still be something of which we can be proud forever.

Yours,
Herman

Lerner and Levin each had different takes on the situation, with the producer apparently inspired in the project by a patriotic spirit, and the situation was not going to be easily resolved.

In the middle of this battle, Lerner was also engaged in putting together *Camelot,* as the musical was now called. But after a smooth pre-production period, the first of the show's numerous problems had already arisen. In September 1959, Gilbert Adrian, who had completed initial designs for many of the show's costumes, suddenly died. Lerner describes seeing the designs for the first time: "When we saw the sketches we were jubilantly impressed. They were original and beautiful and as fanciful as the book."[24] In his memoir, the lyricist implies that Adrian's contribution was a cornerstone of the evolving project, which made his death all the more problematic to the *Camelot* team. In desperation, Lerner turned to Cecil Beaton, the designer of *Fair Lady* and *Gigi,* to beg him to take over the job at the last minute:

To Cecil Beaton

January 28, 1960

Dear Cecil:

No news. No gossip. Business. Business. Business. Business.

Moss, Fritz and I are aware, and have been for a long time, of your determination never to design costumes without doing the sets too. To come to the point quickly, so that you will know whether or not to read the rest of this letter, we all want desperately to talk to you

[24] Lerner, *Street,* 202.

about *Camelot*, and to try to persuade you to make an exception this once. Even though we have all had a wonderful personal relationship together, and affection for you runs high, not for anything in the world would we want to appeal to you on that basis. It would be quite unfair, and from my point of view, unprofessional. Quite the contrary. If you are free to do a show in the fall, and would give us the chance to woo you, we would like to meet with you in February when you come over, and try to excite you about the show and its possibilities.

I assure you that nothing short of the tragedy you know about would have made us ask you to change a perfectly sound artistic position. But the fact is, here we are, wanting you and needing you.

Please let me pick up my mail very soon and find a note in your inimitable doctor's prescription handwriting, saying that you will meet with us when you come over, to discuss it further.

You will be pleased to know that it has been a disastrous theatrical season and *My Fair Lady* is running along not necessarily briskly, but steadily.

We are still ensconced in the Waldorf waiting for our apartment to be ready, which seems to be a more complicated operation than the invasion of Normandy.

Moss is quite impossible since the success of his book,[25] Fritz is in good health, and even though it's hard to believe, I'm more enchanting than ever.

Whether you spurn us or embrace us, I'm delighted you will be here in February, and so look forward to seeing you.

Love as always,
Alan

Unexpectedly, given his intention never again to design costumes without also doing the scenery, as well as being second choice on the project, Beaton agreed to assume the role of costume designer of *Camelot*. Lerner's charming letter had worked its magic. But a problem soon undid this apparently ideal solution. As Lerner explains in the following letter, the fact that a contract had been issued to use Adrian's designs meant that they could not now discard them and start again with Beaton's:

[25] Moss Hart had brought out an autobiographical volume, *Act One*, in 1959.

To Cecil Beaton

February 26, 1960

Dearest Cecil:

Fritz, Moss and I now fall under the sad category called "the best laid plans of mice and men," etc. What has happened is rather complicated and I hope you will bear with me through a rather dull explanation.

As you know, a costume or scenic designer is not permitted by the Union to begin work without a contract. Fritz and I were in Europe for many months, and before we left we gave Adrian an outline of the play. Because of his irrepressible enthusiasm he went immediately to work, sans contract, and completed an enormous amount. When we returned from Europe, and before we realized how very much more was needed, we were hauled up before the Costume Designers Union to explain why we had engaged a man, put him to work, and never given him a contract. We told them, quite honestly, that it was a benign error, that Adrian was not working on speculation, and that we had had all intention of drawing proper agreements when we returned from Europe. We were then instructed to honor that intention and employ someone else to complete whatever designs were necessary.

In the ensuing months we discovered that a great deal indeed was necessary, and hastily wrote you, totally forgetting the obligation we had previously assumed. We now find out that we cannot disregard that obligation, and that the only course left open to us is to use the work Adrian did, and hope we shall find someone who will finish the show and supervise the execution of his designs. To do otherwise would be considerably less than honorable, in view of our pledge to the Union.

In short, dear Cecil, we are in a charming little pickle, not only for ourselves and the show, but with you who graciously was willing to make an exception in our case, and design only costumes. From every view, Fritz, Moss and I were deeply distressed and can only hope you will forgive us for coming to you so impetuously before considering all the other factors.

When we received your letter saying that you would try to work out your schedule to enable you to do the show, we were all "several stories high."[26] To discover it is now impossible, is a real blow, both personally

[26] A reference to Freddy's song "On the Street Where You Live" from *My Fair Lady*.

and artistically. But there it is—and here we are on the good ship Andrea Doria.[27]

When you come in March, I shall ring your phone and pound your door and bully my way back into the bosom of your friendship. I shan't be happy until I know you understand and forgive.

Micheline doesn't get all this. With the ruthless logic of Descartes, she just looks at me and says, "How can you do a show without Ceceel? You are an ass." I quite agree.

Affectionately,
Alan

In the end, circumstances dictated that Adrian's initial designs be implemented and expanded, rather than replaced. Lerner explains that Adrian's widow, Janet Gaynor,[28] "suggested that a disciple of his in California named Tony Duquette be called in to complete the job,"[29] and the producer-writers agreed.

Even if the production team was troubled, at least the cast of *Camelot* was outstanding. Lerner says Julie Andrews was "the first person we thought of for the play," and adds that "she loved the idea."[30] Next up was Richard Burton, the Welsh actor who was rapidly on the way to becoming a major star in Hollywood. Like Rex Harrison, he was not known for his vocal ability, but Lerner says this did not cause the writers alarm "because he is Welsh; and at birth when a Welshman is slapped on the behind, he does not cry, he sings 'Men of Harlech' in perfect pitch."[31] Nevertheless, it was important to make sure that the material they were writing was suitable for him, as they had done when writing material specially for Harrison and Chevalier. By February 1960, Lerner and Loewe were anxious to meet with him to play him the songs they had written thus far. Lerner wrote to try to arrange an appointment:

To Richard Burton

February 4, 1960

Dear Richard:

Fritz and I are so sorry we didn't get to see you while you were here, but we knew that you were up to the nape of your neck in TV, and we

[27] The passenger ship *SS Andrea Doria* sank in 1956.

[28] Actress Janet Gaynor (1906–84) appeared in numerous films of the 1920s and '30s, including *Seventh Heaven* (1927) and *A Star Is Born* (1937).

[29] Lerner, *Street*, 202.

[30] Lerner, *Street*, 194.

[31] Lerner, *Street*, 195.

thought the kindest thing we could do was not to bother you. We didn't realize, however, that you would be departing the second after the program was over.

The show is coming along, not necessarily briskly but steadily, and sometime in the spring we would like very much to get together with you—somewhere. Actually, it's almost necessary that we do, so that we have plenty of time to alter anything vocally that you might require. Although my spies at the Production Center where you made the TV, and at the Blue Angel, tell me you were singing up a bloody Welsh storm, and may pass us for *Rigoletto,* nevertheless it will be a wonderful safeguard for us to meet in the spring.

So do have one of your vast network of representatives let us know when and where, sometime during the months of April, May or June, that we can snatch two or three days from your crowded schedule.

My warmest regards to Sybil, and we will be looking forward to seeing you soon.

Fondly,
Alan

Although brief and jovial, this letter affords an intriguing insight into the author-actor relationship. Lerner and Loewe might have written two of the most successful musicals Broadway and Hollywood had ever seen, but they were still reliant on, and deferential to, the power of the star performer when shaping their work.

Nonetheless, they really had become one of Broadway's leading songwriting teams, and they were constantly bombarded with media requests. Here, Lerner answers ten questions posed to him by London's *Daily Express,* with specific focus on the dynamic of the Lerner-Loewe collaboration:

To Henry Lowrie, Chief of Bureau

London Daily Express

February 26, 1960

Dear Mr. Lowrie:

Here are the answers to the questions you requested.

1. Q: What presented the biggest problem in your relationship?

A: There are no difficulties of compatibility in our relationship. We have been working together for 18 years, and time, mutual respect and admiration and enthusiasm for whatever we are doing simply precludes the possibility. The only problem which is not really a problem is where we work. Loewe likes Palm Springs in the winter, and I am not too mad about it. Our choice of where we work during the summer is also widely dissimilar. But we usually solve it, as it says in the song (ours), "And so rather than do either, we do something else that neither likes at all."

2. Q: How much money have you made jointly?

A: Oddly enough, it's difficult to define. The income from our works is one thing, but at the same time the works themselves create an equity which has a lasting economic value. There is no denying the fact that a successful musical play does bring in large returns. Our joint royalties from the four years of *My Fair Lady*—play and music—is somewhere in the area of a million to a million and a half pounds.

3. Q: Who has the most left?

A: Quite obviously, the government. As is the case in England, large income is a fata morgana. An income such as the one mentioned places one in well over the ninety per cent bracket.

4. Q: When was your partnership under the greatest strain—and why?

A: Boring as it may seem, our relationship has never been under any of the kind you question. The American humorist, Ring Lardner, once wrote a scene where a composer was playing the piano and said to his lyricist about a new melodic line, "What a strain." Said his partner, "then why do you do it?" By that definition, I suppose our greatest strain was, "I Could Have Danced All Night."

5. Q: Do you ever disagree on how a song should be treated? Who usually wins?

A: There are many artistic differences of opinion in a collaboration. It's quite natural. But somehow in the end we always see it in the same way.

6. Q: What do you consider the best song you have written together? The best musical?

A: Melodically, Loewe's favorite composition is "Come to Me, Bend to Me," from *Brigadoon*. Lyrically, my favorite is "I've Grown Accustomed to Her Face." As for the best musical, it's always the one we are working on at the moment. Quite obviously, if we didn't think it would be, we wouldn't be working on it in the first place. It's a form of harmless but essential paranoia.

7. Q: How successful do you think you would have been as a "single"?

A: There is simply no way of knowing. In a collaboration, the combination of two divergent backgrounds, attitudes and taste produce an artistic entity that could only occur with those particular two people.

There is no doubt that had we been successful separately, there would have been a different quality. It may have been equally as successful, but it would not have been the same.

8. Q: Is it harder to come up with a hit song now than when you began your partnership?

A: It is always difficult to write a hit, and we discovered early on that the best way to attempt it, is not to. Because we write exclusively for dramatic use—be it theatre or motion picture—our primary aim is to serve the play. If, along the way, a hit song results, it's a delirious accident, but there is no way of gauging what will find favor with the public. If the play is good undoubtedly there is some kind of emotional truth going on on the stage, and if an audience likes the play, the chances are one or two musical scraps of why they like it, might be liked by the wider public who has not seen the play. In recent times there have been very few popular songs from bad plays.

9. Q: Which comes first, the lyrics or the music?

A: With us, the subject matter comes first, then the title, then the music, then the lyric.

10. Q: What criticism do you have of your partner?

A: Loewe wishes I wouldn't give him such difficult titles to set. I wish he wouldn't write such difficult music for which to write lyrics. We both feel it's most inconsiderate of each other to make each other work so hard.

I hope you will be pleased that we did not take the Fifth Amendment on any question; and we both look forward to meeting you one day soon.

Sincerely,
Alan Jay Lerner

This amusing set of answers shows Lerner deploying his typical weapon—wit—to sidestep potentially difficult questions. In particular, the idea that there were no problems in the relationship is clearly untrue, given the tensions after *Brigadoon* when Lerner went off to write *Love Life* with Weill, and in particular over the first version of *My Fair Lady* when *both* partners went off to write with other collaborators. Yet in this letter, he deflects the topic of their relationship by talking about the fact that they each prefer to work in different places, and finishes with a neat little quotation from Higgins's "I'm an Ordinary Man." Likewise, he drolly misinterprets the word "strain" and answers the questions about money with observations about government taxation. The most serious answers are in relation to Lerner's work itself, and it is fascinating to note that he nominates "I've Grown Accustomed to Her Face" as his favorite song, while Loewe preferred "Come to Me, Bend to Me."

Meanwhile, the tensions regarding the Russian tour of *Fair Lady* reached a head. In spite of Lerner and Loewe's insistence that the tour be canceled, Levin carried on because he perceived that the three of them had given a promise that could not be broken. But Lerner found that instead of the production generating goodwill, the Russians were affronted that the Americans were not planning to send the original Broadway cast on the tour, just as the Bolshoi Ballet had sent its top dancers on their tour of America. Now frustrated beyond words, Lerner wrote strongly to Levin to object to his actions (ironically, it was one day after the musical's fourth birthday on Broadway):

To Herman Levin

March 16, 1960

Dear Herman:

The following has come to my attention:

Ambassador Sobolev,[32] Chief Soviet Delegate to the United Nations, has expressed his outrage at the cast of *My Fair Lady* you are sending to Russia. He has declared this view, among others, to friends who reported it to me. He said that when Russia sends a company of artists to this country, they send the best. We, on the other hand, are sending replacements, road company and even an understudy.

As you know, these are the views held by Fritz and me, and are exactly the views I put forth to the State Department, following your letter to us wherein you attempted to convey your patriotic fervor. It seemed to Fritz and me questionable patriotism to send a company that might bring discredit to the United States. If the attitude of Mr. Sobolev is an indication of what awaits us in the Soviet Union, that is precisely what you will have done.

I suggest you bring this statement of Mr. Sobolev immediately to the attention of the State Department, and move heaven and earth to try to cancel this ill-conceived venture.

You have rocked both companies and created a mountain of ill will, all for the purpose of exposing the play and our government to the possibility of disastrous criticism.

Alan

[32] Arkady Sobolev (1903–64) was a Russian Soviet diplomat who was ambassador to the United Nations from 1955 to 1960, having previously been ambassador to Poland from 1951 to 1953.

However, plans were still too far ahead for the enterprise to be averted, and the US National Company of the show started to prepare for an April 18 opening in Moscow, followed by Leningrad, Minsk, and Kiev.[33] In the event, *Mai Fer Ledi*, as it was translated into Russian, enjoyed immense success on its tour, including a standing ovation on its opening night in Moscow.[34] But sadly, relations between Levin and the writers had hit an all-time low, and not just on the topic of the Russian tour. On March 4, the *New York Times* had reported on a lawsuit over the show: Levin brought an injunction against Lerner and Loewe for selling their rights in *Fair Lady* to CBS "which thereby obtained 'effective control' of the property," according to the article.[35] To make matters more complicated, CBS was signed on to finance the whole of *Camelot* (just as they had *Fair Lady*), to Lerner and Loewe's convenience and therefore probably to Levin's chagrin.[36] No wonder relations between Lerner and Levin were so troubled in this period.

On a more pleasant front, Lerner was elected president of the Dramatists Guild on February 18, replacing Oscar Hammerstein.[37] Although he was later to joke wryly about the worth of this position, Lerner's assumption of the role is yet another instance of his following in the footsteps of Rodgers and Hammerstein (or at least one half of the team, in this case). The reason for Hammerstein's need to stand down as president, however, was sad: he was suffering from cancer, and his death on August 23 cast a shadow over Broadway. Lerner wrote a brief note to Richard Rodgers to express his condolences:

To Richard Rodgers

c. August 1960 [undated]

Dear Dick:

I can only estimate your sadness. But I wanted you to know I was thinking of you and send my deepest sympathies and affection.

Always,
Alan

[33] Sam Zolotow, "Group to Produce for Stage, Films," *New York Times*, March 29, 1960, 47.

[34] Osgood Carruthers, "Moscow Cheers for a 'Fair Lady,'" *New York Times*, April 19, 1960, 15. "'Mai Fer Ledi [photo spread of the Moscow tour],'" *New York Times*, May 1, 1960, SM16.

[35] "Suit over 'My Fair Lady,'" *New York Times*, March 4, 1960, 19.

[36] CBS's participation had been announced on February 9. Sam Zolotow, "'Dear Liar' Plans to Open March 17," *New York Times*, February 9, 1960, 27.

[37] Sam Zolotow, "Rattigan Plans 2 London Shows," *New York Times*, February 19, 1960, 20.

Unbeknownst to either of them at the time, Lerner and Rodgers would team up just over a year later to begin work on a show together.

For Lerner, the majority of 1960 was spent on *Camelot*. The show's debut started to be firmed up: on February 26, its Broadway premiere at the Winter Garden Theatre was set to take place on November 17, and a day later its Toronto preview (which would inaugurate the new, $12,000,000 O'Keefe Center for the Performing Arts) was announced for October 1.[38] In July, further casting was completed, with Roddy McDowall[39] playing Sir Mordred and M'el Dowd[40] as Morgan LeFay.[41] A couple of weeks later, Lerner, Loewe, and Hart suddenly decided to change theaters and hired the Majestic for the production's debut instead of the Winter Garden. The move caused a serious problem, because a single advertisement that had appeared in the *New York Times* in March had sparked mail orders for tickets to the show from members of the public, to the tune of $400,000 (which is what it had cost CBS to underwrite the entire production of *My Fair Lady*). The orders were placed into 60 boxes and shipped over to the Majestic, but even by mid-August the producers refused to advertise the show again because the 60 boxes of orders had not yet been processed. Edwin Knill, the general manager for the show, estimated that these orders would probably mean the first eight to ten months of the show would be completely sold out even before another advertisement was placed. This news item was yet another sign that the show was troubled and apparently being mismanaged, though the article optimistically noted that CBS's investment of an extra $80,000 in *Camelot* (they put in $480,000 this time) "is presumably earmarked for a particularly extravagant scene, in which six fountains will simultaneously spray real water ten feet into the air."[42]

More encouragingly, Julie Andrews arrived very early for rehearsals on this show, getting into New York on August 21,[43] and the cast began work at the start of September. A two-page spread in the *New York Times* on September 18 shows photographs of the company at the first reading, early dance rehearsals, and costume fittings. Most striking of all are two pictures of Julie Andrews, side by side, being kissed in one by Lerner and in the other by Loewe. The caption underlines the reunion of the star of *Fair Lady* with its creators and the article's title—"And Now Fair 'Camelot'?"—provocatively continues that idea, though the question

[38] Sam Zolotow, "Winter Garden Books 'Camelot,'" *New York Times*, February 26, 1960, 23. "'Camelot' Premiere Oct.1," *New York Times*, February 28, 1960, 77.

[39] Roddy McDowall (1928–98) enjoyed a long career acting in films ranging from *How Green Was My Valley* (1941) to the *Planet of the Apes* films.

[40] Actress M'el Dowd (1938–) has appeared in numerous stage and screen productions, though at the time of *Camelot* she was particularly known for her Shakespeare roles.

[41] Sam Zolotow, "Play by O'Casey Due Here Oct. 4," *New York Times*, August 1, 1960, 20.

[42] Arthur Gelb, "Notes Concerning 'Camelot,'" *New York Times*, August 14, 1960, X1.

[43] "Julie Andrews Arrives Here," *New York Times*, August 22, 1960, 22.

mark rightly reminded readers that the success of the earlier show didn't guarantee that of the next Lerner-Loewe effort.[44] Lerner, too, it seems was already having his doubts and was busy making changes to the show when he wrote the following letter to playwright and screenwriter S. N. Behrman:[45]

To S. N. Behrman

September 21, 1960

Dear Sam:

I always seem to wait until I have too much to do before I do anything at all. At this moment we are three weeks into rehearsal, I have all sorts of lyrics to write, [and] the show seems to me as indecipherable as an Eisenhower press conference, so naturally this is the ideal moment to answer my mail.

You were so kind to write me about *Fair Lady*, and I cherish your letter. I must tell you it couldn't have come at a more ideal time. I was right in the middle of one of those lovely periods when I was absolutely convinced I could not write a line and was seriously considering taking up dentistry. So I am doubly grateful, not only for your thoughtfulness but your typically marvelous sense of timing.

We are off Sunday for Toronto and the long out of town junket, returning to New York in mid-November. We open the 19th, and God have mercy on us all.

Will you be here during the winter? I would so much love for us to have an evening together. I shall call you the moment I have recovered from success or failure.

'Til then, with many thanks again,

Fondly,
Alan

After another week's work on the "indecipherable" musical, the entire production made the enormous move to Toronto, where the show had its first preview on October 1, inaugurating the O'Keefe Center. The show opened at 8.50 PM and finished at 12.20 AM, leaving the writers with the job of cutting down the epic show. In Lerner's own words, "Only *Tristan and Isolde*[46] equaled it as a

[44] Seymour Peck, "And Now Fair 'Camelot'?" *New York Times*, September 18, 1960, SM18.

[45] S. N. Behrman (1893–1973) was a distinguished writer of plays (e.g., *Biography*, 1932; *End of Summer*, 1936) and films (including the Rodgers and Hart musical *Hallelujah, I'm a Bum*).

[46] Wagner's epic opera, which typically takes several hours to perform.

bladder contest."[47] However, it is striking that the length of the tryout is often exaggerated: Lerner (the source for most accounts of the night) writes that it lasted "four and a half hours," but the original newspaper reports agree that the national anthems of Canada and the USA were played from 8.40, that the performance itself started at 8.50, and that the curtain came down at 12.20, totaling three and a half hours.[48]

Various aspects of the show were quickly cut at the next available rehearsal, including some of Lancelot's quests, but just as the show itself started to improve, the production's next disaster struck. On October 4, Lerner collapsed from a bleeding ulcer, and was bedridden for over a week, leaving Hart to cut the show down to three hours, fifteen minutes (which was the running time by October 8, as reported by *Variety*).[49] On the day he was discharged, October 15, he walked down his hospital ward to the elevator, looked back while waiting for it to arrive and "saw a hospital bed, obviously occupied, being wheeled into the room" he had just vacated, and discovered it was Hart, who had suffered a heart attack that morning.[50] Although not fatal, the attack was his second and his anxiety was intensified by his father's death on October 5, later reported in *Variety*; he decided not to attend the funeral because he needed to work on the show.[51]

But Hart's illness put him out of action for the foreseeable future; since the director had refused to make changes to the show's written content without Lerner's presence, the lyricist had to go to work on *Camelot* two days after he left the hospital (it was not the same evening, as he described in his book).[52] The news spread throughout the entertainment community, and Lerner received a telegram from Robert Lewis, director of *Brigadoon*, offering to step in and help out. However, Hart had requested not to be replaced for the time being, so Lerner had to refuse the help, even though it came from a favorite, experienced collaborator:

Telegram to Robert Lewis

17 October 1960

DEAREST BOBBY,

I WAS SO TOUCHED BY YOUR TELEGRAM. MOSS HAS ASKED ME TO DO NOTHING FOR THE MOMENT UNTIL THE FULL EXTENT OF HIS ILLNESS

[47] Lerner, *Street*, 214.

[48] See, for instance, Sam Zolotow, "Producers Weigh 'Camelot' Delay," *New York Times*, 36.

[49] "Incoming Shows Hobbled by Usual Star, Script and Staging Troubles," *Variety*, October 12, 1960, 70.

[50] Lerner, *Street*, 216–217.

[51] "Incoming Shows Hobbled," 70.

[52] "Legitimate: 'Camelot' Delay Hits Party Dates; Lerner Succeeds Hart as Stager; Half-Hour Already Cut from Show," *Variety*, October 19, 1960, 57.

IS DETERMINED BECAUSE HE IS HOPING TO REJOIN THE SHOW IN BOSTON. WHETHER THAT WILL BE POSSIBLE OR NOT I DON'T KNOW, BUT IN THE MEANTIME I MUST ABIDE BY HIS REQUEST. I'LL CALL YOU FROM BOSTON. THANK YOU FROM THE BOTTOM OF MY HEART.

MUCH LOVE,
ALAN

Hart's suggestion was that Lerner should take up the directorial reins until he could himself return to the show, hopefully during its next set of previews in Boston (where it was due to open on October 27). In his memoir, Lerner candidly admits that this caused a rift with Loewe, who believed they needed immediate help from a new source, but both the stars of the show and Hart had confidence in him, so Lerner decided to complete the cutting down of the show in Toronto.[53]

It soon became clear, however, that Hart was not going to be able to return before the Broadway premiere, and all he could do was send messages, such as the following telegram (which wryly references King Arthur's "proposition" speech), to encourage Lerner to keep going:

Telegram from Moss Hart

[Undated; c. November 1960]

I AM SO SORRY THE DOCTOR CLAMPED DOWN BUT PROPOSITION, IT'S BETTER TO BE ALIVE THAN DEAD. PLEASE BE OF GOOD CHEER. I AM CERTAIN THE NEW WORK IS GOING TO TURN THE TIDE.

YOUR USELESS BUT LOVING FRIEND,
MOSS

In spite of the continuing problems, public anticipation for the show's Broadway opening ran high, and by the end of October over 40,000 mail orders for tickets had been filed; the show was said to have attained the highest advance box office in Broadway history.[54] Further work was done on the show in Boston, then it moved to New York for an opening on December 3. Perhaps inevitably, the critical reception was disappointing. Robert Coleman in the *Daily Mirror* summed up the general view in saying "it's no *My Fair Lady*," while Howard Taubman in the *New York Times* suggested that Lerner, Loewe, and Hart "badly miss their late collaborator—Bernard Shaw," thereby carping even at their earlier

[53] See Lerner, *Street*, 220–223 for details.

[54] Sam Zolotow, "'Camelot' Sales Continue to Rise," *New York Times*, October 28, 1960, 22.

success by suggesting it was all down to the quality of *Pygmalion*. Outraged by the dismissiveness of the journalists, Lerner's erstwhile collaborator Arthur Schwartz wrote to express his support for *Camelot*'s achievements:

> *From Arthur Schwartz*
>
> [Undated]
>
> Dear Alan,
>
> I am shocked by the notices. I just don't understand Taubman or Kerr or Watts.
>
> You and Fritz have done a superb job and should have been acclaimed. The performances and production are fabulous!
>
> I do believe your run won't be affected by the critics because audiences are bound to react warmly to the feast you have provided.
>
> Mary [Schwartz, his wife] joins me in sending love to you, and will probably write to you too.
>
> Ever,
> Arthur

But Lerner was not too discouraged, initially at least. Sweeping aside the mixed notices, he managed to arrange for Hugh Beaumont to buy the London rights for *Camelot*, with the intention of staging it at the Theatre Royal, Drury Lane, at the end of 1962, which was when the London production of *Fair Lady* was predicted to finish.[55] With Loewe, he announced the formation of an independent film company, Rosebund Productions, with the intention of making a movie out of Anne Piper's novel *Marry at Leisure*.[56] Then on December 28, the writers declared their intention in both *Variety* and the *New York Times* to work on a new show: "Alan Jay Lerner and Frederick Loewe, their musical 'Camelot' firmly ensconced at the Majestic, will do a musical based on the life of Gabrielle (Coco) Chanel,[57] the famous French couturiere."[58] Frederick

[55] Arthur Gelb, "London Will See 'Camelot' in '62," *New York Times*, December 12, 1960, 37.

[56] "Rosemont-Widney Team Maps 'Marry at Leisure' Feature for Britain," Variety, November 9, 1960, 5. The film was later made as *A Nice Girl like Me* (1969).

[57] Gabrielle "Coco" Chanel (1883–1971) was a leading French fashion designer who created the world-famous Chanel brand.

[58] Louis Calta, "Couturiere's Life Seen as Musical; Fashion Figure, Creator of Chanel No. 5, Is Heroine Lerner-Loewe Project," New York Times, December 28, 1960, 23. "Legitimate: Brisson Plans Musical On 'Coco' Chanel (No. 5)" December 28, 1960, 51.

Brisson[59] was announced as the producer, and his wife, actress Rosalind Russell,[60] was named as Lerner and Loewe's ideal star.

This, however, marked the end of the main period of the Lerner-Loewe partnership. Until their brief repairing in the mid-1970s, their only remaining work together comprised revisions to *Camelot,* joint television appearances, and the film adaptations of *My Fair Lady* and *Camelot*. Initially, it was not clear that there would be no follow-up to *Camelot*. On January 9, 1961, *Fair Lady* celebrated its 2,000th performance on Broadway,[61] and during the following week Moss Hart was able to go back to work by attending *Camelot* and briefly meeting the cast.[62] He planned to return (with Lerner) a month later with some revisions to the script and score. Then on February 6, Loewe declared he would take "a sabbatical of twelve to eighteen months to rest and travel."[63] On the face of it, this was not particularly ominous: after all, *Camelot* had only just opened, and with *Fair Lady* still running and *Gigi* having returned to cinemas, Loewe had no financial worries. There had been a long period between finishing work on *Gigi* and the opening of *Camelot,* and a year of rest at this point did not appear to represent a permanent rift. Yet the strain of *Camelot* was showing on both sides. Loewe had returned to his home in Palm Springs, California, while Lerner had sought refuge in Switzerland. The lyricist had also announced a new solo venture to the press, producing television films.[64] Clearly, the pair needed to get away from one another.

Of course, Lerner's regular correspondence continued as usual. The following letter, though just a casual note to wish lyricists Betty Comden and Adolph Green good luck on their show at the Waldorf Astoria in New York, is another reminder of his position in the theater world at the time. Lerner may have met Green through their mutual friend and fellow Harvard graduate, Leonard Bernstein. Here we get a sense of Lerner having been so taken up with *Camelot* that he was unable to engage with much else going on, as well as of his state of exhaustion after illness and manic work:

[59] Frederick Brisson (1913–84) was a Danish producer, with many credits including *The Pajama Game* (1954) and *Damn Yankees* (1955).

[60] Rosalind Russell (1907–76) was the award-winning star of the Broadway musical *Wonderful Town* (1953), as well as films including *His Girl Friday* (1940), *Auntie Mame* (1959), and *Gypsy* (1962).

[61] Sam Zolotow, "Financial Woes Beset New Show," *New York Times,* January 9, 1961, 31.

[62] Louis Calta, "Gobel Will Star in New Musical," *New York Times,* January 13, 1961, 37.

[63] Zolotow, "Financial Woes Beset New Play," 27.

[64] "Lerner's Vidpix," *Variety,* January 18, 1960, 1.

To Betty Comden and Adolph Green

February 7, 1961

Dear Betty and Adolph,

Having missed Christmas, New Year's and the opening of *Do Re Mi*, I was delighted to find out a few days ago that you were opening at the Waldorf because it gave me a marvelous opportunity to write you and wish the good luck for the first three that I missed and also to thank you for your opening night wires to me.

I hear *Do Re Mi* is the biggest thing since Boulder Dam and I can't wait to see it. Many congratulations.

I have been resting my body on top of an alp and as soon as they dig New York out, I'll be back.

Thanks again and much love,
Alan

Returning to New York, on March 20 Lerner and Hart (but not Loewe, who stayed away "on vacation") took the cast back into rehearsal and made various changes to *Camelot*, including the removal of the song "Take Me to the Fair." This brought down the running time by about ten minutes, according to *Variety*, with seven minutes excised from Act 1 and three from Act 2.[65] Audience reactions to the show early in the run had not been good, but with Hart's tightening of the book and direction, suddenly there was new hope for it, if only suitable publicity could be found. By good fortune, *The Ed Sullivan Show* had already planned to have a Lerner and Loewe tribute on March 19, showcasing their main shows (partly in commemoration of the fifth anniversary of *My Fair Lady* on March 15). At Lerner's suggestion, very little of *Fair Lady* was shown, giving way to the stronger aspects of *Camelot*. Julie Andrews, Robert Goulet, and Richard Burton performed several of their numbers, and Lerner reports that on the next morning "there was a line halfway down the block" at the Majestic Theatre, with people suddenly demanding tickets in droves.[66]

Back on a high after success, Lerner played his typical move and planned several new ventures. First, a rumor leaked out on March 29 that he was considering writing his autobiography for Random House, though this idea was short-lived.[67] On April 6, he abruptly announced that he was to start a new show with Richard Rodgers, who was now seeking a new collaborator after the

[65] "Inside Stuff—Legit," *Variety*, March 22, 1961, 72.
[66] Lerner, *Street*, 244–245.
[67] "Chatter," *Variety*, March 29, 1961, 62.

death of Oscar Hammerstein the previous year. Unexpectedly, it was divulged that Lerner and Loewe's separation "might be permanent, as far as the stage is concerned," though they planned to work together on the films of *Fair Lady* and *Camelot*. It is notable that suddenly Rodgers was named as the composer of the possible Coco Chanel musical, if it was to go ahead—the first occurrence of Loewe literally being replaced by another composer on a Lerner project.[68] Another idea was to make a musical out of the Audrey Hepburn-Gregory Peck movie *Roman Holiday*, with direction by Gower Champion.[69] Elaborating on the working methods of the new pairing, Rodgers said he was "flexible" as to whether he planned to set Lerner's lyrics to music (which was mostly, if not always, the case during his collaboration with Hammerstein) or provide Lerner with music before the lyrics were written (as tended to be the case in the Rodgers-Hart and Lerner-Loewe collaborations).[70] Soon after, the film of *Camelot* was announced. In the wake of the *Ed Sullivan Show* special, the daily intake at the box office had risen from $4,000 to $8,000, and the number of mail orders had likewise doubled. Consequently, Warner Bros. quickly recognized the show's potential as a film, and bought the rights in early April for $1.5 million plus 25 percent of the net profit.[71]Lerner left for Europe in mid-April. In Paris, he met with Coco Chanel to discuss the musical about her life.[72] *Variety* quoted him as saying that he "liked being in a country where none of his shows is playing," and certainly France was one of the few major European countries that were slow to embrace *My Fair Lady* and *Gigi*.[73] In early May he took the opportunity to celebrate *Fair Lady*'s third birthday in London[74] and also appeared on TV in New York to present a two-part program on his career to date, for WCBS-TV's *American Musical Theatre* series. The show included songs from rarities such as *What's Up?* and *The Day before Spring*.[75] On July 11, *My Fair Lady* overtook Rodgers and Hammerstein's *Oklahoma!* and became the longest-running musical of all time on Broadway—something of an irony, since the composer of *Oklahoma!* was now planning to team up with the lyricist-librettist of *Fair Lady*.[76] Lerner was abroad at the time, and he spent the summer developing new ideas for projects; in one article, he was even connected with writing lyrics for the new songs for the

[68] Sam Zolotow, "Rodgers and Lerner to Team Up," *New York Times*, April 6, 1961, 35.

[69] Gower Champion (1921–80) was a prolific director-choreographer, whose many productions included *Bye Bye Birdie* (1960), *Carnival!* (1961), *Hello, Dolly* (1964), and *42nd Street* (1980). Sam Zolotow, "Drama Starring Milton Berle Off," *New York Times*, May 10, 1961, 54.

[70] Lewis Funke, "News of the Rialto," *New York Times*, April 23, 1961, 119.

[71] "WB's 'Camelot' Buy: $1,500,000 plus 25% of Net,'" *Variety*, April 12, 1961, 1.

[72] "Chatter," *Variety*, April 19, 1961, 77.

[73] "A.J. Lerner on France," *Variety*, May 3, 1961, 83.

[74] "Chatter: London," *Variety*, May 3, 1961, 86.

[75] "American Musical Theatre," *Variety*, May 10, 1961,

[76] Louis Calta, "'Lady' Will Set a Record Today," *New York Times*, July 12, 1961, 36.

Figure 4.1 Alan Jay Lerner, c.1960. Credit: Photofest

remake of Rodgers and Hammerstein's *State Fair*, though in the end Rodgers's own lyrics were used.[77]

Still away from New York, Lerner was unable to be present for Richard Burton's final performance in the role of Arthur in *Camelot*, so he wrote the following letter to apologize:

To Richard Burton

September 12, 1961

Dear Richard,

I am desolate I won't be in New York for your last performance. Some day—somewhere—about three o'clock in the morning, when we are all tanked to the eyebrows, you will have to get up and give me a personal final performance from beginning to end.

I hope you got a copy of the published version of the play, because in the preface I tried to express my gratitude to you for those grisly days between Toronto and New York. Beyond that, all I can say is that

[77] "Ignore Europe, Shoot Tuners," *Variety*, June 14, 1961, 8.

I suppose you are the best bloody actor in the world and that is all there is to that. Every time I see *Camelot* in the future, I shall be missing you.

I hope all goes well in Rome and if you need any songs to perk up the second half of the picture, let me know. I will be looking forward to seeing you in November.

Until then, bon voyage, happy *Cleopatra*—and again and again, thank you.

Faithfully,
Alan

Though brief, this letter indicates clearly how much Lerner admired Burton's performance in the show—something he would mention again in later correspondence—as well as underlining the pivotal situation of the show in the actor's career. It was his first musical, and a fair hit, but it was also his final stage appearance before filming *Cleopatra,* the movie that launched him to international stardom opposite his future wife, Elizabeth Taylor. Burton is one of many actor legends with whom Lerner was closely associated, and at the height of the writer's career these associations tended to be on projects with which his collaborators were always closely associated (e.g., Leslie Caron and Maurice Chevalier on *Gigi*; Julie Andrews, Stanley Holloway, and Rex Harrison on *My Fair Lady*; Robert Goulet and Richard Burton on *Camelot*).

In the fall, an article about a concert engagement of French actor Yves Montand (who went on to star in Lerner's *On a Clear Day*) indicated just how far *My Fair Lady* had entered the public consciousness. In reporting the program Montand was to sing, Lewis Funke referred to "I've Grown Accustomed to Her Face" as being "from Alan Lerner's and Frederick Loewe's 'You Know What.' "[78] By now, the musical had become a firm classic, and in September, Warner Bros. paid a record $5.5 million in cash for the screen rights to the show, outdoing *South Pacific*'s $2,270,000, which had been the previous record (held by Twentieth Century Fox).[79] This was front-page news, and the names of Cary Grant and Audrey Hepburn were mentioned in connection with the lead roles (though Rex Harrison ultimately recreated his stage role of Higgins onscreen, of course). The article also reported that the original cast album had sold 3,250,000 copies to a total amount of $15,000,000, which was the highest figure to date for an album of any genre of music. Moreover, the Broadway production had been attended by over three million people by this point. These figures are a potent

[78] Lewis Funke, "News of the Rialto," *New York Times*, October 22, 1961, X1.

[79] Eugene Archer, "5 Million Film Offer Made for 'Fair Lady,' " *New York Times*, September 27, 1961, 1.

reminder of Lerner's prominence during this period, not only in theatrical culture but in the national headlines.

Back in New York by early November, Lerner set to work in earnest on his first show with Rodgers. Various articles in the newspapers from the end of 1961 and the beginning of 1962 mention the tentative start of the new partnership, but no real details are given. Rodgers was busy putting the final touches on *No Strings*, a show for which he had written both music and lyrics and which was due to premiere on Broadway in March 1962, so Lerner was not under pressure to write the book for the show they were to do together, at this stage at least.[80] Two brief notes from the period do indicate that he had begun work on it, though, and they also hint at an incredible amount of affection from the lyricist to this most beloved of composers:

To Richard Rodgers

c. January 1962

Dear, dear Dick:

I hope what will come between these covers will make this one of the happiest of your many happy years.

Affectionately,
Alan

To Richard Rodgers

c. February 1962

Dear Dick:

Here are the first two scenes. The rest needs cutting. I'll mail them on to you in a day or two.

XXX
Alan

The kisses in the second note are especially indicative of a pleasant working relationship, since they are the only such to appear in any of the letters that have been unearthed during the research for this book. Lerner later commented of Loewe that "there will never be another Fritz. No relationship will ever be as

[80] Lewis Funke, "Man Running Scared," *New York Times*, March 11, 1962, X1.

close, both professionally and personally."[81] Yet in this period, not only had Loewe left the partnership—apparently to consider writing a piece based on "a property of Oriental background,"[82] according to a news report from December 1961—but these brief exchanges with Rodgers suggest that Lerner *could* potentially have had an equally fruitful and close relationship with someone else (one of the Broadway greats, no less).

Another of Lerner's close collaborations came to a tragic end on December 21, 1961, when Moss Hart dropped dead of a heart attack at the age of 57.[83] Speaking at Hart's memorial tribute at the Music Box Theatre on January 9, 1962, Lerner commented on the warmth of their working relationship:

> What would take perhaps years of association in civilian life, in the theatre takes a handful of weeks. There is no time for detachment and formality, for suddenly you're intensely involved. Suddenly you're exposed. You're close and you discover. And with Moss to discover was overwhelming. What I found was all the things so many had long known before me... Talent? Of course... Knowledge, experience? Without question. But also—one of the rarest and most decently human of human beings.
>
> To work with a director who is an outstanding creator in his own right had its allures, but can also be a terrifying experience. Only those writers who have been directed by Moss can fully appreciate the tact, delicacy and sensitive understanding with which he went about his job. Never once did he try to superimpose his ideas upon you. He saw the play through your eyes, and if he felt that in places you were becoming myopic or astigmatic he became your glasses to enable you to see your own work clearer. Were there ever a disagreement, you won. If you were proven right, he was the first to admit it. If you were proven wrong, he was the easiest person to be wrong with. For in either case, it was always accomplished with warmth and humor. Personalities were never on trial. Only points.
>
> *My Fair Lady* ran long in New Haven. Condensation, not cutting, was required. Moss came to me with a solution. I went to work on it and in so doing found what I thought was a better one, entirely different. The next day, rather hesitantly, I read it to him. He listened, thought, then rose and said, "You dirty dog. How dare you give me an inferiority complex?"...

[81] Lerner, *Street*, 247.

[82] Louis Calta, "Loewe Acquires a New Property," *New York Times*, 47.

[83] "Moss Hart Is Dead; Playwright Was 57," *New York Times*, December 21, 1957, 1.

> I could repeat such instances by the score ... for courtesy, respect for his fellow worker, patience and professionalism were the tools of his trade. These and something more ... something for which in these troubled days of Broadway the theatre cries out so desperately. For in the best sense of the word, Moss brought glamour to the theatre. He felt it was special and was—and became—special to live up to it. As troubled, uncertain ... as tormented as any who toil in these vineyards, he always covered it all with the cloak of dignity and grandeur.
>
> When we who are members of his profession try to console ourselves by remembering what he was and how we knew him, undoubtedly each will select his own private memory. For me, I shall always think of Moss as The Theatre ... and because of him, be prouder of it and love it that much more.[84]

What Minnelli had been to him in Hollywood, Hart was to him on Broadway—the ideal directorial collaborator with a strong personal aesthetic that bonded closely with Lerner's own. But, of course, the Hart-Lerner combination only lasted for two projects, *Fair Lady* and *Camelot*, and the latter was marred by the ill health of both. With the abrupt retirement of Loewe after *Camelot*, in effect Lerner had lost both his perfect Broadway associates within the space of a year.

Never one to look back, though, he moved on with the Rodgers project, and also flirted again with the television medium. In an attempt to emulate the success of the Lerner and Loewe night on *The Ed Sullivan* Show, a further TV special called *The Broadway of Lerner and Loewe* was put together and broadcast by Channel 4 on February 11, 1962. Julie Andrews, Maurice Chevalier, Robert Goulet, Stanley Holloway, and Richard Burton were on hand, and Lerner and Loewe made brief appearances. But the overall effect was less well received than had been the case with the previous show, largely because of a perceived mismatch between performer and song in many instances: Andrews was given "With a Little Bit of Luck" (Holloway's song in *Fair Lady*) while Holloway and Chevalier sang a duet version of "Almost like Being in Love." Jack Gould in the *New York Times* suggested the effect would have been better "had the numbers been exchanged."[85] Though the critical reaction was mixed, the show's high audience figures once more put Lerner in the public eye.

[84] "Alan J. Lerner's Tribute to Moss Hart" in *A Memorial Tribute to Moss Hart at the Music Box Theatre, New York City, January 9, 1962* (New York: Random House, 1962) 21–23.

[85] Jack Gould, "TV: 'Broadway of Lerner and Loewe,'" *New York Times*, February 12, 1962, 36.

In March came the bad news that playwright Russel Crouse, one of Lerner's colleagues from the Dramatist Guild, had been hospitalized. Lerner wrote him a short but typically witty note:

To Russel Crouse

March 22, 1962

Dear, dear Buck:

I was so deeply concerned to learn of your illness but equally gladdened to hear you're on the mend.

I think you would have been pleased to know what a multitude of people worried like hell about you and expressed love and devotion. I being one of them.

I must say however, it seemed a rather extreme device to get out of Dramatist Guild meetings.

Affectionately,
Alan

In his reply a month later, Crouse mentions a hot topic: Lerner's association with Rodgers, with whom Crouse himself had worked on *The Sound of Music* (as co-author of the book with Howard Lindsay):

From Russel Crouse

April 10, 1962

Dear Alan:

I am a little late in answering your note, but I've got a pretty good excuse. It was very nice of you to think of me. I am coming along fine now and expect to be as good as new, except for a few things I left behind at the hospital.

Hope all goes well with you and that the collaboration is moving swiftly and smoothly.

Sincerely,
Buck

Around that time, Lerner also dispatched the following amusing note of rebuttal to one Eric Shrubsole (perhaps a New York-based jeweler), whose company had delivered something to the Lerner family home:

To Eric Shrubsole

April 9, 1962

Dear Mr. Shrubsole,

I was most upset to receive your letter in which you reported that the servants in the house had been rude to your delivery man. Upon inquiry I discovered you were partially right and partially wrong.

There was indeed a kitchen maid who quite possibly could have listed discourtesy among a large array of unattractive traits. She has since been dismissed for other reasons, but denied your accusation heatedly.

On the other hand, what does seem to have been the nub of "the incident" was that your delivery man asked for a tip and did not seem satisfied with the amount forthcoming from the butler. I gather this led to a few guttural monosyllables. As far as the butler is concerned I can indeed vouch for his honesty and courtesy.

Be that as it may—or may not—I am sure that we will both survive the altercation. I continue to regard Shrubsole Corporation with deep respect and I trust you will feel the same of

Yours very truly,
Alan Jay Lerner

Though unconnected to his professional activities, the letter shows how humorously Lerner chose to deal with the world in general.

He also received a letter from Hoagy Carmichael[86] in early May, offering himself as a potential replacement for Loewe as Lerner's collaborator. The proposal was a curious one, for although Carmichael was an accomplished songwriter and actor, he was not known as a Broadway composer.[87] Evidently, he had not yet heard about the Lerner-Rodgers musical that was in the works:

[86] Hoagy Carmichael (1899–1981) was an American musician, actor, and composer, known for writing the songs "Stardust," "The Nearness of You," "Heart and Soul," and "Georgia on My Mind."

[87] His *Walk With Music* (1940), to lyrics by Johnny Mercer, lasted only 55 performances on Broadway. His other theater credits tended to be as one of a team of composers.

To Hoagy Carmichael

May 3, 1962

Dear Hoagy:

I was so flattered to receive your note and equally sorry that I could not see you while you were in town.

Being one of the leading members of your legion of fans I can think of nothing that would give me greater pleasure than to work with you. For the moment, however, I am writing a show with Dick Rodgers which is scheduled for presentation some time next spring. After that I have to work on the motion picture versions of *My Fair Lady* and *Camelot*. How long all that is going to take me I haven't the slightest idea; so for the moment I am, as they say, tied up.

But maybe one day when all of this is over . . . if you're still interested. Let's keep in touch.

Thank you again.

Sincerely,
Alan Jay Lerner

By this time, Lerner and Rodgers had indeed moved ahead with their new show. Instead of the Chanel musical (a project to which Lerner would later return), they decided to go with an idea that Lerner had for a story about a girl with extra-sensory perception. They signed actress Barbara Harris[88] to the lead female role and estimated an opening date of the following March.[89] A starry male lead of gravitas was sought to complement Harris's comedic talent, and Lerner's thoughts seem initially have gone to his old friend Dirk Bogarde, whom he had approached to play Gaston in *Gigi* back in 1958. Though the actor turned down the idea of performing a stage musical, he showed renewed interest in appearing in a movie musical, and Lerner wrote back to express his own keenness on this idea:

To Dirk Bogarde

June 18, 1962

Dearest Chum:

Of course, I understand completely! Naturally, I'm sorry as Hell we shan't be working together, but I do see how you feel, and I'm deeply

[88] Barbara Harris (1935–) was a major Broadway star of the 1960s and went on to appear in numerous films, including Hitchcock's valedictory *Family Plot* (1976).

[89] Sam Zolotow, "Musical to Star Barbara Harris," *New York Times*, May 1, 1962, 34.

touched. Perhaps when this is over, I'll come up with the right idea for a film. We must do something together sometime. I'm still bubbling with youthful energy, but I have a feeling that any minute I'm going to be like Margot leaving Shangri-La. So we must do it quickly, before the skin starts flaking.

Life is excruciatingly dull in New York these days. Our house—which incidentally is simply beautiful—is all shrouded in white sheets, which protect the furniture from unwanted matter, namely me. Only my workroom, the kitchen and the library are defrocked. And what am I doing here alone? Working my ass off, for reasons I have never been able to pin down. I will get over once or twice, however, during the summer. Might you be coming down to St. Paul? We'll be moving into our house at La Colle the beginning of July. It would be marvelous if you were going to be in the neighborhood.

I don't know what to say about Rex [Harrison] and our friend Dickie [Richard Burton]. I gather Rex is charging around like Ivan the Terrible because nobody knows he's in the picture. As for the Wild Welshman, I spoke to Binky [Beaumont] the other day and asked him if he thought Richard was going to do *Camelot* in London. He told me, quite seriously, that if he goes back to Sybill, he will, but that if he stays with Liz, he won't. It's like being lost at sea, except that instead of having a compass to see which way you're going, you have Richard Burton's cock. Hi, ho!

I hope the picture is going well. Give Judy [Garland] my love; but much, much more to Tony.[90] Ask him to drop me a line if he gets a chance. It would cheer me no end. At the moment I feel a little like Anne Frank.

Devotedly,
Alan

It is intriguing to read the penultimate paragraph, which discusses the clashes between Richard Burton and Rex Harrison, the male stars of Lerner's previous two Broadway musicals, while filming *Cleopatra* together in Rome. Especially pertinent is the idea that Burton might have played Arthur in the London *Camelot*, just as Harrison had done *Fair Lady* on both sides of the Atlantic.

In July, Burton was unexpectedly pronounced to be the likely male lead for the new Rodgers-Lerner show. The composer commented that Burton "loves the idea" and "wants to do it" but confessed "we haven't talked money."[91] By August, it seemed likely that screen commitments would probably prevent the actor from

[90] Anthony Forwood, Bogarde's partner.

[91] Louis Calta, "Premise Troupe to Go to London," *New York Times*, July 10, 1962, 29.

taking part, but Gower Champion, the director-choreographer of *Bye Bye Birdie* and *Carnival,* was signed on to head the production team.[92] In an interview on August 12, Lerner confided that "Many songs and the whole musical treatment have become clear in our minds, which, in a way, is half the battle. Actually, only one song has been finished." He also commented on working methods: "There will be many places where I will do the lyrics first and many places where Dick will write the music first." Rodgers added: "We have no fixed procedures.... He's very flexible, and so am I."[93] Considering very little literature has been devoted to the Lerner-Rodgers association, it is fascinating to see how closely—and, apparently, productively—they appear to have worked throughout this period.

September saw *My Fair Lady* finally close on Broadway, after 2,717 performances and a total box office of over $20 million.[94] Reporting on the event, the *New York Times* noted: "At the final curtain, just before the singing of 'Auld Lang Syne'—smiling, no tears—co-author Alan Jay Lerner remarked that among all the credits for the success of the show, one had been pretty much overlooked—the audience. He had a point and we accept it with deep gratitude. The street where the theatre lives does have two sides, and both were at their best with 'My Fair Lady.' It was our show."[95] These comments signify just how intensely personal the musical had been for New York theatergoers during the late '50s and early '60s, and the idea that it was "our show" has certainly been perpetuated during its many tours, revivals, and film adaptation.[96]

Another Lerner milestone in this month was Robert Goulet's final performance as Lancelot in *Camelot.* The actor was the last of the original leads to leave the show, and Lerner was unable to attend due to his hard work on the Rodgers project:

> *To Robert Goulet*
>
> October 6, 1962
>
> Dear, dear Bobby:
>
> In a way I'm glad that work on my new show prevents me from being at your last night. To see the last of the great triumvirate play his final performance would be a sad occasion for me.

[92] Milton Esterow, "Gower Champion to Stage Musical," *New York Times,* August 9, 1962, 18.

[93] Milton Esterow, "News of the Rialto: New Team," *New York Times,* August 12, 1962, X1.

[94] Sam Zolotow, " 'Fair Lady' Plans Final Farewell," *New York Times,* September 11, 1962, 27.

[95] "Au Revoir to a Lady," *New York Times,* October 1, 1962, 30.

[96] For a performance history of *My Fair Lady,* see Dominic McHugh, *Loverly: The Life and Times of "My Fair Lady"* (New York: Oxford University Press, 2012).

Anyhow, old boy. I'm grateful for the time you were there and I cannot help but look upon your extraordinary and well deserved success (in and out of the play) with kind of a vested personal interest and pride.

You're off to a great career! Bless you—enjoy it—and don't let anybody ever talk you into being different from the wonderful fellow you are now.

Thanks for everything! I'll miss you. And "Bon Voyage" —

Alan

By the end of October, the new Rodgers-Lerner show's title was announced: *I Picked a Daisy*. "The subject is extrasensory perception in a contemporary New York setting," the writers confided, and Robert Horton[97] was now signed on as Barbara Harris's leading man.[98] But soon after, Lerner became intensely dissatisfied with his script for the show—a problem that would plague it up to and beyond its Broadway premiere, which was still more than two years away—and rehearsals were postponed in January 1963 to the end of that year.[99] Family illness also contributed to the delay, as did preparations for the screen adaptation of *My Fair Lady*. Lerner mentions both in the following telegram to Jack Warner, in which he also apologizes for his late departure for Hollywood to work on the film:

Telegram to Jack Warner

January 14, 1963

DEAR JACK

I AM SO SORRY ABOUT THE DELAY IN MY ARRIVAL, BUT AS CUKOR PROBABLY TOLD YOU MY LITTLE BOY HAS HAD PNEUMONIA AND MY WIFE HAS BEEN IN THE HOSPITAL. HOWEVER, THE CRISES ARE FINALLY PASSING AND I GIVE YOU MY SOLEMN WORD YOU SHALL BE GAZING AT MY ENCHANTING FACE NEXT WEEK. IN THE MEANTIME I AM HERE IN NEW YORK AND AVAILABLE FOR ANY PHONE CONVERSATIONS.

FONDLY,
ALAN

Once in Hollywood, Lerner started a new draft of his script for *Daisy* and began revising the *Fair Lady* screenplay (at least eight versions of the screenplay

[97] Robert Horton (1924–) is an American actor, well known in this period for his long-running appearance (1957–62) in the television series *Wagon Train*. He appeared in the Broadway musical *110 in the Shade* from October 1963.

[98] Sam Zolotow, "'I Picked a Daisy' New Show's Title," *New York Times*, October 31, 1962, 34.

[99] "Cast Assembled for Shaw's Play," *New York Times*, January 28, 1963, 7.

exist in the University of Southern California's Warner Bros. Archives, mostly dating from 1963). Little correspondence from this period has survived, perhaps because Lerner was so absorbed in these two large projects, but the following letter shows a comical interaction between Lerner and his namesake, journalist Max Lerner (1902–92):

To Max Lerner

February 12, 1963

Dear Max Lerner,

I am enclosing a letter from one of your French fans which came to me by mistake. It is, however, a mistake that has cleared up a great mystery for me.

I have not received any royalties from France for years and I assumed it was due to the fundamental French belief that one only takes money from Americans but never gives them any. Now I understand thoroughly what has happened. Obviously your books are being published under my name, and my songs and plays under yours. So would you please be a good fellow and send me all those royalties you have been pocketing for all these years?

If you're a little short I will be happy to wait until the newspaper strike is over.

Good try, old man.

Sincerely,
Alan

Again, we can see that the theme of Lerner's lack of acceptance by the French public is the subject of his sense of humor.

Another note of interest shows that Lerner approached Random House with the idea of having the scripts of the Lerner-Loewe musicals published in a single volume, rather like the same publisher's edition of the first six stage musicals of Rodgers and Hammerstein:

To Bennett Cerf [of Random House, Inc.]

March 22, 1963

Dear Bennett:

I happened to glance at the best seller list the other day and I see that you are making so much money that it seemed to me you might be interested in a tax loss: namely the one-volume edition of Fritz' and my musicals. It occurs to me this is the sort of thing you should do or the government is liable to get after you for Article II, Section B, which has to do with best seller monopolies.

The reason for this volume goes way beyond the theatre and American culture in general. Its purpose, as I see it, is simply this: it would make me happy. Not only that, but I have some book shelves to fill and how many sets of Samuel Pepys can you have?

I write you during the Lenten period hoping that you are in an appropriate and benevolent mood. If you are at all interested I would love to have lunch with you and discuss it further. If you are not, this is

Goodbye.

Alan Jay Lerner

He also found time to send a brief telegram to his old classmate, now President Kennedy, on the occasion of the foundation of a Council for Arts:

Telegram to President John F. Kennedy

April 1, 1963

DEAR MR. PRESIDENT,

THE DRAMATISTS GUILD APPLAUDS YOUR DECISION TO APPOINT A COUNCIL FOR ARTS AND WISHES TO EXPRESS TO YOU ITS DEEP GRATITUDE FOR YOUR COURAGEOUS LEADERSHIP AND CONTINUING INTEREST IN OUR COUNTRY'S CULTURAL AFFAIRS.

RESPECTFULLY,

ALAN JAY LERNER

PRESIDENT, *THE DRAMATISTS GUILD OF AMERICA*

After several months of work on *Daisy*, Lerner was happy to announce to the world in May that he had "finally completed the book to his satisfaction" and was "well along on the lyrics." Likewise, Rodgers had "composed some of the music."[100] Their relationship had grown, and a day after this announcement, Lerner published an article in honor of the twentieth anniversary of *Oklahoma!*, called "Oh, What a Beautiful Musical."[101] "This was not an operetta, nor a musical comedy," he wrote. "This was a musical play, in which play, music, lyrics and dancing were fused into one living experience. In short, it was a milestone."

[100] Lewis Funke, "News along the Rialto: R&L's 'Daisy,'" *New York Times*, May 12, 1963, X1.

[101] Alan Jay Lerner, "Oh What a Beautiful Musical," *New York Times*, May 13, 1963, SM16.

Seemingly, nothing could go wrong between Lerner and Rodgers, and with the book for their new show now finished the lyricist started to deal with other projects. On May 23, he produced and directed a fundraising birthday celebration for President Kennedy at the Waldorf-Astoria, with performances by Carol Channing, Ann-Margret, Jimmy Durante, Peter Lawford, Robert Preston, Donald O'Connor, Ed Sullivan, Louis Armstrong, and numerous others. Audrey Hepburn, who was about to start shooting the movie version of *Fair Lady*, sang "Happy Birthday" to the president at the evening's climax.[102]

Lerner also started to think about his next stage musical, and his thoughts returned to the show about Coco Chanel for Rosalind Russell and Frederick Brisson:

To Frederick Brisson

June 12, 1963

Dear Freddie:

Thank you for your letter. I will be here most of the summer and as available as Christine Keeler.[103]

I would love to talk to you about the project, and if I have seemed evasive it's not been because I have been avoiding you but because I have been avoiding everybody until I got finished. I think I must need the delusion that I am an outcast.

Love to you both.
Alan

But *I Picked a Daisy* was about to come unstuck. Stories were leaked in mid-June that the December opening might not be met, and it was revealed that Rodgers and Lerner's booking of the Majestic Theatre included an escape clause if they could not finish the show on time. By mid-June, Rodgers had written half the songs and Lerner had done the book, but the lyrics were slow in coming.[104] Another ominous article on June 28 announced that the musical had "two more weeks" before falling through and claimed that Lerner hoped to finish his work by July 8.[105] But three days after this deadline, the inevitable happened, and

[102] Richard P. Hunt, "President Given Birthday Party," *New York Times*, May 24, 1963, 14.

[103] Christine Keeler (1942–) is an English former model, known for her involvement in the infamous Profumo Affair.

[104] Sam Zolotow, "Rodgers Musical Facing 2d Delay," *New York Times*, June 13, 1963, 26.

[105] Sam Zolotow, "'Daisy' Gets Two More Weeks to Decide on Majestic Booking," *New York Times*, June 28, 1963, 16.

the *New York Times* announced, "Failure by Alan Jay Lerner to finish the lyrics for 'I Picked a Daisy' has brought about the cancellation of the show." Busy in Hollywood with the filming of *My Fair Lady*, Lerner refused to say whether this meant the show would not now happen, while Rodgers commented "When and if there's more material, we'll go back to work."[106]

In reality, the collaboration was over. A few days after the announcement, Lerner received an unexpected letter from composer Burton Lane, with whom he had written the score for *Royal Wedding* at MGM:

From Burton Lane

July 17, 1963

Dear Alan,

This is a very difficult letter for me to write. I realize that it may be unwelcome and that you perhaps feel that our past differences preclude our working together again. But I feel I must write it because, in so many ways, it seems a logical step to take and one that could lead to fruitful results for both of us.

I have been severely handicapped because I have not had the kind of steady collaborator one needs in this business. There is no need for me to elaborate on the difficulties this creates.

The possibility of your being available is, of course, what prompts this letter. You and I in the past have done good work together. I feel we could do it again.

Alan, look, even as I write the U.S.S.R. and the United States seem to be nearing a détente, Kennedy is a Berliner, and Harold Rome is about to do another musical for David Merrick.[107] This proves, beyond a doubt, that anything can happen if the desire is there.

I look forward to hearing from you. Best wishes.

Sincerely,
Burt

This was evidently a tempting offer for Lerner, who later claimed he had independently thought of contacting Lane to take over *Daisy*, and on July 25 he

[106] Sam Zolotow, "'I Picked a Daisy' of Lerner and Rodgers Canceled," *New York Times*, July 11, 1963, 22.

[107] David Merrick (1911–2000) was a prolific, award-winning, and notoriously ruthless Broadway producer who staged Harold Rome's (1908–93) musicals *Fanny* (1954), *Destry Rides Again* (1959), and *I Can Get It For You Wholesale* (1962). Merrick did not, in the end, produce Rome's next show, *The Zulu and the Zayda* (1965), as Lane suggests.

leaked the idea to the press, apparently without informing Rodgers of the new plan.[108] (Strangely, *Variety* published a rumor the day before, suggesting Leonard Bernstein had been approached as replacement composer.)[109] Over the summer, while shooting on *Fair Lady* continued, Lerner and Lane agreed to complete the show (whose title was to change) together, and Rodgers bowed out gracefully. The new team spent the rest of the year trying to complete the score to yet another revised version of Lerner's script, but plans to take the show into rehearsal in January 1964 were again frustrated.

It was obvious that *Clear Day* was a challenge that Lerner was struggling to meet, and further drafts of the script were written throughout 1964. In the meantime, however, he started to look at other things to do. In January 1964, he signed up to write the screenplay and lyrics for a movie musical based on Hugh Lofting's *Doctor Dolittle* stories. Lerner was due to co-produce the film with Arthur P. Jacobs, on a budget of $6 million.[110] He managed to engage Rex Harrison to play the title character in March,[111] and Twentieth Century Fox agreed to finance and distribute the project in May.[112] He also continued to pursue the idea of the Coco Chanel musical, though between the complications associated with his divorce from his fourth wife, the plans for the *Dolittle* film, and the continued work on *Clear Day*, he failed to keep an appointment to meet up to discuss the project with Chanel herself, as the following two telegrams show:

Telegram to Coco Chanel

April 10, 1964

I AM SO VERY SORRY THAT PERSONAL PROBLEMS SUCCEEDED IN ROBBING ME OF PROFESSIONAL BEHAVIOR. THIS IS THE FIRST TIME THIS HAS EVER HAPPENED TO ME. MY DESIRE TO BRING THE SPIRIT OF YOU TO THE STAGE REMAINS AT A FEVER PITCH. UNFORTUNATELY, HOWEVER, I CANNOT COMMIT MYSELF TO ONE YEAR FROM SEPTEMBER AS FREDDIE HAS ASKED ME TO DO. ON THE OTHER HAND I CAN MOST DEFINITELY GUARANTEE 18 MONTHS TO 24 MONTHS FROM SEPTEMBER. I HAVE DISCOVERED THAT IT TAKES A MINIMUM OF A YEAR AND A HALF

[108] Sam Zolotow, "'I Picked a Daisy' May Resume with Burton Lane as Composer," *New York Times*, July 25, 1963, 15.

[109] "Say Lerner May Persist on 'Daisy'; Seeks Bernstein?" *Variety*, July 24, 1963, 63.

[110] "Lerner to Write a Movie Musical," *New York Times*, January 6, 1964, 34.

[111] A. H. Weiler, "Harrison and Lerner Reunited," *New York Times*, March 22, 1964, X11.

[112] A. H. Weiler, "Local Views: 'The Cat,'" *New York Times*, May 10, 1964, X9.

TO DO A MUSICAL PLAY PROPERLY AND MY NEW PLAY WILL NOT LEAVE ME FREE TO WORK UNTIL JANUARY. I BEG YOU TO CONSIDER THIS. IF YOU ARE AT ALL INTERESTED I WILL FLY TO SEE YOU DURING APRIL.

WARMEST REGARDS ALWAYS,
ALAN JAY LERNER

Telegram to Frederick Brisson

[April 1964]

FREDDIE BOY,

PLEASE DON'T GIVE UP. I'VE BEEN SICK AS A DOG PLUS MUCH OUTSIDE TROUBLE. OUTLINE ARRIVING MONDAY NIGHT OR TUESDAY MORNING. TRYING TO COME MYSELF WEDNESDAY.

LOVE,
ALAN

By August, Lerner had achieved much less than he had hoped, but at least *Clear Day* started to come into its final form when Louis Jourdan agreed to play the lead part opposite Barbara Harris.[113] It was a common theme of Lerner's shows to try to repeat earlier successes by casting stars with whom he had worked previously (hence the Harrison *Doctor Dolittle,* for instance), and when Richard Burton had turned down the show, *Gigi*'s Jourdan was another obvious choice.

October saw a return to glory for Lerner with the world premiere of the *My Fair Lady* film. A gala premiere saw Hollywood royalty in attendance, as well as the reunion of Lerner and Loewe. In gratitude, Lerner wrote to the film's director, George Cukor, though he had private reservations about some of Cukor's decisions:

To George Cukor

[Undated]

Dear, dear George

There's no doubt of it, you have a future –

Thank you for giving me everything an author could ever want.

Devotedly,
Alan

[113] Sam Zolotow, "Jourdan to Play Lead in Musical," *New York Times,* August 26, 1964, 33.

The brevity of this note speaks volumes: when he was impressed, Lerner normally expressed himself at length, but this polite note masks his frustrations.

Yet the reviews were mostly excellent, and Lerner regained confidence and focus. *Clear Day* was now set for a March 19, 1965, premiere.[114] The lyricist was enjoying his work with Lane and gave an interview with the *New York Times* in which he explained that "I was trying to reach Burton a year ago last summer when I learned that he was on vacation in Maine. When I got him and explained my plans for a partnership, he thought I was replying to a letter he had written to me the day before [reproduced earlier in this chapter] suggesting the same thing." Lane added: "It was then that we knew we were made for each other."[115]

It had been a frustrating period in Lerner's career. The indomitable "Lerner and Loewe" pairing that had given birth to *My Fair Lady* and *Gigi* in the 1950s faltered through *Camelot* and faded not long afterward. His ingenious plan to team up with another celebrity composer, Rodgers, had come to nothing after more than a year of work, as had his attempt to enter the TV production industry. The Arthur Freed Unit had come to an end, and with it Freed's fleeting plan to film *The Day before Spring*. Negotiations with Chanel had broken down. In short, five years had brought little except the troubled *Camelot*. But the year 1964 ended with promise: *My Fair Lady* won the New York Film Critics' Award for Best Picture, and there was every indication that the next new Lerner musical could be a worthy heir to his earlier hit.[116]

[114] "Lerner's New Show Set for Hellinger," *New York Times*, November 5, 1964, 50.

[115] Louis Calta, "Lerner and Lane Work on Musical," *New York Times*, November 21, 1964, 33.

[116] A. H. Weiler, "Film Critics Name 'My Fair Lady' the Fairest of Them All and Harrison the Best Actor," *New York Times*, December 29, 1964, 19.

CHAPTER 5

"Rise and Look Around You"

FROM *CLEAR DAY* TO *COCO*, 1965–1970

Lerner had toyed with the idea of creating a Broadway musical about extra-sensory perception as far back as the late 1940s, and the mystical flavor of *Brigadoon* was an indication of what was to come with *On a Clear Day You Can See Forever*. A draft for an article in the small collection of Lerner papers at the Library of Congress, excerpted below, explains the writer's rationale for the musical:

> What unknown forces are responsible for such phenomena as that of the inanimate flower pot that one day, for no natural or accountable reason, suddenly tumbled from its perch on a table and broke into piece on the floor? It happened in West Virginia in the home of an elderly widow. It happened at the exact instant her little grandson, who had given her the flower pot, was tragically struck down by a car on the streets of Chicago. And during each war, how many times have you read or heard of cases where a dog suddenly and seemingly without cause begins howling uncontrollably, and then you learn later that his master was killed at that precise moment on some distant battlefield?

The article goes on to list other examples of "clairvoyance, precognition, mental telepathy, psychokinesis" as well as reincarnation. Whatever the problems and critical reception of *On a Clear Day*, it is obvious that these subjects were of great personal interest to Lerner, and that he invested a lot of effort in his first post-Loewe musical.[1]

[1] Untitled draft (14 pp.) signed and dated March 9, 1966.

The Boston opening was set for August 1965, thereby putting the much-delayed *Coco* on the back burner once again.[2] Robert Lewis (of Lerner's *Brigadoon*) was now to replace Bob Fosse[3] and Gower Champion, who had both previously been named as *Clear Day*'s director, and Herbert Ross was hired as choreographer. The show attracted widespread press attention for its record high ticket prices of up to $11.90.[4] Rehearsals began on July 26 at the Mark Hellinger Theatre, where *Fair Lady* had found its home for most of its Broadway run, with the press in attendance. "Before the players began to read their parts, Mr. Lane sang the title song, which will be the overture, to his own accompaniment," recounted Sam Zolotow in the *New York Times*. "The cast applauded. During a five-minute break, Mr. Jourdan observed that 'On a Clear Day' was more a play with music than the customary musical. When the script called for songs, Mr. Lane played them. Mr. Lerner sang 'Hurry! It's Lovely Up Here!,' 'Normal,' 'Domestic Champagne Waltz,' 'Marriage Contract,' and 'Tosy and Cosh.' "

Some of these numbers did not make it into the version of the show that ultimately opened on Broadway three months later, an early hint of how difficult the rehearsal and tryout period would turn out to be. As with *Camelot*, coverage of the trouble was widespread: "During the Boston tryout, Mr. Lerner made drastic book revisions. Boris Tumarin, Lois Holmes, Lucille Smith, Margaret Hall, Neil Fitzgerald and Joan White left the cast and Gerry Matthews was added. John Cullum succeeded Louis Jourdan. Robert Downing, production stage manager, resigned and was replaced by Ross Bowman."[5] A later report noted that "In settling Mr. Jourdan's contract, the producers agreed to pay him $2,700 a week for 18 months. If he is not employed during this time, he will get $4,000 a week, which would have been his normal salary. Mr. Cullum is getting $1,200 weekly."[6] In addition to the cast changes, the book was substantially rewritten and various songs were replaced or rewritten, including "Mom," "The Normal Thing to Do," "Marriage á la Mode," and "Don't Tamper with My Sister." Rather like *Camelot*, but to a greater degree, the show had gone into rehearsal with too many weaknesses in the book, so in spite of some effective scenes, it was given a mixed critical reception on its October 17 opening. John McClain in the *Journal-American* called it "a melodious muddle" and Howard Taubman in the *New York Times* said, "Although there are several outstandingly genial elements,

[2] Sam Zolotow, "$610,000 Invested in 'Baker Street,' " *New York Times*, February 18, 1965, 18.

[3] Bob Fosse (1927–87) was the most important Broadway choreographer of his era, winning eight Tony Awards for choreography and one for direction. He was also an agile and sensuous dancer who appeared in a number of films, including *Kiss Me, Kate* and *Give a Girl a Break* (1953), as well as directing his wife Gwen Verdon in several musicals.

[4] Sam Zolotow, "New Lerner Show Scheduled October 16," *New York Times*, July 27, 1965, 24.

[5] "Lerner Musical Delayed," *New York Times*, October 12, 1965, 56.

[6] Milton Esterow, "On Opening Night: Refined Torture," *New York Times*, October 18, 1965, 44.

they do not survive to turn the new musical into the soaring, satisfying unity it ought to be." On the other hand, Norman Nadel in the *World-Telegram & Sun* called it "The first musical hit of the season... a happy wonder and a bewitching, beguiling musical play."

Still, Lerner had much to celebrate that week, with the *Fair Lady* film marking its first anniversary. During the first twelve months after release, it had grossed more than $46 million.[7] Undeterred by the *Clear Day* problems, he cashed in on the publicity and immediately announced *Coco* as his next musical.[8] But although he hoped to have the book finished by "May or June" 1966, there would be a number of setbacks, just as there had been with *Clear Day*, and several more years would pass before the world premiere.[9] At this point, André Previn's[10] involvement as composer of the new show was kept secret, but it is clear from the following letter from Lerner to Arthur Schwartz—apparently a response to the suggestion they might write a musical together, as they almost had in 1953—that Previn was firmly in place in this role:

To Arthur Schwartz

December 1, 1965

Dear Arthur:

I am so sorry I have not gotten back to you sooner but I was in the country, then I had to go to California and I just returned this morning.

I really felt like letting out a whoop when I read your letter! I would genuinely love to work with you again—my only problem being that I have an immediate commitment to do a score with André Previn that goes back a long, long time. He saved time for us to work last winter and because of the delay in the show I really hung him up. I saw him briefly in California and he is coming to New York in January so that we can sit down and discuss plans.

However, neither of us envisages any lasting partnership primarily because of his multifarious activities and also because of Dory,[11] his

[7] "Year-old 'Fair Lady' Film Tops Gross of $46 Million," *New York Times*, October 21, 1965, 58.

[8] Lewis Funke, "New Musical for Lerner?," *New York Times*, November 7, 1965, X1.

[9] Lewis Funke, "They Hope It's Magic," *New York Times*, December 19, 1965, X3.

[10] André Previn (1929–) is a prolific conductor, composer, and arranger, well known for his Hollywood work as the musical director of movies such as *Gigi* (1958) and the composer of *It's Always Fair Weather* (1955).

[11] Lyricist Dory Previn (1925–2012) was married to André Previn from 1959 to 1970. Together they wrote several Academy Award–nominated songs, and in the 1970s she recorded widely as a singer-songwriter.

wife. When it comes to collaborating with André, there is no doubt that she's got a decided edge.

As soon as I get things sorted out I will call you. I'd love to see you both again soon.

I will never forget the kindness and friendship you have both shown.

Faithfully,
Alan

Perhaps Lerner was trying tactfully to avoid the problems that had beset his relationship with Schwartz during their time working together, though he was certainly busy enough with existing projects at this period. The official announcement of Previn's involvement in *Coco* was made on January 23, 1966, and in a ploy that replicated the *Ed Sullivan Show*'s promotion of *Camelot*, NBC arranged a salute to Lerner on *The Bell Telephone Hour* on February 27, to include excerpts from *Clear Day* with Barbara Harris and John Cullum.[12]

February also saw the start of pre-production for another major Lerner project: the film adaptation of *Camelot*. To direct the film he approached Joshua Logan,[13] the veteran director of numerous projects including Rodgers and Hammerstein's *South Pacific* and Harold Rome's *Fanny*, and received an ecstatic response. "I am tremendously moved by this script," he admitted. "It's literate, dramatic, lyric and always wittily told. It gives me a feeling of hope somehow for our theatre world and even—if enough people see it—for the world itself." Logan went on to say that "it must have a faultless production and a brilliant cast" and he assured Lerner that he would be "honored and thrilled to direct it." This was fulsome praise indeed from such a distinguished figure, and Lerner must have been heartened by the promise that they would "work closely together," though in time their relationship was strained. Logan was hired by Warner Bros. in early March, and the long-held plan to put *Camelot* on the screen was finally under way.[14]

In his hunger for plenty (or too much) to do, Lerner also forged ahead with *Coco*, writing to Brisson about his hope to open the new musical at his favorite, "lucky" *Fair Lady* theater:

[12] Lewis Funke, "Lerner Picks a Partner," *New York Times*, January 23, 1966, 93. "Real Nurse Quits 'Doctors' Serial," *New York Times*, January 24, 1966, 43.

[13] Joshua Logan (1908–88) was one of the most respected directors and writers of his generation, with screen credits including *Picnic* (1955), *Bus Stop* (1956), and *South Pacific* (1958), and Broadway work including *Annie Get Your Gun* (1946), among many others.

[14] "Joshua Logan to Direct Film," *New York Times*, March 10, 1966, 29.

Telegram to Frederick Brisson

22 February, 1966

DEAR FREDDIE

I'M OFF TO CALIFORNIA AND WON'T BE HERE FOR THE REST OF THE WEEK. WILL BE AT THE BEVERLY WILSHIRE. PLEASE, PLEASE CONSIDER THE POSSIBILITY OF THE HELLINGER THEATRE UNLESS YOU HAVE DEFINITE REASONS AGAINST IT. STANLEY STAHL IS FAR AND AWAY THE MOST DECENT THEATRE OWNER I HAVE EVER KNOWN AND SOMEHOW IT WOULD BE NICE TO SEE DECENCY REWARDED. HE IS NOW BEING PRESSED FOR NEXT SEASON. HE'LL BE IN TOWN UNTIL THURSDAY NIGHT AND I WOULD BE GRATEFUL IF YOU WOULD AT LEAST HAVE A CHAT WITH HIM ABOUT IT.

LOVE,
ALAN

Of course, the Mark Hellinger was currently host to *Clear Day*, and the fact that Lerner suggested bringing *Coco* there reveals his (correct) suspicion that the theater would be vacant before the year's end.

He was still convinced of the quality of the material though, and a screen adaptation of *Clear Day* was mooted. Though troubled, the show had made its mark on Broadway, and there was interest from several quarters in the screen version, including Leland Hayward, who had wanted to produce the stage version several years earlier. "I continue to be frustrated about *On a Clear Day You Can See Forever*," Hayward commented.[15] "For, I know I could have made a contribution as producer that would have meant the difference between a moderate run and a huge success. As I once told you, I liked the songs that I heard and the book that I read enough to tell you that I would produce or coproduce it for you without an interest or any other compensation. Now, I feel the same way about it as a movie." But Hayward was to be frustrated again. The screen rights were bought by Paramount as a star vehicle for the young Barbra Streisand,[16] and the production was headed by the studio's chief, Howard W. Koch.[17]

By June 1966, five long years after first thinking of writing a musical about Chanel, Lerner had at last drafted the book of *Coco*. Six songs were

[15] Letter from Leland Hayward to Lerner, February 28, 1966.

[16] Barbra Streisand (1942–) is among the most successful singers of all time, as well as a multi-award-winning actress, director, and producer. Her musicals include *Funny Girl* (Broadway, 1964; movie, 1968), *Hello, Dolly!* (movie, 1969), and *Yentl* (1983).

[17] Howard W. Koch (1916–2001) was an American director and producer, whose movies included *The Manchurian Candidate* (1962), *The Odd Couple* (1968), and *Ghost* (1990). Sam Zolotow, "Derwent Awards Announced," *New York Times*, April 22, 1966, 35.

completed, with another eight in half-finished form; *Clear Day* closed in the same month.[18] He visited Chanel in Paris during August and worked further on the score at Previn's Hollywood home in November (during which month he also married Karen Gundersen, assistant editor at *Newsweek*), in the hopes of getting *Coco* on the stage sometime in 1967.[19] *Camelot* went before the cameras in December 1966, with Logan's cast including Richard Harris[20] as King Arthur and Vanessa Redgrave[21] as Queen Guenevere.[22] Though he was on hand to observe some of the filming, Lerner continued to work on *Coco* while still in Hollywood. In March he completed a three-picture deal with Paramount, to include *Paint Your Wagon, On a Clear Day You Can See Forever,* and a completely new project, a screen adaptation of Antoine de Saint-Exupery's *The Little Prince* (the latter to include music by Previn at this point).[23] Joshua Logan was signed as the director of the *Wagon* film in April, and filming was due to begin at the end of 1967.[24] Initially, the intention was for Lerner to adapt his stage script for the screenplay, but in June he hired Paddy Chayefsky[25] to make the adaptation.[26]

Most of 1967 was spent working on *Coco,* which had become Lerner's pet project of the moment; this helps explain the decision not to adapt *Wagon* himself. In April, he sent a full script of *Coco,* including a number of song lyrics, to Cecil Beaton for comments. Beaton, a favorite from Lerner's blockbusters *My Fair Lady* and *Gigi,* was to design the show and got involved from an early stage. In this letter, Lerner asks him for input, comments on the ongoing *Camelot* film, and reveals his hatred of California weather:

[18] Lewis Funke, "On the Rialto: Into the Sunrise," *New York Times,* June 5, 1966, 123. " 'Clear Day' to Close Saturday," *New York Times,* June 8, 1966, 81.

[19] Peter Bart, "Lerner and Previn Completing a Musical about Coco Chanel," *New York Times,* November 9, 1966, 42.

[20] Richard Harris (1930–2002) starred in dozens of films between 1959 and his death, ranging from *The Guns of Navarone* (1961) to the first two *Harry Potter* movies (2001–2).

[21] Vanessa Redgrave (1937–) is a beloved actress and political activist. She is the only British actress ever to win the Oscar, Tony, Emmy, Cannes, Golden Globe and Screen Actors Guild awards. Her many credits include *Isadora* (1968), *Julia* (1977), and *Atonement* (2007).

[22] " 'Camelot' Filming to Start," *New York Times,* December 2, 1966, 41.

[23] A. H. Weiler, " 'Little Prince' Among Men," *New York Times,* March 19, 1967, D17. On October 4, it was suggested that Previn would be the composer of *The Little Prince.* Robert Windeler, "Previn Conducts In Houston Debut," *New York Times,* October 4, 1967, 42.

[24] "Logan to Direct Film Musical," *New York Times,* April 6, 1967, 42.

[25] Paddy Chayefsky (1923–81) was a playwright, novelist, and screenwriter, winning Academy Awards for *Marty* (1955), *The Hospital* (1971), and *Network* (1976).

[26] "Chayevsky to Adapt Musical," *New York Times,* June 21, 1967, 40.

Figure 5.1 Alan Jay Lerner. Credit: Photofest

To Cecil Beaton

April 21, 1967

Dear Cecil:

I am sending you under separate cover the script of guess what? As you will see, some of the lyrics are in. We have about three songs to go plus many incidental bits.

Please, please write me any and all comments and don't be afraid of flattering me (I never get enough) or criticizing. We have been at the barricades too often together to mince words. And I cannot stand Freddie [Brisson] telling me what other people think and don't tell me themselves. If you could see the joy that fills those Danish blue cheese eyes, you would understand.

I read the play to La Mere Brisson[27] last Friday and the reaction was nothing short of overwhelming. She called later to say she wanted to do it. I also read it to Gower Champion, who was equally as enthusiastic

[27] That is, Rosalind Russell.

but we would have to wait a year and a half, which I think must be definitely avoided. I haven't wanted to force any decisions until everything is finished. That should be in the next two or three weeks. The only thing I know is (well not the only thing) that La Mere B does not want Schlessinger. I have a feeling she thinks I mean Arthur Schlessinger.

California has reached a new high in ghastliness and I could not hate it more. It rains all the time. I know how sad you will be to hear that George Cukor has not worked since *My Fair Lady*. As far as I'm concerned, since before *My Fair Lady*. I think *Camelot* is quite marvelous and Josh has done a wonderful job. Time has still not dented Jack Warner's elegance and Vanessa Redgrave gives me a pain in the ass. However, I'm told she is beautiful but we've had very low clouds this winter and I haven't seen her face. Rachel Harrison[28] bit a hole in Robert Mitchum's[29] pants the other night at a party (the truth) and won the Oscar over George Cukor for language. Billy Wilder says that *Georgy Girl* is supposed to be the life of George Cukor.

I expect we'll be going back to New York in about three weeks just in time for the spring round for Truman Capote. I know lots of other fascinating things but you have to write to me first.

Love,
Alan

The summer was spent on yet more work on the *Coco* script, and in early September Lerner flew to London to work on the score again with Previn. By the middle of the month, Lerner was able to tell Brisson that the music was almost complete—but on a more unexpected note, he also disclosed a surprise change of plan regarding the casting of Rosalind Russell as Chanel:

To Frederick Brisson

September 13, 1967

Dear Freddy,

Contrary to previous information as you can see I am still in London. I had a marvelous ten days work with André and all the melodies are

[28] Rachel Roberts (1927–80) was the fourth wife of Rex Harrison. She was a prolific screen actress, with celebrated appearances in *Saturday Night and Sunday Morning* (1960) and *This Sporting Life* (1963).

[29] Robert Mitchum (1917–97) was well known for his appearances in the film noir genre, including *The Night of the Hunter* (1955).

now completed, including the verses. We may have to add one small interlude but that remains to be seen. In any case, it would only be a short afternoon's work for André.

Not only that, but at long last the book is finished to my satisfaction and you should have a copy in your hands by the time you receive this letter. It is still long in the beginning and I don't mean to imply that I have finished work on it, but for the first time there is a beginning, a middle and an end, and the play at least has an architecture. I hope you will agree.

If you do agree then I think you will also feel as André and I do that—as I have been fearing for many months—this is definitely not for Roz and Roz is definitely not for it. I am totally, irrefutably convinced that each would do the other a great injustice. Her special warmth and ingenuousness that shine through her talent and make it unique would, if called upon as it is now written, give the play a softness which would destroy the whole fabric of it. To ask her to bury it completely would be like hiring Merman and asking her not to sing. What the part requires is a certain emotional brittleness; it is a quality someone either has or has not. It cannot be assumed. That particular kind of cracking along on top of the feelings if it isn't natural emotionally and stylistically comes out at best, hard and at worst, heartless. It is the kind of role that is very much in the vernacular of two or three of the leading British actresses and Katharine Hepburn. As for the musical portion, the gay, uninhibited, irresistible zest that Roz uses instead of a voice would be so out of character that she and the songs would be fighting each other all the way with each winding up the loser, not to mention the play. I know we have discussed this before. I know you have been aware of my doubts. Those doubts no longer exist. I now find myself unalterably opposed.

I wish with all my heart I could explain this to Roz myself because aside from my own personal feelings for her, I have very deep respect for her as an artist, and I would be bereft if she in any way misunderstood. I frankly believe she is too intelligent an actress, as well as person, not to see this herself upon reading the play. I am more than certain she would turn it down anyhow. If, by any chance, she sees the role differently than it is, I will do anything to make my position clear to her. (I have been saying "I" when I should have been saying "we" because André is equally as definite as I about her not playing the role. Actually, after reading this draft he called me up and the first thing he said was: "I love it, but this is certainly nothing for Roz.")

It is such a relief to get the thing off my back that I am going to stay over until next week and relax a bit. I will stay here until Friday and then go to Paris until about Wednesday, then home. I will be at the Plaza. I have not been in touch with anybody here because I think we must first cast the part. Obviously, the star will have a say and I don't want to go off half-cocked again. I will call you the instant I am in New York and if you would like me to go to see Roz, wherever she is, I will of course do so.

I hope you are happy with the script. I look forward to seeing you as soon as possible. Be sure not to give any love to Jack Warner and Arthur Jacobs but keep it all for the Brisson family.

Always,
Alan

Since *Coco* had always been intended as a return to the musical stage for Russell, this must have come as something of a shock to Brisson. Lerner was firm in his refusal to allow her to play a part that was meant to be designed for her, and the completion of the script and near-completion of the score meant she had literally been written out of the production.

The reason for Lerner's change of heart becomes clearer in the following letter from four days later:

To Katharine Hepburn

September 17, 1967

Dear Miss Hepburn:

I have been trying to leave you alone until I get back this week but today is Sunday and I have no "hommes d'affaires" to see and I never visit the French in the country because the men wear neckties and everybody stays indoors and so I've been working on the lyric for "Always Mademoiselle." (André did the music while I was in London. I think you'll like it. It's in the "My Man"[30] genre but the melody is stronger and no self-pity. There will be none of the latter in the lyric either.) And so because I have been working on something that I fervently hope will be for you, writing you has become irresistible.

[30] "My Man" is a popular song, originally written in French (as "Mon Homme"), by Jacques Charles, Channing Pollock, Albert Willemetz, and Maurice Yvain. It was made famous in America by Fanny Brice of the Ziegfeld Follies, who recorded it in 1921. Barbra Streisand performed it on her TV special and album *My Name Is Barbra* in 1965, and later sang it as the finale of the film version of *Funny Girl* (in which she portrayed Brice) in 1968.

First of all, I must tell you that our paths have been crossing all week. Monday, I saw Anatole Litvak[31] in Claridge's and we had a bite together. He told me that he had been working on a script for Peter O'Toole[32] called "The Ski-Bum"[33] and that it was not developing well and that it would probably be abandoned. The next day I heard that "Lion in Winter"[34] may be moved forward because Peter O'Toole had suddenly become free. Friday evening I arrived in Paris and as I walked into the hotel, the very first person I saw was Terrence Young [*sic*].[35] Short chat and, unsolicited, he informed me he suddenly had two pictures at the same time: "Mayerling" and "Lion in Winter" because "Lion" was going sooner than expected. Period. The night before I left London, I ran into Sam Spiegel[36] who fixed his misty blue eyes on me and said: "Did you get her?" "Get whom?" said I. He answered with an all-knowing wink, murmured something in classic Estonian in which your name was prominently placed, and disappeared into the night.

Needless to say, any sort of unexpected prompting was hardly necessary to bring you to mind. For the past few weeks my thoughts have not been elsewhere. And since last Monday night I have been elated into orbit. I couldn't possible have made you know on the phone the length, breadth and height of my enthusiasm. Probably, not even face to face either. Unfortunately, enthusiasm in our profession has been so squandered by pitchmen and barkers that by now it rings with the hollow sound of insincerity. However, to me it's still precious stuff and I have never used it either to hoodwink others or myself. So I feel I am entitled to ask you to take mine seriously; and to believe me when I tell you that never in my entire professional life have I ever wanted anyone to play any role in anything I have ever written as much as I want you to play Coco. If you allow me, I will prove it to you by doing anything and everything within the bounds of artistic, legal, economic and social

[31] Anatole Litvak (1902–74) was the Academy Award–winning director of *The Snake Pit* (1948). He was also famous for his French movie *Mayerling* (1936), the 1968 remake of which is mentioned later in Lerner's letter.

[32] Peter O'Toole (1932–2013) was an Irish actor who achieved stardom with *Lawrence of Arabia* (1962) and went on to be nominated for eight Academy Awards.

[33] Possibly based on the novel of the same name by Romain Gary, which had appeared in 1965.

[34] *The Lion in Winter* (1968) is a celebrated film adaptation of the 1966 Broadway play of the same name. The movie won three Academy Awards, including one for Katharine Hepburn (who tied for Best Actress with Barbra Streisand in *Funny Girl*).

[35] Terence Young (1915–94) was a British screenwriter and director, prominent in the 1960s for directing three of the early James Bond films.

[36] Sam Spiegel (1901–85) was a prolific Hollywood producer, with movies including *The African Queen* (1951) and *On the Waterfront* (1954).

reason to make it possible for you to do it conveniently, happily and comfortably.

Because I cannot see anyone but you in the part, I feel I ought to acquaint you with a few of the facts concerning the origin and history of the play to date. The idea was brought to me seven years ago by Freddie Brisson, who is, as you know, producing it. (Actually, we are co-producers but I don't wish to be so-billed.) André and I began working on it roughly a year ago May. It began as a possible venture for Roz. Sometime around late March or early April it became patently clear to André and me that it was not developing into a Roz Russell vehicle. I had a meeting with Freddie and told him. He was most understanding, but suggested withholding the final decision till the play was finished. By June André's and my feeling had hardened into a firm conviction that it never would be or could be a part for Roz and at a meeting with Freddie suggested we begin looking elsewhere. I returned to Long Island to continue work and André and I made a date to meet in London in September, where he would be conducting, to complete the score.

I did not tell Freddie or anyone outside of your intimate circle that I was sending you the script nor shall I until after I have seen you on the coast. I'm sorry that has been delayed a few days. (I have a house here I'm trying to sell that is all entangled in French black tape—red is out this season.) I will be back in New York on Friday and I will call you the instant I set foot in the New World. If you can see me, I'll come right to the coast or anywhere you are.

Please give my love to Gar[son Kanin],[37] Ruth [Gordon][38] and George [Cukor] and I hope and pray I will soon know you well enough to send you the same and not have to remain

Only sincerely yours,
Alan

One of the defining characteristics of Lerner's career is his love of writing for major theater and movie stars, and it is clear from this letter that Hepburn had become the latest in a long line that also included Harrison, Burton, Andrews, Kelly, Chevalier, and Astaire. Even when compared to his letter to Gabriel Pascal in Chapter 2, in which he writes of his burning desire to have Mary Martin play

[37] Garson Kanin (1912–99) was a successful director and writer for both stage and screen. His movies include *My Favorite Wife* (director, 1940) and *Adam's Rib* (writer, 1949).

[38] Ruth Gordon (1896–1985) was an actress and writer. With her husband, Garson Kanin, she wrote *Adam's Rib*, while her movie roles included Maude in *Harold and Maude* (1971).

Eliza Doolittle, Lerner's letter to Hepburn seems unusually extreme and pressing in his warmth of feeling about working with her on *Coco*.

The sentiments continue in the following telegram from a few days later, during which time Hepburn presumably agreed to consider the project:

Telegram to Katharine Hepburn

September 20, 1967

RETURNING FRIDAY, WILL CALL AS AGREED. OFFICE SENDING YOU A CLEAN SCRIPT WITH A FEW CORRECTIONS AND CUTS. AM SO EXCITED AM A PUBLIC NUISANCE. CAN I COME SEE YOU THIS WEEKEND?

REGARDS.
LERNER

But his excitement was soon to be spoiled when the *New York Times* announced on September 27 that "Rosalind Russell will depict Coco Chanel, the French couturier, in "Coco," a musical by Alan Jay Lerner (librettist and lyricist) and André Previn (composer)."[39] Evidently Russell had become aware of Lerner and Previn's plans to transfer her long-planned vehicle to someone else and tried to cling to it while she could. In shock, Lerner wrote to Brisson the following day:

Telegram to Frederick Brisson

September 28, 1967

DEAR FREDDIE:

I LEFT CALIFORNIA WITHOUT CALLING YOU BECAUSE FROM TUESDAY AFTERNOON ON I WAS ALMOST IN A STATE OF SHOCK AND I NEEDED A LITTLE DISTANCE TO REGAIN PERSPECTIVE. I EXPRESSED MY FEELINGS TO YOU VERY CLEARLY BOTH IN MY LETTER FROM LONDON AND IN PERSON ON MONDAY. AND, AS YOU KNOW, I THOUGHT I WAS TO DISCUSS THEM WITH ROZ TUESDAY EVENING. THE HURRIED ANNOUNCEMENT ON TUESDAY MORNING WHICH WAS OBVIOUSLY INTENDED TO PREVENT ANY FURTHER DISCUSSION, NOT ONLY WITH ME BUT ANDRÉ, WAS SIMPLY UNFORGIVABLE. MY OUTRAGE IS MINISCULE COMPARED TO THE SADNESS I FEEL FOR ROZ WHO IS A GREAT ARTIST AND A GREAT WOMAN AND DOESN'T DESERVE THIS. IT WAS INEVITABLE THAT THE ANNOUNCEMENT

[39] Sam Zolotow, "Rosalind Russell to Star in 'Coco,'" *New York Times*, September 27, 1967, 43.

> WOULD PRODUCE A COMMENT FROM CHANEL IN PARIS AND, AS USUAL, WHAT SHE HAD TO SAY DIDN'T HELP ANYTHING. SO THAT THE AIR MAY BE CLEARED LET ME TELL YOU THAT I DID NOT SAY THAT KATHARINE HEPBURN WOULD PLAY THIS ROLE. I DID SAY THAT I DID NOT THINK ROZ WAS RIGHT FOR IT AND MENTIONED THE SAME THREE PEOPLE I MENTIONED TO YOU IN MY LETTER. HEPBURN HAPPENED TO BE THE ONLY ONE CHANEL HAD EVER HEARD OF. THE QUESTION NOW IS THE PROCEDURE FOR THE FUTURE. THE PUBLIC ANNOUNCEMENT HAS NOT CHANGED ANDRÉ'S AND MY CONVICTIONS. I SUGGEST THAT WE SAY AS LITTLE AS POSSIBLE TO THE PRESS AND THAT WE DO NOT DENY YOUR ANNOUNCEMENT. THAT WOULD BE TOO UNFAIR TO ROZ. I FURTHER SUGGEST THAT WHATEVER IS SAID MUST HAVE OUR MUTUAL APPROVAL. AND FINALLY, IN A FEW WEEKS FOR A REASON TO BE MUTUALLY AGREED UPON, I SUGGEST THAT ROZ ANNOUNCE HER WITHDRAWAL. I WILL SAY NOTHING TO ANYONE UNTIL I HEAR FROM YOU.
>
> ALAN

While *Coco* was causing all these problems, the movie of *Camelot* was about to be premiered. Lerner received a letter from producer Jack Warner in early October to indicate his admiration for Lerner's work and to bring him up to date on final edits. "Just heard the first test record of the sound track from the picture *Camelot*. Unless I am a sucker for a left hook, it is really phenomenal!" he declared. "As soon as the album is completed I will have our record company send you several of them. I now realize how great this score and lyrics are! Am sure the public will go for this album in a very huge way." He also reported that "Josh [Logan] is coming over tomorrow to see the minute cuts I made in the "Guenevere" number," showing the level of Warner's involvement in the movie. The film had a gala charity premiere on October 25 at the Warner Theater on Broadway.[40] Sadly, the reviews were as mixed as they were at the Broadway premiere. "It is still the same sort of clutter of supernaturalism ornately displayed with conventional romantic realism, all set to music, as it was on the stage," commented reviewer Bosley Crowther, "only more so, because of the extravagance of Warner Brothers and the massiveness of the Panavision screen."[41] Still, the box office receipts were excellent, and Richard Harris was quickly signed on to a new Lerner project: the screen adaptation of *Clear Day*, opposite Barbra Streisand (a surprising move, given Lerner's later impatience over Harris's behavior).[42]

Not one usually to bear a grudge, Lerner moved to try to patch things up with Rosalind Russell after *Camelot* had opened. At the end of October he wrote to

[40] Enid Nemy, "One Long, Shining Night: Camelot," *New York Times*, October 26, 1967, 51.

[41] Bosley Crowther, "Screen: 'Camelot' Arrives at Warner," *New York Times*, October 26, 1967, 53.

[42] A. H. Weiler, "From San Francisco to France," *New York Times*, November 5, 1967, D17.

try to arrange a meeting with her during his spell in Hollywood for the West Coast premiere of the new film, to smooth things over:

To Rosalind Russell

October 30, 1967

Dearest Roz:

I'll be coming to the coast sometime within the next week—presumably in time for the premiere of *Camelot*—and I long to see you. Not so much to sit down and retrace the itinerary that led to the Terrible Misunderstanding. Frankly, I don't think we could, and even if we could, it doesn't seem relevant.

All I know is that whatever any of us may have done was done innocently, with good intention and with good will. I know it is true of you and Freddie. I only hope and pray that you know it is true of me, too. Frankly, I don't think any of us could make a living on a riverboat.

Rather than the past, I would like to see you about the future, and try to find the most graceful and innocuous way of sparing you any public embarrassment. Needless to say, you could not be damaged. An incident like this turns to a feather when weighed against a career such as yours. Nevertheless, embarrassment is bad enough and I am determined to find a way to reduce it to the palest blush possible.

Only by knowing the depth of my affection and respect could you measure my sadness for the discomfort this may have caused you. You are one of the most human beings I have ever met, and there ought to be some kind of game preserve for people like you where things like this simply don't happen.

Devotedly,
Alan

With this duty performed, Lerner now moved to find backing for *Coco*. Hepburn was confirmed in the role to the press in mid-December (though it was claimed that Julie Christie[43] was Chanel's personal preference for the role), and at the same time it was announced that Paramount Pictures, with whom Lerner currently had a close relationship thanks to the *Wagon* and *Clear Day* deals, would finance the whole of *Coco*. Additionally, they had "made a pre-production deal

[43] Julie Christie (1941–) won an Academy Award for *Darling* (1965), but is perhaps best known for her appearance in the blockbuster *Doctor Zhivago* (1965).

for the movie rights to the show," estimated at $1.5 million.[44] Lerner had an unerring ability for financing his shows, as can be seen from CBS's backing of *Fair Lady* and *Camelot*, and *Coco* was to be no exception.

Finishing the show, however, was by no means easy. The year 1968 was taken up with his production of the film of *Paint Your Wagon*, for which he wrote a handful of new songs with Previn, and with preparation of the screenplay of *Clear Day*, which was due to start filming in December. It is evident from the following letter written to Hepburn in May 1968 that *Coco* was still undergoing rewrites and that Hepburn sensed the show would not go into rehearsal in November as planned. In vain, Lerner still hoped it would go ahead since this was the only gap in Previn's ever-increasing international conducting schedule:

To Katharine Hepburn

May 18, 1968

Dear Kate:

Freddie and I had lunch last week with Peter Shaw[45] and Benny Thau[46] and they reported to me your fear that I would not be ready for rehearsals in November and that ergo, the play would have to be postponed. Needless to say, I was quite surprised because, as I told them, you didn't seem to be worried about that when I saw you, and knowing the way you gave me what-for for being late for appointments, it seemed to me highly unlikely you would have kept silent if you thought I was going to be late for rehearsals. However, I certainly did not doubt their veracity. And further proof came to me in a letter from Cecil Beaton in which he told me of reading an interview with you in which you said again that the chances are *Coco* would be postponed.

I can only assume that the cause of your concern must have been something someone said or wrote or printed after I left the Riviera. Whoever he was, he has never in his life been so thoroughly and conclusively wrong. He is not only wrong, but if he would care to make a gentleman's bet of any amount up to my entire worth at this moment, I would be enchanted to make him a little poorer, too.

[44] "Katharine Hepburn to Star in a Musical on Broadway," *New York Times*, December 16, 1967, 48.

[45] Peter Shaw (1918–2003) was a producer, the head of production at MGM, and a representative for Katharine Hepburn at the William Morris Agency. He was married to actress Angela Lansbury.

[46] Benjamin Thau (1898–1983) was MGM's production chief.

Furthermore, even if I wanted to postpone rehearsals (which I most definitely don't—I can't wait) I cannot because November is the only time that André Previn will be available in the foreseeable future. Therefore, barring crippling illness, atomic war, planetary collision, or your wishes, rehearsals will begin in November, and that's that, period, end of statement, to be sworn to and notarized if and when you so desire.

Now to business.

The rewrite is coming along extremely well. I think (and pray) you will be pleased with the change. It will all be ready for you to read when you return at the end of June—by which time I also hope we will have found a director. I know that Peter [Shaw] will be discussing this problem with you when he sees you, so I won't go into it here.

I understand you have moved to La Garoupe. I lived there once many years ago. Is Lady Norman[47] still around or alive? I never forgot her because one afternoon she walked over to see me and, with a canny look in her eye, said: "Mr. Lerner, are you aware of the fact that your play *My Fair Lady* has almost the identical plot as Bernard Shaw's *Pygmalion*?" I told her that it had been brought to my attention and, after wagging a bony finger at me, she disappeared into the foliage. I am certain that if she hears you are going to play Coco Chanel she will come over one evening to warn you that there is a couturier in Paris with the same name.

A friend of mine saw a part of *Lion in Winter* cut together and said it's superb and that you give the greatest performance of your career. I hope the picture is going well and I'm looking forward to the end of June when you are back here again.

Faithfully,
Alan

This forthright manner was typical of Lerner's relationship with Hepburn, who became one of his closest friends. But her worst fears were to be realized, and in September it was announced that the musical had been again postponed to the middle of the following year, pending the completion of *Wagon* and *Clear Day*.[48]

For his fiftieth birthday on August 31, 1968, Lerner received special messages from many of his friends, including one of his oldest, record producer Goddard

[47] Lord and Lady Norman Aberconwy bought 100 acres on the French Riviera in the early twentieth century. They created the villa and garden at Cap D'Antibes known as La Garoupe, and Lady Norman became a famous socialite.

[48] Sam Zolotow, "Musical Is Made from 'Bus Stop,'" *New York Times*, September 4, 1968, 40.

Lieberson. The Liebersons had written Lerner a poem and sent him a clock on the occasion, and he wrote the following to thank them (humorously referring to the poet e. e. cummings in his salutation):

To Goddard Lieberson

September 10, 1968

Dear e.e. cock:

The clock is so beautiful that when I look at it I almost forget that it's like Utter-McKinley ticking away my remaining minutes.

It was fiendishly kind of you and I shall treasure it as long as I am around to see it. Please thank Brigitta for me, also. However, I must tell you that if you think this sort of gamesmanship is going to make me ease up on the tennis court, you're one hundred percent right.

As if reminding me of my ephemeral state were not enough, the poem is so charming and witty and skillful that while my heart is filled with gratitude for your thoughtfulness and for our long and close friendship, it has shriveled the rest of me with an inferiority complex. In fact, there is every possibility that I may not be able to write another lyric and will have to sell your clock in order to pay my alimony.

So, thanks, old boy. And come back and see us soon. Mealtime is never the same without you.

Aye,
Alan

The fall saw Lerner significantly rewrite *Coco,* and in the New Year he had good news for Hepburn:

Telegram to Katharine Hepburn

January 9, 1969

DEAR KATE:

ANDRÉ AND I HAVE A WHOLE NEW SHOW TO GO OVER WITH YOU WHICH WE ARE TERRIBLY EXCITED ABOUT. WE REALLY THINK IT'S SOLVED.

WHEN WILL YOU BE BACK? CAN'T WAIT TO SEE YOU.

PLEASE CABLE ME AT PARAMOUNT.

MUCH LOVE, AND HAPPY NEW YEAR FROM BOTH OF US,

ALAN

Similarly, to Brisson he was able to announce a working script and score for the show:

To Frederick Brisson

January 16, 1969

Dear Freddy,

At long last!

It was our tacit understanding that the next time you would hear from me would be when I would have something to talk about: namely, the revised show. I will be back on Tuesday, and I'll call you the instant I arrive, so we can get together during the week—because, I'VE GOT IT. Despite *Paint Your Wagon* and *Clear Day*, André and I have been working during the last month, and we are continuing to do so here in New York. We have written three more songs, and aside from extra lyrics here and there, and one recitative business, the score as far as songs is concerned, is complete. The reason I am writing you, however, is to tell you about the area in which we've been working, because it is complicated and costly, and I thought perhaps it would give you a little time to think about it before we meet.

You undoubtedly remember that on many occasions Cecil spoke to us about the Czech film-stage technique called Laterna Magika. (Hepburn, by the way, also spoke to me about somehow using film in the play.) At one point, Cecil wanted all of us to go to Prague to see the technique. I heard it was being performed at the San Antonio Exposition, and early in October, I flew to Texas, and André and I went to see it. For our purposes, it is not only sensational, but indispensable. There are three screens used. One square on either side of the stage, and a rectangular one upstage. In case you didn't see it, the trick is that the people walk on and off the screens.

The man who controls the rights in this country is a fellow named R. J. Cassel. I met him when I was there, and discussed with him the possibility of our acquiring the rights for dramatic use. It would also mean using the Czech inventor-director, who would help us prepare the stuff. Fortunately, Mr. Cassel's lawyer is Arnold Weissberger, and Irving Cohen had a couple of meetings with him in New York, so that he (Irving) could talk to you about it authoritatively when the time came to do so.

When Cecil was on the Coast for *Clear Day,* I went over the outline with him, and he, for the first time, was highly enthusiastic and elated. Also, about a month ago I had to have breakfast with Bluhdorn,[49] and brought up the subject to him. I told him that if we use the process, it will undoubtedly mean an increased budget on the show. He gave us his official blessing. I did not go into specifics because that is something you are far better equipped to handle than I. I merely wanted to start getting him used to the larger figures.

I have finished a step-by-step outline a couple of weeks ago, and expect to have the first act by the end of next week. André and I are completely excited about it. If we can pull it off, we'll have the goddamnedest show anybody ever saw.

I've been trying to reach Hepburn for the last three weeks. She's been flying around Italy somewhere. It is crucial that we get together with her as soon as possible. André leaves for London on the 25th, but will be available in London from February 1st through 5th. I gather that Hepburn will be there then. So will Cecil. It might very well be that we will have to fly over and meet with them all during that time. Anything that you can do to help me locate Hepburn and set this all up, incidentally, I would greatly appreciate.

I'll call you Tuesday.

Love to you and Roz.

Always,
Alan

The letter is an excellent interface with Lerner's strategic thinking about his projects (even if his ideas didn't always work). While finishing two movie projects, he managed to complete most of the writing on *Coco,* hold meetings with his designer, pursue the logistics of using new technology in the show, talk to the person who could approve the financial implications of using such technology (i.e., Bluhdorn), and convey all of this to the producer, as well as prompting him to track down Hepburn.

In February 1969, Lerner celebrated his twenty-fifth year in show business with a benefit dinner at the Waldorf-Astoria Hotel.[50] Filming of *Clear Day* continued in America throughout the first few months of the year, and the

[49] Charles Bluhdorn (1926–83) was an American industrialist who owned the conglomerate Gulf+Western Industries. They controlled Madison Square Garden, Simon & Schuster publishing, and Paramount Pictures (from 1966). Under Bluhdorn's control, Paramount grew to become the number one studio at the box office. Their backing of *Coco* is the reason for Lerner's reference here.

[50] "Dinner for Alan Jay Lerner," *New York Times,* January 16, 1969, 46.

troublesome movie of *Paint Your Wagon* reached completion, way over schedule and over budget. With these problems to contend with, Lerner struggled to give Hepburn enough attention on *Coco*. He also spent time and effort on the "Laterna Magika" film material for use in the show's flashback scenes. Again, he had to write to the actress to beg her patience during this busy time, after receiving an angry phone call from her:

To Katharine Hepburn

May 10, 1969

Dear Kate,

I am dictating this on the phone to New York before catching the plane.

You have been poisoned with such an unfortunate idea of me that any minor change in schedule, even for the most pertinent reason, immediately becomes proof positive of my undependable character. The fact is, *no* change in schedule is ever frivolous with me, and certainly not this one.

As you know, I came out here with the Texan and the Czech to work on the film section of *Coco*. The Texan revealed himself to be a lunatic, and I had to get rid of both of them. Since then I have been researching other processes, preparing a preliminary budget, and discussing additional financing with Paramount. Yesterday afternoon was devoted to a full scale meeting on the publication and recording of the *Coco* score.

I intended returning Thursday night but was under the impression that you were going away for the weekend. Yesterday I found out that you were staying in town, and this morning I got my eardrum punctured. I was only calling to say I was returning tonight.

I have since spoken with Freddie, who tells me you were expecting me for a meeting. I had no idea a meeting had been planned.

Kate, I have been working on this project for three years. It is far and away the most important thing in my professional life and I love it. I also adore you and I'm devoted to you, whether you do the play or not, and even though at times I could kill you (primarily because you could kill me). But I wish you would stop thinking of me as some kind of irresponsible, undisciplined will-of-the-wisp, and please, please, don't torpedo this venture for reasons that may not be right.

I'm in great shape to get on an airplane, and I'll probably land a couple of hours ahead of the plane... what more do you want? At least that's something, isn't it? Dear, dear Kate... please!

Yours through thick,
Alan

Normally, Lerner wrote deferentially to colleagues who were annoyed with him, but here his frankness further illustrates the candor (and thereby affection) of his relationship with Hepburn.

August brought the announcement of the opening night of *Coco*, now set for December. The theater was to be the Mark Hellinger, as Lerner had hoped all those years before, and because of the elaborate set, the show would preview for four weeks in New York, rather than undergoing out-of-town tryouts.[51] Talking to the *New York Times* at the first rehearsal on October 13, Lerner commented that the piece was "all about people who work in fashion, about the creation of elegance," and, more specifically, "an independent woman who refuses to compromise. Not only did she create the uniform for the emancipated woman, but she is, I suppose, the most emancipated woman I've ever met. She doesn't feel any less womanly not being married or not having children."[52] The writer also compared Chanel to Hepburn herself: "In her life, she too has been a very independent woman. An independent woman in every sense of the word. They're both career women, but they've never lost one ounce of femininity. They're intensely feminine women. What was that Chanel said to me? 'There's no future for a woman trying to be a man.'" In these ways, the musical was perhaps more heavily influenced by Lerner's personal encounters with Chanel than might be assumed, which in turn inspired the casting of the strong Hepburn rather than the softer Russell.

Mel Gussow's article further described the rehearsal: "As the show's musical director, Robert Emmett Dolan, played the piano, Mr. Lerner sang the score, beginning with 'Turn on the Lights' [which was later cut]. Seventeen songs later, Miss Hepburn stood in for Mr. Lerner and sang the last song, one of the seven she has in the score." Once more, Lerner had to juggle several projects at the same time. Three days into rehearsals for *Coco, Paint Your Wagon* had its premiere. As was the case with most of his musicals in the 1960s, the reviews were very mixed, not least because the cast (including Lee Marvin, Clint Eastwood, and Jean Seberg) were not typical musical theater figures, but the $20 million budget had at least guaranteed a lavish affair.[53] It further struggled with having been given an "M" ("Mature," i.e., suggested for mature audiences only) rating by the Motion Picture Associations Code and Rating Administration, rather than "G" for "General," thereby reducing the potential size of the audience.[54]

[51] Louis Calta, "'Coco,' with Singing Katharine Hepburn, Due Dec. 18," *New York Times*, August 6, 1969, 28.

[52] Mel Gussow, "After 12 Years, 'Coco' Is in Rehearsal," *New York Times*, October 14, 1969, 52.

[53] See, for instance, Vincent Canby, "Screen: Amiable 'Paint Your Wagon,'" *New York Times*, October 16, 1969, 56.

[54] A. H. Weiler, "Paramount Seeks a 'G' for 'Wagon,'" *New York Times*, October 31, 1969, 37.

Figure 5.2 Alan Jay Lerner, Moss Hart, and Frederick Loewe working on *Camelot*, 1960. Credit: Photofest

Similarly, when *Coco* opened on Broadway on December 18, the critical reaction was variable. Rehearsals had been difficult on all fronts, with particular tension between Lerner and Beaton, who blamed Lerner for all the show's weaknesses. The following letter from the lyricist hints at the tense backstage atmosphere:

To Cecil Beaton

4 December 1969

The idea that I would blame a poor matinee on the hats is an amusing conceit, but not mine. *That* ridiculous I am not.

I have a sad, fleeting feeling that when at last the work is finished and the show has opened, I'm going to discover that I'm deeply hurt by your mystifying attitude toward me on this show. For the moment, all I can care about is trying to make the show as good as possible—and I need your help—with enthusiasm or without. But believe me, I'm not a blame-dodger.

Aye,
Alan

Eventually, the pair put this behind them, but Beaton was to suffer almost as much as Lerner on *Coco*, since his designs were negatively compared to Chanel's own. Clive Barnes in the *New York Times* was particularly vicious, saying, "Mr. Beaton has never struck me as a particularly accomplished designer—although his dresses were often pretty—and nothing in *Coco* causes me to revise that opinion.... The time is meant to be 1954, but the costumes did not seem appropriate to either the time or the place."[55] On the other hand, he admitted, "The show has two great things going for it. One is the well-scrubbed and gallant radiance of Katharine Hepburn. I adored her through everything. The other is the occasionally acerbic wit and even occasional wisdom of Alan Jay Lerner's book." The writer must have been delighted to have come out of the stress with such praise.

Undaunted by the mixed reviews, Lerner and the cast proceeded to make an album of the show. It was common to make changes to musicals before committing them to record, and in this brief note to Hepburn we can see the kinds of decisions this involved:

To Katharine Hepburn

[Undated; early January 1970, preceding *Coco* recording]

Kate dear,

I have been examining the dialogue surrounding "Gabrielle" and leading into "Coco." I think much of it could be tightened, and that it is too much for a record. But at this point I wouldn't tighten my belt if my pants were falling off. Therefore, I suggest you do it exactly as it is, with the possible exception of condensing the opening speech as indicated below. In any event, I will be there when you record it, providing my tailor can get my suit of armor ready in time.

With it all, I love you dearly, which shows two things:

1. I have taste
2. I am also a masochist

Aye,
Alan

[55] Clive Barnes, "Theater: Katharine Hepburn Has Title Role in 'Coco,'" *New York Times*, December 19, 1969, 66.

COCO
My father was a champagne salesman. I adored him and I lived for his occasional visit. Six weeks before my first communion, he came for the afternoon. I pleaded with him to take me away with him.

In the following letter, the album has by now been recorded, and the increased warmth of affection from Lerner to Hepburn is noticeable in comparison to their early encounters:

To Katharine Hepburn

[Undated; c.January 1970]

Dearest Kate,

Here are the tapes—with some technical imperfections which, of course, won't be on the finished product.

YOU ARE MARVELOUS! All the excitement and the emotion that is on the stage somehow leaps out at you. It's really a tingling performance and everybody who has heard it is jubilant—including me.

Because of the time problem, the dialogue sequence between "Gabrielle" and "Coco," therefore in "Gabrielle" itself, had to be omitted. I assure you that good as it was, it is not needed in order to get the full impact of the number; and although the decision was not made by me, I fully endorse it.

You will notice an imperfection at the end of "Always Mademoiselle," but that is an imperfection in the tape, not the recording. It's really a thrilling performance and if you stick with it I think you've got a hell of a future.

And speaking of the future and the new year, all the happiness this world can offer will fall far short of what I wish for you. Bless you, bless you, bless you!

Always,
Alan

Lerner also found time to write a letter to one of his idols, Irving Berlin, thereby beginning an infrequent but tender correspondence that shows once again how much he respected and loved the writers of his youth. In this letter, reference is made to a "book," which was a bound collection of Berlin's complete published song sheets. He sent copies of this collection to a number of his favorite songwriters, and Lerner's copy became one of his most treasured possessions. The letter also alludes to a portrait Berlin painted of Barbra Streisand during *On a Clear Day*:

To Irving Berlin

January 5, 1970

Dear Irving,

If anyone wondered if I had any hobbies, and looked through my desk, I think he would decide that I am a collector of unfinished letters to you. Your kindness and generosity to me over the last year has touched me so deeply that every letter I started to write seemed inadequate, and I put it away "for-when-I-had-more-time." I finally have more time, but I feel just as inadequate.

To begin with, that book! I opened the package late one night, not knowing its contents, and as I began to flip through the pages I found myself crying. The quantity—the quality—and that you should have sent me a copy in the first place! Any time anyone in our profession, or in any profession, needs a bit of humbling, he ought to take a look at that book. The volume of your work staggers the mind as much as it moves the heart, and I thank you from the bottom of mine for sending it to me.

The painting of Barbra is a sheer delight. I love having it. I had no idea you dipped the brush.

Now that *Coco* has opened, I am anxious for you to come and see it and to hear what you think. As you know, the critics were less than cordial, and André and I came off like two white cops in a Watts riot. I think André wrote a lovely score, but he damaged himself with the orchestrations. Although he didn't do them, he supervised them. In any event, the score certainly sounds better on the album, which I will send you as soon as it comes in.

It's a strange world in which to be writing these days. The critics seem to be trying to articulate what they think the kids want. The big hope is that one day they'll do it so well, the kids will rebel against *them*, and they'll all go away and leave us alone.

I heard you were in Paris. I hope you had a good time, and I do look forward to seeing you.

Thank you again. I feel proud and honoured to be on your "mailing list," and belatedly, a happy, happy new year.

Faithfully,
Alan

Berlin's reply was similarly cordial:

From Irving Berlin

January 9, 1970

Dear Alan:

What a nice letter.

I knew how occupied you have been the past year so really didn't expect you to rush into any thank you letters. Besides, I still have some unanswered mail in my desk drawer that dates back to the Ed Sullivan Show.

Seriously, I was delighted with your letter and thank you for all the generous things you say.

I do want to see *Coco*. Sometime soon I will call your office to get a couple of house seats.

I read some of the reviews. However, I've talked to several people in our business who have seen the show and they raved about it. Only last night I heard Barry Farber[56]—one of the better night talk shows—speak about *Coco*. He loved it and couldn't understand the critics. Besides, with over $130,000 a week business, who needs critics.

I would really like to see you sometime. I've been an admirer of yours for many years. Not alone for your great talent, but for your energy, drive and guts to keep working at it so successfully.

With my best to you for the new year.

As always,
Irving

Berlin's entrance into Lerner's life at this moment nicely underlines the changes in the Broadway and Hollywood musical the lyricist had witnessed during the 1960s. Gone was the "dream factory" atmosphere of Freed's MGM unit, which had facilitated the creative freedom of *An American in Paris* and *Gigi*. In its place were overblown "road show" screen versions of established Broadway shows like *Paint Your Wagon, Camelot,* and *My Fair Lady* (whatever their undoubted virtues). Lerner's stage productions were few in number, and after the end of the relationship with Loewe, his collaborations with Lane and Previn were unhappy and uneven. Neither *Clear Day* nor *Coco* was quite right.

[56] Barry Farber (1930–) is one of the most respected journalists of his generation, and at the time of Berlin's letter was the all-night host of a hit show on WOR AM radio.

Regardless of Lerner's excellent contributions to both of these, his wit and suavity were of a world that was different from the decade's major musicals by a new generation of writers, from Kander and Ebb's dark *Cabaret* (1966) to Jerry Herman's big and brash *Hello, Dolly!* (1964). In particular, the nudity, open sexuality, and drugs in *Hair* (Off-Broadway, 1967; Broadway, 1968) were matched by a rock score that took musicals in a more rebellious direction. Lerner made his feelings clear a few years later:

> Since the mid-sixties, the musical theatre has been fumbling, stumbling and groping for the right direction, not certain whether rock is genuine nourishment or merely intravenous feeding. In or out of theatre, rock is primitive stuff, extremely limited dramatically, popularized by the young for the young. Although youth has many glories, it has never been a period distinguished for judgment and that is no less true today. What has misled many who should know better is the vastness of the young population and the vastness of their attendant purchasing power, the two together creating an impression of an important new sound instead of just a loud one. Increasing the volume will never turn a belch into an aria....
>
> I am convinced that the audience for genuine theatre is still there waiting and wanting to be seduced again, in spite of inflation, apathy and all other sociological ills. Because I believe that and believe it deeply, I cannot be pessimistic about the future.
>
> Besides, if musicals disappeared, what would I do with myself? Eh?[57]

Reflecting this reactionary position, two of Lerner's next projects would reunite him with his favorite composer on old-fashioned projects. But the new wave of writers had caused him to ponder: the turn of the decade saw him form a new collaboration with an edgy young film composer to write a musical version of one of the most controversial novels of the twentieth century.

[57] Alan Jay Lerner, "Introduction," *The New York Times Great Songs of Broadway* (New York: Quadrangle, 1973), 8.

CHAPTER 6

"Matters of Consequence"

COLLABORATIONS OLD AND NEW, 1970–1974

Aside from his conventional professional correspondence, Lerner regularly wrote to friends and acquaintances about his life and work. The letter that opens this chapter was written to John Lahr,[1] critic at the *New Yorker,* after Lerner had read his biography of his father Bert Lahr,[2] *Notes on a Cowardly Lion* (1969). Lahr's many acclaimed performances include the Lion in the movie of *The Wizard of Oz* (1939) and Estragon in the first US productions of Samuel Beckett's absurdist play, *Waiting for Godot* (1956). Lerner pays tribute to the actor's talent and warmth of personality in this letter, but he also can't resist referring to Lahr's review of *Coco* in the concluding paragraph (he included the new cast album of the show with his letter):

To John Lahr

January 28, 1970

Dear Mr. Lahr:

I just finished reading your book about your father and I couldn't help but write you and tell you how deeply moved I was.

I knew your father quite well and he was to me one of the most extraordinary performers I have ever seen. Certainly "Waiting for Godot" was one of the rare experiences I have ever had in the theatre.

[1] John Lahr (1941–) is a veteran New York critic, as well as the biographer of several important entertainment industry figures, including Frank Sinatra and Noël Coward.

[2] Bert Lahr (1895–1967) was a popular American actor. He was prolific in many genres on stage and screen, with appearances in musicals including *Life Begins at 8:40* (1934), *DuBarry Was a Lady* (1939), and *Two on the Aisle* (1951) on the stage, and *The Wizard of Oz* (1939) and *Rose Marie* (1954) on the screen.

I went backstage on opening night and was still unsuccessfully trying to hold back the tears and saw him in his dressing room. I threw my arms around him and said something inadequate like: "You were magnificent." He whispered in my ear: "Alan, will you tell me what the fuck this play is about." There is no doubt he was not only great show business but great theatre.

In case you are wondering how I knew him, when I first graduated from college I wrote radio programs for a while, including variety shows, and on more than a few occasions he was the guest star. I'm glad to say he was pleased and on several occasions called me up to help him doctor a script for him. (Incidentally, we "met" at your apartment one day. I think you were three or four at the time.) I loved him dearly and one of the things I most regret is that I never found the right idea for a show for him.

In 1958 The Lamb's Club gave a Testimonial Dinner to Fritz Loewe and me and your father appeared on the dais as one of the speakers. His opening line was: "Fritz Loewe and Alan Lerner have raised the standards of the musical theatre so high that I haven't been able to get a job for eight years." Great line.

I read your review of *Coco* with great interest. I would be less than human not to say that I would have preferred a more favorable one, but I thank you for being the only critic who reviewed the play. For some reason, this is the one country that insists that every play a man writes be better than his last, and when it is not it is usually either dismissed or ridiculed. So I am grateful to you for being so un-American. Enclosed is a copy of the score of *Coco* which, if you have time to listen to, you'll either like more or less. If it is less, forgive me. If it is more, I forgive you.

Please give my regards to your mother.

Sincerely,
Alan Jay Lerner

The reviews of *Coco* had indeed been mixed and disappointing for Lerner. John Chapman in the *Daily News* headed his review "*Coco* Belongs to Kate Hepburn, Leaving Not Much for the Rest of Us," and Martin Gottfried in *Women's Wear Daily* noted somewhat harshly that "Alan Jay Lerner's book isn't a story—it's an engraving on the side of a building. Andre Previn's music is orchestrated for the movies, so thick you have to eat it with a spoon. Directing it is like moving an elephant. Seeing it is like riding one. And the elephant is white." Equally condemnatory was Richard Watts Jr. in the *Post*: "A surprisingly dull show, seriously handicapped by an inferior book and a very minor score." Hepburn, however, was uniformly praised, and Lerner's witty book was arguably given far too little credit for this. His lines for Hepburn were often extremely amusing, for instance, in a scene in which she dictates letters such as "Dear Pablo, I hear your wife has just left you and I want to wish you continuing good luck." But the critics went to town in damning the show, which had the largest budget of any Broadway musical to date ($900,000).

Undeterred as usual, Lerner proceeded with his varied portfolio, including writing occasional articles. In February 1970, he was asked to compose a profile of Frank Sinatra for *Cue* magazine, and wrote to send the singer-actor a copy:

To Frank Sinatra

February 17, 1970

Dear Frank:

I don't know if you know it but *Cue* has asked about one hundred critics from all over the country to name their bests over the last thirty years. It had to do with their April issue, which celebrates their 30th year in existence. As best singer, you're the first Democrat to win anything by a landslide since Roosevelt in 1936. *Cue* asked me to write an article about you, which I did with pleasure. I am enclosing a copy. I hope you like it. I meant every word.

I get news about you from Silent Sam.[3] I hope I'll get it first hand very soon.

Faithfully,
Alan Jay Lerner

The flattery of the letter and article was possibly strategic, as Lerner was soon to approach Sinatra to star in a new film.

Katharine Hepburn had only signed up to play in *Coco* until April 1970, and both Lerner and Brisson were keen to replace her with another movie actress. By March, nobody had been found to take over, so Hepburn agreed to extend her appearance to June 13. Their thoughts for her replacement initially went to Gloria Swanson,[4] star of *Sunset Boulevard* (1950), someone whose talents were different from Hepburn's but whose presence would have undoubtedly attracted

[3] Sam Spiegel.

[4] Gloria Swanson (1899–1983) was one of the most popular actresses of the silent movie era, and later made the successful transition to sound. Her most famous role, Norma Desmond in *Sunset Boulevard* (1950), memorably required her to play a faded silent movie star, and she was nominated for an Academy Award. Lerner's ex-wife Nancy Olson also appeared in the film, which perhaps brought about their acquaintance.

huge audiences.[5] In mid-March, she traveled to Hollywood to audition for Lerner and Brisson, but the lyricist had to cancel the appointment. Swanson did not receive the message to say he could not appear in Palm Springs as promised, and on March 24 she sent him an irate telegram, capped with the words: "I've seen more humiliation and disrespect in these three days waiting for your arrival in Palm Springs than in all my fifty-five years as a performer." Lerner quickly dispatched an apologetic reply:

Telegram to Gloria Swanson

March 26, 1970

DEAR GLORIA

I'M DEEPLY SORRY THERE HAS BEEN THIS CONFUSION AND THAT I WAS UNABLE TO GET TO PALM SPRINGS OVER THE WEEKEND. I THOUGHT THAT THE MESSAGE I SENT YOU MADE IT CLEAR BUT IT MUST HAVE LOST SOMETHING IN TRANSLATION. I ALSO WANT YOU TO KNOW THAT THE PROPER WORK CAN ONLY BEGIN IN NEW YORK AFTER APRIL 8TH WHEN WE CAN MEET AND WORK TOGETHER REGULARLY. IF THE JUNE 13TH DATE SEEMS SHORT NOTICE PERHAPS WE COULD EVEN EXTEND IT. IN ANY CASE, I BEG YOU TO RECONSIDER. I TRULY WOULD LOVE TO SEE YOU DO IT AND I THINK YOU WOULD BE MARVELOUS AND HAVE A GOOD TIME, SO DO FORGIVE ME NOT ONLY FOR LAST WEEKEND BUT FOR STILL HOPING.

ALAN

It seems the pair managed to patch up their differences, but not to the extent of agreeing a contract; in later interviews, Swanson claimed that the producers had refused to pay her the same rate as Hepburn.[6]

In April, Hepburn extended her stay to June 27, and after much persuasion agreed to record a fifteen-minute segment from the show (including her song "Always Mademoiselle") for the Tony Awards broadcast on April 19. Lerner wrote to thank her:

[5] Louis Calta, "Gloria Swanson Will Audition for Miss Hepburn's 'Coco' Role," *New York Times*, March 18, 1970, 41.

[6] "I only wanted what Katie received. Nothing more, nothing less. That wasn't too much to ask, was it?" Bob Thomas, "Gloria Swanson Upset by False 'Coco' Reports," *Nevada Daily Mail*, July 19, 1970, 8.

To Katharine Hepburn

[undated; c. April 1970]

Dearest Kate:

You were absolutely marvelous today.

I thought so, the director thought so, the producer, everyone.

I know you hated doing it, but Sunday night will present the first good reason they invented the goddamn medium at all.

Thank you for doing it. I've had intestinal spasms ever since I asked you. But you were simply wonderful.

Always,
Alan

In June, Hepburn once again extended her contract, this time to August 1.[7] She was then succeeded by French actress Danielle Darrieux,[8] whose performance was well reviewed by several newspapers. Mel Gussow in the *New York Times* noted, "For the first time, one hears the entire score sung... [and] Alan Jay Lerner's lyrics seem to grow in stylishness and intelligence." He concluded, "The part and the clothes suit Miss Darrieux splendidly."[9] But her run in the show was to last only four weeks, bringing *Coco*'s Broadway run to an abrupt end on October 3.

With the casting problems on *Coco* still brewing, mid-June had seen the premiere of Lerner's latest stage-to-screen adaptation, *On a Clear Day You Can See Forever*. Re-teaming with director Vincente Minnelli and designer Cecil Beaton (both of *Gigi*), Lerner hoped the former's visual style and a revised script and score would help bring clarity to the troubled show, which had already been reworked several times for stock presentations. But last-minute changes, including the excision of songs like "Wait Till We're Sixty-Five" and "Who Is There among Us Who Knows" after they had been filmed, left large portions of the movie without songs. It ran over two hours, and in spite of the vibrant performance of Barbra Streisand, the plot's engagement with extra-sensory perception and regression still failed to provide a coherent story line. *Variety*'s review revealed an additional reason the critics might not have been in a good mood: "It turned out that the print screened for review was not the final 129 min. version but a longer 143 min. answer print, with four additional scenes, including a

[7] "Miss Hepburn Extends Role of Coco to Aug. 1," *New York Times*, June 2, 1970, 35.

[8] Danielle Darrieux (1917–) is a distinguished French actress, whose work spans from the musical movie *Le Bal* (1931) to an appearance in *L'Heure Zéro* (2007). Aside from *Coco*, she appeared in the stage musical *Ambassador* in London (1971) and on Broadway (1972).

[9] Mel Gussow, "Stage: Miss Darrieux Becomes Coco," *New York Times*, August 7, 1970, 28.

song by [Jack] Nicholson and the pictures [*sic*] most elaborate musical production number, all of which were subsequently cut."[10] Still, Vincent Canby in the *New York Times* said he was "eventually hypnotized into a state of benign though not-quite-abject permissiveness,"[11] and most of the critics found something to admire. On a budget of $10 million, the film made roughly double that figure at the box office.

Shrugging his shoulders, Lerner lost no time in choosing a new movie project, namely, a musical adaptation of Antoine de Saint-Exupéry's short novel *The Little Prince* (1943). To appear as the pilot, Lerner's thoughts immediately went to his favorite actor, Richard Burton, who had not only excelled in *Camelot* but whom Lerner had also wanted to appear in *Clear Day*. He wrote to Burton in early August and received a reply that indicated the star's interest. "Am fascinated and always have been by *Le Petit Prince*," he wrote, "and am even more fascinated by the idea of your treatment of it. Will it take long to do? What form will it take and a myriad other questions?" While developing the film, Lerner also started to develop a new stage musical. *Lolita, My Love* was the most daring show of Lerner's career. Based on Vladimir Nabokov's controversial novel *Lolita* (1955) and its equally contentious film version by Stanley Kubrick[12] (1962), the musical was Lerner's attempt to deal with a more mature subject matter in line with Broadway's increasing trend toward gritty themes. Working on the show during the fall of 1970, Lerner turned to a new composer to write the score. John Barry[13] was well known at the time for his connection with the James Bond franchise, and although he was still in his thirties, he had already won two Academy Awards. His theatrical pedigree was less established: his only professional credit was the score for *Passion Flower Hotel* (1965), which had a brief run (148 performances) in London. The partnership had potential though, and they completed most of the score by November.

Norman Twain[14] was in charge of the production, and rehearsals were slated to start on January 4, 1971.[15] At the end of November, Lerner and Barry chose

[10] Rick, "Film Reviews: On a Clear Day You Can See Forever," *Variety*, June 17, 1970, 16.

[11] Vincent Canby, "Screen: 'On a Clear Day You Can See Forever' Begins Its Run," *New York Times*, June 18, 1970, 53.

[12] Stanley Kubrick (1928–99) was among the most revered filmmakers of his generation, with movies including *2001: A Space Odyssey* (1968), *A Clockwork Orange* (1971), and *Eyes Wide Shut* (1999).

[13] John Barry (1933–2011) was the Oscar-winning composer of *Born Free* (1966), *The Lion in Winter* (1968), *Out of Africa* (1985), and *Dances with Wolves* (1990), as well as twelve of the Bond movies. He also composed five musicals, including *Passion Flower Hotel* (1965).

[14] Norman Twain (?–present) is a theater and film producer. His Broadway productions include *Bajour* (1965) and *Henry Sweet Henry* (1967), though he is also credited with the movies *Lean on Me* (1989) and *Heavens Fall* (2006).

[15] "'Lolita' to Appear as Musical in '71," *New York Times*, November 4, 1970, 41.

Figure 6.1 A publicity shot for the movie version of *My Fair Lady*, with George Cukor (director), Jack L. Warner (producer), Alan Jay Lerner and Cecil Beaton (designer). Credit: Warner Bros. Pictures/Photofest

Tito Capobianco,[16] best known for his work in the opera world, to direct the show. As with *Little Prince*, Burton was Lerner's first choice to star in the show,[17] but he turned it down, as did Michael Redgrave (Lerner had previously offered him Higgins in *Fair Lady*, of course).[18] British actor John Neville[19] was signed instead.[20] During this period, Lerner's correspondence is sparse, but he did find time to write to two good friends. For Christmas 1970, Irving Berlin had sent Lerner another painting, and he wrote profusely in January to thank his hero:

[16] Tito Capobianco (1931–) is a celebrated and prolific opera director who was prominent in this period for his productions at the New York City Opera.

[17] Jack O'Brian, "Off the Grapevine," *Toledo Blade*, December 7, 1970, X3.

[18] "Musical 'Lolita' by Lerner-Barry Headed for B'way," *Variety*, November 4, 1970, 55.

[19] John Neville (1925–2011) was a British actor whose work ranged from classical roles with the Old Vic company in London in the 1950s to a regular stint on *The X-Files* on television in the 1990s. Prior to *Lolita, My Love*, he had taken over from Keith Michell in the 1958 West End production of *Irma La Douce*.

[20] Lewis Funke, "The Rialto: And Julie Harris 'Drinks a Little,'" *New York Times*, November 29, 1970, 119. "Neville to Bow in Musical as the Humbert of 'Lolita,'" *New York Times*, December 16, 1970, 54.

To Irving Berlin

[undated; c. January 1971]

Dear Irving:

The painting at Christmas just simply made me cry. How incredibly kind you are! And as for the painting itself, it is a joy—so original and gay and young—and decorative. I really love it more than you can imagine. You share so much with me and I feel so inadequate about being able to tell you what it means to me and how proud I am by your attention and thoughtfulness.

One day when I come back from the road—March 30—could I call you or call on you? God, I would love to see you again.

We'll be opening March 30th with *Lolita, My Love*. Would you come to the opening or the preview? I'll be in touch from Philadelphia for your answer.

Thank you again, dear, dear Irving.

Always,
Alan

While rehearsing the show, he also wrote a brief note of thanks to Robert Lewis, who had sent Lerner a book on Nabokov:

To Robert Lewis

[Undated; early February 1971]

Dearest Bobby:

I was re-reading the book you sent me on Nabokov and I suddenly had the sickening feeling that the letter I had written in my head I had never put on paper—i.e., the letter to thank you for 1st thinking of me and 2nd and much more important, the book. It's the gift not the thought that counts, I always say.

Seriously, it was so kind of you and I appreciate it more than I can say.

We are in the middle of rehearsals and—and—well, what can I tell you about rehearsals you haven't had ulcers about. Will you come to the opening? March 30. Will be in Philadelphia from the 15th [February] to March 15th if you're in the mood. I'll be staying at the Barclay.

Thank you again—and

Much love always,
Alan

This letter hints at the trouble the show was in, and unfortunately Lerner's ulcers anticipated what was doomed to be his biggest flop. The main problem was the story, which was regarded as distasteful: a European professor called Humbert Humbert falls in love with his landlady's teenaged daughter. Commenting at the time of casting, producer Twain optimistically declared that the show would be "the epitome of tastefulness." But ultimately the situation that had been acceptable as an abstract thought in Nabokov's novel became unpleasant when acted out on stage (though, of course, Kubrick's film had shown that a dramatized version could be successful). In mid-February, Capobianco resigned as the director and was replaced by British actor-director Noel Willman, who had previously directed the unsuccessful musicals *Darling of the Day* and *Love Match*, as well as hit plays like *A Man for All Seasons* and *A Lion in Winter*.[21] Things did not seem to improve. After the Philadelphia tryout, the show was closed down for ten days, returned to New York for an extra rehearsal period, and then re-opened at Boston's Shubert Theater on March 15. The planned Broadway opening was delayed to April 13, and Annette Ferra[22] was replaced in the role of Lolita by Denise Nickerson.[23]

In spite of all the problems, one of the few aspects of the show that everyone agreed was successful was the song "Sur Les Quais de Ramsdale, Vermont," performed by Dorothy Loudon[24] as Lolita's mother, Charlotte. *Variety* called it "the only song rouser... a Piaf-style lilt," and the *Boston Herald Traveler* noted that Loudon's "massive contribution to the excellent first act makes you sorely miss her in the second."[25] Lerner obviously appreciated her too, as can be seen from the following note, apologizing for the difficult time she had endured in the production:

[21] Louis Calta, "'Lolita' Puts Off Broadway Debut," *New York Times*, February 19, 1971, 26.

[22] Annette Ferra (known as Christina Ferra-Gilmore) (1955–) is an American actress (*The Alfred Hitchcock Hour*) and casting director.

[23] Lewis Funke, "Rising Rivers," *New York Times*, March 21, 1971, D1.

[24] Dorothy Loudon (1925–2003) won the Tony Award for her performance as Miss Hannigan in the original production of *Annie* (1977). She had the misfortune to appear in a number of notorious flops—including *The Fig Leaves Are Falling* (1969), *Ballroom* (1980), and *Annie 2* (1990), alongside *Lolita, My Love*—but her work generally received high praise.

[25] Samuel Hirsch, "*Lolita My Love*, New Musical by Lerner-Barry, Opens at Shubert Theater," *Boston Herald Traveler*, March 24, 1971, 27.

To Dorothy Loudon

[Undated; March 1971]

Dearest Dorothy,

There's a conspiracy somewhere against decent people.

I can offer nothing—damn it—except a shoulder, my prayers, my affection—and a blanket offer to do whatever you wish to do.

Always,
Alan

Another nine performances took place, but it was no good: on March 27 *Lolita* closed down in Boston, never to re-open.[26] The show left a deficit of $900,000 according to *Variety*, which probably put a stop to Lerner's hopes to "revise the show for a possible New York opening in late spring or early fall."[27]

In April, Lerner heard from composer Jule Styne (*Gypsy, Funny Girl*), who had the idea of turning Shaw's *Major Barbara* into a musical. After the severance of his working relationships with Previn, Lane, and now Barry, Styne was perhaps another obvious partner for Lerner. It was also natural to look to another Shaw play in an attempt to emulate Lerner's biggest success (which was still *My Fair Lady*, of course). But Lerner was slow to respond, much to Styne's irritation. "I haven't heard from you, so I am going to assume that you aren't interested," he wrote. "As I have first-rate other talent who want to work with me, who I know would be excited about this fascinating project, I intend to pursue it with them." On receiving this, Lerner finally replied:

To Jule Styne

April 20, 1971

Dear Jule,

First off, I'm dying to work with you. You have fewer bigger fans than I.

The problem for me is *Major Barbara*—not because it wouldn't make a good musical. I think it could make a great musical. It's trying to reconcile myself to doing another Shaw play. I'm afraid it would be begging comparison for me, for you, too.

[26] " 'Lolita, My Love,'' *New York Times*, March 30, 1971, 23.
[27] " 'Lolita My Love' folds in Boston,'' March 30, 1971, 1 and 62.

What I have been turning over in my mind the last few days was trying to see if I could get it out of that period, at least. But Shaw is deceptively stubborn. It is for this reason, and this reason only, that I have been slow getting back to you; and it is for this reason, and this reason only I have decided I cannot do it.

But if you ever say I don't want to work with you again, I'll sue you for libel.

Thank you for asking me and merde for *Some Like It Hot.*

Faithfully,
Alan

Styne's reply was much more cordial:

From Jule Styne

April 22, 1971

Dear Alan:

Since you write such beautiful letters and I get such prompt answers, I have decided that even if we never work together—one day someone may do a musical based on our letters to one another. It will be called "THE LERNER-STYNE LETTERS."

I am very happy to know that you feel about me as I do about you. Somewhere...sometime...there has to be a great work yet to be accomplished by us.

I admire your working so hard on *Lolita* and know that something good will come out of it since you feel as you do about it.

Let's keep these letters coming.

Obediently,
Jule

For the first time in years, Lerner was now without a partner (he didn't explore other properties with Styne), and he launched himself fully into finishing his screenplay for *The Little Prince* without a composer. Previously, the project had been linked with Previn, Barry, and even Burt Bacharach,[28] but after a decade of flops and near-misses without his old partner, it was time for Lerner's reunion with his greatest collaborator, Fritz Loewe. During the summer of 1971,

[28] Burt Bacharach (1928–) is an American songwriter of numerous hit songs, many of them written with lyricist Hal David. Together, they wrote the Broadway musical *Promises, Promises* (1968).

Loewe was persuaded by Lerner's agent to come out of retirement for one last musical, and in late August it was confirmed that not only would he and Lerner write the score for *Little Prince* together, but they would also revise and expand their songs for *Gigi* and bring it to the stage for the first time.[29] The *Gigi* project had been rumored in 1969, but it was only now that work was to begin.[30] In late September, the composer left for London, where he and Lerner started to write together again, and returned to the United States to complete *Little Prince* in the winter.[31] Among many friends who were delighted by the re-teaming, Lerner heard from his old friend, actor Douglas Fairbanks Jr., who said "I have just dashed off a quick, happy note to Fritz wherein I proclaim with my own form of 'hosannas' at the news of you both collaborating once again. What with the President's concessions on the International Monetary Debate being announced, the formal end of the India-Pakistan war being proclaimed, a slight improvement in Ulster terrorism and the Stock Market being up, this news is about as good a Christmas present as the world could find."[32]

Back in New York, Lerner took time out to inaugurate the second series of the "Lyrics and Lyricists" program at the 92nd Street "Y," at which he spoke about and performed a range of his songs, including "You Haven't Changed at All" from *The Day before Spring* and "I Talk to the Trees" from *Paint Your Wagon*. (The event was recorded live and later released on record and CD.)[33] Then it was on to Loewe's house at Palm Springs, where work was completed. In March 1972, they were interviewed for a feature on their re-pairing, in which they played down their previous differences and focused on their artistic harmony. Loewe commented that "I've always thought *The Little Prince* could only be done by Lerner.... He has a poetry, a knowledge of a treatment for a musical that's his personal, magnificent talent." For his part, Lerner said "We continue with the same kind of enthusiasm we had in the beginning, tempered by a little experience.... The main difference in working with Fritz as to compared with working with anyone else—the real difference, which I never appreciated until now—is enthusiasm."[34]

[29] Leonard Lyons, "Lyons Den," *Bangor Daily News*, August 30, 1971, 9.

[30] See, for instance, Dan Knapp, "*Gigi* May Make Another Comeback," *Los Angeles Times*, December 24, 1969, A7.

[31] David D. McNicoll, "Luther—With Some Humor," *Sun-Herald* [Sydney], September 26, 1971, 109.

[32] Douglas Fairbanks Jr. (1909–2000) followed his father into screen acting. His early movies were from the silent film era, but his most successful pictures (including *The Prisoner of Zenda*, 1937) were talkies. Letter of December 23, 1971, from Fairbanks Jr. to Lerner (private collection).

[33] John S. Wilson, "Lyricist's Craft Is Lerner's Topic," *New York Times*, December 14, 1971, 56. An edited version of the event is available on DRG Records 5175.

[34] "Lerner and Loewe Return for Musical," *Boca Raton News*, March 3, 1972, March 3, 1972, 7.

Around this time, Lerner went to see the new movie version of Kander and Ebb's hit show *Cabaret*, directed by Bob Fosse, and was struck by its original qualities, as he told its producer, Cy Feuer:[35]

To Cy Feuer

March 1, 1972

Dear Cy,

I saw *Cabaret* last night and I've got to tell you that in my not-so-humble opinion, it is the best screen musical I have ever seen in my life. What you and Bob have wrought is nothing short of a miracle. And Bobby's direction is so imaginative, so controlled—every scene has such an idea behind it—every performance, every moment, in fact, that it is simply the most brilliantly directed musical film ever produced. Just when I thought we would be paddling forever through the dungfields of Norman Jewison[36] and Tom O'Horgan,[37] you and Bobby have really restored my faith and made me happy I'm in the musical theatre.

I thank you both from the bottom of my heart.

Faithfully,
Alan

Though it is unclear from this message, it seems likely that this helped Lerner think to ask Fosse to appear as the Snake in *The Little Prince*.

In March, it was also widely rumored that Paramount had been pursuing Frank Sinatra for the role of the Pilot in the film.[38] Sinatra had announced his retirement in March 1971, so it would have been a coup to get him to return to work, but Stanley Donen,[39] veteran director of *Singin' in the Rain*, who had

[35] Cy Feuer (1911–2006) produced some of the most successful musicals of all time, including Frank Loesser's *Where's Charley?* (1948), *Guys and Dolls* (1950), and *How to Succeed in Business without Really Trying* (1961).

[36] Norman Jewison (1926–) is a director and producer, known for films such as *In the Heat of the Night* (1967) and *The Thomas Crown Affair* (1968). Lerner is referring to Jewison's recent direction of *Fiddler on the Roof* (1971) in this letter.

[37] Tom O'Horgan (1924–2009) directed the Broadway productions of *Hair* (1968) and three musicals that opened in 1971: *Jesus Christ Superstar, Lenny,* and *Inner City. Hair* was still running at the time, giving O'Horgan an incredible monopoly over Broadway, which explains Lerner's remark.

[38] See, for instance, "Sinatra Is Sought for 'Prince,'" *Pittsburgh Press*, March 29, 1972, 51.

[39] Stanley Donen (1924–) is the acclaimed director or co-director of numerous classic films, including *On the Town* (1949), Lerner's *Royal Wedding* (1951), *Seven Brides for Seven Brothers* (1954), *Indiscreet* (1958), and *Charade* (1963).

been signed to direct *Little Prince,* vetoed this casting. Two years later, when the movie had been finished, Donen declared that he "didn't think [Sinatra] would be right for 'The Little Prince.' The part calls for a man who must allow himself to be dominated by a six-year-old boy. It's difficult for me to imagine Frank relating to a child in such a way.... I didn't want to risk the movie on him."[40] The article also said, "Neither did Donen eagerly anticipate Sinatra's indomitable presence on a set. Frank calls the shot on the working hours, how many takes he will agree to do, and other facets of movie making which belong traditionally to the director." Therefore, after an extensive search that included approaches to leading actors Nicol Williamson,[41] Robert Goulet, Gene Hackman,[42] and Richard Harris, Broadway veteran Richard Kiley[43] (of *Man of La Mancha* fame) was cast as the Pilot in July.[44]

Lerner spent the remainder of 1972 completing work on the two musicals, especially on revising the new stage script for *Gigi.* A draft of the latter dated October 27, 1972, in the Gloria Swanson papers at the University of Texas at Austin shows Lerner was developing it at this time; Swanson was approached to appear in the production as Aunt Alicia or Mamita but didn't accept.[45] During the fall, lavish casting was confirmed for most of the roles, including Alfred Drake (*Oklahoma!, Kismet, Kiss Me, Kate*) as Honoré, Daniel Massey (*She Loves Me, Star!*) as Gaston, Maria Karnilova (*Fiddler on the Roof*) as Mamita, and Agnes Moorehead (*Citizen Kane, The Magnificent Ambersons*) as Aunt Alicia. In December, the production was firmly announced for early the following spring, to debut in San Francisco for a brief tour before reaching Broadway.[46] But casting problems with the title role meant that it was not until March 1973 that Terese Stevens, a little-known pop singer from England, was announced as Gigi. Edwin Lester, producer of the pre-Broadway version of the show (Saint Subber[47] was to take over for the Broadway transfer), commented that the role of Gigi had been the most difficult to cast: "We needed a girl who could appear to be 16 years old,

[40] Vernon Scott, "Sinatra's Out for Director," *Reading Eagle,* December 9, 1974, 21.

[41] Nicol Williamson (1936–2011) was a celebrated classical actor, who also appeared in numerous films and the Broadway musical *Rex* (1976).

[42] Gene Hackman (1930–) won Academy Awards for *The French Connection* (1971) and *Unforgiven* (1992), among several dozen films in a 53-year career in Hollywood.

[43] Richard Kiley (1922–99) was a beloved stage and film actor, well known for appearing in the Broadway productions of *Kismet* (1953), *No Strings* (1962), and *Man of La Mancha* (1965).

[44] Earl Wilson, "It Happened Last Night," *Sarasota Herald-Tribune,* April 24, 1972, 7B. Joyce Haber, "Kiley Is the Man of 'Little Prince,'" *Los Angeles Times,* July 31, 1972, F12.

[45] Gloria Swanson Papers, Harry Ransom Research Center, University of Texas at Austin, box 183, folder 7.

[46] Jack Gaver, "Lerner, Loewe Create Stage Version of 'Gigi,'" *The Hour,* December 6, 1972, 42.

[47] Arnold Saint-Subber (known as Saint Subber) (1918–94) was an important theatrical producer, well known for his association with the plays of Neil Simon.

could sing, dance and act. We had every talent agency in the country looking for us and I personally auditioned 38 aspirants." In the end, Katharine Hepburn (appearing in London at the time) recommended Stevens to Lerner, and after auditions with the creative team (including director Joseph Hardy[48] and choreographer Onna White)[49] she was hired.

Lerner was especially busy during 1973, with the filming of *Little Prince* taking up the first half of the year (including a six-week location shoot in Tunisia) and rehearsals for *Gigi* starting in April. The show opened in San Francisco on May 15 and moved to Los Angeles seven weeks later.[50] This scheduling proved awkward for Lerner, similar to previous occasions when he had been trying to work on a Broadway project in tandem with a movie. This time, he faced serious clashes with Stanley Donen, who significantly reshaped the screenplay of *Little Prince* without permission, while *Gigi* opened to mixed reviews in California. Headlines such as the *Washington Post*'s "Gigi having revival pains adapting to stage version" were typical of initial impressions of the new show, with the general feeling being that the five new songs and various new scenes did not match up to the quality of those familiar from the movie.[51] "Say a Prayer for Me Tonight" was cut from the film score, and "The Parisians" was also excised during the San Francisco part of the tour. A profile in the *Christian Science Monitor* began with an ominous indication of the strain of putting the show on stage: "It was the morning of opening night in Los Angeles. Alan Jay Lerner had been up since 6 o'clock. Not nervousness so much as habit. He'd been up at that hour every morning during the agonizing weeks of rewriting after the stage version of "Gigi" opened in San Francisco. That's when he works best and there was much to do."[52] The article included comments from Lerner on his relationship with Loewe and on their ideas for improving *Gigi*:

> We've worked together 30 years... longer than any team in the history of the musical theater.... It was the greatest release, like coming home again, just as if those intervening years had never happened. We sat down and talked it through and got wildly excited and then threw it all out the next day and talked new ideas—just the way we used to do. He has such faith in me and I in him. When you work with someone

[48] Joseph Hardy (1929–) is the Tony Award–winning director of *You're a Good Man, Charlie Brown* (1967) and the 1974 film version of *Great Expectations*.

[49] Onna White (1922–2005) was the choreographer of the Broadway productions of *The Music Man* (1957), *Half a Sixpence* (1965), and *Mame* (1966), among others.

[50] Jack Gaver, "*Gigi* Goes to Broadway," *Times-Union*, Warsaw, Indiana, May 1, 1973, 5.

[51] Leroy F. Aarons, "Gigi Having Revival Pains Adapting to Stage Version," *The Washington Post*, July 31, 1973, 17.

[52] Joseph N. Bell, "Profile: Lerner & Loewe & 'Gigi,'" *Christian Science Monitor*, August 30, 1973, 7.

that closely, you never have the feeling that you have to show them constantly that you can still write, that you have to prove yourself with every lyric. There's none of that with Fritz. He never kept a bar of music I didn't like and I've never kept a word he didn't like. I understand his talent, and he understands mine.... We'd had so much fun with "The Little Prince," that it seemed like a marvellous idea. So we just kept going with "Gigi."

Our troubles started with the song that introduces Gigi—"I Can't Understand the Parisians." It was right for Leslie Caron, but it was all wrong for Terri [Stevens]: it made her sound brash and tomboyish and not a little girl about to bloom into something else. Because "Gigi" is thin in plot, you *have* to feel for that girl. She was growing up in a manless world, and she had yearnings that were special and her very own. That sense simply wasn't there. So at the top of the list of what had to be done after we opened in San Francisco was a new song to introduce Gigi, a touching song that really gets into her thoughts.

To me, a ballad that says something penetrating about one person is the toughest thing of all to write. I can write clever things, patter things, rather quickly. But when it comes to digging into somebody with a ballad—I just never know. You want to say it in terms of the character in a fresh way, try to find the special image to capture *that* moment with *that* girl.

It finally took me three weeks to write "The Earth and Other Minor Things." I got the idea rather quickly, and Fritz wrote a beautiful melody to my title—which is the way we work. But then I holed up in my room to write and thought I was going to have a nervous breakdown before I could finish it. When the pressure is on, the temptation is always to settle before you're satisfied.... We put it all in 10 days before we finished in San Francisco... and it was a new show. Almost overnight, there were lines at the box office.

One of the unfortunate happenstances of the last 10 years, is not so much that young people with some musical talent have been overpraised as that the older and more experienced professionals have been so despised by the press that a lot of them are afraid to go back to work in their own medium—including a lot of fine playwrights like Paddy Chayevsky, who won't write for the theater any more.

Take the rock phase of the musical theater, for example. I like good rock as much as anyone else, but I also know it has no dramatic value. I know as a craftsman you can't explore character with it, can't dramatize nuances of feeling, can't phrase. That's one of the things that makes Fritz's music so marvellous: he phrases music so I can write the way we

> speak—"I've grown accustomed to her face." But when everything is at the mercy of sound, then the lyricist is a pawn. I think rock will gradually disappear from the theater. There are some fine rock composers, but there will never again be another "Hair" score that blew so much fresh air into the field.
>
> Yet many gifted young composers are contemptuous of the musical-theater form itself. The danger of revolt is always that a lot of good things are thrown out with the bad. The musical theater has been around since Offenbach, and there are certain pillars that hold up the house—things that make the great musicals—and they are always going to be there. My sadness is when I see someone who doesn't deserve it being overpraised while he is alienating people who have loved and supported the musical theater. The desire to attract the young has driven away a lot of people who have always cared about the theater. The theater has never been for one age group—and it never should be.

Finally, when asked whether *Gigi* would be the final Lerner-Loewe collaboration, Lerner responded: "I don't think so. I think Fritz will write again. I hope so. When I asked him a couple of weeks ago, he just said: 'Oh, my boy, I'm tired, I'm tired.' So I told him I'd mess around for a few months and then come back and see if he felt like doing something new. And that's what I'll do."

Meanwhile, the atmosphere on the set of *The Little Prince* had been tense almost throughout, as the following letter from Lerner to Stanley Donen reveals. Evidently Donen had heard that Lerner had been appalled by his liberal rewrites of the screenplay, and Lerner wrote to defend himself, while reminding the director that they needed to remain civil for the good of the film:

> *To Stanley Donen*
>
> May 11, 1973
>
> My dear fellow,
>
> Bob Evans[53] reported to me that you are in high dudgeon these days because it has reached your ears via Sam Spiegel that I am no longer a member of your fan club and that I have expressed doubts about your ability to make *The Little Prince* the picture I had hoped it would be. Or something to that effect.

[53] Producer Robert Evans (1930–) is responsible for hit films such as *True Grit* and *The Italian Job* (both 1969), and was head of production at Paramount.

It so happens that except for one brief nod at The Guinea in October I have not seen the redoubtable Sam since last August. However, I must confess that there have been a few other friends in the profession—namely, Kate Hepburn, Billy Wilder, Irene Selznick, Peter Viertel, John Kohn and Rex Harrison—to whom I have recounted my adventure in Tunisia, to wit: that upon my arrival I was handed a completely rewritten script that was dated a few days after I had left London the previous month. They seemed to be as appalled as I by your brutal disregard of professional ethics, especially when they all knew how enthusiastic I had been about our relationship up to that point. It would not surprise me at all if my little anecdote were repeated to others, including Sam.

And there you are. That is the whole story. And now, I suppose you'll rewrite it.

Really, really, Stanley! What did you expect me to say about you? Are you a nut, too?

Robert Coote is in London. I spoke to him before he left New York, and he is most anxious to do the picture. So please get in touch with him if you have not already.

I hope all is going well. What a fool I would be to hope differently. After all, it is not possible for me to have a hit and you to have a flop with the same picture.

Yours,
Alan

It seems there was also tension between Lerner and Bob Fosse, to whom the lyricist wrote the following letter:

To Robert [Bob] Fosse

May 11, 1973

Dear Robert:

I have spent a good part of the year writing you congratulatory notes, and in one of them I mentioned how marvelous I think THE SNAKE number is. What obviously happened was: you were too inundated with letters of acclaim you didn't read mine carefully—which is a shame because they are usually terribly well-written and frequently amusing.

Anyhow, I was delighted to hear from you and to know that even though I'm an author you are interested in what I thought.

Aye,
Alan

Shooting on the film was completed in late August, but Paramount decided to delay release until December 1974, intending it to be their big Christmas family film. This would allow further editing of the film to take place, as letters later in this chapter reveal.

The following is another example of one of Lerner's everyday letters that hint again at his personality:

To George A. Warde, American Airlines

October 20, 1973

Dear Mr. Warde:

Letters of complaint must be as boring to the reader as they are to the writer—even a professional writer such as I, and I would never have added my contribution had it not been for one of the American Airlines ladies at one of the airports—a lass I used to know years ago when I used to fly American Airlines. She asked me why she had not seen me lately and I explained it to her graphically. She took me aside and pleaded with me to write to the American Airlines office as a favor to her. It seems that the rudeness and brusqueness of the American Airlines stewardesses are quite well known and, according to her, I would be doing the decent people at American Airlines a favor by recounting to the management my experiences.

To put the matter in some perspective, I fly thousands and thousands of miles a year, and this is the first such letter I have ever written, or felt the need to write. Let me give you one or two examples of the "courtesy" of the American Airlines stewardesses.

1) Last year flying from New York to Los Angeles I discovered a friend of mine in economy. I was in First Class. During the flight I walked back to say hello. The stewardess in economy stopped me, literally blocked the passage and told me to return to First Class. I said: Do you mean I am not allowed to visit a friend in economy? She said, in the ice-covered tones of a storm trooper: Not on my plane. She said it so loudly that several rows turned around to see what was happening.

2) A few weeks ago I had to bring a small dog from New York to Detroit. I placed him in the proper box and told the stewardess I would hold him in my lap for a few moments to quieten his fears and then I would place him under the seat as I usually do on TWA or any of the airlines I have ever flown. Said the stewardess: This plane will not leave the ground until that box is under your seat, upon which she left and

returned with some tape to tape up the box. The last time this happened to me on American Airlines I got off and waited one hour and took TWA, where I had no trouble. Unfortunately, on this occasion I had to be in Detroit and I had no alternative but to obey the orders of this ill-mannered, unfeeling, intolerable creature. Needless to say, the dog threw up, and it was all rather messy.

I had two or three similar experiences several years ago and have successfully avoided taking American Airlines until recently. I read that the company is in the process of reorganization, and I can certainly understand why. I am on the road directing a play of mine, *Gigi*, and I have gone out of my way to make certain the company of some fifty people is never booked on your airline.

Returning from London via Pan American the other day, I found myself seated next to an American Airlines official, and I told him of my misadventures. He nodded sadly and said: Yes, yes, we know that happens. Please write.

I have no idea why American Airlines has successfully cornered the market on all the rudeness that flies in the skies. I can only say, Sir, that it makes "the good life" the emptiest of promises, and I cannot help but feel sorry for some of the more civilized personnel. It is on their behalf, I suppose, that I write.

Very truly yours,
Alan Jay Lerner

As Lerner mentions in this letter, he had been present at additional performances of *Gigi* on its tryouts in St. Louis, Detroit, and Toronto, where it played for three weeks before previewing at Broadway's Uris Theatre from November 7 and opening on November 13. In spite of Lerner's hard work, not only on the writing but also the direction (he had taken over from Joseph Hardy in Detroit), as well as the replacement of Terese Stevens with her understudy Karin Wolfe,[54] the reviews were sadly mixed, ranging from Martin Gottfried's rather crude "It is as big and stylish as a discount store" (*Women's Wear Daily*) to Douglas Watt's comment in the *Daily News* that the show "struggles to evoke once more the chic and rapture of the Lerner-Loewe film classic." The show closed in February 1974 after a disappointing 103 performances.

From this, Lerner moved on to one of the most potentially exciting collaborations of his entire career. Lerner's name had been linked with the composer Leonard Bernstein on at least three prior occasions: once in connection with a

[54] Karin Wolfe (1944–) is an American actress whose credits include the soap opera *Days of Our Lives* (1972–75).

possible musical in the late 1940s, once in 1957 when they wrote a celebratory piece for their alma mater, Harvard University, and very briefly when Richard Rodgers had dropped out of *I Picked a Daisy* (which became *On a Clear Day*). In the fall of 1973, they finally agreed to write a Broadway musical together. Although Bernstein had considered writing several shows in the 1960s, none of them came to fruition, so this would be his first musical since his masterpiece, *West Side Story* (1957). Its subject was to be a history of the White House, though its exact nature was yet to be decided. The collaboration was firmly in place, and in November 1973 Lerner wrote the following amusing message to Bernstein on the occasion of the composer's return to Harvard to give his famous Norton Lectures:

To Leonard Bernstein

November 19, 1973

Dear Son:

I want to congratulate you on your splendid record at Harvard. The Cambridge Police has notified me that you have broken the thirty day record for parking tickets. As for your liquor bills, they are still at M.I.T. being computed. And who is this girl Mary Juana? Why is she so expensive? Can't you find a nice, sensible Jewish girl? And what about graduating sometime? At fifty-four you should be able to make it now.

Amen.

Saint [Subber] and I went to see *Via Galactica*[55] the other night and I'm afraid we'd better forget about Peter Hall.[56] I cannot hold him to account for the imbecility of the material, but he is certainly to blame for the rank amateurishness of the presentation. Anything that could be done to kill any emotion he successfully accomplished. The demands of the scenery made it impossible to put the orchestra in the pit and as a result, the string section is somewhere behind a panel, the brass is in the ladies' room and there is a moog synthesizer (how do you spell it?) that I believe is telephoned in from across town. Any director whose priority list places the sets above the music is hardly our man.

[55] *Via Galactica* (1972) is a rock musical with music by Galt MacDermot, who had success with *Hair* (1967) and *Two Gentlemen of Verona* (1971). It ran only seven performances and is a notorious flop.

[56] Peter Hall (1930–) is a distinguished English director who founded the Royal Shakespeare Company in 1960 and was director of the Royal National Theatre in this period. He was married to actress Leslie Caron when she was filming Lerner's *Gigi*.

I spent a week in California on *Gigi* and now I am back and about to start on our opus. I know that in those cloistered surroundings the theater must seem light years away, but I couldn't resist dropping you a line.

Tobago was lovely. I can't wait for June.

If you get a chance, call me when you get back—if you come back.

Always,
Jean-Paul Lambeau

The show would eventually become *1600 Pennsylvania Avenue*, but it was still more than two years from completion. This time, Bernstein's busy concert schedule would be the main reason for the delay. Nonetheless, this jovial letter set the tone for what seemed to be a largely happy writing process, even though the production itself turned out to be another sad disaster for Lerner.

He started to draft the libretto in November, and progress had already been made by Christmas, at which point he wrote the following short message to Irving Berlin, who had by now become a good friend:

To Irving Berlin

December 21, 1973

Dear Irving,

It's very hard not to think of you most of the year, but it's impossible at Christmas.

I do hope you are well. I hope you have a lovely holiday. And I wish I could add to your life a particle of the joy you have brought to mine.

Faithfully,
Alan

Replying in February 1974, Berlin commented on the apparently perfect match of Lerner and Bernstein:

From Irving Berlin

February 6, 1974

Dear Alan,

I'm sorry to have waited so long with my thanks for your nice holiday message. Frankly, I've had one of my "let-downs" and it took me longer to snap out of this one. However, I feel much better now.

I was deeply touched by your note and thank you for your thoughtfulness.

I haven't had a chance to see *Gigi*. I understand it's doing well, but it is not the block-buster that I rooted and hoped for, but you seem to keep going.

I was interested and pleased with the news about your future plans, especially the show you are doing with Leonard Bernstein. He is one composer who not alone can read, write and conduct music, but can write a good tune. The man who wrote the lyrics for *My Fair Lady* and the guy who wrote the music for *West Side Story* is a pretty good combination.

Again, many thanks for your note and my best to you.

Always,
Irving

In the same period, Lerner also heard from Lehman Engel,[57] conductor of many Broadway shows and the author of a number of books on musicals. His latest volume focused on song lyrics, and he wrote to ask for Lerner's permission in reproducing some of his lyrics for the book. Lerner's humorous reply masks a curiosity about which lyrics were required (and ultimately he only gave permission for a portion of Engel's list of 23 lyrics to be included):

To Lehman Engel

January 8, 1974

Dear Lehman,

Not only did I not faint when I received your letter—I was overjoyed to hear from you—especially when you wish to offer me money, albeit only $10.00.

Your request to include some of my lyrics is, of course, rhetorical, providing the chapter on me begins: "Not since Robert Burns and the Cavalier poets..." but I expect that's what you intend to do anyhow. Naturally, I would most appreciate it if I could see the chapter before it goes to print, and suffice to say I wish you all the best luck in the world on the project.

Faithfully,
Alan

[57] Lehman Engel (1910–82) conducted numerous shows on Broadway, including *Li'l Abner* (1956) and *Take Me Along* (1959).

The first few months of the year were spent on three activities: continuing work on *1600 Pennsylvania Avenue*, trying to fight for changes to *The Little Prince*, and writing a series of "footnotes" for use in a "cavalcade of American music" to be staged by New York's City Center in April. The following letter to Irving Lazar, Lerner's agent at the time, reveals Lerner's feelings on all three musicals:

To Irving Lazar

March 14, 1974

Dear fellow,

Sorry I missed you in New York, but as I trust somebody told you, I was in Haiti for a week—which was very quiet, very sunny, and I got a lot of sleep and a lot of work done and enough color to blend in with the natives.

The show with Lenny is coming along great. We're having a marvelous time and about seven numbers are in various stages of completion. He goes on tour the beginning of July and we both feel the show will be finished by then. He returns in November for rehearsals.

I don't know whether you're up to date on *The Little Prince*, but although the overall picture is good, the first half is slow and the sequence when the Rose sings "Be Happy" is an absolute abomination. As a reflection of Donen's exalted view of love, women and mankind, the role is played by a hooker and sung and danced in a manner that can only be described as a cross between Carrie Fernell and Ann Corio. I'm not certain how Bob feels about it, but I *know* that Frank Yablans[58] is as revolted as Joe Tandet,[59] Fritz and I are, and we are trying to set up a meeting with him in New York to see what can be done. Donen refuses to change it, giving among his arguments that Peter Bogdanovich[60] thinks it's terrific. (No fool, Bogdanovich.) I'm sorry that you have not had a chance to see the picture because I can't believe that your own violent reaction wouldn't help.

[58] Frank Yablans (1935–) is a producer and screenwriter. He was president of Paramount from 1971 to 1975.

[59] A. Joseph Tandet (–2009) was an attorney and the associate producer of *The Little Prince*. He later produced another musical version of the story, *The Little Prince and the Aviator*, on Broadway, though it closed in previews. In 2008, he published a brief memoir of his exploits, called *The Lawyer and the Little Prince*.

[60] Peter Bogdanovich (1939–) is the acclaimed director of *The Last Picture Show* (1971). In 1975, he directed a cult flop musical film, *At Long Last Love*, which featured over a dozen Cole Porter songs.

City Center is doing a sort of five week celebration of American music of the twentieth century for which I supplied some footnotes. I hope for the sake of the City Center that it works. For myself, I couldn't give more of a damn.

I saw Gar[son Kanin] and Ruth [Gordon] the other night and they are tremendously excited about "Dreyfus." It sounds terrific.

I hope all is well Chez Lazar. Give Mary my love. I'll see you at the opening of Ascot.

Aye,
Alan

In any event, Lerner's ambivalence toward the City Center show was to be well placed. When it opened on April 11, the reviews were harsh, with Clive Barnes commenting in the *New York Times* that he was "surprised how close to all wrong the show came."[61] Lerner also came in for blame for certain aspects of the show's organization, and received, for instance, a letter from Burton Lane's lawyer, Arnold Weissberger, asking why Lane's name had not been credited since one of his songs was to be performed. Lerner wrote the following letter of defense, explaining that his participation in the show had been very marginal and was essentially an act of charity on his part:

To Arnold Weissberger

March 20, 1974

Dear Arnold,

The best way to answer your letter is by simply enumerating the facts, all of which, if you are so inclined, you can check with Chuck Eisler at the City Center.

1. I had absolutely nothing to do with the advertisement.

2. I have really very little to do with the whole project. I supplied a *very brief* connecting commentary which took me a few days to prepare. I passed by rehearsal once for five minutes and I have never even attended a full rehearsal—nor intend to.

3. It was only because of your letter that I really examined the ad at all.

4. I had absolutely nothing to do with the selection of the songs, but I do know Burton's name is mentioned and I believe something of his is being performed and I will check on it today.

[61] Clive Barnes, "Play: 'Music! Music!' from '95 to Now," *New York Times*, April 12, 1974, 22.

I also don't know why Stephen Sondheim's name isn't mentioned, although the show ends during the '60s before his last three hits. I know that something from *West Side Story* and *Gypsy* is being used.

In other words, I really don't know much about this thing at all—which is just the way I want it. What I did I did for the City Center, on the promise that I would not be bothered after handing in the script, because I am hard at work on another project.

But nevertheless, it *is* an outrage that Burton's name was not mentioned. Please assure him it had nothing to do with me. He has no greater fan than I, and I have always liked him more than he liked me.

The defense rests.

Affectionately,
Alan Jay Lerner

P.S. Since writing the above I called the City Center and found out that Dan Dailey broke his leg yesterday. Can Burton [Lane] do a time step? Or can you?

A week later, Lerner and Loewe were surprised to win the Tony Award for Best Score for *Gigi*—so much so, in fact, that neither attended the ceremony to accept the award.[62]

By May, much of *1600* had been drafted, but Bernstein was busy with the premiere of his new ballet with New York City Ballet choreographer Jerome Robbins,[63] *Dybbuk*. Lerner wrote to wish him good luck, as well as to speed him on his way back to work on the musical:

To Leonard Bernstein

May 15, 1974

Dear Lenny,

Blessings tonight. I can't wait to see it and hear it.

If Jerry [Robbins] wants any changes after tonight I'll put a contract out on him.

[62] Steven R. Weisman, "'River Niger' and 'Raisin' Win Tonys," *New York Times*, April 22, 1974, 46.

[63] As choreographer, director, and/or producer, Jerome Robbins (1918–98) worked on the hit musicals *On the Town* (1944), *The King and I* (1951), *West Side Story* (1957), *Gypsy* (1959), and *Fiddler on the Roof* (1964). He anthologized his own work in *Jerome Robbins' Broadway* (1989).

I'm starting the second act and waiting for you like Duse for D'Annunzio. The room is ready, the piano has been tuned, the plane is revved up and I have fired my children.

Hurry.

Always,
Alan

Lerner was obviously having a wonderful time with the show, and for once he was not responsible for its slow progress. Over the summer, he managed to work further with Bernstein, who held a press conference in September to announce the production. Don Oberdorfer of the *Washington Post* reported that the musical was "planned to celebrate the U.S. Bicentennial" in 1976, and Bernstein was quoted as saying, "The subject is the White House from 1800 to 1900, from the time it was built for John Adams until the time it acquired its name under Teddy Roosevelt....All this century is seen from the kitchen through the eyes of the blacks, who have been the only consistent inhabitants of that house. We are trying to tell that terribly important story of the little white lie that our country has been living with since its inception—by which I mean the big black lie."[64] In the end, the simplicity with which Bernstein explained the show's premise did not characterize the piece as it appeared on Broadway, but its strong theme explains both the composer and lyricist's desire to write the musical.

During the summer, Lerner also sent the following letter to a young writer, Ed Brown, who was trying to create a musical. Though the piece seems not to have made it to the stage, the letter is interesting for its insights into Lerner's varied thought processes about writing and putting on a show; it is also surely of note that whereas Lerner is sometimes portrayed as being self-absorbed in his career, this letter shows him giving extensive help, and criticism in a tactful way, without hope of any personal gain:

To Ed Brown

August 5, 1974

Dear Ed,

I enjoyed meeting you and your wife so much on Friday and I must say your entire project sounds fascinating.

[64] Don Oberdorfer, "Bernstein, Lerner Planning Musical," *Windsor Star*, September 6, 1974, 44.

Figure 6.2 Designer John Truscott, director Joshua Logan and Alan Jay Lerner look at a scale model of the set for the movie version of *Paint Your Wagon*. Credit: Photofest/ Paramount

I read the outline and listened to the songs over the weekend, understanding, of course, that the outline is only a beginning and its principal purpose at this point is only to give a background for the songs.

Let me begin with what I think is right about it:

The idea is theatrical and exciting and fresh. The music is, for the most part, first rate and, I think, captures some of the excitement of the theme itself.

Before I tell you what I think is wrong with it, I beg you to bear in mind that I am the fellow who turned down the dramatization of *Teahouse of the August Moon* because I didn't think it would work; and many years ago, when no less a figure than Moss Hart showed me the score for *The Music Man*, we both agreed that it would only be fair to the producer to advise him not to produce it. I offer these credentials to enable you to keep what I have to say in perspective.

1) I have found over the years—and used it in good stead—that when one has a fantastic story to tell that one wishes to be taken seriously, there must be a character on the stage that the audience can

identify with, who represents their disbelief. It is as if before the audience can say, "Oh, come off it," somebody on the stage does it for them and puts them at ease. As that character, through the dramatic action of the play, begins to accept the fantasy, seriously and emotionally, he brings the audience along with him. That character is missing. Without that character the fantasy becomes an obvious creation of the author. The people on the stage become the mouthpiece of the author. What one arrives at, then, is spectacle rather than drama. A recent glaring example of this kind of dramatic mistake was *Via Galactica*, directed by no less an artist than Peter Hall—and lasted one week.

2) Before a play can be about ideas it has to be about people.

3) Because in this case one is dealing with a legend that may, in fact, be rooted in some historical truth, it seems to me in order to do the nobility of that legend justice, the play should be written in a language that, whatever its style, cannot be colloquial. This is where, I believe, the lyrics fall short. The play is larger than life, which I love—but the language is in the contemporary idiom, which cheapens the high purpose.

4) My last point is personal rather than dramatic. The truth of Atlantis is much more fantastic than any fantasist can create. The tragedy of its decline and fall, if one is to believe the ancient myths, is a more pertinent lesson for our times than the one presented in this version. Simply stated, the legend is that a paradise was destroyed by greed and a lust for power. The souls who perished in the cataclysm of Atlantis have returned in the bodies of contemporary man and are being given another chance. It's a great theme. I long for that feeling to permeate the play.

The physical and visual ideas that you outlined for the production are marvelous. But first of all the play must be a good play. A number of years ago Abe Burrows[65] was directing his first play on Broadway. He called his friend George S. Kaufman[66] and said to him: "George, they want to use a treadmill in the play. Is that a good thing?" Kaufman thought for a moment and said: "What do they say on it?" That's my point.

[65] Abe Burrows (1910–85) was a leading figure on Broadway, working (as director and/or writer) on *Guys and Dolls* (1950), *Make a Wish* (1951), *Two on the Aisle* (1951), *Silk Stockings* (1955), and *How to Succeed* (1961).

[66] George S. Kaufman (1889–1961) was a playwright, director, and producer, with an incredible range of credits from writing material for the Marx Brothers to directing *Guys and Dolls* (1950). Of note is his book for Gershwin's *Of Thee I Sing* (1931) and his collaborations with Moss Hart and Edna Ferber.

I hope some of these notes may be of assistance. If you disregard them I won't blame you and with all my heart I wish you the greatest success.

Kindest regards to you and your wife.

Faithfully,
Alan Jay Lerner

With *1600* well on its way, Lerner made a last-ditch attempt in September to make improvements to *The Little Prince,* with which he and Loewe were both dissatisfied and which was due for release in November. First, he wrote to Stanley Donen to try to repair the relationship and to suggest a few changes that might help the film:

To Stanley Donen

September 25, 1974

Dear Stanley,

I saw the picture yesterday and I'm enormously encouraged. I think you did a terrific re-editing job and although it is obviously difficult to be objective at this point, especially when one views it alone and not with an audience, I do feel hopeful.

If you are still open for any minor suggestions, I would like to offer the following:

1) As the Little Prince goes from planet to planet—as you remember, Fritz wrote "Be Happy" as "flying music"—would it not be possible to use it? I do think it would be gayer and more fitting.

2) The Rose is so charming now that the dance is out, would you consider using both choruses of the lyric—or at least have her sing the first chorus while he is next to her and have the second chorus be heard as he gets farther and farther away from the planet? Or at least restore the verse to the song. I do think it would add more of a moment to their relationship.

3) There's no question that taking out "Matters of Consequence" was a good move. Unfortunately, as you undoubtedly know, there is an awkward blend when the Little Prince begins the scene with "Do they also eat baobabs?" Would it be possible to cut the baobab reference and begin with just eating flowers?

4) "I'm On Your Side" is much, much better. I just felt that the last chord could be held just a little longer and the end of the number extended two seconds to give it a finish.

5) "I Never Met a Rose" seems to work pretty well now, but what would you think of either:

a. Using the original orchestration and even though he puts the megaphone to his mouth, not let it change his tonal quality.

or

b. If you feel strongly about the Horace Heidt orchestration, at least keep the tonal quality even.

6) I wish you would reconsider that famous line being said by the Fox in the wheatfields. I know you have a cut of it with Kiley saying it himself and it really gives the line the importance it should have. It seems a little cutie-pie this way for so important a moment in the Pilot's character development.

7) When the Pilot first hears the laughter in the heavens it seems a little faint. I've heard it much stronger and I'm certain it would help.

8) The overture at the moment seems neither fish nor fowl. Wouldn't it be better to hear "Little Prince" and "Closer and Closer" in their entirety rather than a sort of mumbo-jumbo of themes? Personally, I wouldn't care if we just heard an establishment of "The Little Prince" theme and then played "Closer and Closer" over and over. It would make for a very gay beginning.

9) I think a couple of helpful snips could be made in the planets. The Napoleon line by the Historian, for example. And I wish we could tighten up the General.

Please think all this over, especially the overture and the wheatfield line, and try to forget the suggestions came from me. And congratulations again on all the work you've done.

Alan

Having received no reply, he then wrote to Frank Yablans, president of Paramount Studios, to suggest changes to the soundtrack album of the film that was to be released in conjunction with the movie:

To Frank Yablans

September 30, 1974

Dear Frank,

Nixon's representative told me that he had spoken to you on Friday and that I should send along suggestions for the album and that you would do what you could. They are enclosed.

Needless to say, I did not receive an answer to my letter to Mr. Donen (rhymes with Onan) which is about par for the course. I don't know if it's allowed, but last Thursday on Yom Kippur when praying for the dead, I mentioned his name.

Again, thank you for everything. You have in me a long-term municipal bond of friendship eager to be cashed.

Love to you and Ruth,
Alan

Notes on *The Little Prince* Album

1) I have suggested to Stanley that the opening overture music under the credits needs re-doing. If he does it, it will provide a perfect opening for the album. If he doesn't, we would be better off with no overture at all and begin the album with "I Need Air."

2) "I Need Air"—on the album it should be done without the verse, "It's A Hat" etc., and begin with the chorus "I Need Air." That means that to do a clean job it will probably require a 4 to 8 bar introduction to the vocal.

3) "I'm On Your Side"—in the film it is cut to one chorus. I would suggest that on the album the original two choruses be included.

4) "Be Happy"—the verse has been cut out of the film, plus the first chorus of the song. I think the album should include the verse and the two vocal choruses. I don't think any additional orchestration would be needed for that—but an ending will have to be added.

5) "You're A Child"—It will probably be able to stay as it is, although I have not heard the way it ends because the Lamplighter sequence is not in the film. It may need an ending.

6) "I Never Met A Rose"—there is in existence a marvelous orchestration that was used in the screen tests—the one used by Robert Goulet. I strongly, *strongly* suggest that it be used instead of the "rickety-tick" version that Donen uses in the picture. If there is any problem about matching Kiley's voice to it, we do have that orchestration on tape and I'm certain Kiley would come in and re-record it for nothing.

7) "Why Is The Desert"—I don't know how long it runs, but it will probably be all right as it is.

8) "The Snake In The Grass"—all right as it is, *minus* the one or two lines of dialogue that Donen added during the song.

9) "Closer And Closer"—The dance section should be edited out and what would help enormously would be the re-recording of one *full* chorus of the song in tempo. The orchestration is there, it simply has to be re-recorded for the album.

10) "Little Prince"—OK as it is.

All the changes suggested above could be accomplished in one three hour session with the orchestra in London. I don't know what the English recording rates are, but I will find out and send them along under separate cover.

Some of Lerner's suggestions were apparently adhered to, at least in connection with the editing of the film, and he was happy that some changes were made, as he wrote to the film's star, Richard Kiley, in October:

To Richard Kiley

October 10, 1974

Dear Richard,

I have been working so hard I did not notice your play[67] was opening.

Needless to say, I couldn't be happier about the results and your reviews. Congratulations!

I saw a re-edited version of the picture and it's 100% better. Whether it's "good" or just "better" is hard for me to say.

I'm off this weekend to Europe for a couple of weeks. I'll be in touch.

Love to Patty.

Aye,
Alan

But sadly, what had been intended as a great reunion for Lerner and Loewe was something of a critical disaster. Vincent Canby in the *New York Times* summed up the general opinion when he said that "it's too abstract and sophisticated to be of interest to most children and too simple-mindedly mystic and smug to charm even the most indulgent adult.... This score, the first Lerner-Loewe collaboration since *Gigi* and *Camelot*, is full of lovely things that are a total waste in these barren circumstances."

For his part, Lerner made his feelings about the film quite clear in *The Street Where I Live*: "[Loewe] wrote the most beautiful score, filled with melody and bubbling with the innocence of youth. Alas, it never was heard on the screen as he had composed it. The director, someone named Stanley Donen, took it upon himself to change every tempo, delete musical phrases at will and distort

[67] *Absurd Person Singular* is a play by Alan Ayckbourn that opened on Broadway on October 8, 1974.

the intention of every song until the entire score was unrecognizable. Unlike the theatre, where the author is the final authority, in motion pictures it is the director. And if one falls into the hands of some cinematic Bigfoot, one pays the price for someone else's ineptitude. In this case the price was high, because it undoubtedly was Fritz's last score."[68] The golden collaboration was over, and Lerner was frustrated because he believed their work to have been excellent. Certainly the finished movie is a disappointment compared to the heights of *Gigi*, but the eleven-track soundtrack album, now available on CD, reveals the high quality of the short creative burst brought about by the re-teaming of Lerner and Loewe.

[68] Alan Jay Lerner, *The Street Where I Live* (London: Hodder and Stoughton, 1978), 248.

CHAPTER 7

"I Remember It Well"

OLD FRIENDS, 1975–1980

Lerner spent much of 1975 working on *1600 Pennsylvania Avenue*, a project on which he and Bernstein placed great hopes. In August, he wrote to his fellow lyricist, Ira Gershwin, with whom he had worked on *An American in Paris* back in the early 1950s, to apologize for failing to appear in a tribute evening to him. He also described progress on the new show and confessed that it had kept him so busy that his correspondence had lapsed:

To Ira Gershwin

August 6, 1975

Dearest Ira,

I have been locked up for so many months with Lenny Bernstein on the show we're doing that I have hardly known what was going on in the world. When I came up for air a few days ago I found out about your evening, and I am heartsick that I didn't know about it and did not communicate with you on the appropriate night. Be that as it may—and unfortunately it is—all I can say is, instead of an evening it should be a national holiday, and I'm as sad I missed it as I am not knowing about it.

I think of you so often, so much more often than you know. I can't tell you how many times your name pops into the conversation. In spite of all the scrabble games I lost to you, you and Lee[1] and Roxbury Drive and the fun we had when the "group" was still all together will always be one of my most precious memories.

[1] Leonore Gershwin, Ira's wife.

> The new show is almost finished and, as usual, it's been a sweat. But it's been exciting working with Lenny. (Incidentally, even though we were at college together the first time we ever talked about writing together was in your house in 1951.) I haven't even wondered how it will do but I suppose underneath I feel the way I usually do; astonished if it's a success and outraged if it isn't.
>
> Please give my love to Lee. I don't think I will be out your way before rehearsals, but I hope to be sometime after the first of the year. I'll come by to give you a belated hug and either cry on your shoulder or get a hug in return.
>
> Devotedly,
> Alan

Lerner's letter suggests that although he wasn't sure of the quality of the piece, he had particularly enjoyed working with Bernstein. Significantly, given the musical's rapid demise on Broadway, many months had gone into the writing; this was not a show that had been thrown together quickly. Nevertheless, the composer and lyricist struggled to find backing for the production, partly because it was such an ambitious piece and partly because Lerner's recent projects (especially *Lolita* and *The Little Prince*) had all flopped. In August, the show even lost its producer, Saint-Subber,[2] who gave up when he realized the money was impossible to obtain and the script still problematic.[3] Lerner and Bernstein then turned to Roger L. Stevens,[4] a dear friend of Bernstein's and the chairman of the Kennedy Center in Washington, where the show was booked in for one leg of its out-of-town tryout. He agreed to produce the show with Robert Whitehead,[5] a Canadian who had helmed some hit plays and a couple of less-successful musicals.[6] In September Lerner managed to secure the backing of the Coca-Cola

[2] Arnold Saint-Subber (1918–94) established his career by producing *Kiss Me, Kate* (1948) and had a particularly fruitful working relationship with Neil Simon, seven of whose plays he produced. In 1973, he produced Lerner's *Gigi* on the stage.

[3] Jack O'Brian, "By…Jack O'Brian," *Schenectady Gazette*, August 28, 1975, 14.

[4] Roger L. Stevens (1910–98) was (like Lerner) educated at Choate and went on to become one of the most important theatrical producers of the twentieth century, a fact that won him a special Tony Award in 1971. Among his successes were *Cat on a Hot Tin Roof* (1955), *Bus Stop* (1955), and *West Side Story* (1957), as well as landmark revivals of *On Your Toes* (1983), *Death of a Salesman* (1984), and *She Loves Me* (1993).

[5] Robert Whitehead (1916–2002) enjoyed a long career on Broadway, producing works such as *A Man for All Seasons* (1961) and *The Prime of Miss Jean Brodie* (1968). His musical productions included *Goldilocks* (1958), *The Conquering Hero* (1961), and *Foxy* (1964).

[6] Tom Shales, "Tuning Up for '76, a Bernstein-Lerner Musical at the Center," *Washington Post*, September 17, 1975.

Company, which underwrote the entire production to the tune of $900,000.[7] Mel Gussow in the *New York Times* reported that "The Coca-Cola participation came about because of Lerner's boyhood friendship with John Paul Austin, board chairman of the Coca-Cola Company." Gussow also reported that Frank Corsaro[8] (best known for his operatic work) had been hired as the director and quoted Lerner as saying, "The show is primarily concerned with those moments when people tried to take the White House away from us.... I started thinking about it after the last election. The White House seemed to be getting rather remote from the country." Lerner also briefly described his collaboration with Bernstein: "Naturally any time you're writing with a new composer, or lyricist, you do influence each other, and you should, in order to produce a new voice of your own. With Lennie, I usually write the lyrics first. With Fritz [Loewe] I used to write the lyrics second."

But it was not to be the success that Lerner and Bernstein intended. From the very beginning, it was apparent that the musical was not quite ready to go into production. On the first day of rehearsals, January 21, 1976, the press were invited to interview the cast and crew, as was traditional, but Tom Shales's report of the event in the *Washington Post* hinted at the troubles to come: "It was a chance for composer Leonard Bernstein and lyricist-playwright Alan Jay Lerner to explain what '1600 Pennsylvania Avenue,' their new $900,000 White House musical, is really about. They didn't, but they tried."[9] He went on to say that "Much of [the press conference] was given over to arguments over what the play is trying to say." It also emerged that Ken Howard,[10] the actor who was to play nine of the American presidents over the course of the show, had been hired only a week earlier.

By all accounts, rehearsals were difficult, and the musical opened for its Philadelphia previews on February 26 to a mixed critical reception. William B. Collins complained in the *Philadelphia Inquirer* that it was "a big, long musical that makes the rest of us feel as bad as they do." Even worse, he referred to Lerner's "leaden lines" and Bernstein's "music to feel lousy by," and said the show's prospects were "bleak."[11] However, Jonathan Takiff's assessment in the *Philadelphia Daily News* was more balanced. "While I take issue with the

[7] Mel Gussow, "Coke Backs Lerner-Bernstein Show," *New York Times*, September 17, 1975, 38.

[8] Frank Corsaro (1924–) was a leading director at the New York City Opera from 1958, and later staged Handel's *Rinaldo* at the Metropolitan Opera (1984). He had directed several plays on Broadway, including Bette Davis in the successful *Night of the Iguana* (1961), but this was his first Broadway musical.

[9] Tom Shales, "'1600 Pennsylvania Avenue,'" *Washington Post*, January 21, 1976, B1–B2.

[10] Ken Howard (1944–) appeared in the successful Broadway musicals *Promises, Promises* (1968) and *1776* (1969) before *1600 Pennsylvania Avenue*.

[11] William B. Collins, "Giants of the Stage Produce a Puny '1600,'" *Philadelphia Inquirer*, February 27, 1976, 3-D.

pomposity and implications of Alan Jay Lerner's book, I find his lyrics chock full of wit, cunning and sharp insight," he wrote, adding that Bernstein "has wrought a musical mix that is highly eclectic and demanding, often endowed with brilliance."[12] Evidently, much work needed to be done: the first performance lasted a reported three hours and 45 minutes, and in Philadelphia both the director and choreographer[13] left the show (though their contribution had been praised in the Philadelphia reviews). They were replaced by Gilbert Moses[14] and George Faison,[15] both of whom had, in recent seasons, produced critically acclaimed work that dealt sensitively with racial issues. This was significant because the portrayal of the African American characters in the musical was one of its weakest elements. An hour was cut from the show before it reached Washington in March, but the number of presidents depicted was increased to thirteen from eight, thereby complicating the plot further.

Critical reactions to the piece improved in Washington, where the *Washington Post*'s appraisal was complimentary to the show's overall aims while admitting that "the play is still in a state of flux."[16] The *New York Post* even went so far as to announce that "The Potholes Are Gone from '1600 Penn Av.' " and reported that the opening night performance in Washington on March 24 "won enthusiastic audience acclaim."[17] The article continued: "It has had its troubles, but most of them appear to have been surmounted.... Both the book and the score were extensively reworked, and an official opening at the capital's National Theater was delayed twice to allow for more changes in the production." Suddenly, the show was deemed "light-hearted," "tuneful," "brisk," and "brightly colorful," and the article ended by stating that "Both the singing and dancing are superior to most musicals' opening nights."

But the New York critics disagreed when it finally reached Broadway on May 4, deeming it "a colossal embarrassment" (*Women's Wear Daily*) and "an impossible enterprise" (*Daily News*). The concept and staging never quite

[12] Jonathan Takiff, "Lerner & Bernstein's Stars & Gripes," *Philadelphia Daily News*, February 27, 1976, 34.

[13] The original choreographer was African American Donald McKayle (1930–), responsible for landmark musicals such as *Golden Boy* (1964) and *Raisin* (1974). He also choreographed the Disney film *Bedknobs and Broomsticks* (1971).

[14] Gilbert Moses (1942–1995) had directed the musical *Ain't Supposed to Die a Natural Death* in 1971, winning him a Tony nomination and a Drama Desk Award. He was later very active on television.

[15] George Faison (1945–) choreographed *The Wiz* (the hit African American version of *The Wizard of Oz*) earlier in 1975, as well as *Via Galactica* (1972)—ironic, given Lerner's disgust on seeing the latter show in its one-week run (see Chapter 6).

[16] Richard L. Coe, "On and Off the Avenue," *Washington Post*, March 25, 1976, C1–C2.

[17] "The Potholes Are Gone," 20.

worked, and in reply to a supportive telegram from his friend Katharine Hepburn, Lerner admitted defeat:

To Katharine Hepburn

May 6, 1976

Dearest Kate,

It was a lot better than when you saw it, but I guess all work and no play closes Saturday night.

Thank you so much for your telegram. I'll call you next week. I'd love to see you.

Always,
Alan

The show lasted just one week, and on closing night Lerner wrote a poignant note to his collaborator, communicating his grief at the disastrous reception the show had received:

To Leonard Bernstein

May 8, 1976

Dearest Lenny,

I'm sad this show has been the agony it has been for you. I have loved working with you, being with you—and I shall treasure our moments of excitement together always.

I can't say anymore. This day is a killer. And tonight a pogrom.

I hope we can work again—I do.

Love always,
Alan

Though *1600* had experienced a rough road to Broadway, Lerner did have something to celebrate. March 1976 saw a major New York revival of *My Fair Lady*, produced by Herman Levin, with whom Lerner had patched things up after their disagreements in the latter stages of the first Broadway run. The original designs, costumes, and orchestrations were adopted and only lightly tweaked for the revival, and both the original direction and choreography were revisited. Even Robert Coote returned to his old role of Pickering. Commenting on this approach, Levin said: "Outside of the fact that intelligent actors interpret their parts according to their particular abilities there is no change.... This is the classical musical show of the American theater. I think a classical musical has every right to be done over, just as a classical play is done."[18] The critics agreed with Levin's opinion: Clive Barnes said that the show "can still dance all night—and does," while Walter Kerr declared that there was "no reason why this shouldn't run as long as there's justice, and a thirst for lilting bewitchment, in the world."[19] Only a few weeks later, these same critics would describe *1600* as "tedious and simplistic" (Barnes) and a "moralizing bore" (Kerr), but at least Lerner could be proud of the continued success of his indisputable masterpiece from 1956.

Perhaps ready for something nearer the lightness of *Fair Lady* after the severity of *1600,* in June, Lerner hit upon the Melvin Frank[20] film *Buona Sera, Mrs. Campbell* (1968) as the basis for his next musical. The plot concerns an Italian woman who has slept with three American GIs within ten days during the War and is unsure which of them is the father of her daughter. She convinces all three to contribute toward the child's maintenance, but encounters problems when the men return to her village for a reunion and discover the truth. To write the score for *Carmelina,* as it would be called, Lerner turned one last time to Burton Lane, and Herman Levin came on board to produce, following their reconciliation during the *Fair Lady* revival. "I think his new lyrics are the best he's ever done," commented Lane of Lerner's initial work on the show. They had decided to finish the score and then write the dialogue afterward, so that "the score won't be cemented into the book," Lane continued. "And dialogue does come rather easily to Alan."[21] Work began in the fall of 1976, but in the winter Lerner departed for Australia to attend a conference on musical theater at the Sydney Conservatorium of Music; Stephen Sondheim[22] and Harold Prince[23] would be among the other participants.[24] During the journeys to and from the conference, he started another project, which turned out arguably to be his masterpiece of

[18] Richard Eder, "Levin Back on Street Where She Lived," *New York Times,* March 22, 1976, 21.

[19] Clive Barnes, "'My Fair Lady Is Restored to Broadway in Fine Form," *New York Times,* March 26, 1976, 20. Walter Kerr, "Stage View: 'My Fair Lady' Is 20 Years Stronger," *New York Times,* April 4, 1976, D1.

[20] Melvin Frank (1913–88) wrote or co-wrote the screenplays to the movies *White Christmas* (1954), *Li'l Abner* (1959; also directed), and *A Funny Thing Happened on the Way to the Forum* (1966; also produced).

[21] John Corry, "Broadway: Lerner and Lane Back Together Again for the Fourth Time," *New York Times,* March 25, 1977, 52.

[22] Composer-lyricist Stephen Sondheim (1930–) is the winner of eight Tony Awards, an Academy Award, and a Pulitzer Prize, among others. His musicals include *Company* (1970), *Follies* (1971), and *A Little Night Music* (1973).

[23] Harold Prince (1928–) is a legendary producer and director, whose rich body of work ranges from producing *West Side Story* (1957) to directing *Sweeney Todd* and *Evita,* two of the biggest Broadway hits of 1979.He has won 21 Tony Awards to date.

[24] Sally White, "Alan Jay Lerner Here in January," *The Age,* November 1, 1976, 2.

the decade: a memoir about writing *My Fair Lady, Gigi,* and *Camelot,* which would eventually become *The Street Where I Live.* The book was dictated to his secretary and later edited by Lerner in print form; this approach perhaps explains why some factual slips made their way to print, including a misquotation of part of his own song, "I Could Have Danced All Night."[25]

Back in New York, in mid-February 1977 he participated in a tribute to Ira Gershwin with various colleagues including Arthur Schwartz. Then in March Lerner and Lane announced *Carmelina* to the press, by which time about half of the score had been completed. Lerner had reverted to writing the lyrics after the music had been composed, in contrast to his approach with Bernstein, though he would not sit in the room while Lane wrote the music, which was his procedure with Loewe.[26] Bernstein came back into Lerner's life briefly when Goddard Lieberson, the beloved record producer, died of cancer on May 29. A close friend of both Bernstein and Lerner, Lieberson had also produced the original cast albums of *My Fair Lady* and *West Side Story,* among many others, and the composer and lyricist were devastated, as is clear from the following letter:

To Leonard Bernstein

[Undated; early June, 1977]

Dearest Lenny:

Your letter touched me so. I can't tell you how happy I was to hear from you. I have thought of you often and lovingly and only kept away because I did not want to remind you of last year's pain in the middle of this year's.

Oh, how terrible it is about Goddard. I was away for a week and only heard last night at midnight when I returned. Dear, dear chum—be happy. We are at the wrong end of time and I am determined not to waste a moment or miss an opportunity. We must, we must, we must.

Yes, I have gotten over *1600* because I am writing furiously. I have sold a book to Viking and I've about 1/3 finished a new musical. I'll tell you about it when I see you—after this agonizing week is over.

I'll be seeing you any minute, I suspect, but I wanted to write you first.

Thank you again for your sad, darling note. What a year!!

Always,
Alan

[25] Alan Jay Lerner, *The Street Where I Live* (London: Hodder and Stoughton, 1978), 90.
[26] Corry, "Broadway: Lerner and Lane Back Together Again," 52.

In July, Levin approached legendary Broadway director-choreographer Jerome Robbins to direct *Carmelina*. Although Robbins was ambivalent about the idea, he agreed at least to develop the show with them. But over the summer, Levin and Lane clashed, and the producer walked away. In October, Lerner wrote to Robbins to update him on the situation, and to propose Roger Stevens—who had been a staunch ally on *1600*—as a replacement for Levin:

To Jerome Robbins

October 19th, 1977

Dear Jerry,

Here is the play in its last version of the summer season.

The opening is still the way you first heard it, but that is only because I have not finished the new lyric. The way I am doing it now, it is exclusively Vittorio's number. I will quote the first two lines because they may give you an indication:

Twilight in San Forino—thank you, dear Lord.
All day in San Forino I am so bored.

He curses his fate having to stay in this poor excuse for a village, indicates the house wherein lives the reason he is there—then ends under her balcony imploring her to emerge. Instead, Fat Rose comes out. Then it goes on roughly the same.

In Scene 4, because the song for the three Americans is still vague, the dialogue leading up to it is also. That whole moment needs a total conception. I have a few notions, but we have not addressed ourselves to them as yet.

Without going into unnecessary detail, the question of management is now open. It was neither of my doing or desire, but unfortunately there was, shall we say, a clash of personality between Burt and Herman, and Herman decided as much as he loved the show, and as happy as he and I were to be working together again, he cared more for the level of his blood pressure.

If by any blessed happenstance we could join forces—meaning you, Burt and I—I am certain we could make an arrangement with Roger Stevens to take care of the sordid business. That is, of course, if you like him as much as I do. I believe he would give us the maximum support with the minimum of interference. I have never known anyone to behave better than he did when my recent ship went down.[27]

[27] That is, *1600 Pennsylvania Avenue*.

I was sorry to hear you were not feeling well and I hope it is both trivial and brief. I also hope reading the play will not dampen your enthusiasm. We can meet any day next week (or night) that is convenient for you. Until then—

Faithfully,
Alan

Stevens came on board as producer, and Robbins continued to discuss the show with Lerner and Lane, but in February 1978 he abruptly pulled out, citing lack of time and the fact that what he called the "light Mozart-Goldoni" aspect of the piece, which is what had interested him in the show, had failed to emerge.[28] This was a setback, and with the addition of casting problems, the show was not ready to open until 1979.

Meanwhile, Lerner had continued to send and receive his usual mix of business and personal letters. For instance, in October 1977 he received a request from Lotte Lenya, Kurt Weill's widow, to allow her to instigate a revival of *Love Life*, a piece of which she was apparently very fond. In his reply, Lerner admitted to having doubts about his own work on the show, perhaps compounded by its conceptual similarities to the recent *1600*, but made his affection for her, and for Weill's music, very clear:

To Lotte Lenya

October 27, 1977

Dearest Lenya,

I wish I loved the book and lyrics as much as I love the music.

What do you want to do with it? I ask only out of curiosity and not because your answer will condition my judgment. I could never say "no" to you, so automatically that means yes.

I will be in New York for the indefinite future and I am available to be consulted or ignored with equal affection.

Love,
Alan

[28] Letter from Jerome Robbins to Burton Lane, February 7, 1978, Jerome Robbins papers, New York Public Library.

He also replied to a request from fellow lyricist Sammy Cahn,[29] who was evidently planning a book on lyric writing and wanted to know what Lerner's favorite rhymes of his own writing were. Though Cahn did later publish a *Songwriter's Rhyming Dictionary*, it did not contain contributions from other lyricists, so it is interesting to see which of his own couplets Lerner was proud of:

To Sammy Cahn

January 24, 1978

Dear Sammy,

I don't know what to say. I have been moving and somehow your letter got put somewhere and I only read it over the weekend—two months late.

Am I too late to join the club? In the hopes that I am not, I am enclosing a one-page bio and a photo.

As for my favorite rhymes, I have never thought of myself as being particularly skillful at "clever-cleverness." If backed against the wall, however, I suppose I would choose:

"Besieged/Noblessly Obliged" [from "What Do the Simple Folk Do?," *Camelot*]

"Sport/Rigor Mort' " [from "The Seven Deadly Virtues," *Camelot*]

"Budapest/Ruder pest" [from "You Did It," *My Fair Lady*]

I think the idea for the book is marvelous. I hope to see you soon.

Faithfully,
Alan Jay Lerner

In April, he heard that Felicia Bernstein, the composer's wife, had been suffering from lung cancer and wrote to offer his sympathy (tragically, she died soon after on June 16):

To Leonard Bernstein

April 26, 1978

Dear Lenny:

I have been lost behind a pad for the past several weeks and only just heard about Felicia and what she has been enduring.

[29] Sammy Cahn (1913–93) won Academy Awards for his lyrics for the songs "Three Coins in the Fountain," "All the Way," "High Hopes," and "Call Me Irresponsible." Of his five Broadway musicals, only *High Button Shoes* (with Jule Styne, 1947) was successful.

What can I do other than say that I am thinking of you and her—with love and sympathy—and with impotent rage at the frivolous cruelty of whoever is up there.

Always,
Alan

He also started to pursue *The Little Prince* once more, this time from the point of view of publishing the songs in a readily available form. Some of them had been published individually at the time of the film's release but were now practically unobtainable. Lerner had always considered the score to be among his and Loewe's finest, yet little had been done to exploit it after the failure of the movie, so in this letter to his friend Charles Bluhdorn, chairman of the conglomerate that owned Paramount, he makes the first steps toward a possible songbook:

To Charles Bluhdorn

May 31, 1978

Dear Charlie,

I was so upset—as I know you were—about Stanley Donen's butchering of the script and score of *The Little Prince*, but it undoubtedly meant a great deal more to me because I know it was Fritz's last score.

I would love to try to do something with that score and I was wondering if there were any way I could acquire, by some arrangement, the publishing right from Paramount Music. At the moment the score just lies there fallow, of no use to anyone.

I am well aware that this sort of thing is undoubtedly handled by someone in a less exalted position than you, old friend, and I would be grateful if you would tell him to call me or tell me who he is so I can call him.

Comment va la famille? Bien, j'espere. I see your driver from time to time who tells me you are well and who always promises to send you my warmest regards. I hope he does. If he forgot,

Warmest regards,
Alan Jay Lerner

In the fall, *The Street Where I Live* was released to generally enthusiastic reviews, and Lerner publicized it internationally. For instance, he gave an interview in the UK-based *Guardian* in September in which he talked about his early ambitions to be a composer, his study of French and Italian literature at Harvard, and his love of writing poetry, topics that were not usually the focus of his discussions with journalists. He also contrasted Loewe's musical style with that of Gershwin, and explained how he loved Loewe's "chanson style which is marvelous for writing lyrics."[30] Mel Gussow's review of the book in the *New York Times* stated, "In a time when gossip can masquerade as literature, what a pleasure it is to encounter in print such an urbane and intelligent writer as Alan Jay Lerner.... Mr. Lerner is gentlemanly, demanding on himself and hopelessly in love with the theater."[31]

The nostalgia involved in revisiting the creation of his three great hits set the tone for various of Lerner's activities in the immediate future. The book brought him widespread acclaim, and the collaboration with Lane marked the continuation of a partnership that had started 40 years earlier with *Royal Wedding*. Columnist John Corry remarked: "The big Broadway musical frequently has been pronounced dead, and the talent that could put one together frequently has been thought to be off doing other things. Now there is 'Carmelina,' which will employ virtually all the talent you have ever heard of at work on a big Broadway musical, and which will open in New York at the end of March. It will have music by Burton Lane, lyrics by Alan Jay Lerner and a book by Mr. Lerner and Joe Stein.[32] It will also have Peter Gennaro[33] as choreographer, Oliver Smith as set designer and Donald Brooks[34] as costume designer. If you do not know what these people have done in the theater, then you simply have not been paying attention. If you do not know what the director has done, you haven't been paying attention at all. The director will be José Ferrer."[35] Plainly, Lerner had put behind him the disappointments of *Lolita* and *1600* and had joined forces with some of the greatest names in musical theater for *Carmelina*. The only marked difference with the project was the presence of a co-librettist (Joseph Stein, the award-winning book writer of *Fiddler on the Roof*). Having been criticized in recent times for his scriptwriting, Lerner was manifestly trying to make a difference here.

[30] Alex Hamilton, "A Good Word for Broadway," *The Guardian*, September 16, 1978, 11.

[31] Mel Gussow, "Books: Alan Jay Lerner Is Lyrical without Music," *New York Times*, November 25, 1978, 13.

[32] Joseph Stein (1912–2010) wrote the books for musicals such as *Fiddler on the Roof* (1964), and *Zorba* (1968).

[33] Peter Gennaro (1919–2000) choreographed *Fiorello!* (1959), *The Unsinkable Molly Brown* (1960), and *Annie* (1977), among others.

[34] Donald Brooks (1928–2005) was a fashion designer whose work on Broadway included *No Strings* (1962), the modern clothes for Lerner's *On a Clear Day* (1965), and Lerner's final show, *Dance a Little Closer* (1983).

[35] John Corry, "Broadway," *New York Times*, December 22, 1978, C2.

The next letter was probably Lerner's last of 1978. He had been asked to name his ten favorite living song writers for a book project and came up with the following list, which contains a preponderance of Broadway names (of these, he had worked with Bernstein, Lane, and Rodgers, and had discussed working with Bacharach and Styne) mixed with a couple of more contemporary figures:

To Carol Orsag, Managing Editor, The Book of Lists

December 26, 1978

Dear Ms. Orsag,

In answer to your letter about the Ten Best Modern Songwriters, I must assume that you mean the Ten Best Songwriters alive and writing. On that list, in alphabetical order, my choice would be:

1) Burt Bacharach
2) Leonard Bernstein
3) & 4) Kander & Ebb
5) Burton Lane
6) Richard Rodgers
7) Paul Simon
8) Stephen Sondheim
9) Jule Styne
10) Jimmy Webb

Sincerely,
Alan Jay Lerner

The New Year brought with it the excitement of the rehearsals for *Carmelina*. These started in the third week of January, and by now operatic bass Cesare Siepi[36] and Georgia Brown[37] (the original Nancy in *Oliver!*) had been cast in the lead roles, adding two more distinguished names to the lineup. Lerner wrote briefly to his friend, novelist Herman Wouk, to inform him that he would be in Washington in March. In spite of some typically self-derisory comments, he seemed quietly confident about the new show's chances of success:

[36] Cesare Siepi (1923–2010) was a world-class bass who was best known for his Verdi and Mozart roles. His two Broadway efforts (*Bravo Giovanni*, 1962, and *Carmelina*) were both disasters.

[37] Georgia Brown (1933–1992) was an actress and singer, best known for creating the role of Nancy in Lionel Bart's *Oliver!*

To Herman Wouk

January 31, 1979

Dear Herm,

I'm in the middle of rehearsal of a new musical (I must be out of my mind) so forgive me if this is brief.

1) Your book is terrific.

2) The musical, called *Carmelina,* is opening at the Kennedy Center on March 6th, so I will be in Washington all month unless chased out.

3) I have thought about "Marjorie"[38] many, many times over the years. Let's talk about it when I am there.

4) I miss you and it was good to receive your letter. All I usually hear from my old friends these days is thump, thump, thump.

I am not aging gracefully. I have lost a good deal of my charm but I am still very nice.

Can't wait to see you.

Faithfully,
Alan

But like *1600, Carmelina* was to have problems with its tone, book, and structure that would make the tryouts problematic. In anticipation of the March 21 opening in Washington, Lerner, Lane, Ferrer, and Stein gave a joint interview that attempted to paper over the problems. The show was destined to flop, but the interview contained some interesting comments from Lerner about the process of putting the show on the stage:

> I had been in Italy the summer before, three summers ago. I was in Capri, sitting on a rock and toasting and having a little vino and I thought, "My heavens, why don't I ever have this feeling in the theater any more?" Just ease and gentleness and charm and joy. When Burton mentioned "Lovers and Other Strangers" [a film that Lane had proposed for musical adaptation], the memory of that feeling bubbled to the surface again, and we settled on the subject that eventually became "Carmelina." The plot is a true story I had read in The London Times many years ago. We discovered a film had been made of it, "Buona Sera, Mrs. Campbell," which concentrated on the man, not

[38] Wouk's novel *Marjorie Morningstar* (1955) had been made into a film with Natalie Wood in 1958. Evidently, Wouk was proposing a musical treatment.

> the woman. Burton and I saw it together, and we both felt it should be about a woman who lives a lie for 16 or 17 years. In those little Italian villages, the widows are sort of the "duennas," and that's what was fascinating. This woman was the most respected lady in the community, but she was the widow of a man she made up. . . . We saw a play about a lovely Italian village, not three Americans. The woman has been living a lie like in a Goldoni play. It's a love story, too, because she has a lover, and she cannot say anything about it because she lives this chaste life as a widow. . . .
>
> I spent a lot of my youth in Italy. My mother lived in Venice. I had gone to Italy many, many times, so life in a little Italian community is not unknown to me. . . .
>
> [The music] has to have a little larger-than-life quality, like a Neapolitan street song. With the book and lyrics, too, the whole idea is not to write it so it requires an Italian accent, but to write it in that special cadence that Italian in English has. . .If it needs an Italian accent, it's written badly. . . .
>
> I first saw Siepi at the Met about 16 years ago in "Don Giovanni." I went every time he did it. I was so enamored of him I asked him to lunch and said, "If I ever have an idea for a musical, would you consider it?" He said, "Do I have to sing every night?" I said, "Yes, you have to sing every night." Time went by. One day my secretary mentioned him and I said "Oh my gosh." He happened to be passing through New York, so we made an appointment and as he walked in he said, "Well, it took you quite a while to think of an idea, didn't it?"[39]

The Washington reviews of the show were tepid ("*Carmelina* makes *Sarava*[40] look good," smirked Kevin Kelly in the *Boston Globe*),[41] but the Broadway premiere was fixed for April 8 and the production moved ahead as planned. Nervously, Lerner wrote to thank producer Stevens in advance of the opening, acknowledging his support on a second consecutive stressful project:

[39] Don Shirley, "'Carmelina' Is Rich in Creative Talent," *Sarasota Herald-Tribune*, March 16, 1979, 13C–15C.

[40] *Saravá* is a musical by Mitch Leigh and N. Richard Nash. It opened on Broadway on February 23, 1979, and ran for 132 performances.

[41] Kevin Kelly, "'Carmelina' Makes 'Sarava' Look Good," *Boston Globe*, March 28, 1979, 40.

To Roger Stevens

April 6, 1979

Dear Roger,

My affection for you runs so deep that the words could not come harder—even if it were a lyric. As far as this show is concerned, had it not been for your kindness and fairness I think we would have gone from the Kennedy Center to Menningers.[42]

So once again, I thank you. I hope your faith in *Carmelina* will be rewarded. God knows, you deserve it.

Much love to you and Christine,
Alan

Speaking to the *New York Times* a week before opening, Lerner confessed that he had, as usual, been agonizing over the lyrics of the show: "Yesterday I went all day on two lines. . . . I started at 6 a.m. and finished at 2 p.m. I won't tell you what the lines were. You'd think, 'How could that take so much time?' All right, I'll tell you: 'Why does he make my feathers fly / and get my dander up so high?' I was trying to find more lyrical ways of saying, 'Why does he irritate me so?' " He also commented on the opening scene and on the show's overall approach: "You have to tell the audience on what level it's going to be thinking and feeling that night. . . . 'Carmelina' uses the artifices of the *commedia dell'arte*. It's a romantic farce. I want to make the style clear"[43].

When the show opened on Broadway, it was to mixed reviews. But they were by no means as condemnatory as those for *1600* had been. Indeed, Clive Barnes in the *New York Post* said that "Lerner's lyrics twist in the sunlight of his invention—fantastic. Nowadays, only Stephen Sondheim has this gorgeous gift for lyric language." But he, and all the reviewers, had to admit that the show was professional yet old-fashioned. On a Broadway scene that was currently reveling in musicals like *Sweeney Todd* and the open-ended run of *A Chorus Line*, there was no place for *Carmelina* and it closed after a couple of weeks. Lerner summed up the situation simply to Irving Berlin in this short note:

[42] A psychiatric hospital.

[43] Eleanor Blau, "Lerner and Lane Make Music Again," *New York Times*, April 1, 1979, D7.

Figure 7.1 Clint Eastwood, Alan Jay Lerner, Joshua Logan, Lee Marvin, and Jean Seberg in a publicity shot for the movie *Paint Your Wagon*. Credit: Photofest/Paramount

To Irving Berlin

April 12, 1979

Dear Irving,

It was so sweet of you to think of me on opening night.

Unfortunately, it turned out to be an occasion that required more courage than humility. However, fool that I am, I will be at the post soon again.

My affection always,
Alan

If his confidence was knocked by the obvious disappointment of *Carmelina*, Lerner was soon to be comforted by yet another nostalgic event. On May 14, a benefit for the Theater and Music Collection of the Museum of the City of New York brought together a stellar cast for by far the biggest celebration of Lerner and Loewe's talents that they would ever witness. Julie Andrews and Rex Harrison performed numbers from *My Fair Lady* and danced together for the first time since they had left the original London production; the other participants included Louis Jourdan, Hermione Gingold, John Cullum, Alfred Drake, George Rose,[44] Kitty Carlisle Hart, and Reid Shelton. The evening closed with Lerner reading from *The Street Where I Live* and performing three numbers with Loewe at the piano: "If Ever I Would Leave You," "They Call the Wind Maria," and "Camelot." The gala was extraordinary for Lerner, who admitted that "I would be lying if I did not say I was touched and honored.... But the special occasion for me is to be on stage with Fritz Loewe again after all these years."[45]

The lyricist wrote to thank all of the participants personally after the night: reproduced below are his letters to Douglas Fairbanks Jr. (who performed "Thank Heaven for Little Girls"), Julie Andrews, Agnes de Mille (who restaged and introduced two dance numbers from *Brigadoon*), and Anna Sosenko, who was responsible for putting together and producing the entire evening. Sosenko had hired Lerner as a radio scriptwriter at the very start of his career, so it was particularly appropriate that she should be in charge of this tribute almost four decades later.

To Douglas Fairbanks

May 17, 1979

Dear old chum,

How can I ever thank you for helping to make Monday evening the most memorable night of my life?

Aside from the charm and artistry of your performance, there was that special affection, tempered by years and years of friendship that came over the footlights and gave me that extra warm feeling that—well, I might as well say it—brought tears to my eyes.

I don't know or understand why you did not receive the letter I sent you after the opening night [of *Camelina*] thanking you for both your telegrams. It will probably turn up one day. I remember saying that it was unfortunate that the opening night turned out to be an occasion for courage and not false humility.

It was so nice for Fritz and me to be able to spend a little time with you and Mary Lee at Irene's on Tuesday night and I look forward to our lunch in June.

[44] George Rose (1920–88) was an English actor who first appeared on Broadway in 1946 in a production of *Henry IV, Part One*. For Lerner, he played Greff in *Coco* (1969), for which he received a Tony nomination, and then won a Tony for playing Alfred Doolittle in the revival of *My Fair Lady* in 1976.

[45] Judy Klemesrud, "A Broadway Gala for Lerner and Loewe," *New York Times*, May 15, 1979, C12.

I only hope that Fritz remembers he lives in Palm Springs and finds his way home.

Thanks again, old boy. It was a special evening because of special people like you.

Devotedly,
Alan

To Julie Andrews

June 11, 1979

Dear, dear Julie,

Forgive me for not writing you sooner, but I left for Europe a couple of days after that evening that you helped to make so memorable.

I suppose in many ways it was the most moving night of my life—in fact, it was like seeing half my life all over again.

You were as lovely as ever and my only regret is—as I said in my book—that you are not in the theatre where I could see you as often as I wished.

Thank you for the effort and the joy. My blessings are with you always.

Love to you and Blake [Edwards].

Aye,
Alan

To Agnes de Mille

June 11, 1979

Dear, dear Agnes,

Forgive me for not writing you sooner, but I left for Europe a couple of days after that evening that you, more than anyone, made so memorable for me.

I cannot tell you how moved I was, not only by the fact of your being there, but the words you spoke. Fritz and I were sitting together at the rear of the theatre and I found myself clutching his arm to keep from making a slobbering ass of myself.

No one knows better than I how much you contributed to Fritz's and my career, and if I never told you before how grateful I am to you, let me do so now.

Oh Agnes, dear Aggie—I don't mind getting older, but I do miss the beginnings.

Bless you and thank you.

Much love,
Alan

To Anna Sosenko

Dear, dear Anna,

Little did I think, when I left your employ way back in the 16th century to hurl myself into "la vie du theatre" with Fritz, that it would be you who would sum up our career and give me the most rewarding, moving, beautiful night of my life. For there's no doubt that what you did for us on the stage of the Winter Garden Theatre was all of that and more. How can I ever thank you?

When you told me months and months ago what you intended to do and the galaxy of talent you intended to corral, I did not think it would be possible. I guess I had forgotten what a determined, incredible lady you are and what a fantastic theatrical flair you have.

It was a stunning night, one I will never forget, and one for which I will always be in your debt and humble at your feet.

When can we do it again?

Bless you and thank you from the bottom of my heart.

Much love,
Alan

Lerner also alludes to the gala in the following letter to J. W. Fisher, one of the co-producers of *Carmelina*, who had written to Lerner in the hopes of resurrecting the show, perhaps in London. It is clear from Lerner's response to this suggestion that he was angry at not having been heeded more during the tryout period, and that he felt the show could have been improved and turned into a success with his guidance:

To J. W. Fisher

May 17, 1979

Dear Bill,

I'm so sorry for the delay in answering your letter. It was so touching and filled with so much hope and good will that it deserved an instant reply. Unfortunately, I was in the hospital for a week (nothing serious—a bad infection in my leg that had to be drained) and the moment I was released from medical bondage I was thrown into the preparations for the Tribute to my dear old partner Fritz Loewe and me that took place at the Winter Garden Theatre last Monday night for the benefit of the Museum of the City of New York. It was one of the most memorable evenings of my life and I dearly wished you had been there.

Seeing Rex and Julie Andrews, Louis Jourdan, Hermione Gingold, Alfred Drake and all the people we have worked with over the years on one stage made for a joyous and emotional reminder of how wonderful the theatre can be. After strolling over the hot coals with me for all those weeks it would have given me such pleasure to have been able to share the evening with you.

As for the future of *Carmelina,* I have too much respect for you not to be completely honest. I only hope that in doing so it will not be misconstrued as egomania.

I have never known a musical where the fixing was as possible and the doing as impossible. Unfortunately, the same impossibility still exists. As long as the management refuses to look at the track record and decide whom to bet on, there is no way of making *Carmelina* the musical experience that it was inches away from being.

Let me be more precise. *Carmelina* was not a traumatic, shattering experience for me. It was a frustrating and aggravating one. It was my 14th musical. I have won Drama Critic's Awards, three Tony Awards and three Academy Awards. Of the seven musical films that have ever won Academy Awards, I have written three of them. In the theatre, had someone invested in every show I have ever written, he would have made 42 times his investment. I have produced and/or co-produced four musicals, including *My Fair Lady* and *Camelot.* Yet all that experience was equated by the producers with that of a man of glaring emotional instability, who has only written three shows in his entire life, one of which was *Carmelina.* I suddenly found myself regarded as part of a team of "tempermental nuts."

When it became apparent there was an obvious stalemate between the librettist and the composer, none of the producers looked at the track record and made what would have seemed to me an inescapable decision of whom to follow. If the composer refused to co-operate, a request to the Dramatist Guild would have settled the matter once and for all and the composer would have been sent home. In other words, had I been you, I would have told Mr. Lane to either co-operate or leave.

I have no idea what lies in the future for *I Remember Mama*, but—parenthetically—it is interesting to note that the morning after it opened out of town, when a difference of approach between the composer and the lyric writer became apparent, it did not take the producer very long to make a judgment. He did not send Richard Rodgers home. They replaced the lyric writer, Martin Charnin.[46]

A show is fixed as follows: Find the trouble spot. In our case, it was the first ten minutes. And write immediately. When Fritz and I were uncertain, we would try one way, then another way, then another way, until a solution was found. Out of town with *Paint Your Wagon,* 6 songs were written in 10 days. Two were discarded, four were retained. In *Camelot,* with Moss Hart, our director, in the hospital, I rewrote the entire play from scene two to the penultimate scene in the second act. Moss Hart sent word from his oxygen tent that he wanted no one to direct the play but me, so I did as I was bid. Two new songs were added. One was dropped. A new set was built and all the work was accomplished in four weeks. True, it was never a perfect play, but I can assure you it was far closer to the mark than *Carmelina.* In the case of *Camelot,* there was no problem with the management because Moss, Fritz and I were the management. The second week we were in Washington, Jose Ferrer wanted to quit. He told me so. The reason for his discouragement was the creative stagnation and because he himself had no strong opinion that might have tilted the scale.

Can *Carmelina* be rewritten until it realizes its obvious potential? My God, yes! Joe and I could probably do it in a week—if proper musical assistance was brought in, not necessarily to write any new songs, but someone with enough musical knowledge to fill the theatre with Neapolitan street music instead of those zippy 1928 orchestrations.

But none of this will happen. I know it. And therefore I cannot help but be pessimistic. I love *Carmelina.* It should have been an enchanting evening. It could have been, but it never will be.

I think that *Carmelina* would fare even worse in London than it did in New York. The essential element in the musical theatre today is style. *Sweeney Todd* is a brilliant triumph of style over content. In England there is an acute awareness and appreciation of style, even more so than here. The man who could have given *Carmelina* the style it required was

[46] Ironically, Lerner's argument here does not help him, because *I Remember Mama* was a huge flop, running just 108 performances in 1979. Charnin both wrote and directed the show, and it was his replacement as director that was more significant.

the director Frank Dunlop,[47] who did *Scapino* so brilliantly in London and then New York. He heard *Carmelina,* loved it, understood it and wanted to do it. He was rejected by Mr. Lane.

No, dear Bill, my suggestion is to leave it alone and hope that Ernie Martin, who seems to love it so dearly, will decide to schedule it as part of the Los Angeles Civic Light Opera season next summer.

I'm sorry I cannot be as enthusiastic as I know you would like me to be. It is not a role I come by easily or naturally. But as I said in the beginning, I felt I owed you my honest opinion.

You are a wonderful man and the theatre needs more like you. I dearly hope that this experience will not discourage your continuing participation.

Faithfully,
Alan Jay Lerner

The lyricist had decided to move on. Since nostalgia rather than innovation was the order of the day, Lerner was fully supportive of the suggestion of reviving *My Fair Lady* with Rex Harrison and *Camelot* with Richard Burton—the return of the original leading men to Lerner's two most successful stage musicals. *Camelot* was slated for 1980, with *Fair Lady* to follow the next year. Lerner was plainly thrilled at the thought of Burton returning to the role of Arthur in particular, and never hid his opinion that the actor was definitive in the part. When the possibility of the *Camelot* production arose in June, he wrote to Burton with the theater and movie scripts and explained that he proposed to tighten the piece if the actor agreed to appear in it:

To Richard Burton

June 25, 1979

Dear Richard,

Don Gregory[48] and Mike Merrick[49] got in touch with me on Friday and told me to send you a script of *Camelot.* The fact that there is even a modicum of hope was enough to give me a three day high.

[47] British director Frank Dunlop (1927–) held positions at the National Theatre and the Young Vic Theatre, which he founded in 1969. His play *Scapino* was based on a character from the commedia dell'arte and toured the world, including New York. He went on to direct a major revival of *Camelot* with Richard Burton in 1980.

[48] Don Gregory (1934–) is a Broadway producer with credits including *Clarence Darrow* (1974), *The Belle of Amherst* (1976), and the Lerner revivals discussed in the remainder of this chapter.

[49] Mike Merrick produced *Camelot* (1980) and *My Fair Lady* (1981) with Don Gregory, and has worked with various other companies including the Royal Shakespeare Company.

Having been out of the country so much over the last ten or twelve years, I wonder if you realize the almost legendary proportions that *Camelot* has taken on. Undoubtedly, a good deal of it is due to its identification with the Kennedy legend, but a great deal of it is due to the score and the cult that has grown up among those who were fortunate enough to have seen you in it. Only two weeks ago on TV there was one of those movie dramas about a man who became unhinged following the Kennedy assassination and during the entire two hour show he constantly sat at the phonograph listening to you sing *Camelot*. There is hardly a day goes by when there is not a reference to it in the newspapers. My son, who is at college, said to me recently: Dad, maybe you think you are known for *My Fair Lady*, but I can tell you that with the kids I know it is because of *Camelot*.

In short there is an overwhelming audience longing to see you in *Camelot*—most of them to see you for the first time. When one considers what happened to Yul Brynner and *The King and I*,[50] there is no question that Richard Burton in *Camelot* would be the largest theatre attraction in modern times—even more than Rex in the revival of *My Fair Lady*.

In perusing the script after all these years, I found several places where, with a little bit of work, I could strengthen some of the scenes. I started to indicate them in the script but then decided to wait to hear from you. There were also several moments in the film which I would like to incorporate, ergo, I am enclosing the movie script also.

In thinking back over the original production, I think great mistakes were made in the designing of the sets and costumes. I would like to get more of the rugged, Dark Ages feeling into the show and a little less Disneyland. But again, more about that, if and when.

We missed you at the Lerner and Loewe night at the Winter Garden last month. It was an incredible evening and I know you would have enjoyed it.

Please give my warm regards to your dear wife and I look forward to hearing from you.

Aye,
Alan

[50] Yul Brynner (1920–85) was the original star of Rodgers and Hammerstein's *The King and I* (1951). In 1977, he headlined a major Broadway revival of the show, which became a commercial success, and he took the show to London in 1979.

The *Fair Lady* revival was a little more complicated. It was Harrison's special ambition to take the show back to London as well as Broadway. But the British producer Cameron Mackintosh[51] had just put together a production of the musical that was touring the British provinces, subsidized by the British Arts Council, and he now wanted to bring it into the West End. Lerner had not been expecting this, but when he was invited to take over the direction of the production and tighten some of the performances, he was genuinely excited. However, he was unhappy with some of the musical changes that had been made to the show, particularly in the dance music, and wrote to insist that they be put back if he were to take on the job of director:

To Cameron Mackintosh

July 25, 1979

Dear Cameron,

I was delighted by the news—and deeply impressed with your hustle. I know that you are Scottish, but you must have some Jewish blood somewhere.

I am reasonably optimistic that with co-operation from the cast and an intractable point of view, which I have, the performances can be sharpened, made more exciting, more romantic, and—if you will—more Shavian (as I see it). I can only hope Peter Bayliss[52] can be persuaded to join the company.

What I am deeply concerned about, however—and this is really for Gillian[53]—are any and all changes that were made that changed the music. The intrusion of another style of orchestration, which happens any time the fundamental arrangement was not based on a Loewe composition, cheapens the entire production and, I am convinced, is an invitation to flying brickbats. I do not mind the shift in the ballroom sequence, and I do understand the scenic problems in returning it to its

[51] Sir Cameron Mackintosh (1946–) is the most successful British musical theater producer of all time, with credits including *Cats* (1981), *Les Miserables* (1985), *The Phantom of the Opera* (1986), *Miss Saigon* (1989), and *Mary Poppins* (2004).

[52] Peter Bayliss (1922–2002) was a British actor whose work included appearing in *The Matchmaker* (1956) in New York, in *The Red Shoes* (1948) and *Darling* (1965) on film, and numerous television programs. Mackintosh did succeed in attracting him to the production of *My Fair Lady* for the role of Doolittle.

[53] Gillian Lynne (1926–) is a veteran British choreographer, perhaps most closely associated with her work on *Cats* (1981) and *The Phantom of the Opera* (1986).

traditional spot at the end of Act I, but tell Gillian that somehow a way must be found to preserve the "Embassy Waltz."

This is also true of "Get Me To The Church On Time." The attempt to individualize is admirable and I am sure would be more successful if it were done to the original music. Gillian must give her creative attention to reshaping that number. I probably would feel a little softer about it if it were more successful than the original version, but it is definitely not. There is a very structured shape to that production musically that was created by a genuine composer who knew what the hell he was doing. It must be restored.

I told Fritz, as lightly as I could, that there had been a few added modulations and his blood pressure rose alarmingly. It is one thing for changes to have been made when neither of us knew about it. If he thought that I would be involved in a production that would countenance the dismemberment of his music, I think he would have every justification for lopping my head off.

I say all this not because I am a traditionalist, but because I know that the musical fabric has been seriously discolored by the changes that were made, and the show has suffered accordingly. To me it is no different than if someone came along and rewrote the lyrics to "Get Me To The Church On Time."

The restoration of the music bears very strongly on the amount of help I can give. So please, please give it your first priority.

I'll call you on Monday and, knowing you, I'm certain you will have solved everything by then.

Aye,
Alan

Rex Harrison was palpably upset about the Mackintosh production, since he realized that it would be impossible for him to bring his version of the show to London at the same time, but Lerner wrote to comfort him that the public would always be interested in seeing Rex Harrison in *My Fair Lady*. Toward the end of the letter, he also mentions a project with Michel Legrand[54] (to be called *The Mountains of Peru*) on which he was planning to work, though it never came to pass:

[54] Michel Legrand (1932–) is a French conductor and composer. He wrote the musical *The Umbrellas of Cherbourg* (1964) and won an academy award for the song "The Windmills of My Mind."

To Rex Harrison

August 3, 1979

Dearest Chum,

I know you and Mercie[55] must have had a glorious trip and I can only tell you that sitting here in this sweltering city and thinking of you strolling the deck of your personal QE2 put a hell of a strain on our friendship.

I was in Europe at the beginning of the week and passed through London for one day and heard about (and read about) this irritating production of *My Fair Lady* that now seems to be coming into the West End. At the risk of boring you with details which you may already know, let me review quickly the background of this production.

Two or three years ago it was the idea of Cameron Mackintosh and some of his associates to create some kind of government-sponsored repertory of well-known examples of the musical theatre. To that end, he was able to persuade the London Arts Council to support him. All very noble, so far. It was decided that *My Fair Lady* was to be the first production of this new experiment. They wrote to Fritz and me and we saw no reason to withhold the rights. I personally felt it was very healthy for the musical theatre in general. We gave them our blessings along with a contract. In that contract, I may add, they were given the right to bring the show into the West End, if they decided to do so. There is no loophole in the contract that would make it possible for us to withdraw that right. I might further add that the London Arts Council contributed £150,000 towards the financing—a goodly sum. All of these arrangements took place almost a year before Merrick and Gregory came to you with the idea of reviving *My Fair Lady* with you recreating your original role.

In June, after we saw it in Nottingham, I had a rather tense and lengthy session with Mackintosh in which I told him how I felt about what we saw. I could not insist that he not bring it to London because, as I mentioned above, I do not have that right. I told him in no uncertain terms, however, that I thought the entire affair was disgraceful and he would be leaving himself open to a barrage of criticism. I told him it would not be *My Fair Lady* that would suffer—the judgment is already in on that—it would be he and his production. About a fortnight later when I was back in the States I received a phone call from him telling me

[55] Harrison was married to Mercia Tinker, his sixth wife, from 1978 to his death in 1990.

that they could not procure a theatre. I sighed with relief and thought that was that.

To my astonishment, I received a call from him a week ago informing me that he had indeed found a theatre, the Adelphi, and he intended to open his production in London on October 11th.

So now the dilemma became mine. Do I help and try to improve the show before it comes in, or do I simply let it sail into London and sink to the bottom? What disturbs me is that there is always the possibility that it will not simply sink to the bottom because it is *My Fair Lady* and there is a whole generation that did not see the original. However, I am convinced that at the very best it could not possibly run more than a few months.

Nevertheless, it seems to me that should you, two years after playing in the States, decide to bring it to London, Mackintosh's production, or any other production, cannot possibly influence the success of Rex Harrison in *My Fair Lady*. If Mackintosh's version receives bad reviews, when you open everyone will say: at long last, here is the real *My Fair Lady*. If he gets away with it, when you open the reaction must be: if you thought you saw *My Fair Lady* two years ago, you had better come and see it with Rex Harrison. Although I do not mean to compare *My Fair Lady* to *Hamlet*...for argument's sake, if there is a bad production of *Hamlet,* it never prevents people from coming to see a good one.

The one thing I personally do care about is that any production that comes to the West End not be tasteless and vulgar, and Mackintosh's is. As long as he has a theatre, I have pleaded with him to remove what I consider vulgar, and at least present it decently. Mainly, I would like the songs well-sung so that this new generation can't say the score is overrated. Other than that, I frankly don't give a goddamn what happens, and in all sincerity, neither should you. If I were you I would not waste one sleepless moment on it. It is not worth it. You are impervious. You are operating on a level so far beyond this that there is no way your production could be affected. It isn't even worth saying: it's too bad. It is not even a pain in the ass. As far as you are concerned it is nothing. Absolutely nothing. And it you ever think differently, I beg you to remember again that night at the Winter Garden theatre in May, just two years after a rather successful, tastefully produced revival of *My Fair Lady,* and how, when the audience heard you say "Damn, damn, damn" there was an ovation the like of which I cannot recall in the theatre, and they hadn't even seen you yet! If you think anybody in the world can damage that magic, I suggest you change wines immediately.

So please, old boy, dismiss Mr. Mackintosh from your mind. I have told him in no uncertain terms to hold his tongue as far as the press is concerned or I will publically wash my hands of his effort. The only reason I am reluctant to do so now is because of the participation of the London Arts Council.

As you have undoubtedly heard, all the necessary approval was given for Patrick Garland.[56] I understand when I first expressed my reservations, you misunderstood that expression as a sign that I would not approve of him. We must not have any more of that. We have known each other too well and I believe our friendship is too strong for me not ever to be totally frank with you at all times. If I was really trying to say no, believe me, I would have said it. I would expect no less from you. Of course, we are bound to have differences of opinion as we go along. But I am always on your side and you will never have to read between the lines to divine what it is I am trying to say. If I am not clear, ask me point blank—and I will do the same with you. If I am ever not detailed enough in my reasons for or against something, please tell me and I will try to be more explicit. You and I went through *My Fair Lady* together without one unpleasant word between us and there is no reason why that should change now. And it won't. I love you, and you know it.

I hear you are playing a German general in Ireland. No doubt an imitation of Franz Allers.[57] I am so pleased he will be able to help us.

In two weeks I will be off to Paris to start work with Michel Legrand. I think we have found an interesting subject. I will be there well into the autumn. As soon as I know my address I will pass it along to you and maybe we can join up somewhere for "a jaw over supper."

Give my love to Mercie. I can't wait for next August. Have a nice Ireland and I'll see you very soon.

Affectionately always,
Alan

P.S. I must tell you I think that Merrick and Gregory are terrific. I've had several meetings with them. I love their enthusiasm. And I have great

[56] Patrick Garland (1935–2013) was a British director whose many credits include two stints as the artistic director of the Chichester Festival Theatre. He directed the musical *Billy* (1974) in the West End.

[57] It is not entirely clear who the "German general" was that Lerner referred to, but clearly he is making a joke about Franz Allers (1905–95), the German conductor of the original production of *My Fair Lady*, whose relationship with Harrison was tense.

respect for their professionalism and determination. I think we're in good hands.

Lerner's comments about the Cameron Mackintosh revival of *Fair Lady* in this letter are evidently exaggerated in order to calm down Harrison. In truth, the London revival was a great success for all involved, and it also introduced Lerner to his eighth and last wife, Liz Robertson,[58] who played the role of Eliza to enormous acclaim in the production. The *New York Times* called her "a dazzling new Eliza Doolittle" and "unquestionably a star."[59] Among the many good wishes Lerner received for opening night, probably the most poignant came from Stanley Holloway, the original Doolittle, whom Lerner wrote to thank. The return to London and to *My Fair Lady* ended a troubled decade on a high:

To Stanley Holloway

November 2, 1979

Dear Stanley,

As Eliza would say, "How kind of you to think of me." I showed your telegram around to everyone and they were all as touched as was I.

The show went beyond my wildest expectations, but *My Fair Lady* is never the same without you.

My love to the family and to you always.

Faithfully,
Alan

[58] Liz Robertson (1954–) is a British actress whose many credits include *I Love My Wife, Song and Dance, The Music Man,* and *The Phantom of the Opera* in London.

[59] William Borders, "A New Fair Lady Delights London Theatregoers," *New York Times,* November 26, 1979, C15.

CHAPTER 8

"Another Life"

THE FINAL YEARS, 1980–1986

Lerner's critics and biographers often focus on a perceived European aesthetic in his writing, and he regularly visited the Continent on holiday, as well as having been educated at Bedales School in England. Many of his musicals are set in Europe, including *Brigadoon, An American in Paris, My Fair Lady, Gigi, Camelot, On a Clear Day* (in part), *Coco,* and *Carmelina,* and several of his collaborators were of European descent or training. His life therefore came full circle with his move to London in the 1980s. It became his main home during his work on most of his remaining theater, film, television, and book projects. Lerner's sudden death in 1986 cut short a career that was still full of promise: he left incomplete a musical version of *My Man Godfrey,* a film version of *The Merry Widow,* and a television series about the history of musical theater. He was also supposed to write the lyrics for Andrew Lloyd Webber's[1] *The Phantom of the Opera,* until his final illness forced him to withdraw. One or more of these might have provided the career resurgence he longed for but never enjoyed.

New productions of his classics kept his name in the news, however. The Burton revival of *Camelot* was scheduled to open in the late spring of 1980 and preview in Toronto (where it had received its world premiere in 1960) before coming into New York. Harrison's revival of *Fair Lady* was then planned to follow it with a New Orleans tryout and national tour before reaching Broadway in the summer of 1981. But there was already a major problem. Harrison and Lerner were determined to have an English actress in the role of Eliza and had cast a relative unknown, Cheryl Kennedy,[2] in the part. But American Equity ruled against her and said Eliza should

[1] Andrew Lloyd Webber (1948–) is the British composer of a string of hit musicals including *Jesus Christ Superstar* (1970), *Evita* (1976), *Cats* (1981), and *Sunset Boulevard* (1993).

[2] Cheryl Kennedy (1947–) had appeared extensively in musicals in the United Kingdom before the *Fair Lady* revival, including *Half a Sixpence* (1963), *Jorrocks* (1967), *First Impressions* (1971), and *Flowers for Algernon* (1979).

be played by an American. Lerner supported Harrison's outrage at the decision and wrote to Mike Merrick, one of the revival's producers, to beg him not to stage the show in light of this ruling:

To Mike Merrick

February 6, 1980

Dear Mike,

I was appalled to learn this morning that Equity had ruled against Cheryl Kennedy.

Although you have a signed contract from the Dramatist Guild which gives you the rights to produce *My Fair Lady*, I beg you, for your own good and for the good of the play, to abandon it. I agree with Rex's position entirely that to do *My Fair Lady* with an American girl, especially after our recent experience, is self-defeating and doomed.

This is a painful decision to make, but I deeply believe there is no alternative.

What an outrage!

Faithfully,
Alan Jay Lerner

Eventually, after a series of appeals, an outside arbiter ruled in favor of Kennedy, but she struggled vocally during the tour to the extent that she had to be replaced on Broadway by an understudy, Nancy Ringham[3]—who was an American.[4] The *Camelot* revival was no less troubled, and the original Guenevere, Kathleen McKearney, had to be replaced after three weeks' rehearsal by Christine Ebersole,[5] who went on after three days of rehearsal and two previews.[6] When the show opened in New York on July 8, Ebersole received positive reviews, but the acclaim was mostly Burton's: the *New York Times* said "he remains every inch the King Arthur of our most majestic storybook dreams,"[7] though the actor

[3] Nancy Ringham's (1954–) Broadway credits include *The Will Rogers Follies* (replacement cast, 1992) and *Follies* (revival, 2001).

[4] The events leading up to Kennedy's replacement are described at length in Patrick Garland's memoir of Harrison, *The Incomparable Rex* (London, 1998).

[5] Christine Ebersole (1953–) is an actress and singer, whose extensive career in theater, film, and television included a well-received revival of *Oklahoma!* on Broadway in 1979.

[6] Michiko Kakutani, "From Ado Annie to Guenevere in a Week," *New York Times*, June 12, 1980, C15.

[7] Frank Rich, "Stage: Burton Stars in Revival of 'Camelot,'" *New York Times*, July 9, 1980, C15.

struggled through the run and had to withdraw in March 1981 due to back surgery.[8]

The third Lerner-Loewe Broadway revival of 1980 was *Brigadoon,* which opened at the Majestic Theatre on October 16. Its major feature was the return of Agnes de Mille to restage her original choreography, and Lerner was clearly thrilled:

Telegram to Agnes de Mille

October 16, 1980

DARLING AGNES,

WHAT A PITY I CANNOT BE THERE TONIGHT BUT I WOULD PROBABLY WEEP MY WAY THROUGH IT RECALLING ALL THE YEARS WE HAVE WORKED TOGETHER. THANK YOU FOR BEING THERE AGAIN.

ALL MY LOVE AS ALWAYS,

ALAN

He also paid tribute to the choreographer's skills in a newspaper article on October 12, in which he talked about how "in this computerized, dehumanized, directionless society we have created for ourselves—or allowed others to create for us—there is once again a longing for feeling, melody and a more affectionate view of humanity,"[9] hence the then-current trend of revivals of post-*Oklahoma!* musicals. The *Brigadoon* production received several enthusiastic reviews in the press, including one from Frank Rich, who described it as "a miracle that is pure Broadway."[10] A month later, back in the UK, *Gigi* was revived at the Haymarket Theatre, Leicester, in a new production featuring British names such as Hugh Paddick[11] and Betty Marsden.[12] Though it failed to transfer to London, this meant that all the main Lerner and Loewe shows apart from *Paint Your Wagon*

[8] "Names in the News," *The Day,* April 4, 1981, 29.

[9] Alan Jay Lerner, "Once Again, There Is a Longing for Melody," *New York Times,* October 12, 1980, D1.

[10] Frank Rich, "Theater: 'Brigadoon' Dances In," *New York Times,* October 17, 1980, C3.

[11] Actor Hugh Paddick (1915–2000) was well known for his appearances on the radio program *Round the Horne* in the 1960s, as well as the original production of *The Boy Friend* (1953). He also appeared as Pickering in the London production of *My Fair Lady* after Robert Coote departed the show.

[12] Betty Marsden (1919–98) was a British actress, specializing in comic roles on stage and radio. Michael Billington, "Gigi," *The Guardian,* November 29, 1980, 13.

were currently to be seen in major British or American revivals, and Lerner's period of nostalgia was at a climax.

The main projects that he pursued in 1981 were a Broadway musical with composer Charles Strouse[13] and a new, liberal film adaptation of the operetta *The Merry Widow*. He signed up to write the screenplay and lyrics in mid-April while in New York to lend a hand to the writers of *Copperfield*,[14] a new musical based on Dickens's *David Copperfield* that was struggling on its way in to New York (the producers were Merrick and Gregory of the *Fair Lady* and *Camelot* revivals),[15] and spent the spring working on the first draft.[16] The intention from the start was to involve international star tenor Plácido Domingo[17] in the film, with Barbra Streisand as a favorite to play the titular Widow in the reconceived storyline; others they discussed included Julie Andrews, Audrey Hepburn, Christopher Plummer,[18] Mikhail Baryshnikov,[19] Michael York,[20] and Kenneth MacMillan[21] (as the choreographer). From the start, though, there were problems in obtaining the rights to adapt *The Merry Widow* so liberally. Although Lerner wanted nothing more than to be left simply to write the screenplay, he was urged by Terence Pritchard, of Chardmark Productions, to write a synopsis that could be used in brokering the deal. Lerner replied in slight exasperation at the delays to the film:

[13] Charles Strouse (1928–) is well known as the composer of the hit musicals *Bye Bye Birdie* (1960) and *Annie* (1977), though his compositional career has lasted over 50 years and is rich and varied.

[14] *Copperfield* had music, book, and lyrics by Al Kasha and Joel Hirshhorn. It ran 26 previews and 13 regular performances.

[15] Carol Lawson, "Broadway," *New York Times*, April 3, 1981, C2.

[16] Letter from Terry Pritchard to Robert Lantz, March 27, 1981. Information on this project all comes from letters and documents in the private collection of Liz Robertson.

[17] Plácido Domingo (1941–) is one of the most important and versatile opera singers of the latter half of the twentieth century. His operatic roles encompass both major and lesser-known works by Verdi, Wagner, Mozart, Puccini, and Donizetti, among others. He has also appeared in films of Verdi's *La traviata* (1982) and *Otello* (1986).

[18] Christopher Plummer (1929–) is a film, theater, and television actor. His best-known musical appearance is in the film *The Sound of Music* (1965), and he won a Tony Award for his appearance in the short-lived Broadway show *Cyrano* (1973).

[19] Mikhail Baryshnikov (1948–) is a dancer, choreographer, and actor, well known for his distinguished career in ballet.

[20] Michael York (1942–) is a prolific stage and screen actor. His major musical credit is the film version of *Cabaret* (1972), though he has appeared in numerous important non-musical films. In 2006, he played King Arthur in a tour of Lerner's *Camelot*.

[21] Kenneth MacMillan (1929–92) was a major figure in British ballet, creating many new works and acting as Artistic Director of the Royal Ballet from 1970 to 1977. In 1993, he created the choreography for a revival of Rodgers and Hammerstein's *Carousel* at the Royal National Theatre in London, and won a Tony Award for this piece of work when the production went to Broadway.

To Terence Pritchard

August 19, 1981

Dear Terry,

Although I am cursed with understanding your problems, as far as doing a synopsis is concerned I must decline. I do not write good synopses—most authors don't—and there are people who work in studios for $50 a week who know how to do this sort of thing with some experience.

As far as the score is concerned, I have indicated in the script that almost all the songs will be included, which, as I also pointed out in the prologue, will be the first time the entire score will be heard on the screen. But I cannot say at this moment in what order the songs will be heard, because to make that decision I need the assistance of the director and the musical director, as I mentioned in the prologue.

I must confess to be more than a little impatient to get on with the project, complete with whatever drafts and changes are necessary, have my meetings with a musical director and finish the lyrics. Some of them, like "The Merry Widow" waltz, I have already begun.

I am very worried about being caught in a squeeze because of my obligations to Charles Strouse and the new show, and I must say I find it rather disheartening to hear that it takes three weeks even to translate a contract. Be that as it may, enclosed is the musical synopsis you sent me and I hope it all can be solved as quickly as possible, so that we can all get on with it.

Sincerely,
Alan Jay Lerner

In September, a new rewrite of the screenplay was requested in order to satisfy the original writers' estates, and Lerner was furious at the extent of the changes ("It's like doing an all-white *Porgy*. Yes?" he wrote underneath the letter suggesting the new format). Streisand was approached in early November, but anticipated being too busy with the filming of *Yentl*[22] to take part, even though she promised to read the screenplay. Hollywood was suffering financially during the fall of 1981, and with the kind of casting and personnel ideas Lerner was pursuing, he ultimately had to agree to rewrite his first screenplay:

[22] *Yentl* (1983) is a major film project co-produced, co-written, directed by and starring Barbra Streisand.

To Terry Pritchard

November 30, 1981

Dear Terry,

The Merry Widow, as we know, has been filmed twice in the last forty years by MGM. It is no coincidence that in order to preserve a semblance of the original plot the major ingredient that has made *The Merry Widow* endure had to be junked—namely the score. Even a wizard such as Ernst Lubitsch[23] was unable to incorporate the music into a plot that was conceived at the turn of the century as a stage conceit. Even in the glorious days of Jeanette MacDonald and Nelson Eddy, when operetta flourished on the screen, it was impossible to present both plot and music on the screen and preserve some form of the reality that the screen requires.

The intent in this present version is to reverse the tradition and put the score of *The Merry Widow* on the screen in the only way it can be done, which is by photographing the stage production itself on the stage. In so doing, the outline of the original plot can be retained, but the songs will take on an added meaning because of their relationship to the plot that surrounds this stage version. There is no validity to the criticism that the photographed stage production could be any operetta of that or any other period. The situations were so devised to heighten the pertinence of the songs of *The Merry Widow* and *The Merry Widow* alone. It would not work with *Annie Get Your Gun, My Fair Lady,* or any operetta by Stoltz or Leo Fall.

In this year of 1981 one cannot go from dialogue to music as it is done in the theatre without stamping the entire project as hopelessly old-fashioned. The motion picture is too real a medium to permit it. This is especially true when one deals with operetta music, no matter how great it may be. One can photograph an opera, as Joe Losey[24] has just done with *Don Giovanni,* but it becomes an art piece for a limited

[23] Ernst Lubitsch (1892–1947) was a major figure in the early days of sound film. His musicals included *The Love Parade* (1929), *Monte Carlo* (1930), and *The Smiling Lieutenant* (1931). His version of *The Merry Widow* (1934), which Lerner refers to in this letter, starred his regular collaborators, Maurice Chevalier and Jeanette MacDonald.

[24] Joseph Losey (1909–84) was an American director, well known for his screen versions of three Pinter plays, including *The Servant* (1963). In 1979, he released a film of Mozart's *Don Giovanni,* which Lerner alludes to in this letter.

audience. One can make a film of the stage musical *Annie*,[25] because the plot has a relevancy to human emotions in 1981. There is no way under God's heaven that the story of a widow from an imaginary country, who is so rich that her failure to marry a fellow countryman would cause financial havoc to the country of her origin, can be expected to relate to any human emotions in 1981. It is a pure and simple operetta plot, totally remote to our times.

To present my credentials for this seemingly authoritarian point of view, there have been seven musicals in the past that have won Academy Awards, and I have written three of them.

Despite the fact that almost the entire score of *The Merry Widow* will be, for the first time, presented on the screen, and despite the fact that the bones of the original story will be retained while the plot is being presented on the stage, I am now asked to rewrite the present material for reasons that are not artistic, but purely legal, i.e. to placate the widows of the original book who objected strenuously to the first two productions of *The Merry Widow* where the plot was retained and the music was not. This seems to me the shabbiest excuse for rewriting in all my experience as a writer, both for the stage and the screen.

Nevertheless, by sheer craftsmanship instead of creation, I will attempt to bring the surrounding story more into a relationship with the one on stage by making the lady a widow and by rewriting some of the incidents in her life so that they mirror the action on stage. In so doing let me state that in my opinion it will not improve the work and my total effort will be to see that it impairs it as little as possible.

What matters in *The Merry Widow* is the score. As Robby Lantz[26] pointed out, no one ever comes out of the theatre whistling the plot. Although I am fully aware that rewriting was always necessary, once a director is involved, rewriting to preserve something that time has proven to be unworkable is not a task I look forward to with any inspirational glee. Nevertheless, it shall be done and God help us all.

Sincerely,
Alan Jay Lerner

If the references to his "credentials" and "craftsmanship" seem a little pompous, surely Lerner was justified in being so annoyed. As a young writer at MGM,

[25] Perhaps *Annie* (1977) was especially in Lerner's mind because he was collaborating with its composer, Charles Strouse, at that point. The film version of the show was released in 1982.

[26] Robert Lantz (1914–2007) was a major talent agent, with clients including Leonard Bernstein and Bette Davis.

he had been treated with respect and his creativity had been nourished. Now, the atmosphere of the film industry had turned from art to business and he was expected to respond to demands, in spite of being a long-established, Academy Award–winning screenwriter.

With all this simmering in the background, Lerner was also hard at work on *Dance a Little Closer*, the musical he was writing with Charles Strouse. Though the idea dated back to sometime in 1979, the show was announced in May 1981. Lerner admitted, "There is not much to say at this stage of the game—except that we're doing it, and love it and are optimistic."[27] It was to be based on Robert Sherwood's 1936 play *Idiot's Delight* and was intended as a vehicle for Liz Robertson, whom Lerner had married in August.[28] On the same day, the Harrison revival of *Fair Lady* opened on Broadway. In spite of some reservations about the production and performances, the critics concluded that "they simply do not write shows like this anymore."[29]

Though Lerner was heavily involved in the production of *Closer*, the official producer was to be Frederick Brisson, who had helmed *Coco* for Lerner. Nobody else had yet signed on to the show. Therefore, when Lerner read a news item about a possible creative team and casting gossip in *Variety*, he wrote to encourage Brisson to keep as quiet as possible about the production for the time being:

To Frederick Brisson

November 30, 1981

Dear Freddie,

I noticed a story in Variety about *Idiot's Delight* which included the names of both Herb Ross[30] and Twyla Tharp.[31] Even James Coburn's[32] name snuck in.

I feel very strongly that as much as is possible we should keep the publicity under wraps, and only publicize the facts when

[27] Carol Lawson, "Broadway," *New York Times*, May 1, 1981, C2.

[28] "Lerner Weds Actress He Directed as Eliza," *New York Times*, August 19, 1981, C17.

[29] Mel Gussow, "The Stage: 'My Fair Lady' Returns," *New York Times*, August 19, 1981, C17.

[30] Herbert Ross (1927–2001) was a producer, director, and choreographer. In his early days as a performer, he appeared in musicals such as *Something for the Boys* (1943). On film, he choreographed *Funny Girl* (1968) and directed *Goodbye Mr. Chips* (1969) and *Funny Lady* (1975). He choreographed Lerner's *On a Clear Day* (1965) on the stage.

[31] Twyla Tharp (1941–) has choreographed for many of the world's great ballet companies. Her Broadway work includes *When We Were Very Young* (1980), *Catherine Wheel* (1981), *Singin' in the Rain* (1985), and *Movin' Out* (2001).

[32] Actor James Coburn (1928–2002) enjoyed a 45-year career that included almost 70 movies.

they become facts. As you know, Twyla Tharp, who, incidentally, impressed Charles and me very much indeed, also wants to direct as well as choreograph. Whether she should or not is unimportant at this moment, but we did tell her that we would not be showing the play to anyone else until we meet again on February 8th, and she is given the complete first Act to read. If her enthusiasm is such that she becomes involved emotionally with the project, it will be easier at that time to discuss what her function will actually be. But I certainly don't want to seem like a liar when I tell her no one else has seen the play until that date.

Neither Charles nor I said anything about James Coburn, but I believe he has been telling people about it, which is his business, I suppose. If the press at any time ask any of us about it, I think we should merely tell the truth, which is that there has been a discussion with him but that nothing is definite.

As of this moment, all that I know to be true is that Charles Strouse and I are writing it, you are producing it and Liz Robertson will be the leading lady—whether it be done in America first or in England. The truth of the matter is I would probably not have written the play in the first place if it hadn't been for my desire to write a vehicle for Liz, whose talents, as you will see from her television show, are vast and varied. In fact, and I say this quite objectively, I don't know anyone on either side of the ocean who can do everything from operetta to raunchy pop the way she can.

Charles and I finished another song while I was in New York, which makes seven so far. My plan at the moment is to be back in New York mid-January for a month, and then Charles will return to London with me for a month mid-February.

It was good talking to you and I look forward to seeing you a week from Thursday, which turns out to be December 10th.

Fondly,
Alan

Meanwhile, the problems with *The Merry Widow* continued. The more time went on, the more Lerner was being pressured into returning the operetta to its original state. Yet his intention had always been to create a new scenario with the songs interspersed as comments on the action rather than presented as part of the story. Spending January working on *Dance a Little Closer*, Lerner then returned to London in February, reread his script, and wrote to the film's producers to give them his feelings on the project:

To Terry Pritchard and F. Marks

February 9, 1982

Dear Chaps,

This seems to be a propitious moment to go on record about what's happening to *The Merry Widow*, both from a script and casting point of view. I would like to remind everyone that in the beginning we had a rather tight script that most certainly needed work, but nevertheless had a kind of integrity—if I may sound pompous for a moment—and a conception. To put it succinctly, my conception was that the story that revolved around *The Merry Widow* should be bitter-sweet and be designed so that at the climax of the film, hopefully, the audience would be moved to tears. The gaiety would be provided by the lyrics and, of course, the music on the stage. But my contribution would be the lyrics, i.e. to keep them gay and bright and amusing. The gayer and brighter the music and lyrics are, the more touching and moving would be the end of the play. I never once thought of this as a "delightful" evening at the cinema. My ambition was for it to be exciting, beautiful and moving. Moving, moving, moving!

I re-read the script the other day and I found it wandering far from what I hoped it to be. For example, I think "Vilia" appearing near the end of the film is infinitely sentimental and deprives the end of its sentiment. Something gay should be happening on stage.

I don't think it is possible for anyone to see what I mean until the lyrics are written. Therefore, it becomes necessary for everybody to take it on good faith. I have just been through an experience with "Idiot's Delight" in which—no matter what the ultimate result of the work might be—the question arose whether or not it was a truly romantic story. I kept saying nobody could tell that until the songs that revealed the people were written. Why write in dialogue what I intend to do in verse? Since the addition of four new songs, suddenly, from somewhere, everybody now thinks it's a terribly romantic play. Why? Because two songs in the first Act make you cry and are deeply revealing of the two leading people. I think it is clear why I mention this in connection with the change that will occur in *The Merry Widow* when the lyrics are written.

Robby [Lantz] has reported to me that Baryshnikov is now being considered for the Baron. How the Baron is going to dance has contorted me into a Rubic cube of confusion. On the other hand, I agree that the part written for him is inadequate. Whether or not it can be strengthened I don't know until I try, but it certainly seems to me that the spinning of an interweaving set of love stories could stand the addition of one more explored a little more deeply and dramatically.

Finally—and this I know if I know nothing else—the lady who plays the Widow has to be a singer. Elizabeth Taylor would be a farce. The fact that Audrey Hepburn was dubbed in *My Fair Lady* literally finished her career and did the picture no good at all. As far as I can tell these days, it is the picture and the writing that make the star and not the other way around. Barbra Streisand has had her share of flops and so have Clint Eastwood[33] and Burt Reynolds.[34] To start making concessions to the bankers at this stage is to embark on the road to disaster.

Perhaps because I have been away from everyone for a few weeks, I have the feeling that the project is becoming splintered in some strange way and the original intention is getting lost—at least the original intention as I understood it and wrote it.

I will be returning to London within the next ten days and my intention is to go to work immediately on the lyrics so pre-recording can begin in April as advertised—providing, I assume, we have a leading lady, whoever she is, and as much as I admire her, I sure don't think Elizabeth Taylor is it. Nor, if I may be forgiven the repetition, do I think lightening up the picture into some kind of Hungarian comedy is the way this picture should end. I would like to see floods of tears and the audience swimming up the aisle when the picture ends. There is no catharsis like it and to be strictly commercial, there is no surer way to have a hit. Believe me, if Ali McGraw had recovered from leukemia or if Eliza had married Freddie in *My Fair Lady*, the eight song hits in that show would hardly have been worth it, and *Love Story* would have been Marcus Welby.

Having said my piece, I will now withdraw into my cocoon, but before I do so I send you both all my affection.

Aye,
Alan Jay Lerner

After further work on the script, the project was temporarily abandoned because the estates and producers would not agree with Lerner's approach.

[33] Clint Eastwood (1930–) is a multi-award-winning director, producer and actor whose dozens of movies include the film version of Lerner's *Paint Your Wagon* (1969).

[34] Burt Reynolds (1936–) is an actor and director. His many screen appearances include *Smokey and the Bandit* (1977) and *Boogie Nights* (1997).

It hardly mattered, though, because he had plenty of work left to do with Charles Strouse on *Dance a Little Closer*. In mid-February, they agreed that Lerner would direct the show, thereby making his official Broadway directing debut. "Someone has to look down the road to see what the play should be," he commented, "and I think I have that vision."[35] He also gave new versions of his "Lyrics and Lyricists" talk about his work from time to time, for example at Winfield House on February 25, for the US ambassador to Great Britain.[36] Liz Robertson sang a number of his songs, and they performed "I Remember It Well" together. In March, while working on the new show, Lerner wrote to Richard Burton to ask him to appear as a guest in one of Robertson's cabaret performances at the Duke of York's Theatre in April:

To Richard Burton

March 8, 1982

Dear Richard,

I couldn't help but see your picture in the paper last weekend and it did my heart good to see you looking so much better. My God, what a rough year you had!

Will you be coming back through London again in the near future? If you are, I have a question—or call it a favour—to put to you. I know how you hate the telephone, so I am writing to you instead.

When Liz was down in Chichester last summer, she did a one-woman show on a Sunday night which was so successful she had to give two more performances. As a result, she has been asked to bring it to London and do it at the Duke of York's, starting Sunday night April 18th, as a sort of cabaret, i.e. late Saturday night from 11 to 12.30 a.m. and Sunday evening at 8 p.m. At each performance various chums, like Placido Domingo, Vera Lynn[37] and Harry Secombe,[38] are going to appear with her (one at a time). If, by chance, you *are* going to be in London, would you consider coming on and perhaps doing "Camelot"? Or "How to Handle"—or whatever? It would all be very informal and hopefully good fun. If it will not be possible, or if the whole idea makes

[35] Carol Lawson, "Broadway," *New York Times*, February 19, 1982, C2.

[36] Script and documentation in Liz Robertson's private archive.

[37] Vera Lynn (1917–) is a singer and actress, perhaps best known for entertaining British troops during the Second World War. She was called "The Forces' Sweetheart."

[38] Harry Secombe (1921–2001) was an actor and singer, known for appearing on the BBC radio series *The Goon Show* and in musicals such as *Pickwick* (London, 1963; Broadway, 1965).

you look longingly at the canal, you don't even have to bother answering this letter. And God knows there will be no love lost. If, on the other hand, it might entice you, you, or somebody on your behalf, can reach me here in London.

No matter what, if you do come through London we would love to see you—even for a quick moment.

I have been back and forth from America several times because of the new show, which seems to be coming along very well. I successfully avoided seeing *Camelot*. The Irishman,[39] against all persuasion, insisted upon bringing it back to New York. With the memory of your performance still fresh in everybody's mind, after a few staggering weeks he took to the hinterlands again. It's still playing somewhere, but I haven't bothered to look. The last thing I heard was that they arrived in Buffalo on the night of the biggest blizzard in ten years.

Wagner[40] sounds absolutely wonderful and I hope you're enjoying it. At least you get to go to Venice.

Do take care of yourself and whether I hear from you or not, my affection follows you.

Aye,
Alan

More than 20 years on from the original *Camelot*, Lerner's affection for Burton, and his reverence for his talent, remained very high.

Originally, the plan had been to put *Dance a Little Closer* into rehearsal in August 1982, to arrive on Broadway by December, but it was not ready in time. Casting took place over the summer and was announced in September: joining Liz Robertson were George Rose, a veteran of Lerner's *Coco* and the 1976 *Fair Lady* revival, and Len Cariou,[41] who had appeared in Strouse's *Applause*.[42] Further delays were then incurred because Brisson struggled to find backing for the show, as he admitted in January 1983: "We would normally be in rehearsal now, but the money didn't fall in as easily as it did in the past.... I have done 21 shows on Broadway. This is the first time I haven't been overcapitalized."[43]

[39] Lerner is referring to Richard Harris, who had taken over from Burton in the anniversary revival of *Camelot*.

[40] *Wagner* (1983) is an epic film about the life of Wagner, in which Burton played the great German composer.

[41] Len Cariou (1939–) is a Canadian actor, well known for creating the role of Todd in Sondheim's *Sweeney Todd* (1979) on Broadway. His other Broadway credits include *Applause* (1970), *A Little Night Music* (1973), and *Teddy & Alice* (1987).

[42] Carol Lawson, "Broadway," *New York Times*, September 3, 1982, C2.

[43] Lawson, "Broadway," C2.

With the show on the backburner until the funds could be raised, Lerner was delighted when he was approached with the possibility of reviving the *Merry Widow* project:

To John Pringle

December 15, 1982

Dear John,

What a delightful surprise discovering it was you at the other end of the phone! And delightful surprises are in short supply these days.

I am enclosing the script, which, as you will see, was created with the music of *The Merry Widow* in mind. However, it is quite obvious that the story does not depend at all on what music is used. There is a large library of beautiful operetta literature that is available, most of which is in the public domain. In the script you will read I actually indicated more music than I expected to use in order to keep the Lehar estate happy.

The budget, I had discovered, was in the neighborhood of $7,000,000—but that included a large sum paid to the Lehar estate plus a very costly sequence chez Franz Josef which is not necessary—plus—all those *Merry Widow* stage scenes inserted for the estate. As you will see, it's fundamentally a very intimate story.

In any case, I hope you at the very least enjoy it and at the very most might be interested in doing it.

I'll be in London for a few days over Christmas and I'll certainly call you. No matter what happens with the script, it will be a joy to see you after all these years.

Aye,
Alan

As for *Dance a Little Closer*, it finally went into rehearsal on March 7 ahead of a Broadway opening at the Minskoff Theater on May 11.[44] The weekend before the opening, the *New York Times* published an article about the show, including an interview with Lerner about his adaptation of the source material, *Idiot's Delight*: "What I've tried to do is preserve the fundamental structure of the play and to replace some characters who would not be relevant today with characters

[44] Lawson, "Broadway," C2.

I think are," Lerner commented.[45] "This is a book musical in a day when there are very few book musicals; the theater today is a theater of magnificent productions and tap-dancing. But I just fell in love with this play, and thought it was time to do it, for a whole series of reasons." Ironically, the critics would point to the overwhelming nature of the show's sets—which included a skating rink—as one of its flaws, and it was uniformly panned. The musical closed after just one performance. But even during the previews, Lerner was philosophical about its chances: "I feel differently about success than I did before," he said. "Naturally, I would like it, but primarily I would like to avoid humiliation. It's very strange; people think that the longer you are in the public eye, the more immune you become to what people will say about you. It's not true; you become more vulnerable. You don't mind being criticized so much, as long as you feel you are being criticized on the level of your effort, instead of dismissed. I think in the theater you fundamentally get more or less than you deserve, and you don't get 'A' for effort. I've had a lot of failures, but most of the time when I haven't fared well with the critics, I think they were right—although I might have resented it at the time."

It seemed that Lerner had indeed come to accept critical appraisal more philosophically. In writing to thank Irene Selznick for sending him a copy of her book, *A Private View,* which had just been published, the lyricist expressed regret about the show's disaster but overall contentment with his new life:

To Irene Selznick

[Undated; 1983]

Dearest Irene,

Your book is a marvel. It is so "felt" and so perceptive and honest and intensely readable and moving. In some ways I felt I was meeting you all over again—and loving you all over again.

I was shattered to hear of your illness—but I know—I really know you will conquer it. Too much love is going with you.

For myself—you know. (Alas!) But I have never been happier. I would rather have Liz than all the hits in the world.

We're going back home to London but I'm sure we'll be back before the summer is over—this time with time for friends and not the goddamn theatre.

Bless you. Thank you for the book. My love goes with you always.

Alan

[45] Leslie Bennetts, "Alan Jay Lerner Brews a Political Love Story," *New York Times,* May 8, 1983, H1.

In August, Lerner was involved in a car accident that left him unable to work on his shows for a period, but he made himself busy by completing most of the research for a new book project: a history of musical theater. By the end of November he was able to write to his publisher, Collins Ltd., that it was "gathering momentum" and that "all the research is finished—minus one book."[46] He also met with the BBC that month to continue ongoing discussions about creating a 10-hour television series to tie in with the book, though he made it clear that the series would be made only after publication of the book; in the end, after numerous discussions and correspondence in 1984, the series was abandoned so that Lerner could focus on his theater work. Around the same time, he also agreed to work with Burton Lane on a revised version of *Carmelina*, to be retitled *Someone in April*. The following letter to David Aukin,[47] a budding theater producer who later ran the Royal National Theatre, shows that Lerner and Lane were about to recommence work on the musical by writing some new songs:

To David Aukin

November 28, 1983

Dear David,

Thank you for your letter.

I must confess that I never quite knew what was wrong with *Dance a Little Closer*, but I knew something was and I think you have put your finger squarely on it. I am not only convinced you are right but there is another interest in it and I am withdrawing it. What a clever man you are!

I think Armand Gerrard sent you a script of *Someone in April*, which used to be called *Carmelina*. Burton Lane, the composer, is coming over in a couple of weeks and we are going to do two or three more songs for it. I have always loved that property and had it been handled as a small piece of "commedia dell'arte," which is what I tried to do—sort of Goldoni—it would have worked. Ironically, the one paper that tore it to pieces was the New York Times. Two months later the critic was replaced by Frank Rich who wrote Joe Stein a letter telling him that he

[46] Letter from Lerner to Roger Schlesinger, November 25, 1983. Copy in Liz Robertson's private archives.

[47] David Aukin (1942–) is a producer. He was artistic director of the Hampstead Theatre and the Leicester Haymarket Theatre, executive director of the Royal National Theatre, and head of film at Channel 4.

could not understand the Times review, and had he been there...! And of course he was there, two months later.

Do think about it and give me your astute opinion.

Hope all is going well. Some day, somehow, I am sure we will work together.

Best wishes.
Aye,
Alan

The intention was for the revival to begin in Norwich and later come into London, where it was hoped the show's fate would be kinder than it had been on Broadway. This would then be followed by a New York transfer. In the first months of 1984, Lerner worked concurrently on the book, documentary series, and the new material for *Carmelina*. His progress on the latter is preserved in the following series of letters to Lane. Because the lyricist was in London and the composer in the United States, much of this work was done via correspondence. As a result, this is probably the greatest insight we have into the relationship between Lerner and one of his composers, demonstrating how they exchanged ideas and, in particular, Lerner's approach to the show in question. Mention is made of the director, Hugh Wooldridge;[48] the producer, Armand Gerrard;[49] and various suggestions of actresses to play the title role:

To Burton Lane

January 24, 1984

Dear Burt,

I think I mentioned to you the way things work over here. There are several beautiful theatres outside London, such as the Theatre Royal at Nottingham, Bristol and many others—the best of which is Norwich, which is managed by a man named Dick Condon.[50] He is, by reputation, the most intelligent and "show-wise" of all the regional managers. When one is about to do a new play, one goes to Condon first.

[48] Hugh Wooldridge is a director and producer, whose credits include international productions of *Jesus Christ Superstar* and *The Rocky Horror Show*, as well as the annual *Night of 1000 Voices* at London's Royal Albert Hall.

[49] Armand Gerrard is a producer and general manager, with numerous credits including a UK tour of *Calamity Jane* (1996).

[50] Richard Condon (1937–91) was an impresario and theater manager. He took charge of the Theatre Royal, Norwich, from 1972.

With that in mind, I prepared as clean a script as I could and it was sent off to him. We heard yesterday that not only does he love it, but will co-finance it and we can open in Norwich. It may not seem much in New York, but over here it's quite a coup.

We are not certain when the theatre will be available, but June is the ideal time for rehearsal. With a good show and the proper bookings, it could come into London at the end of September or the first week in October with most of the investment recouped. If the first scene of this play cannot be fixed by June, then we better forget about it completely. So, I think June is a reasonable date.

What I intend to do is to write several versions of that opening scene and then we can all decide which one we want. In one of the versions I would like to include the prologue, "Come With Me to San Forino." So could you send me either a lead sheet or a cassette, or preferably both? I also need the prayer.

I started to work on "You Never Told Me" and there is a big problem for me about it. Could the first two bars be repeated so I could have question and answer? As it is, there really is no room for the title except the opening line, when it would be coming too soon. The alternative would be if I write a lyric based on this melody and then you fiddled round with it. Either way is alright with me but I can't do it the way it is.

I spent last evening with Armand [Gerrard] and Hugh [Wooldridge] and we went over schedules, etc. Their number one choice for Carmelina—and with good reason—is a girl over here named Julia McKenzie.[51] First of all because she's incredibly talented: there is no better singer on the British stage. She also has a television series, so she's a big star all over the country. She doesn't look Italian, but with a black wig and darkened skin, she's such a good actress, she can probably pull it off. She may even be able to sing "I'm a Woman" and not make it sound like an anthem for Women's Lib, the way Georgia [Brown] did. She's extremely feminine.

General auditioning would begin around the end of April. Through his connections with the opera and ballet world, Armand is searching for a Vittorio.

There is a brilliant orchestrator over here named Ian MacPherson. What Armand and Hugh intend to do is give him the music and let him orchestrate and record an overture which would be sent to you for your

[51] Julia McKenzie (1941–) is a television and stage actress. She has a strong association with the musicals of Stephen Sondheim, and is also television's *Miss Marple*.

approval. But before that, of course, we need copies of all the music, so the sooner you could get them to me, the better.

I promised the boys that I would have the opening scenes ready by 1st March. That gives us plenty of time for decisions. They were both devastated at the thought of cutting "Why Him?," so I have an idea for a long verse for it which I will write and send to you. As I told you, over here they adore that song. As a matter of fact, there's a huge charity gala at Drury Lane on 26th February and Liz [Robertson] has been asked to sing it—that, and nothing else!

Anyhow, I think that brings you up-to-date. I would really appreciate it if you could get the music to me as soon as possible.

I am glad you and Lynn [Lane] enjoyed your holiday. I can't imagine anyone not being transported by Venice. . . .

Aye,
Alan

To Burton Lane

February 10, 1984

Dear Burton,

Received your letter this morning and yesterday all the music from Chappell's. I also had a long talk with Joe [Stein] on the phone yesterday morning.

Joe feels very strongly, and I think he is right, that the sooner we get to "Someone in April" the better. That is, after all, when the play really begins. Therefore, the question is how to establish everything that has to be established in the opening scene with as much dispatch as possible.

Secondly, there is no question that "Love Before Breakfast" has to go.

I have not disregarded any of your suggestions but it seemed to me they were prolonging the opening scene instead of shortening it. Joe and I talked over one rather revolutionary idea, which is to begin with the prologue and have no songs in the opening scene but merely write it as a play so that the first song inside the play would be "Someone in April." I said that I thought there was a way of doing both "Why Him" and "Time For a Love Song" in the balcony scene. I am not sure about that until I try it, which I will do this week. I am still working on various versions of the opening scene which would include "Why Him" and "Time For a Love Song" with a new song in the balcony scene.

As for my coming to New York, there is simply no way that I can. However, Joe said he thought he could come over the first week in April.

I must tell you in all honesty that I am not 100% certain it is going to be possible to get this play on when the producers would like to. Jane Lapotaire[52] has signed to do something for the National Theatre and Julia McKenzie has another commitment. I think the casting is going to be very difficult and without a smashing Carmelina, there is no point in doing the show at all, even if all the writing meets our mutual approval.

At the moment, Hugh Wooldridge is directing another play and will not be available to us for another ten days. At that time, we can sit down and have some long meetings about everything. In the meantime, I will keep working and keep you informed of progress.

I hope you are happy in the new apartment.

Best to you both from both of us.

Aye,
Alan

To Burton Lane

February 24, 1984

Dear Burt,

Received your letter this morning.

About casting: as I told you, Jane Lapotaire is signed by the National Theatre and the only reason I bring it up is because I think that with the exception of Gemma Craven[53] (who is a possibility), you are not going to find a better voice than Lapotaire's. After all, no matter what you thought of "Dear Anyone,"[54] she did Piaf's complete repertoire and knocked them in the aisles!

Chita Rivera[55] is of course sensational but really too old—and I don't think you could get her in the country. She's now playing Liza

[52] Jane Lapotaire (1944–) is a British stage and screen actress. She was well known in this period for creating the title role in *Piaf* (1978) for the Royal Shakespeare Company; for its move to Broadway in 1981, she won a Tony Award.

[53] Gemma Craven (1950–) is an Irish actress who appeared in the movie musical *The Slipper and the Rose* (1976) and the BBC drama *Pennies from Heaven* (1978). Her stage credits include *They're Playing our Song* (London, 1980), for which she won an Olivier Award.

[54] *Dear Anyone* (1983) was a flop West End musical.

[55] Chita Rivera (1933–) is an actress and singer, whose credits include creating the role of Anita in *West Side Story* (1957). She was celebrated at the Kennedy Center Honors in 2002.

Minnelli's mother[56] and Liza Minnelli could play Gia's mother! Bernice Massi[57] you could not get in the country. That I can assure you—and besides she means nothing over here. Millicent Martin[58] is terrific and a dear friend of Liz's but she's happily ensconced in *42nd Street*, lives in America and has no desire to come back to London. Besides, she's 50, which I think is much too old.

Mary Tyler Moore[59] is a possibility. I am having a meeting tonight with Armand and Hugh and I will bring it up.

I think I have a decent outline for the opening scene which I will write up and send off to you in a day or two.

Hope you are at last moved. Best to you both.

Aye,
Alan

P.S. Needless to say, "Love before Breakfast" will be out and replaced with "You Never Told Me." I will do a lyric "sort of" based on the music and we can take it from there.

AJL

To Burton Lane

February 27, 1984

Dear Burt,

This is what I think is the cleanest and clearest and most immediately audience-absorbing way of doing the first scene.

No prologue. The curtain rises on Vittorio in mid-afternoon preparing the cage for the evening's business. He sings a big soliloquy ending with "Time For a Love Song" in which he pours out his troubles in anger and frustration, which should be a big number—two choruses of

[56] In Kander and Ebb's *The Rink* on Broadway.

[57] Bernice Massi (1933–) appeared in numerous Broadway musicals, including *No Strings* (1962) and *What Makes Sammy Run?* (1964).

[58] Millicent Martin (1934–) is an English actress and singer. Her credits include *The Boy Friend* (1954) on Broadway, *Expresso Bongo* (1958) in London, and *That Was the Week That Was* (1962) on BBC TV.

[59] Mary Tyler Moore (1936–) is an American actress, known for *The Mary Tyler Moore Show* (1970). She starred in the short-lived Broadway musical *Breakfast at Tiffany's* (1966) and the movie *Thoroughly Modern Millie* (1967).

the song plus the interlude in the middle besides the beginning which has to be written. I thought I would write a lyric for your perusal.

"Why Him?" with a verse in which she tells of men who have been interested in her and whom she has found attractive—but of course done nothing—and can't understand why this man should disturb her. This man who never says a word, never makes an advance, etc., then the chorus.

Replace "I Must Have Her" with a dialogue statement of his determination to do something about her tonight before the Americans return and all the memories are re-aroused, ending with a reprise of "It's Time For a Love Song"—the last line being changed to: "It's time and the time is tonight!." Naturally, I would fix the previous lines to accommodate the rhyme change.

The balcony scene: as planned with "You Never Told Me." I will do a lyric based on the melody you sent me—but not quite.

How does this strike you? I can't believe there is a more effective way of doing that opening scene—and I love being able to reprise "Time for a Love Song."

The hottest contender for Carmelina—and interested—is Gemma Craven, but what about Jill Clayburgh?[60] I don't know if she would be interested or if we could get her into the country but she's a wonderful actress and came from musicals, and let's face it, Carmelina doesn't have to sing like Mimi! She has to have a good voice and be able to put over a song.

There was a huge charity benefit last night at Drury Lane. Liz sang "Why Him?," got about five laughs and the response was tremendous. They do love that song over here.

Getting back to the vocal requirements of Carmelina, if you had seen all the musicals in town which I had hoped you would do while you were here, you would have seen how extensively body mikes and electronic sound is used. It's almost expected. They like a lot of noise over here. Even the dialogue is carefully miked so when the singing is brought up a bit, it doesn't change the tone of the show.

How are your new digs?

All the best.

Aye,
Alan

[60] Jill Clayburgh (1944–2010) was an American actress. She was Academy Award–nominated for the movies *An Unmarried Woman* (1978) and *Starting Over* (1979), and appeared in *The Rothschilds* (1970) and *Pippin* (1972) on Broadway.

P.S. A very good set designer and lighting man have been set and the choreographer should be selected within the next couple of weeks—so things are moving.

P.P.S. I forgot to mention Vittorio. Everybody's favourite seems to be Denis Quilley[61] who did *Sweeney Todd* over here. He has a fantastic voice and is a wonderful actor. He did one of the Franco Zeffirelli/Eduardo de Felippo plays with Joan Plowright and does Italian to a fair-thee-well. He is coming by Tuesday night to hear about the play and I will do two of the songs for him.

AJL

To Burton Lane

April 28, 1984

Dear Burt,

Received your letter this morning and I am sending you the revised opening scene which I completed about a month ago but was waiting until I had more to send.

If I seemed in my last letter to be preoccupied with matters not pertaining to the play, let me assure you my intention was only to fill you in on the possibilities and problems. The fact is, no matter what we write and how good it is, unless we can cast it—there is little chance of getting it on—and frankly, I don't want to spend a lot of time and travel unless I know there is going to be a production.

So far, no one has turned the play down because they don't like it. It has either been we don't like them or the ones we did like had conflicting commitments. The exception was Diana Rigg,[62] who liked it but didn't think it was for her—or so she said.

It's been a long winter and I have been working hard and am exhausted and so is Liz—so we are off on holiday today till mid-May. I will be in touch with you when I get back.

Aye,
Alan

[61] Actor Denis Quilley (1927–2003) appeared in numerous musicals in London, ranging from *The Boys from Syracuse* (1963) to *Anything Goes* (2003).

[62] Diana Rigg (1938–) is a prolific actress, with credits ranging from Emma Peel in TV's *The Avengers* to the James Bond film *On Her Majesty's Secret Service* (1969). Her work in musicals includes the movie of *A Little Night Music* (1977), the American flop *Colette* (1982), and the original London production of *Follies* (1987).

To Burton Lane

May 25, 1984

Dear Burt,

Returned from Capri last night and found your letter waiting.

To keep the book straight, the reason for my "depression" (which it really wasn't) last Fall was because of the automobile accident I had in August. I can't stand being incapacitated and it took a long time before I could move around well.

Because I am not good at sitting around doing nothing, I have been working on a new book for the last few months (not autobiographical—about the musical theatre). Collins, who is the biggest publisher over here, is publishing it as soon as I can get it finished and the BBC want to do it as six 1-hour television shows some time in 1985. I also have started thinking about a new musical for Allan Carr[63] and Jerry Minskoff[64] with a young up-and-coming composer over here.

I have been afraid all along there would be problems about casting *Someone in April*. I have just spoken to Armand Gerrard and as you have probably heard, it seems to be off—certainly for the next six months. I don't agree with you that it is simply a matter of getting the play right and we will find the right company.

I must also tell you in all honesty that one of the problems we have had has been that damn album which, because of the orchestrations, makes the score seem old-fashioned. I think Armand will confirm this with you, so for the last few auditions, I have been doing it myself with a pianist, who plays the score rather Italianate and it works fine. I agree with you that the book could be stronger in the beginning but I assure you that that has not been the problem.

Whenever Armand gives me the word, I will drop everything and go back to work. In the meantime, have a good summer and best to you and Lynn.

Aye,
Alan

It is interesting to see in this series of letters a dual focus between Lerner and Lane's discussion of what needed to be changed or added to the show and the

[63] Allan Carr (1937–99) was a hugely successful producer, with credits including the film *Grease* (as co-producer, 1978) and the Broadway musical *La Cage aux Folles* (1983).

[64] Jerome Minskoff (1915–94) was a theater owner and producer, whose projects included *Irene* (1973) and *King of Hearts* (1978).

practicalities involved in putting it on the stage. In the case of the writing, they usually agreed on the work's flaws, but they seemed to disagree on the way to move the production forward. Lane thought that if they perfected the show, they would easily find a theater and star, whereas Lerner felt it was important to know who was going to play Carmelina so the musical could be revised around her. The lyricist also seemed more aware than the composer that until theaters and actors could be lined up, all the time they were putting in on the writing was speculative. Tensions had been constant through most of Lerner's relationship with Lane, even though the quality of the work they produced was often very high (especially the songs). In the following letter to David Grossberg, his close friend and attorney, Lerner is open about his exasperation with Lane. He also gives some interesting details about a revival of *Gigi* that had been proposed for America, with Louis Jourdan taking Maurice Chevalier's role of Honoré Lachailles:

To David Grossberg

29th May 1984

Dear Dave,

Just got back from Capri. Even though the weather was dicey, we both had a wonderful rest—the first since *Dance a Little Closer* and the hospital last summer—and I am full of piss and ginger!

Lots of things. One at a time.

As far as *Gigi* is concerned, an American tour is really not to my interest. It most certainly *is* to my interest for Cameron [Mackintosh] to do it over here where—whether he goes to Toronto with it or not—it will definitely play the Old Vic for two months and if it is well cast, well presented and well received, it can be moved to another theatre which is the usual route these days. In other words, I would rather gamble on a first class run here in London, away from Tams-Witmark, etc. So any way you want to get me out of that American business, go right ahead. You could say, for example, that I don't approve of the changes in the book and I am not anxious to have it done unless I am present, which I can't be—or maybe you can quibble about the royalties. I don't care as long as it is cancelled once and for all.

What am I doing now? I am working like the very devil on the book and also starting with Gerard Kenny[65] on *My Man Godfrey*. I promised

[65] Gerard Kenny (1947–) is an American songwriter, with hits including "New York, New York (So Good They Named It Twice)," "I Made It through the Rain," "Fantasy," and "I Could Be So Good for You."

Allan Carr to have some sort of outline for him by mid-summer. In order to do that, I have to see if Kenny and I have a future together and write some songs.

As far as *Carmelina* is concerned, it is really in the lap of the Gods. Of course it needs work and of course I am willing to do it, but Armand [Gerrard] agrees with me that we can't move unless there is the possibility of a cast on the horizon. Burton's idea that if you make the show as good as you can possibly make it, the rest will follow, is simply not true—at least not here. Not only that, what was primarily wrong with *Carmelina* in the States was the style. It should have sounded like Italian street music and not like an old-fashioned Broadway musical. The sets should have been small and looked Italian and the costumes should not have made the people look like "the folks on the green" instead of real people. The truth of the matter is—and I haven't really told this to Burton—that everybody here likes the book and the problem is the music. Knowing what I go through writing anything with Burton Lane, I just don't want to tackle it unless I can see a production. As for the notion of some day bringing it back to Broadway, I think that's crazy. I am not sure that even if it were hailed over here, I would want it back on Broadway. For obvious reasons it doesn't do me any good, so why take the chance?

The head of P.B.S. is coming over June 10th for a meeting with the B.B.C. and Goldcrest Films about my book. They all have written me they want to do it. The question is, can it be set up financially? Goldcrest is cleaning up these days. Besides being a major investor in *Gandhi*,[66] they have the new *Tarzan* picture and three extremely successful TV series over here.

When Irving [Cohen] was over last year, he said he was going to initiate, or try to, an audit of *Camelot* and *Paint Your Wagon*. Any news?

Oh yes! One very important thing. I don't know what's happening with that Goddamn album of *Dance a Little Closer*, but we certainly have no contract. Liz signed something which I assume has the usual clause saying that the artist may not record her songs elsewhere for five years. She is about to make an album and we are going to do three songs from *Dance a Little Closer*. If they ever do release the U.S. album, they will need a contract from me. In that contract, there will have to be a clause releasing her from that restriction. Do you think we should so notify Chandler whatever-his-name-is now or just go ahead and do it?

[66] *Gandhi* (1982) is an epic biopic about Mohandas Karamchand Gandhi. It won eight Academy Awards on its release and was a huge financial success.

What is most important is that she be not liable for anything. The producer of the album over here brought this to my attention today. Please write me your thoughts about it.

That's all.

Love and kisses,
Alan

Lerner's candor in this letter is striking: he clearly no longer enjoyed working with Lane and was keen to focus his activities in London now he had moved his life there.

He continued to work on his book about musicals, but more slowly than anticipated, as he confessed to his publisher in April:

To Roger Schlesinger, Collins Publishers

April 16, 1984

Dear Roger,

A few years ago, Tom Courtenay[67] did *Hamlet* somewhere out in the provinces and one night he was horrified to discover that Edith Evans[68] was in the audience. She came back after the performance, went in to see him and said: "It's coming."

So is the book. A little slower than perhaps I might have hoped, so I fear spring will be a little late this year.[69] The truth is, I have been working so hard, I am exhausted and before I go any further, I am going to take three weeks off. When I return, I will read what I have written and with renewed energy you will receive the bulk from me in June.

On May 25th, the head of Public Broadcasting in America is coming over to sit down and work out a deal with the BBC and Goldcrest/Primetime. I think their plan is to do it in late spring of 1985.

I think I am pleased with what I have so far and I hope you will be too.

All the best.

Aye,
Alan

[67] Tom Courtenay (1933–) is a stage and screen actor, who was at one point married to Cheryl Kennedy (of the 1981 revival of *My Fair Lady*). He is known for his screen appearances in *Billy Liar* (1963) and *Doctor Zhivago* (1965).

[68] Dame Edith Evans (1888–1976) was one of the greatest actresses of the twentieth century, encompassing over 150 roles in more than 60 years.

[69] "Spring Will Be a Little Late This Year" is a song by Frank Loesser.

In the summer of 1984, Lerner resumed work on what would be his final, incomplete musical, *My Man Godfrey*. Like *Dance a Little Closer*, it was based on 1930s material, this time a screwball comedy starring William Powell[70] and Carole Lombard[71] (1936). Lerner teamed up with a new collaborator to write the music, Gerard Kenny, who was then perhaps best known for penning the hit Barry Manilow[72] song, "I Made it Through the Rain." They had started talking about the show the previous fall (as Lerner indicates in his letter to David Grossberg, earlier), but the writing could only begin in earnest after the opening of *Closer*. The producer was to be Allan Carr, who was then represented on Broadway by *La Cage aux Folles*, and Lerner had ceded the librettist duties to Kristi Kane, an American playwright in her mid-twenties. Writing to his manager, Robert Lantz,[73] in August, Lerner was able to report that the project was going swimmingly:

To Robert Lantz

August 14, 1984

Dear Robby,

Re: *My Man Godfrey*

Just a quick note because I am in the middle of a three-day recording session with Liz on her new album—which incidentally is going to be wonderful.

Kenny and I had a positive love feast with Allan Carr. We played him three incomplete songs which gave him a sense of the style and I gave him a general idea of my approach to the adaptation and we are all three going to take a house by the sea together. I told him now that we have finally solved the approach, things will soon be getting on to paper. All I can say is, he is planning a March rehearsal—about which I said nothing. Gerard Kenny has to go to New York to see his ailing father this week. Allan will be there and they are going out together Thursday night—with Kenny's wife.

[70] William Powell (1892–1984) was a major star at MGM, best known for his appearances in the *Thin Man* films.

[71] Carole Lombard (1908–42) was a popular actress in Hollywood screwball comedies of the 1930s. She was killed in a plane crash at the age of 33.

[72] Barry Manilow (1943–) is a singer and songwriter. His hit songs include "Mandy" and "Could It Be Magic." He has also composed two musicals, *Copacabana* (1985, TV; 1994, UK stage) and *Harmony* (1997).

[73] Robert Lantz (1914–2007) was an agent to numerous major stars, including Bette Davis and Leonard Bernstein.

He also loves you dearly and said he thought you were the most intelligent, charming, co-operative gentleman he has met in the theatre! So, between the three of us, he is in a cocoon of happiness.

About *The Merry Widow*, I only wrote two lyrics and they only fit the story I was working on, not *The Merry Widow*.

So everybody is happy except Collins who are beginning to wonder where the hell their book is. And so am I.

That's all.

Love and kisses,
Alan

In September, suddenly *Carmelina* was on the cards again, which caused Lerner a problem: in addition to *Godfrey* and the history book on musicals, he had agreed to revise his work on *Gigi* for its London stage premiere the following year. He tried to squeeze in some more work on the show with Lane when actress Raquel Welch[74] (who had previously replaced Lauren Bacall in *Woman*

Figure 8.1 Alan Jay Lerner in 1980. Credit: Photofest

[74] Raquel Welch (1940–) is an American movie star, with films including *Bedazzled* (1967) and *Myra Breckinridge* (1970).

of the Year on Broadway) showed interest in the part of Carmelina in October, but in January he decided to take a backseat in the production. He also wrote a sample episode for the proposed BBC TV series to accompany his book and submitted it in October, as well as beginning the revisions to *Gigi*. All this would keep him busy for the rest of 1984.

In early December, he wrote the following letter to Sydney Gruson, *New York Times* correspondent, editor, and publishing executive, who was one of Lerner's lifelong friends. The letter is an excellent reflection of the lyricist's savage wit and good humor among those he was closest to. It also alludes to early details of the London *Gigi* for which John Dexter, best known for his work in the operatic sphere, was to be the director:

To Sydney Gruson

6th December 1984

Dear Chum,

I am sending you a book written by a man who I always told you should be the critic of the New York Times, but what can I expect from a journalist who makes the blanket statement he does not believe in "the conspiratorial interpretation of history"—which I assume includes Julius Caesar?

Anyhow, putz, you will find this an absolutely brilliant and penetrating book which should, with any luck, cut through the ice surrounding your frozen journalistic cortex.

Why I love you, I don't know. I can't believe after all the wives and associated women, I have a latent homosexual streak. Christ, you are not even pretty.

With it all, it was wonderful seeing you over here and my fondest dream is to lure you with pleasure, wine, women and the indescribable charm and wit of my company to moving here permanently—or, at least, semi-permanently. I will even find a Golf Club that will allow you in!

We are off to Egypt on the 21st and I hope the thought of my contracting diarrhoea, cholera and malaria will add to the joy of your Christmas season.

Give Marit my love—and of course sympathy—and a big hug for Christmas.

Aye,
Alan

P.S. "Gigi" is galloping ahead and goes into rehearsal in April. Louis Benjamin and Jerry Minskoff have worked out a partnership for the production and John Dexter is indeed a genius. I think it will be opening in Norwich for May for about a month and it would be great if you were here sometime around then to come up and see it.

Later that month, he met up with Kristi Kane and had a two-day meeting about their ideas for *My Man Godfrey*. In the following two letters to Allan Carr, Lerner gives his initial impressions about Kane and her work and also makes some suggestions about casting and staging. Additionally, he announces that he was to be honored with the Songwriters Hall of Fame's Johnny Mercer Award the following March, a distinction of which he was evidently extremely proud:

To Allan Carr

December 17, 1984

Dear Allan,

Kristi is a charming and bright lady and we had a most interesting two days together. I think it would be unfair not to pass on to you my initial reactions.

First of all, there is the problem that she has never written a musical and no one knows better than you what a complicated form it is. We discussed many ideas, two of which disturbed me considerably, and I told her so. One was that she wanted to eliminate the scavenger hunt because she thought it is cruel that Irene (Lombard) becomes aware of it herself and begins to grow as a human being. I think I may have convinced her. Her second random thought was that Godfrey's old girl from Boston should appear in the last scene, which I told her I definitely thought was unnecessary. Fundamentally, it is one of the best last scenes I can remember in a romantic comedy and it should be toyed with with considerable restraint.

I think I am right in assuming that one of the reasons you wanted a book writer called in was to expedite the project so that it would be ready for September rehearsals, but there are so many other things that are involved that would make September impossible. Mainly, for example, the director. Secondly, the cast. I do my best work when I know for whom I am writing.

I had lunch with Alan Bates[75] last week who is immensely interested and enthusiastic. He and his agent are coming by on Wednesday to hear some of the songs. He told me that his agent in California whispered to him that Malcolm McDowell[76] was also being considered. As much as I admire McDowell, I think he would be a great mistake. He is simply not man enough and Godfrey should be a man in every sense of the word, who has done some considerable living. The other possibility is someone who has become an overnight star over here named Charles Dance,[77] because of *The Jewel in the Crown,* the thirteen-hour television series that knocked England off its bum last year and is by far the best television series ever made. I believe it's coming to America starting in January. Dance is a little younger but a man and, I am told, sings very well. But, needless to say, he is not in the same class as Bates who is pure magic on the stage. I know *A Patriot for Me*[78] didn't do well in California but that has nothing to do with anything. One can't blame an actor for appearing in a play that doesn't work.

The girl is also a major question. Have you any ideas? I have one which is—I appreciate—too much to hope for—Meryl Streep[79] started her career as a singer. I realize she's probably booked up until 1994, but there is no harm in asking. My God, wouldn't she and Bates be something?

Bates seems to be available for September rehearsals at this moment but I don't see how commitments can be made until the elements come together. In the meantime, I will exert my world famous charm to try and keep him in line.

Returning to the director for a moment—have you thought about Tommy Tune? Surrounded by the right people, I think he could be quite marvelous.

[75] Alan Bates (1934–2003) was a popular British actor who appeared in a range of films, including *Whistle Down the Wind* (1961), *Zorba the Greek* (1964), and *Women in Love* (1969).

[76] Malcom McDowell (1943–) is an English actor, nominated for a Golden Globe for his appearance in *A Clockwork Orange* (1971).

[77] Charles Dance (1946–) is an English actor who has appeared in a range of projects including *The Jewel in the Crown* (1984), *Alien 3* (1993), and *Rebecca* (1997).

[78] *A Patriot for Me* (1965) is a controversial play by John Osborne. Bates had recently starred in a revival.

[79] Meryl Streep (1949–) is one of the most revered actresses of her generation. She has been nominated for a record 18 Academy Awards, of which she has won three, and 28 Golden Globe Awards, of which she has won eight (also a record).

In any event, there is one quintessential aspect of the show and that is it must be the most elegant musical since *My Fair Lady*. To really work with the kind of score Gerard and I are writing, it needs ladies and gentlemen. Not only that, it is about the rich and the chic.

My final suggestion is that I am going to New York on March 16th because on the 19th, I am to receive The Songwriters Hall of Fame Award for lyric writing. It is only the third they have given in their existence—so I am, for the moment, quite unbearable! It would be lovely if Gerard and I and Kristi—if it still be she—and you could meet in New York for a couple of days of bringing each other up to date. Gerard and I will show you the new songs, etc.

I have been working my head off for the last month or two and that plus my daughter's illness has left me a little on the ropes, so Liz and I are going away Friday for the holidays and will be back on January 4th. I think "Jingle Bells" would just about finish me off, so we are going to Egypt.

From January 4th on, I will be here until that date in March, so do let us try and communicate at your convenience when I return.

Have a wonderful holiday. I look forward to the New Year and *My Man Godfrey* with effervescent enthusiasm.

Faithfully,
Alan

After the painful disaster of *Dance a Little Closer*, one can only admire Lerner's enthusiasm and optimism in thinking *My Man Godfrey* could be "the most elegant musical since *My Fair Lady*." He believed there was no reason that he could not enjoy success with the new musical, and threw himself into it with as much energy as ever. The Mercer Award was also well timed to boost his confidence, as is apparent from this follow-up note to Carr:

To Allan Carr

December 21, 1984

Dear Allan,

I just re-read the letter concerning the Award. I don't want to present myself to you in any false colours. The letter actually says the following:

"We are honored that you have agreed to accept the 'Mercer Award.' This award has been presented only three times in the sixteen year history of the Hall of Fame. Ginger Mercer is expected to come to New York to personally present the award to you as John always thought you are the greatest."

Lovely to talk to you last night. I will be back January 4th. If Kristi wants to call me about anything, please tell her to do so.

Have a wonderful holiday and a "highly successful" New Year.

Aye,
Alan

Back in London after his Egyptian vacation, Lerner resumed work on *Godfrey* in January 1985. His commitment to this show meant that when complicated changes to *Carmelina* were being requested from all sides, he finally decided to hand over the revision of the script to Joseph Stein. The following is his reply to a letter from Hugh Wooldridge, who had met with Lane and Stein in New York and drawn up a plan of action:

To Armand Gerrard

14 January 1985

Dear Armand

"Someone in April"

I read Hugh's letter with great care and there are so many points of view about this play that what I would like to suggest is that, if he will, Joe Stein write it to his, Burton's and Hugh's satisfaction. Joe and I invariably agree about everything, so I have complete confidence that I would be happy with anything he writes (including a rearrangement of the songs).

I confess that I have my doubts about beginning with "Carmelina" because nobody knows who the hell anybody is, but perhaps it will be alright.

I have no objection to cutting out "It's Time For a Love Song," although it might be a bit much to introduce it at the very end of the play for the first time. Too operetta for me.

I also have my doubts about all the wives reprising "The Image of Me" because it has no emotional value. The reason it does with Florence is because her husband is the one who thinks he can't have a child.

I don't understand the idea for Gia. Songs are about one thing and I wouldn't know how to write a song about three different men. Doing what? I am also rather fond of the one she sings, but—as I said above—if everybody agrees it should be taken out, I will try and think of something else.

Finally, "I Must Have Her" is a stiff and will be no matter what lyrics are put to it. It's not the fault of the melody, it was just an idea that didn't work. I would rather reprise "Carmelina" with new lyrics.

In all honesty, I must say that I rather like the show the way it is, with the suggestions that were made previously, i.e. "You Never Told Me" and "Time For a Love Song" beginning and ending Scene I. What will be the music to end Scene I now? Or is it the general consensus that no music is needed?

Anyhow, I leave the whole thing up to Joe. I simply have too much work to do to sit down and try and re-write this play so that everybody is satisfied when it is finished. None of the three of us was completely happy with it and Burton was quite violent about it, so I shall relieve the tension by being a "go-alonger." If it's alright with Joe, it will be alright with me.

Aye,
Alan

When the project became even more entangled later in the year, Lerner permitted Lane to work with another lyricist, Barry Harman,[80] on a few new songs for the show, in order for it to be ready to go ahead while Lerner was working on *Godfrey* and *Gigi*. In the following letter to Sydney Gruson, he outlines his other recent activities, which included a rare (for Lerner) occasional song, "Brocades and Coronets," written in honor of the six-month-old Prince Harry, younger son of Prince Charles:

To Sydney Gruson

28th January 1985

Dear Syd,

Knowing that your reading habits are reduced to the New York Times and trash—I assume you have given up pornographic literature out of envy—I am enclosing a review from the Atlantic Monthly which I do not think will amuse you at all. But that's what I'm here for, isn't it, pal? I really don't know how you get along without me in New York. And frankly how I get along in London without you.

[80] Barry Harman (1952–) is a writer and producer. He wrote the book and lyrics for the musicals *Olympus on My Mind* (1986) and *Romance/Romance* (1987).

Are you and Marit coming over in February? I don't know why, but in all your daily phone calls I have forgotten to ask you.

Liz and I will be in New York March 15th. I collect my award for being brilliant at the Waldorf March 18th. I hope you and Marit can come. Also, Alan Carr is giving a large dinner in my honour the night before at a place to be designated, so if you have a drag outfit[81] left in the closet I hope you will come and pay homage. I promise to put you next to Porter.

I have been working my butt off. Gerard Kenny, who is writing *Godfrey* with me, will be in New York and we can play you some of the songs. We will be a little over half finished by then.

On February 15th, Liz sings the lullaby we have written for young Prince Harry before the Royals at the Barbican. I think it came off quite well. It is called "Brocades and Coronets."

Any news from your side? Or are you still leading that boring life that you cherish so?

I received a couple of pompous letters from Welles[82] which I'm sure were Photostats. Did you receive a couple, too? I have written him a sympathetic but caustic reply.

Give my love to Marit and a boot in the arse to you, old chum.

Aye,
Alan

After a month of working on the lyrics, he also wrote to Carr to update him on the progress of the songs for *Godfrey*:

To Allan Carr

February 1, 1985

Dear Allan,

<u>Progress Report</u>

Accomplishments to date:

1. Opening song, "Garbage Isn't What It Used To Be"—finished, minus four lines, including musical interlude introducing Godfrey in speech/song in the middle of the number.

[81] A reference to *La Cage aux Folles*.

[82] Benjamin Welles, another of Lerner's lifelong friends.

2. During it, he mentions the difficulty of "selling those bloody apples on the corners" and he gives them all away. I would love to have 1000 balloons shaped liked apples fall from the ceiling and on to the audience.

3. "I've Been Married"—finished, music in the hands of Alan Bates.

4. "Miss Hilary Bacon of Beacon Hill"—finished, music being delivered to Alan Bates this week.

5. "Will I Ever Fall in Love Again—Not I Yi Yi Yi" (rumba)—music completed, lyrics one half.

6. "Run For The Train"—Harlem—music completed, lyrics one half.

7. "Some People"—completed, but there will be a second chorus which Godfrey sings to the audience and which I am well into.

8. An absolutely beautiful new song for the second act called "It Was You Again," sung by Irene. Wherever she went in Europe and looked at the gondolier, or the hotel porter, or the maître d'hotel, "it was you again." No lyrics.

9. The second act will open at the pier when the two sisters came back from Europe. Comedy song by custom officials and Irene and Cornelia called "Anything To Declare?" Not started.

10. "Dancin' The Blues Away"—finished.

By the time we arrive in New York in mid-March, I imagine seven or eight will be completed. As it lays out, there will probably be eleven numbers in the score, not counting reprises with additional lyrics.

There will definitely be a tango for Mrs. Bullock and her teacher as we discussed.

The score is being written roughly to the outline which seemed to be satisfactory to Kristi. I told her when we met that there were two or three scenes that were so musical, it would be preferable if I wrote them. She agreed. But of course they will not be chiseled in granite.

Do you think Tommy Tune will be available? As I mentioned on the phone, Foster Brooks[83] would be sensational if he's not too expensive. I think I mentioned Alyson Reid,[84] the girl who is playing the lead in the movie of *Chorus Line*.

The score will be completed without doubt by June 1st at the latest.

That's all.

[83] Foster Brooks (1912–2001) was an actor and comedian, known for playing an amusingly drunken character in many of his performances.

[84] Alyson Reid (1958–) appeared as Cassie in the movie version of *A Chorus Line* (1985), as well as stage productions including Lerner's *Dance a Little Closer*.

Hope you're well, happy and enjoying a life of fame and fortune and that this year will be your most successful of all.

Much love.

Aye,
Alan

The old *Merry Widow* project briefly returned into view in February, when Plácido Domingo raised the possibility of making it. He was due to record an album of operetta arias, *Vienna, City of My Dreams,* in the spring of 1985, and his agent, Margherita Stafford,[85] mentioned the *Widow* project to Lerner. By now, it was clear that the original authors' estates would never allow the operetta to be used, so Lerner suggested using his original scenario interspersed with extracts from other Viennese pieces of the same style and period. Allan Carr became interested in the film, and in the following letter Lerner explains its back history to him, as well as a possible way forward:

To Allan Carr

February 5, 1985

Dear Allan,

Never did I think I would be sending you the enclosed, but yesterday I was on the phone with my old friend, Margherita Stafford. She told me she had been discussing Placido with you and that you mentioned to her you had heard I had once written a script for him and would I send it to you. Ergo, I am sending it to you.

Placido and I go way, way back. Believe it or not, he began his professional career as the understudy to Freddie Eynsford-Hill in the Mexican production of *My Fair Lady,* which was produced by my brother. He had expressed a desire to do a film of *The Merry Widow* and two young English producers, along with Margherita, came to me. At the time I was busy contemplating my navel and I undertook to do it. After reading *The Merry Widow,* however, it seemed absurd to try and do it the way it was, so I decided to write a Schnitzlerian[86] plot. (He's back in vogue again, incidentally. Two plays at the National.) Sort of like *La*

[85] Margherita Stafford (1927–2008) was a leading agent of various major opera singers, whom she managed with her partner David Law under the Stafford Law firm.

[86] Arthur Schnitzler (1862–1931) was a controversial Austrian author. One of his plays, *Reigen,* depicts characters before and after the sexual act, and it was turned into a French-language film, *La Ronde,* in 1950.

Ronde with *The Merry Widow* songs interspersed on the stage, and with new lyrics the songs would have a double meaning.

After finishing the bloody thing, the two widows of the original book, who think their dead mates wrote the greatest thing since Genesis Book I, were absolutely horrified and permission to proceed was refused.

Then we all decided to keep the script and interpolate instead of *The Merry Widow* some of the great songs of that era. They would be just as wonderful for Placido. Alas, however, by that time the two Limeys had run out of money and had to abandon the project.

As a result of Margherita's prodding last night, I got it off the shelf, dusted it and le voici, as they say in the *Cage aux Folles*.

Finished the second Act ballad over the weekend, "It's Always You," and I hope you will be as pleased with it as I am.

Margherita says you're in California, so I hope that is where you are because that's where the script will be.

Love.

Aye,
Alan

P.S. By coincidence, I received a call last week from one of the ex-producers who is now working in Australia who asked me to send him a script. He asked if I thought Liz would be interested. I think—unbiased—she might be quite marvelous. Audrey Hepburn has already said she would play Frieda.

Lerner also wrote to Stafford herself, assuring her that he had sent the screenplay to Carr:

To Margherita Stafford

February 7, 1985

Dear, dear Margherita,

I have met charming people in my life and I have met efficient people, but I must admit you are the only one who is both.

Mike Allen called me last night—thanks to you, of course—and we had a very interesting and, I think, profitable chat. He knew nothing about the lullaby and was astounded that EMI was so cavalier about it. He said he would make enquiries and get back to me today.

In the course of conversation, *The Merry Widow* script came up, which I have tentatively retitled *The Waltz Goes On*—and to my surprise he had read it two years ago and loved it. I also found out, before talking to him, that EMI has now some affiliation with the ubiquitous Allan Carr. How he waddles around in so many places is a wonder. Incidentally, I sent the script off to Allan with a note detailing its history and how it had been rewritten so that some of the famous songs of the operettas of the day could be used instead of *The Merry Widow*.

We had a long talk about my book and the plans of the BBC, Goldcrest and public television in the U.S. I am having lunch with Mike Wooller[87] of Goldcrest tomorrow, and I will drop it into the conversation. There is no doubt that Julius[88] would be wonderful for it and I will certainly recommend him most enthusiastically. I am also preparing a brief outline of the series for you and it will be in your hands before the weekend.

Between finishing the book, the television series, the musical I am writing for Allan Carr, which is to go into rehearsal in September (hopefully with Alan Bates), and another musical that I am bursting to write as soon as I can get to it, I have what is called a filled plate.

Liz and I would love to see you and David. I will call you next week and perhaps we can arrange a dinner.

Much love from both of us to both of you.

Aye,
Alan

Though it had only occasionally been mentioned in previous correspondence, Lerner's next project to reach the stage was the London revival of *Gigi*. He had extensively re-conceived the show since its Broadway incarnation. This version would rearrange some of the material so that, for instance, the show would now start with "Paris Is Paris Again" rather than "Thank Heaven for Little Girls"; no doubt he hoped this would help avoid unflattering comparisons with the movie version. The key to the reconception was that whereas the Broadway production had seemed to swamp what was basically an intimate story, this London version would be more like a chamber show. Still, it was important to have some excellent actors to take on the well-loved characters. Key among these was the British

[87] Mike Wooller (1927–96) worked in various branches of production and management in television and became a founding member of Goldcrest Films and Television in 1981.

[88] Conductor Julius Rudel (1921–) was on Stafford's artists' roster and she had suggested him as a suitable candidate for conducting the musical numbers for Lerner's television series.

actress Sian Phillips,[89] who had starred in a London revival of *Pal Joey* (1980), and Lerner wrote to encourage her to take the part of Aunt Alicia, enclosing a copy of the Broadway cast album:

To Sian Phillips

February 27, 1985

Dear Miss Phillips,

"GIGI"
I was delighted to hear that you were pleased with the script. My hopes would be dashed if you didn't do it.

The enclosed record is from a production (ghastly, I might add) that was done on the West Coast but it does include "The Contract" in the second act—which incidentally is done much too slowly—and "Paris Is Paris Again."

Aunt Alicia also does a duet of "The Night They Invented Champagne" with Mamita that ends the first act and the two ladies reprise it again in the second act just before Gigi goes to Maxim's. So, all in all, I think there will be enough singing to keep you busy. The most important item of course is "The Contract" which does work a treat.

I hope you like it and, if I am not being too optimistic, I look forward to working with you.

Sincerely,
Alan Jay Lerner

In March, Alan Bates agreed to appear in *Godfrey*, and this gave the production just the boost it needed. Indeed, on March 22 the show was announced in the press, and there seemed no reason to think it would not now happen.[90] But Lerner was still unhappy with Kane's work on the book, and the following letter is one of a number in which he gently tried to cajole her into a different direction:

[89] Sian Phillips (1933–) is a Welsh actress, known equally for her many classical roles and her appearances in films such as *Becket* (1964) and *Goodbye, Mr. Chips* (1969).

[90] Enid Nemy, "Broadway," *New York Times*, March 22, 1985, C2.

To Kristi Kane

March 27, 1985

Kristi my love,

Enclosed is a copy of the lyrics to date. I will send you more as we get along.

I hope you will forgive me if for a moment I sound pseudo-professional, but from prehistoric experience I have found the following:

1. The great danger is to contribute too much. The screenplay is so bloody good. I ran into David Lean[91] in California and we were talking about it and he considered it one of the best comedies ever made on the screen—with which I agree. I know that twice I adapted plays: once I did as little as possible and had a hit and the other I did a huge re-write and had a flop! It's really all there and just needs carefully editing. For example, the more I get into the writing of the score, the less important the maid becomes.

2. At this point, I beg you not to worry about music and lyrics. The ideas for lyrics after a certain point will flow from what you write rather than the other way round. My job is to take the emotion and condense it into a lyric.

3. And finally—run the picture as often as you can. I have seen it over twelve times myself and run it every couple of weeks. I am constantly finding in it new things that I didn't see before.

It was lovely being with you in New York and I look forward to the whole project with high enthusiasm.

Call me any time about anything.

Gerard saw Allan Carr who was thrilled about Alan Bates and is coming over to see him as soon as he is well enough.

The weather here is lousy and I envy you.

Best love,
Alan

Another project in which Lerner was involved in his final year, but which has largely been overlooked, is the Broadway show *Teddy and Alice*. It told a fictionalized account of the relationship between Teddy Roosevelt[92] and his daughter during

[91] Sir David Lean (1908–91) was a film director and producer, whose famous epic films included *The Bridge on the River Kwai* (1957), *Lawrence of Arabia* (1962), *Doctor Zhivago* (1965), and *A Passage to India* (1984).

[92] Theodore "Teddy" Roosevelt (1858–1919) was president of the United States from September 14, 1901, to March 3, 1909.

his time at the White House. The idea was to use music by John Philip Sousa[93] and add lyrics by Hal Hackady,[94] with some new songs by Richard Kapp[95] and a book by Jerome Alden.[96] Lerner gave some input at the early stages, no doubt because of his long-term association with the director, Stone Widney, who had been stage manager on *Paint Your Wagon*, assistant director on *My Fair Lady*, production assistant on *Camelot*, and production supervisor on *Clear Day, Coco*, and *Dance a Little Closer*. In the following letter, he offers some initial thoughts on how the piece could be sharpened:

To Stone Widney

8th April 1985

Widney, dear boy,

I can't go through the play scene by scene because, if anything, that's for later on when you and the fellows have read the following notes and decided if they have any validity.

After reading the script two or three times, I have a very strong feeling about both Teddy and Alice. Teddy first.

What I miss is more of Teddy the President. I think I mentioned in New York that in any dramatized biography you have to assume that the audience knows nothing about the character and/or precisely what he did, in this case, as President.

Specifically, he was always keenly aware that he became President by accident and was determined to be re-elected and receive the mandate of the people. In 1902 he took three steps which he did not realize at the time because of opposition in both Congress and the press, which made him so popular with the people that it practically guaranteed him re-election.

1) He persuaded Congress to establish a Bureau of Corporations with powers to inspect the books of all business involved in inter-state commerce. In order to get the Bill through, he promised Congress

[93] John Philip Sousa (1854–1932) was an American composer, remembered for his large catalogue of marches.

[94] Lyricist Hal Hackady's (?–) credits include *Minnie's Boys* (1970), *Ambassador* (1971), and *Goodtime Charley* (1975).

[95] Richard Kapp (1936–2006) was an American conductor who founded the ensemble Philharmonia Virtuosi of New York.

[96] Jerome Alden (1921–97) was a playwright and screenwriter, whose work included a play about Theodore Roosevelt, *Bully*.

he would ask for nothing more. Instead, he used the power of the Presidency in a way no other President since Lincoln had done before.

2) He brought a successful law suit against the Northern Securities Company, the huge combine of railroads put together by J. P. Morgan, John D. Rockerfeller, Harriman and James Hill. As I remember, that was the occasion that brought J. P. Morgan to the White House. I would love to see that scene, or some of it.

3) In order to settle the coal strike which he felt was against the public welfare, he threatened to call in the army unless both Union and Management came to the White House and mediated a solution. Which they did. Contrary to his nickname of "Trust-buster," he was for regulation not for dismemberment. In other words, against the will of the powers that be. He really was an imperial President who used the full powers of his office. I deeply miss some of that in the play, certainly enough to understand what kind of President he really was and why the acceptance of challenge was a product of his personality.

As for Alice, there are many moments when I find her obnoxious. "Boo-hiss" and "scrumptious" and all such terminology that may have been indigenous to the period, makes my skin crawl. When I read that she shot the lights out from the train, she seems to me like a spoilt brat. I would like to feel a little more that she understood her father as well as went her own merry way. Fundamentally, more wit and charm to go with her self-indulgence. I don't mean that she manipulates her father but she should be a little more irresistible.

I think there are too many love songs by Nick and Alice. Sousa was not a good writer of operettas. Anyhow, the love story is really between father and daughter rather than Alice and Nick.

When I first heard the play, "The Stars and Stripes Forever" ended the first act. It was absolutely smashing and I hope to God it can be restored.

In the second act, I do have a positive sequence to suggest for the last half of the second act. (Incidentally, the first act is too long as you all probably know.) The sequence is that before the election, we find out that Alice has made up her mind about Nick. Next, Teddy is overwhelmingly re-elected. Jubilation. But his jubilation is interrupted when Alice tells him she wants to get married. The idea of using "Can I Let Her Go?" as first a ballad is brilliant. He sings it and when he makes up his mind that he can't stand in her way, the song becomes the march and the march becomes the music of the wedding. I think the combination of the wedding and the march will be both emotional and thrilling. A fantastic end to the play.

Parenthetically, I think Edith's song is terrific and I love the re-enactment of San Juan Hill. The beginning is also wonderful.

In general, there is an embarrassment of riches. What I am aching for is the sharpening of Teddy and my desire to fall in love with Alice. There is such a danger that because of the vocal requirements you may end up with an operetta-like Alice and that would be disastrous.

I hope you find some of these first-blush thoughts constructive. As far as Teddy is concerned, for God's sake don't worry about his being too political a figure. There is nothing he did—certainly in his first term of office—that anyone can object to. The "Square Deal" is a far cry from the "New Deal"—if that's what the backers are worried about.

Incidentally, I think Eleanor's resume a la Bronte could be told in a less expository way by Alice and give us a chance to see her sympathy and understanding of her father. I would also love to find out from Alice about her father's physical weakness as a child which made him the way he is.

I think that's all at the moment. If I have any more thoughts, I will get them off to you.

Aye,
Alan

In the end, the show opened in late 1987, more than a year after Lerner's death, and Widney left it in Washington during its disastrous out-of-town tryout. Lerner was credited as "artistic consultant." Speaking at the time of its November 1987 Broadway premiere it was noted by Len Cariou, who played Teddy, that this billing was earned, and that the idea for the show came during Widney and Lerner's research on *1600 Pennsylvania Avenue*.[97] In his opening-night review of the show, Frank Rich declared, "If the show's creators had any respect for the dead, they would not give the defenseless Mr. Lerner partial artistic 'credit' for a show that makes his own unsuccessful Presidential musical, '1600 Pennsylvania Avenue,' seem like 'My Fair Lady' by comparison."[98] Yet from the letter to Stone Widney, Lerner seems to have had passionate ideas about the piece, even if he also implies that lots of work was needed.

Ironically, *1600 Pennsylvania Avenue* itself was the subject of the next letter. Lerner had remained on good terms with Leonard Bernstein after the show's untimely demise, but this was the first time a revival had been seriously

[97] Jeremy Gerard, "Len Cariou Does a Bully 'Teddy and Alice,'" *Chicago Tribune*, November 12, 1987. Accessed online: http://articles.chicagotribune.com/1987-11-12/features/8703250415_1_night-music-richard-kapp-demon-barber (22 August 2012).

[98] Frank Rich, "Theater: Teddy and Alice," *New York Times*, November 13, 1987.

suggested. Bernstein wrote to ask whether Lerner would allow someone else to come in and revise the show's book, and he invited Lerner to revise his own lyrics. In his reply, Lerner indicates his willingness to allow the project to take place, and although he expresses a keenness to work on the lyrics himself, he even permits Bernstein to bring in someone else to do that too. The letter is mostly of interest, however, for his ideas on why the show didn't work in its original form:

To Leonard Bernstein

April 16, 1985

My dear old chum,

Robby [Lantz] passed on to me your interest in trying to reshape and make something out of *1600*. I gather that although there is no schedule you would like to get it done some time before the tri-centennial.

To get to the point: of course a fresh eye is needed. Even though I've had an eye implant and don't wear glasses any more (can you believe it?), I don't think this brand new one will be sufficient, and I would welcome a writer with ideas on how to re-organise and rewrite.

As far as the lyrics are concerned, I suddenly seem to have taken a new lease on life and am scribbling like fury. I have a musical [*Gigi*] in rehearsal here in July which John Dexter is directing, and am two-thirds through the score of another that Allan Carr plans to put in rehearsal sometime in the autumn. Besides that I am just completing a huge tome for Collins on a history of the musical theatre since Offenbach. So if the right time for you should be impossible for me, and time adjustments cannot be arranged, as much as I would dislike it I would understand if you had to turn to someone else for any additional lyrics. But I truly hope that will only be the last resort. I would love to have another crack at it.

It is very interesting how *1600* started because Robby remembers its inception one way and I have a clear memory of it in another. Originally I wanted to do five episodes which were critical in the history of the White House. I remember that I thought the entire production would look like a rehearsal, on the theory that democracy is still rehearsing. Robby, on the other hand, is convinced that the original intention was to write a sort of "Upstairs, Downstairs" history of the White House—without the upstairs. In other words, it would be told strictly through the eyes of a multi-generational servant family. What I think we got was a mixture of both with moments of the black experience thrown in, all of which added up to a horse with three heads. I still vote for the "upstairs" story—perhaps now even more than ever because the upstairs material is fresher and we have been surfeited with the history of the blacks in America. Another reason is because I don't—and didn't—do that sort of thing very well. But, I am open to any and all approaches.

In any event, I have some two thousand books and crates of pre-play material that are finally about to be shipped over to me and I will be able to examine all those early versions.

I am, at long last, not happily married but ecstatically so to a smashing lady—we've been together for five years and married for four, a track record for me. We bought a house too quickly that was and is too small, but we have finally got around to looking for a place large enough to accommodate all that I left in storage. I adore living in London and I've had the most wonderful five years of my life here. So whenever we meet—which I hope will be soon, somewhere—prepare yourself for a bubbling version of your old Virgo friend.

I hear the new *West Side Story*[99] album is terrific. We have been in Spain for a few days on hol and this is our first day back, but I've already ordered a copy.

I think of you often. And always with love.

Aye,
Alan

In spite of Lerner's enthusiasm, the revival never came to fruition in Lerner or Bernstein's lifetime.

However, the rewritten *Gigi* made it to the stage in the early fall of 1985. It was ready to go into rehearsal in late July, but hit a snag at the last minute when Loewe suddenly withdrew permission for the extra songs that had been written for the 1973 Broadway production to be used. Since "Paris Is Paris Again" was a particular cornerstone of Lerner's reconceived book, he wrote to Loewe in an attempt to persuade him to let him use it:

To Frederick Loewe

July 15, 1985

Fritz,

There has been so much legal back and forthing about what songs can or cannot be used in "Gigi" that I thought, perhaps, I could cut through it all by giving you a history of the enterprise over here.

[99] Bernstein had recorded *West Side Story* with the opera singers Jose Carreras and Kiri Te Kanawa for Deutsche Grammophon.

The idea of bringing "Gigi" to London originated over a year and a half ago with Cameron Mackintosh, who, as you know, did "My Fair Lady" and did us proud. It was while Cam was planning it that John Dexter, who certainly in everybody's opinion is one of the best directors in the world, became involved. What Dexter had in mind, and God knows I agreed with him and I am sure you would, too, was to capture the intimacy of the film—which, as we know, did not have the usual M-G-M production numbers, etcetera—but, at the same time, not be haunted by the film. It would be a true theatrical piece and not what Gerald Bordman, in his authoritative History of the Musical Theatre when writing about "Gigi," said: "Lerner and Loewe's enchanting film musical was lifted off the screen and set down uncomfortably on the legitimate stage. The translation from film script to play script was mere hack work." So what Dexter had in mind, for example, was to begin on a bare stage and create Paris before our eyes, the restaurant in the Bois, thereby giving it a fresh, theatrical, as opposed to cinematic, beginning. Scenes would move gracefully from one to the other musically and it would, in a sense, become a little theatrical jewel, as the film was a cinematic jewel. Honoré would narrate a little more than he did to maintain the flow. But the first essential was to find a genuinely superb Gigi.

When Cam's schedule became overcrowded—he is doing three new companies of "Cats" all over the world, plus a musical version of "Les Miserables" at the Royal Shakespeare, plus Andrew Lloyd Webber's "Song and Dance" in New York, all within three months—Sir Louis Benjamin of Moss-Stohl, Jerome Minskoff (who is now functioning a great deal over here—he is involved in eighteen plays) and Helen Montagu, who is David Merrick's silent assistant in London on "42nd Street" and an immensely experienced and respected lady, all joined forces to bring it to the West End. Had we waited for Cam, we would have lost John Dexter and Cam understood that and gave us all his blessing.

The cast that Dexter has assembled is superb and he found a Gigi aged nineteen, who will probably be the next Audrey Hepburn. She is enchanting looking, sings well and is a smashing little actress. The sets and costumes are ravishing and "Gigi" will be the most elegant musical since "My Fair Lady."

To help the movement from scene to scene, in two places "Paris Is Paris Again" suddenly became really an integral part of the play, and the charm of Amanda Waring[100] (Gigi) really gives "Wide, Wide World" the touching importance it never had.

[100] Actress Amanda Waring (1966–) has appeared in the musicals *From Here to Maternity* and *Love off the Shelf*, in addition to the title role in *Gigi*. She is the daughter of the actress Dorothy Tutin and the actor Derek Waring.

I did a lot of work theatricalizing the script, fundamentally in the transitions, and writing extra half-choruses here and there to the film score, also to assist in those transitions.

We are playing in one of the choice theatres in London, the Lyric Theatre, which we would never have got except that Moss-Stohl owns the theatre.

Rehearsals are to begin a week from today and last week was the first time we heard that you only wished songs from the film to be used. If your desire was conditioned by the success of Louis Jourdan's production, let me assure you it was dreadful and only successful in places because of Louis combined with "Gigi." When I read the script, I told Dave Grossberg to make certain it never appeared within 150 miles of New York. Even Cam, when he saw it, was appalled.

Also, the fact is at this point that management has rights that cannot be withdrawn. The Dramatists' Guild Law and the law over here is that only one of the authors' signatures is required. The reason for this is that if the other author (or authors) is unhappy, he can have his version done by someone else. Because I signed the contract with the full confidence that you would be as pleased about the production as I, the producers now have the right to the stage version.

So what we are really discussing is two songs, and you must know that if either does not work I am certainly not going to leave it in. But you are at a disadvantage because you have not seen or heard the girl, and have not been party to all the meetings with Dexter and cannot see how artfully he has blended the entire production.

There is simply no comparison to what will appear on the stage at the Lyric Theatre to any other version of "Gigi" there has ever been, at least in English. And, I repeat, anything that needs changing or dropping will be.

Isn't it wonderful about the Kennedy honours?

Aye,
Alan

The change of tone between this and Lerner's letters to Loewe of 1956, when they were at the height of their fame and intimacy, is noticeable, but Lerner keeps his patience in spite of Loewe's evidently having dragged his feet. The final sentence refers to the fact that Lerner and Loewe had just been invited to receive Kennedy Center Honors in December of the same year, yet another sign of the nostalgia that had developed for their collaborations even as Lerner was continuing to produce new work with other composers.

Gigi opened in September to mixed reviews, most of which blamed Dexter's "stiff" direction as one of the main problems.[101] For Lerner, it was a great disappointment, as he confided to Loewe after the event, but at least the *Gigi* brand name guaranteed reasonable advance sales:

To Frederick Loewe

October 8, 1985,

Fritz,

I thought it was about time to give you a progress report on "Gigi." First, the good news.

The show is an unqualified smash. In a small theatre of less than 1,000 seats, we are doing close to £60,000 a week, which is a house record for the Lyric Theatre. The audiences adore it, there are lines at the window every day, the advance is around £250,000 and seats are being sold into April and May.

The album has been made and I will send you a copy as soon as it is off the press. I think you will like it about as much as I do, which is that it is adequate. As you know, we only have ten men in the pit and the man who sings "Gigi" has had throat problems since we opened.

The not-so-good news is that John Dexter, who came heralded with an immense reputation, turned out to be a disaster, never directed the actors, and lit the whole thing like an opera. The opening night was very wobbly and the notices reflected it. However, Beryl Reid[102] who plays Mamita, whether she remembers her lines or not—more often not—can do no wrong with the British public. Jean-Pierre Aumont,[103] although charming, suffered from lack of direction.

Since it has opened, I have gotten more lights on the stage and better performances, and the subsequent reviews in the Sunday papers and magazines were much better than the dailies. The dailies took up so much space criticizing John Dexter there was hardly room to talk about anything else.

[101] Matt Wolf, "Classic 'Gigi' Flops Again," *Associated Press/Mid Cities Daily News,* October 1, 1985, 6.

[102] Beryl Reid (1919–96) was a British actress, nominated for a Golden Globe for her performance in *The Killing of Sister George* (1968).

[103] Jean-Pierre Aumont (1911–2001) was a French actor who played numerous roles on stage and screen, the latter including *Heartbeat* (1946) with Ginger Rogers and *Lili* (1953) with Leslie Caron.

But, bit by bit, the show is getting in shape. Sian Phillips, who plays Aunt Alicia, is superb, and the little girl, Amanda Waring, is an adorable Gigi.

The sum total is that the audience likes it better than I do, and undoubtedly better than you would. What does work is the small size of it, which seems appropriate for the intimacy of the story—and the British do love romance. There is no question it will run for at least a year and possibly more. The theatre manager, who is a very wise old bird, is convinced it will run over two years. However long it runs, you can add another year for touring the provinces. In order to protect the territory, I have asked Dave [Grossberg] to make certain there are no more stock and amateur rights in England while the show is running first class.

Needless to say, "Gigi" is being played constantly on the air, and once the album comes out—next week—I know it will get a lot of performances. The principal disc jockeys here are all good friends of mine, and the most important man on the air, David Jacobs,[104] has become one of my closest friends. "On The Street Where You Live" is his theme song and he plays us four or five times a week.

I will see you in Washington.

Love to Francine.

Aye,
Alan

He also wrote the following two letters to Burton Lane after the opening, keeping in touch with him about the emerging revisions to *Carmelina*. Lane had visited Lerner in London over the summer with Barry Harman (the new lyricist) and they had discussed their mutual ideas for the new version. Lane wrote to thank Lerner for his hospitality, to suggest a London revision of *Clear Day* for Liz Robertson, and to ask whether he would join Lane in giving permission to a new small New York record company, Premier Recordings, to record some of the songs from their aborted *Huckleberry Finn* of three decades earlier. The following two letters are Lerner's brief replies to these enquiries, and are his last surviving letters to Lane:

To Burton Lane

October 7, 1985

Dear Burt,

Sorry I have been so long in answering, but I have been over my head with "Gigi" which opened to justifiably "iffy" notices, but to an audience

[104] David Jacobs (1926–2013) was a popular British radio broadcaster, associated with programs such as *Juke Box Jury, Any Questions?* and *The David Jacobs Collection*.

response that, as far as I'm concerned, is far more than it deserves. It actually opened to a larger advance than "42nd Street," the audiences adore it, and seats are selling into April. So I suppose I shouldn't complain. Unfortunately, I have to like it, too, so next week I am going to do a little work on it.

I think "Clear Day" for London would require an enormous rewrite and I don't know if I am up to doing another revival at this moment. Maybe next year, after I get another new show under my belt.

As far as Copenhagen is concerned, if they are interested I say let them have it.

I was very impressed with Barry and I will put down on paper the opening we talked about. I actually had dinner with Hugh over the weekend.

I hope all is well.

Aye,
Alan

To Burton Lane

October 8, 1985

Dear Burt,

Fascinating about the "Finn" score.

The only song that troubles me is "When You Grow Up You'll Know," for which, I think, the lyric is very old-fashioned. Does it have to be included?

Other than that, I certainly have no objections, and as far as the financial arrangements are concerned, whatever you agree to is all right with me.

Best to you both.

Aye,
Alan

December 8 brought the long-awaited Kennedy Center Honors, where Lerner and Loewe were joined by soprano Beverly Sills,[105] actress Irene Dunne,

[105] Beverly Sills (1929–2007) was a highly respected and popular soprano, specializing in *bel canto* repertoire. Upon her retirement, she became an administrator, most notably as general manager of the New York City Opera and as chairman of the Metropolitan Opera.

comedian Bob Hope,[106] and choreographer Merce Cunningham[107] at a White House reception and evening performance for one of the country's highest honors. Rex Harrison and Louis Jourdan introduced the Lerner and Loewe section, which included "Paint Your Wagon" and "I Talk to the Trees" sung by Robert Goulet and Liz Robertson; Michele Lee[108] singing "Almost Like Being in Love" from *Brigadoon*; "I Remember It Well" sung by Don Ameche and Maureen Stapleton; Goulet performing "If Ever I Would Leave You," and Robertson singing "I Could Have Danced All Night." The segment ended with Anthony Newley and the company joining forces in "With a Little Bit of Luck."[109] Obviously, it was a great night for Lerner, and in the following letter he thanks Goulet for his contribution. Reference is also made to a possible Las Vegas production of *Camelot* that Goulet was considering. He had asked for Lerner's permission to do it, in light of the fact that the book would be considerably edited down:

To Robert Goulet

January 7th, 1986

Dear Bobby,

Thanks for your letter. It was wonderful seeing and hearing you in Washington.[110] My God, what a weekend! I only wish Fritz had been there. (If you quote me, no deal on "Camelot.")

As far as Vegas is concerned, I really know nothing about the territory, so I must let you be the judge. On the one hand, Douglas Fairbanks Jr. played "My Fair Lady" in a circumsized version, and on the other, considering the trouble we had getting the final curtain of "Camelot" down before breakfast, I don't know how it could be condensed. But of much more importance is your own feeling about it. You are the one who would be playing it, and I should think twelve performances would drive anybody bonkers.

I don't know what is happening with Richard Harris but for safety's sake I had better check his itinerary.

[106] Bob Hope (1903–2003) was one of the most important entertainers of the twentieth century, remembered especially for his series of "Road" movies with Bing Crosby and Dorothy Lamour.

[107] Mercier Cunningham (1919–2009) was an esteemed dancer and choreographer, notable for his role in the American avant-garde, including collaborations with composer John Cage.

[108] Michele Lee (1942–) is an American actress and personality, whose musical theater appearances have included *How to Succeed* (1961) and *Seesaw* (1973).

[109] Copy in the Paley Center, New York. Information on the program from http://www.paleycenter.org/collection/item/?q=robert+kennedy&p=3&item=T86:0249 (accessed: 22 August 2012).

[110] That is, for the Kennedy Center Honors.

Let's keep in touch.
Your wife is adorable. You look smashing. Stay that way.

Faithfully,
Alan

But sadly, the emotional high of the Kennedy Center was to mark Lerner's last major public appearance. Back in London in the New Year, he hoped to start work on a musical based on Gaston Leroux's *The Phantom of the Opera* to music by Andrew Lloyd Webber. It was a logical move for the lyricist. On the one hand, the material provided the opportunity to write a musical based on a classic romantic love story, exactly his sort of fare. On the other, it was natural that Lerner should want to collaborate with by far the most successful composer of musicals of the decade, following on from his collaborations with other giants of the field like Weill, Loewe, Bernstein, Lane, and even Rodgers, even if some of these resulted in projects that were unsuccessful or aborted. Yet Lerner's smoking habits had finally caught up with him and he was diagnosed with pneumonia, so he agreed to relinquish the lyric writing on *Phantom* to Richard Stilgoe:[111]

To Andrew Lloyd Webber

March 20, 1986

Dear Andrew,

This bloody pneumonia has really done me in. I actually have to go back into hospital today.

I really don't see any way that all my parts will be reassembled on time to do the show and I am desolate. All the more so because I had a whiff of an exciting collaboration.

When I am finally, truly well and no longer look like "The Phantom of the Opera," I will call. If there is still time to do one or possibly two lyrics, perhaps I can throw in a few rhymes.

Thank Richard for me for his professional courtesy and understanding and there is no doubt in my mind you are going to have a wonderful hit.

Aye,
Alan

[111] Richard Stilgoe (1943–) is a British songwriter, whose varied career has included writing the lyrics for the original 1984 version of *Starlight Express*.

In late March, though, it was confirmed that instead of pneumonia, Lerner had contracted lung cancer. The following letter, which is the last of this collection, finds Lerner trying to crack one final joke and remain optimistic even in the face of death. But he clearly knew his chances were poor, and in April, after returning to New York and bring admitted to the Memorial Sloan-Kettering Cancer Center, he died on June 14 at the age of 67:

To Andrew Lloyd Webber

March 31, 1986

Dearest Andrew,

Who would have thought it? Instead of writing *The Phantom of the Opera,*[112] I end up looking like him.

But, alas, the inescapable fact is I have lung cancer. After fiddling around with pneumonia they finally reached the conclusion that it was the big stuff.

I am deeply disconsolate about *The Phantom* and the wonderful opportunity it would have been to write with you. But I will be back! Perhaps not on time to write *The Phantom,* but as far as I am concerned this is a temporary hiccup. I have a 50/50 chance medically and a 50/50 chance spiritually. I shall make it. I have no intention of leaving my beautiful wife, this beautiful life and all of the things I still have to write. As far as I am concerned it is a challenge, and I fear nothing.

But I shall be thinking of you, and Sarah [Brightman],[113] and Richard [Stilgoe], and Cameron [Mackintosh] all the way, and I know you will have the success God knows you deserve. It is a wonderful score and I am heartbroken that I cannot get a crack at it.

I will be in touch with you over the summer just to let you know I am up and around and thinking of you, and I hope with all my heart that one day we will have a chance to work together.

Blessings always to you and Sarah.

Aye,
Alan

[112] Completed by Lloyd Webber with lyricists Stilgoe and Charles Hart, *The Phantom of the Opera* opened on October 9, 1986, in London's West End, where it continues its run. It is currently the longest-running musical in Broadway history.

[113] Actress Sarah Brightman (1960–) originated the role of Christine in *The Phantom of the Opera,* and was Lloyd Webber's wife at the time of the show's opening.

Lerner's premature death cut short his career just as it was on the brink of renewal. Personal happiness had brought a sense of purpose, and intellectually he was ready for new challenges. The potential success of *Phantom* would have replenished his fortune, and perhaps he would have gone on to write other musicals with Lloyd Webber. *My Man Godfrey* might equally have proved a hit, albeit not on the scale of *Phantom*, and the BBC series on musicals would have allowed him to end his career with a survey of the genre that was the focus of his all-consuming passion. Yet even without these, his legacy of great songs, shows, and films speaks for itself. True, his final decade did not bring the critical raves and commercial success of his earlier days. But with a catalogue of musicals including *An American in Paris, Brigadoon, Camelot, Gigi,* and, most especially, *My Fair Lady,* Lerner ensured that America had grown accustomed to his face—not just for "one brief shining moment," as King Arthur has it in *Camelot,* but forever.

TIMELINE

August 31, 1918: Born in New York City
September 1936: Arrives at Harvard
March 29, 1938: Premiere of *So Proudly We Hail!*
April 8, 1938: New York debut of *Fair Enough*
October 1939: Announces *The Little Dog Laughed* (unproduced)
June 26, 1940: Marries Ruth Boyd
October 8, 1942: Premiere of *Life of the Party* in Detroit
November 11, 1943: Broadway premiere of *What's Up?*
November 1944: Begins work on *The Day before Spring*
June 1945: Starts to draft *Brigadoon*
November 22, 1945: *The Day before Spring* opens on Broadway
February 1946: MGM takes up option on screen version of *The Day before Spring* (incomplete)
October 1946: *Brigadoon* announced to the press
March 13, 1947: Broadway premiere of *Brigadoon*
April 1947: Splits with Frederick Loewe
June 1947: Divorces Ruth Boyd
July 1947: Announces new collaboration with Kurt Weill
September 1947: Marries Marion Bell
October 7, 1948: Broadway debut of *Love Life*
January 1949: Starts to write *Royal Wedding*
September 15, 1949: Divorces Marion Bell
March 19, 1950: Marries Nancy Olson
May 1950: Reunites with Loewe and starts to write *Paint Your Wagon*
February 1951: MGM buys screen rights to *Brigadoon*
March 1951: *Royal Wedding*
October 1951: *An American in Paris*
November 12, 1951: Broadway premiere of *Paint Your Wagon*

March 1952: Begins first attempt at *My Fair Lady*
March 20, 1952: Wins Academy Award for screenplay of *An American in Paris*
April 1952: Considers writing musical version of *Casablanca* with Loewe
September 1952: Considers movie version of *The Girl of the Golden West*
October 1952: Abandons first attempt at *My Fair Lady*; severs collaboration with Loewe
February 1953: Starts work on new songs for movie version of *Paint Your Wagon* with Arthur Schwartz
March 1953: Signs contract to write musical of *Li'l Abner* with Schwartz
October 1953: Starts writing screenplay of non-musical *Green Mansions* for MGM
November 1953: Ends collaboration with Schwartz; Burton Lane takes over as composer of *Li'l Abner*
December 1953: Undertakes further work on *Huckleberry Finn* for MGM. Production on movie of *Brigadoon* begins
August 1954: Resumes work with Loewe on *My Fair Lady*; abandons *Abner*
September 1954: Premiere of movie version of *Brigadoon*
April 1955: Plans musical adaption of *Saratoga Trunk*
March 15, 1956: *My Fair Lady* opens on Broadway
April 1956: Abandons *Saratoga Trunk*
May 1956: Begins work on screenplay of *Gigi* without Loewe
February 1957: Loewe agrees to write score for *Gigi*. Lerner directs rehearsals of National Tour of *My Fair Lady*
March 15, 1957: World premiere of songs dedicated to Harvard, with music by Leonard Bernstein, at Carnegie Hall
March 27, 1957: Revival of *Brigadoon* opens at City Center, New York
April 21, 1957: *My Fair Lady* wins six Tony Awards. Lerner moves to Paris to work on *Gigi*.
October 1957: Announces work on *Father of the Bride* with Loewe; divorces Nancy Olson
December 1957: Abandons work on *Father of the Bride*
December 25, 1957: Marries Micheline Muselli Pozzo di Borgo
April 1958: Loewe suffers heart attack and cannot attend London premiere of *Fair Lady*
May 15, 1958: *Gigi* receives world premiere screening. Lerner and Loewe consider musical version of *Life with Father*
February 1959: Lerner and Loewe start work on *Camelot*
February 18, 1960: Lerner elected president of Dramatists Guild
April 18, 1960: *My Fair Lady* receives Russian premiere
October 1, 1960: First performance of *Camelot* in Toronto
October 4, 1960: Lerner hospitalized for bleeding ulcer

October 14, 1960: Lerner takes over direction of *Camelot*
December 3, 1960: Broadway debut of *Camelot*
April 6, 1961: Announces new collaboration with Richard Rodgers
February 11, 1962: *The Broadway of Lerner and Loewe* TV special is aired
September 30, 1962: *My Fair Lady* closes on Broadway
October 1962: Announces details of *On a Clear Day You Can See Forever* with Richard Rodgers
Early 1963: Works on screenplay of *My Fair Lady*
May 23, 1963: Produces birthday celebration for President Kennedy at the Waldorf-Astoria
July 1963: Collapse of collaboration with Rodgers; Burton Lane takes over as composer of *On a Clear Day*
January 1964: Agrees to write screenplay and lyrics for *Doctor Dolittle*
October 1964: *My Fair Lady* movie is released to cinemas
December 1964: *My Fair Lady* wins New York Film Critics' Award
March 8, 1965: Divorces Micheline Muselli Pozzo di Borgo
October 17, 1965: Broadway premiere of *On a Clear Day You Can See Forever*
November 15, 1966: Marries Karen Gunderson
January 1966: Announces collaboration with André Previn on *Coco*
February 27, 1966: Tribute to Lerner screens on *The Bell Telephone Hour*. Pre-production on movie of *Camelot* begins in the same month.
August 1966: Visits Coco Chanel in Paris to discuss *Coco*
October 1967: Charity premiere of *Camelot* film in New York
1968: Writes new songs with Previn for movie of *Paint Your Wagon* and screenplay of *On a Clear Day* for Barbra Streisand
February 1969: Celebrates twenty-five years in show business at the Waldorf-Astoria
October 16, 1969: Premiere of *Paint Your Wagon* movie
December 18, 1969: Broadway premiere of *Coco*
June 17, 1970: Movie of *On a Clear Day* opens in cinemas
November 1970: Announces stage adaptation of *Lolita* with music by John Barry
March 15, 1971: *Lolita, My Love* opens in Boston tryout, but closes before reaching Broadway
September 1971: Lerner and Loewe reunite to write score for *The Little Prince* and revision of *Gigi* for the stage
Early 1973: Filming of *The Little Prince* takes place
May 15, 1973: Stage version of *Gigi* opens in San Francisco
November 1973: Starts to write *1600 Pennsylvania Avenue* with Bernstein
November 13, 1973: Broadway premiere of *Gigi*
April 11, 1974: Premiere of City Center show *Music! Music! Music!* for which Lerner wrote some "footnotes"

April 21, 1974: Lerner and Loewe win Tony Award for Best Score for *Gigi*
April 30, 1974: Divorces Karen Gunderson
December 10, 1974: Marries Sandra Payne
December 1974: *The Little Prince* is released
1975: Extensive work completed on *1600 Pennsylvania Avenue*
March 25, 1976: Anniversary revival of *My Fair Lady* opens on Broadway
May 4, 1976: *1600 Pennsylvania Avenue* opens
Fall 1976: Work begins on *Carmelina*
1976: Divorces Sandra Payne
January 1977: Lerner appears in musical theater festival in Australia and starts work on memoir *The Street Where I Live*
March 1977: Announces *Carmelina* to the press
May 30, 1977: Marries Nina Bushkin
Fall 1978: Publication of *The Street Where I Live*
April 8, 1979: Broadway premiere of *Carmelina*
May 14, 1979: Tribute to Lerner and Loewe at Museum of the City of New York
Summer 1979: Briefly discusses collaboration with Michel Legrand on *The Mountains of Peru*
November 1979: Major revival of *My Fair Lady* in London, with direction by Lerner
July 8, 1980: New York premiere of revival of *Camelot*
October 16, 1980: New York revival of *Brigadoon*
April 1981: Begins work on film adaptation of *The Merry Widow* and briefly works on *Copperfield*
May 1981: Announces *Dance a Little Closer,* with Charles Strouse
August 1981: Divorces Nina Bushkin
August 18, 1981: Marries Liz Robertson; Harrison revival of *My Fair Lady* opens on Broadway
February 1982: Agrees to direct *Dance a Little Closer*
May 11, 1983: *Dance a Little Closer* opens on Broadway
August 1983: Involved in a car accident; spends the rest of the year researching a history of the musical theater
Summer 1984: Begins work on *My Man Godfrey* with Gerard Kenny
October 1984: Starts to revise *Gigi* for London stage premiere
January 1985: Hands over *Carmelina* revisions to Joseph Stein and continues work on *Gigi*
February 15, 1985: Premiere of lullaby for Prince Harry, "Brocades and Coronets," with music by Gerard Kenny
March 1985: *My Man Godfrey* announced to the press
April 1985: Completes some initial work on *Teddy and Alice*
September 17, 1985: Premiere of *Gigi* in London

December 8, 1985: Receives Kennedy Center Award with Loewe
January 1986: Discusses collaboration with Andrew Lloyd Webber on *The Phantom of the Opera*
March 31, 1986: Withdraws from *Phantom* after diagnosis of cancer
June 14, 1986: Dies in New York

APPENDIX

Just prior to going to print, the following brief letters came to light. Since neither Loesser nor Prince is otherwise represented in the book, and each message has a point of interest (not least the idea of a *Don Quixote* musical over a decade before *Man of La Mancha*), I was delighted to be able to include them here at the last minute.

D.M.

To Harold Prince

June 9, 1956

Dear Hal:

I have thought about *Don Quixote* many times. I wish I knew how to do it.

I am still looking, so please communicate any ideas that may pop into your head.

Fondly,
Alan

To Frank Loesser

February 2, 1966

Dear Frank,

You must think I'm a lunatic. I really had a blackout about that whole episode. What do you think it means?

Anyhow, at the slightest provocation I would be delighted to supply all medical documentation to prove that I am *not* a lunatic, although I must admit our particular branch of dramatic arts has never distinguished itself for sanity.

Be all that as it may, I would like to apply again for the job of lunch companion and I beg you to reconsider my application. I have to go away for a few days and will be back Tuesday. I offer you Wednesday, Thursday, Friday or any lunch hour the following week. I do hope you will select one of them.

My apologies again. I really do look forward to seeing you.

Yours rationally,
Alan

REFERENCES

Archival Sources

THE LETTERS REPRODUCED IN THIS BOOK ARE DRAWN FROM THE FOLLOWING ARCHIVES:

Library of Congress: Alan Jay Lerner collection, Arthur Schwartz collection, Burton Lane collection, Leonard Bernstein collection, Joshua Logan collection, Irving Berlin collection, Roger Stevens collection

New York Public Library: Hanya Holm papers, James Barton papers, Jo Mielziner papers, Brooks Atkinson papers, Leland Hayward papers, S. N. Behrman papers, Comden and Green papers, Richard Rodgers papers, Frederick Brisson papers, Katharine Hepburn papers, Richard Kiley papers, Jerome Robbins papers, Agnes de Mille papers

Yale University: Goddard Lieberson collection, Theatre Guild Collection

Wisconsin Historical Society: Herman Levin papers, Moss Hart papers, Edna Ferber papers, Howard Lindsay and Russel Crouse papers

USC: Arthur Freed Collection, Jack L. Warner collection

Boston University: Dirk Bogarde collection, Irene Mayer Selznick collection

Harvard University: Marietta Peabody Tree papers

Kent State University: Robert Lewis collection

St John's, Cambridge University: Cecil Beaton papers

Margaret Herrick Library, Academy of Motion Picture Arts and Sciences: George Cukor papers

Harry Ransom Center, University of Texas: Gloria Swanson papers

Swansea University: Richard Burton papers

Kurt Weill Foundation: Lotte Lenya

John F. Kennedy Presidential Library: White House Files

Gershwin Foundation: Ira Gershwin

Private collections: Liz Robertson, Cameron Mackintosh, Andrew Lloyd Webber, Vera Goulet, David Grossberg

Select Bibliography

Julie Andrews, *Home* (New York: Doubleday, 2008).

Stephen Banfield, *Sondheim's Broadway Musicals* (Ann Arbor: University of Michigan Press, 1994).

Geoffrey Block, *Enchanted Evenings* (New York: Oxford University Press, 1997; rev. New York: Oxford University Press, 2009).

Saul Chaplin, *The Golden Age of Movie Musicals and Me* (Norman, OK: University of Oklahama Press, 1994).

Stephen Citron, *The Wordsmiths* (New York: Oxford University Press, 1996).

Cheryl Crawford, *One Naked Individual* (New York: Bobbs-Merrill, 1977).
Barry Day (ed.), *The Letters of Noel Coward* (London: Methuen, 2007).
Howard Dietz, *Dancing in the Dark* (New York: Quadrangle, 1974).
Lehman Engel, *The American Musical Theater* (New York: Macmillan, 1975).
Lehman Engel, *Words with Music* (New York: Schirmer, 1972).
Hugh Fordin, *MGM's Greatest Musicals: The Arthur Freed Unit* (New York: Da Capo, 1996).
Patrick Garland, *The Incomparable Rex* (London, 1998).
Benny Green (ed.), *A Hymn to Him: The Lyrics of Alan Jay Lerner* (London: Pavilion Books, 1987).
Otis Guernsey (ed.), *Broadway Song and Story* (New York: Dodd, Mead and Co., 1985).
Otis Guernsey (ed.), *Playwrights, Lyricists, Composers on Theater* (New York: Dodd, Mead and Co., 1974).
Moss Hart, *Act One* (New York: St Martin's Griffin, 1989).
Edward Jablonski, *Alan Jay Lerner: A Biography* (New York: Henry Holt, 1996).
Gene Lees, *Inventing Champagne: The Worlds of Lerner and Loewe* (New York: St. Martin's Press, 1990).
Alan Jay Lerner, "Introduction," *The New York Times Great Songs of Broadway* (New York: Quadrangle, 1973).
Alan Jay Lerner, *The Musical Theatre: A Celebration* (London: Collins, 1986).
Alan Jay Lerner, *The Street Where I Live* (London: Hodder and Stoughton, 1978).
Glenn Loney, *Musical Theatre in America* (Westport, CT: Greenwood, 1984).
Jeffrey Magee, *Irving Berlin's American Musical Theater* (New York: Oxford University Press, 2012).
Ken Mandelbaum, *Not Since Carrie* (New York: St Martin's, 1992).
Bill Marshall and Robynn Stilwell (ed.), *Musicals and Beyond* (Exeter: Intellect, 2000).
Dominic McHugh, *Loverly: The Life and Times of "My Fair Lady"* (New York: Oxford University Press, 2012).
Ethan Mordden, *Beautiful Mornin'* (New York: Oxford University Press,1999).
Ethan Mordden, *Coming Up Roses* (New York: Oxford University Press, 1998).
Ethan Mordden, *The Hollywood Musical* (New York: St Martin's, 1981).
Marni Nixon, *I Could Have Sung All Night* (New York: Billboard, 2006).
Richard Rodgers, *Musical Stages* (New York: Da Capo, 2002).
Doris Shapiro, *We Danced All Night: My Life behind the Scenes with Alan Jay Lerner* (New York: William Morrow, 1990).
Rick Simas, *The Musicals No One Came to See* (New York: Garland, 1987).
Larry Stempel, *Showtime* (New York: W. W. Norton and Co., 2010).
Steven Suskin, *More Opening Nights on Broadway* (New York: Schirmer, 1997).
Steven Suskin, *Opening Night on Broadway* (New York: Schirmer, 1990).
Steven Suskin, *Show Tines* (New York: Oxford University Press, 2010).
Richard Traubner, *Operetta* (New York: Oxford University Press, 1983).

Websites

The Harvard Crimson: www.thecrimson.com
Internet Broadway Database: www.ibdb.com
Internet Movie Database: www.imdb.com
The New York Times: www.nytimes.com
Time Magazine: www.time.com
Variety: www.variety.com

INDEX

√$39.95